Understanding the Social World of the New Testament

The New Testament is a book of great significance in Western culture yet is often inaccessible to students because the modern world differs so significantly from the ancient Mediterranean one in which it was written. It is imperative to develop a cross-cultural understanding of the values of the ancient Mediterranean society from which the New Testament arose in order to fully appreciate the documents and the communities that they represent.

Dietmar Neufeld and Richard E. DeMaris bring together biblical scholars with expertise in the social science to develop interpretive models for understanding such values as collectivism, kinship, memory, ethnicity, and honor, and to demonstrate how to apply these models to the New Testament texts. Kinship is illuminated by analysis of the Holy Family as well as early Christian organizations; gender through a study of Paul's view of women; and landscape and spatiality through a discussion of Jesus of Nazareth. This book is the ideal companion to study of the New Testament.

Dietmar Neufeld is Associate Professor of Christian Origins in the Department of Classical, Near Eastern and Religious Studies at the University of British Columbia, Canada. His publications include the edited volume *The Social Sciences and Biblical Translation* (SBL/Brill 2008).

Richard E. DeMaris is Professor of Theology at Valparaiso University, USA. His publications include *The New Testament in its Ritual World* (Routledge, 2008) and he is on the editorial advisory board of *Religious Studies Review*.

Understanding the Social World of the New Testament

Edited by

Dietmar Neufeld

and

Richard E. DeMaris

Routledge
Taylor & Francis Group

LONDON AND NEW YORK

First published 2010
by Routledge
2 Park Square, Milton Park, Abingdon, Oxon, OX14 4RN

Simultaneously published in the USA and Canada
by Routledge
270 Madison Ave., New York, NY 10016

*Routledge is an imprint of the Taylor & Francis Group,
an informa business*

Typeset in Sabon by
HWA Text and Data Management, London
Printed and bound in Great Britain by
CPI Antony Rowe, Chippenham, Wiltshire

British Library Cataloguing in Publication Data
A catalogue record for this book is available from the British
Library

Library of Congress Cataloging-in-Publication Data
Understanding the social world of the New Testament / edited by
Dietmar Neufeld and Richard E. DeMaris.
p. cm.
Includes bibliographical references (p.) and indexes
1. Bible N.T. – Social scientific criticism. 2. Israel – Social
conditions. I. Neufeld, Dietmar. II. DeMaris, Richard E.
BS2545.S55U53 2009
225.8′301–dc22   20090218-1

ISBN13: 978–0–415–77581–6 (hbk)
ISBN13: 978–0–415–77582–3 (pbk)
ISBN13: 978–0–203–86514–9 (ebk)

ISBN10: 0–415–77581–7 (hbk)
ISBN10: 0–415–77582–5 (pbk)
ISBN10: 0–203–86514–6 (ebk)

Contents

Illustrations

Figures

Tables

Contributors

Alicia Batten is associate professor of Religious Studies at the University of Sudbury, a bilingual institution federated with Laurentian University in Sudbury, Ontario, Canada. She has published articles in a variety of journals including the *Catholic Biblical Quarterly* and *New Testament Studies*. Forthcoming books include *What Are They Saying About James?* (Paulist 2009) and *Friendship and Benefaction in James* (Emory Studies in Early Christianity 15; Deo 2009). She is currently working on the economic and social significance of adornment for women in early Christianity.

Pieter F. Craffert is professor and chair of the Department of New Testament and Early Christian Studies at the University of South Africa in Pretoria. He is the author of *The Life of a Galilean Shaman: Jesus of Nazareth in Anthropological-Historical Perspective* (Cascade Books 2008). His research interest focuses on historical Jesus research and the use of anthropological models and insights for understanding New Testament and early Christian texts and societies.

Dennis C. Duling (PhD, University of Chicago), National Endowment for the Humanities Fellow and recipient of the Kenneth L. Koessler Distinguished Faculty Award (Canisius College), is translator of, and commentator on, "The Testament of Solomon" (*Old Testament Pseudepigrapha*, Doubleday 1983), annotator of "The Gospel of Matthew" (*HarperCollins Study Bible*, SBL 2006), and author of *Jesus Christ Through History* (Harcourt Brace Jovanovich 1979) as well as many social-scientific articles on Matthew and Paul. His most recent book is *The New Testament: History, Literature, and Social Context* (Thomson/Wadsworth 2003).

David A. Fiensy is dean and professor of New Testament of the Graduate School of Biblical Studies and Ministry, Kentucky Christian University. Among his publications are *Prayers Alleged to be Jewish* (Brown Judaic

Studies; Scholars 1985); *The Social History of Palestine in the Herodian Period* (Studies in the Bible and Early Christianity; Mellen 1991); and *Jesus the Galilean* (Gorgias 2007). His research interests include the socio-economic life in Galilee in the first century CE.

Alan Kirk is professor and chair of the Department of Philosophy and Religion at James Madison University, Harrisonburg, Virginia. Recent publications include *Memory, Tradition, and Text: Uses of the Past in Early Christianity*, co-edited with Tom Thatcher (Brill 2005), and "Tradition and Memory in the *Gospel of Peter*," in *Das Evangelium nach Petrus* (De Gruyter 2007). His current research includes applications of memory theory to problems in the origins and history of the Gospel tradition.

Margaret Y. MacDonald is professor of Religious Studies at St Francis Xavier University in Antigonish, Nova Scotia, Canada. A past President of the Canadian Corporation for Studies in Religion, her previous books include *The Pauline Churches: Institutionalization in the Pauline and Deutero-Pauline Writings* (Cambridge University Press 1988), *Early Christian Women and Pagan Opinion: The Power of the Hysterical Woman* (Cambridge University Press 1996), *Colossians and Ephesians* (Sacra Pagina; Liturgical Press 2000), and *A Woman's Place: House Churches in Earliest Christianity* (with Carolyn Osiek and Janet Tulloch; Fortress 2006). Funded by the Social Sciences and Humanities Research Council of Canada, her current research project investigates children and childhood in early Christian house churches.

Bruce J. Malina is professor of Biblical Studies at Creighton University. He has studied in the US, Rome, and Jerusalem and has degrees in philosophy, theology, and biblical studies. He received an honorary doctorate from the University of St Andrew in Scotland (1995). He is associate editor of *Biblical Theology Bulletin*, Catholic Biblical Quarterly Monograph Series, and editor of a series called Paul's Social Network: Brothers and Sisters in Faith (Liturgical Press 2008–). He is a founding member of the Context Group: Project on the Bible in its Cultural Environment. His books include *The New Testament World: Insights from Cultural Anthropology* (John Knox 1981; rev. edn 1993 and 2001) and a series of New Testament Social Science commentaries with Richard L. Rohrbaugh and John J. Pilch (Fortress 1992–).

Halvor Moxnes is professor of New Testament at the University of Oslo. His earlier studies were on Paul, *Theology in Conflict: Studies in Paul's Understanding of God in Romans* (Brill 1980). During studies in the US he became interested in the cultural context of New Testament writings and used peasant economics in a study on Luke, *The Economy of the Kingdom:*

Social Conflict and Economic Relations in Luke's Gospel (Fortress 1988). In recent years he has focused on the historical Jesus, and used space theory and studies of masculinity in *Putting Jesus in His Place: A Radical Vision of Household and Kingdom* (Westminster John Knox 2003). He is presently engaged in a project to read the early historical Jesus studies in light of emerging European nationalism in the nineteenth century.

Peter Oakes teaches New Testament at the University of Manchester. His interest in constructing models of first-century situations came to expression in *Philippians: From People to Letter* (Cambridge 2007); his new book, *Reading Romans in Pompeii: Paul's Letter at Ground Level* (SPCK/Fortress 2009); and an article, "Contours of the Urban Environment," in Todd Still and David Horrell (eds) *After the First Urban Christians* (T & T Clark 2009). He also published an article on methodology in Bruce W. Longenecker and Kelly Liebengood (eds) *Engaging Economics* (Eerdmans 2009).

Carolyn Osiek recently retired as Charles Fischer Catholic Professor of New Testament at Brite Divinity School at Texas Christian University. She taught for 26 years at the Catholic Theological Union at Chicago. She holds a doctorate in New Testament and Christian Origins from Harvard University, and is a past president of the Catholic Biblical Association and the Society of Biblical Literature. Her teaching and research interests are in areas of social life, family, and women in early Christianity.

John J. Pilch is adjunct professor of Biblical Literature at Georgetown University, Washington, DC, and former clinical professor of preventive medicine at the Medical College of Wisconsin, Milwaukee. Recent publications include "The Usefulness of the 'Meaning Response' Concept for Interpreting Translations of Matthew's Gospel" in Dietmar Neufeld (ed.) *The Social Sciences and Biblical Interpretation* (SBL and Brill 2008) and 20 articles on disease topics in the *New Interpreter's Dictionary of the Bible* (Abingdon 2006–10).

Jennifer Pouya recently completed her ThM thesis at Brite Divinity School and has begun doctoral studies at Vanderbilt University. She has published one article, "Kierkegaard and the Jewish Shadow," and has presented on Matthew at American Academy of Religion and Society of Biblical Literature meetings. She is interested in the ways in which New Testament texts have been used as rhetorical weapons.

Richard L. Rohrbaugh is the Paul S. Wright Professor of Religious Studies, Emeritus, at Lewis and Clark College in Portland, Oregon. His academic research has focused on the social and cultural setting of early Christianity and especially on the way ethnocentric readings by contemporary western scholars have altered the meaning of New Testament texts. He has authored numerous articles and nine books, including *The New Testament in Cross-Cultural Perspective* (Cascade 2007), *Social Science Commentary on the Synoptic Gospels* (with Bruce J. Malina; Fortress 2003), and *Social Science Commentary on the Gospel of John* (with Bruce J. Malina; Fortress 2001). He is an avid fly fisherman and hiker.

Eric C. Stewart is assistant professor of Religion at Augustana College, Rock Island, Illinois. He is author of *Gathered Around Jesus: An Alternative Spatial Practice in the Gospel of Mark* (Cascade 2008) and co-editor of *In Other Words: Essays on Social Science Methods and the New Testament in Honor of Jerome H. Neyrey* (Sheffield Phoenix Press 2007) and *The Social World of the New Testament: Insights and Models* (Hendrickson 2008). His research interests include cultural geography, Greek rhetoric, gossip networks, and espionage.

Risto Uro is university lecturer of New Testament Studies and acting professor of Biblical Languages at the University of Helsinki. His recent publications include *Thomas: Seeking the Historical Context of the Gospel of Thomas* (Continuum 2003), *Explaining Christian Origins and Early Judaism: Contributions from Cognitive and Social Science* (edited with Petri Luomanen and Ilkka Pyysiäinen; Brill 2007), and *Sacred Marriages: The Divine–Human Sexual Metaphor from Sumer to Early Christianity* (edited with Martti Nissinen; Eisenbrauns 2008). Uro's current research interest is focused on the role of ritual in the formation of early Christian religion.

Ritva H. Williams is associate professor of religion at Augustana College, Rock Island, Illinois, a liberal arts college related to the Evangelical Lutheran Church in America. She is the author of *The Bible's Importance for the Church Today* (Augsburg Fortress 2009) and *Stewards, Prophets, Keepers of the Word* (Hendrickson 2006). She is currently working on a project exploring dietary purity issues in early Christianity and its social milieu.

Preface

With so many excellent translations of the Bible available, which render ancient Greek and Hebrew into clear and even colloquial English, it is easy to miss how foreign the Bible and its world really are to us. Translations mask the foreignness, so it is crucial for biblical scholars to foreground the very different world in which the Bible was composed. That is the primary aim of this book. It will serve as guide to the reader unfamiliar with the world of ancient Mediterranean culture.

This is not the first book of its kind, but it is the latest and, we hope, the best. The circle of biblical scholars that pioneered the study of the ancient Mediterranean world from a cross-cultural and anthropological perspective, The Context Group, has already collaborated on several very useful books, beginning with *The Social World of Luke-Acts* (Neyrey 1991). For those who prefer the format of a dictionary or encyclopedia, *Biblical Social Values and Their Meaning* has much to offer (Pilch and Malina 1993). Many contributing to those earlier volumes have contributed to this book, but we extended our recruiting to include scholars who are developing new approaches to the biblical text. After all, social-scientific criticism has advanced remarkably in the last two decades, and we wanted to be as up to date as possible. We also chose to focus not on individual biblical books or the Bible as a whole but specifically on the New Testament.

The volume represents the fruit of a collaboration between Richard E. DeMaris and Dietmar Neufeld, but it is not our first joint effort. Since 2005 we have served as co-chairs of the Social-Scientific Criticism of the New Testament section, which is sponsored by the Society of Biblical Literature. Together we have programmed many sessions for the SBL's annual meeting. The collegiality and cooperation generated by this work, together with regular contact with scholars from around the world who have helped advance a cross-culturally informed interpretation of the New Testament, inspired us to try our hand at something new. The idea for this book and the recruitment of an international cast of contributors to it grew quite naturally out of our several pleasurable and rewarding years as co-chairs.

Our common task as teachers gave us further impetus to put together a book of this kind. We both teach university undergraduates for the most part, Dietmar at a large public school, Richard at a small private one. The two institutions are rather different, yet we both introduce students to the New Testament and have become acutely aware of the problems the text poses, no matter what translation one uses. As the idea for a book gestated, thoughts turned to our students, who would benefit from a comprehensive interpretive framework that would enable them to grasp the ancient Mediterranean world. Because the New Testament is moored in the values of ancient Mediterranean society, an awareness of, and sensitivity to, those values is basic for understanding the text. It is pedagogically essential, therefore, to direct students' attention to the cultural values of the Roman world in which the New Testament and ancient Christianity emerged. To do so, this volume will introduce the ancient Mediterranean's value system through an interlocking set of interpretive models developed by anthropologists and presented by the contributors. Our aim is to familiarize students with the relevant interpretive models of the social sciences as essential aids for understanding the New Testament.

To be sure, studies of the New Testament using social-scientific insights abound, but they limit themselves to a small portion of the New Testament or a single interpretive model. Our volume presents an ensemble of complementary models that is broad enough to address a representative selection of New Testament texts. The strategic selection of both models and texts results, we believe, in an excellent guide for students, one that illuminates ancient Mediterranean culture and the New Testament.

We could not have undertaken the project we had in mind without significant assistance from many colleagues; it is beyond our reach to have control of all the interpretive models in this volume. So we owe a great debt to the book's many contributors, and also to our students who inspired us to envision it. The greatest expression of gratitude, however, goes to two indispensible companions, Sarah, friend and partner of Richard, and Viola, friend and partner of Dietmar.

Dietmar Neufeld and Richard E. DeMaris

Abbreviations

ABR	*Australian Biblical Review*
AHR	*American Historical Review*
ANRW	*Aufsteig und Niedergang der römischen Welt.* Edited by H. Temporini and W. Hasse. Berlin, 1972–
AQ	*Anthropological Quarterly*
ASR	*American Sociological Review*
ATANT	Abhandlungen zur Theologie des Alten und Neuen Testaments
ATLA	American Theological Library Association
BAR	*Biblical Archaeology Review*
BBB	Bonner biblische Beiträge
BBR	*Bulletin for Biblical Research*
BDAG	Bauer, W., F. W. Danker, W. F. Arndt, and F. W. Gingerich. *Greek–English Lexicon of the New Testament and Other Early Christian Literature.* 3rd edn, Chicago, 2000
Bib	*Biblica*
BJRL	*Bulletin of the John Rylands University Library of Manchester*
BJS	Brown Judaic Studies
BTB	*Biblical Theology Bulletin*
BZNW	Beihefte zur Zeitschrift für die neutestamentliche Wissenschaft und die Kunde der älteren Kirche
CBQ	*Catholic Biblical Quarterly*
CP	*Classical Philology*
CQ	*Classical Quarterly*
EGL	Eastern Great Lakes (SBL regional meeting)
FF	*Foundations and Facets*
FRLANT	Forschungen zur Religion und Literatur des Alten und Neuen Testaments
HR	*History of Religions*
HTR	*Harvard Theological Review*
HvTSt	*Hervormde teologiese studies*

IG	*Inscriptiones graecae.* Editio minor. Berlin, 1924–
JAAR	*Journal of the American Academy of Religion*
JBL	*Journal of Biblical Literature*
JJS	*Journal of Jewish Studies*
JQR	*Jewish Quarterly Review*
JSJSup	Supplements to the *Journal for the Study of Judaism*
JSNT	*Journal for the Study of the New Testament*
JSNTSup	*Journal for the Study of the New Testament*: Supplement Series
JSOT	*Journal for the Study of the Old Testament*
JSP	*Journal for the Study of the Pseudepigrapha*
LCL	Loeb Classical Library
List	*Listening: Journal of Religion and Culture*
LXX	Septuagint (Greek Old Testament)
MT	Masoretic (Hebrew) Text
MWBS	Mid-Western Biblical Studies
NIDB	*New International Dictionary of the Bible*
NIGTC	New International Greek Testament Commentary
NovT	*Novum Testamentum*
NRSV	New Revised Standard Version
NTAbh	Neutestamentliche Abhandlungen
NTS	*New Testament Studies*
PJ	*Palästina-Jahrbuch*
PTMS	Pittsburgh Theological Monograph Series
QS	*Qualitative Sociology*
RelSRev	*Religious Studies Review*
ResQ	*Restoration Quarterly*
SBL	Society of Biblical Literature
SBLDS	Society of Biblical Literature Dissertation Series
SBLMS	Society of Biblical Literature Monograph Series
SBLSymS	Society of Biblical Literature Symposium Series
SBS	Stuttgarter Bibelstudien
SR	*Studies in Religion*
ST	*Studia theologica*
TDNT	*Theological Dictionary of the New Testament.* Edited by G. Kittel and G. Friedrich. Translated by G. W. Bromiley. 10 vols. Grand Rapids, MI, 1964–76
VC	*Vigiliae christianae*
WUNT	Wissenschaftliche Untersuchungen zum Neuen Testament
ZNW	*Zeitschrift für die neutestamentliche Wissenschaft und die Kunde der älteren Kirche*

Introduction

Richard E. DeMaris and Dietmar Neufeld

The New Testament opens with four accounts of Jesus's life followed by a narrative about the growth and expansion of a small circle of Jesus's followers westward from Jerusalem to other cities in the Roman empire and ultimately to Rome. At one level these are simple, straightforward stories about the founding and spread of a new faith. Yet a closer reading reveals narratives that are complex and puzzling. Countless modern readers find this true not only of the four Gospels and the Acts of the Apostles but the entire New Testament.

How do we best make sense of the New Testament, a book of great significance to western culture yet often baffling? What is needed is an interpretive framework that enables the reader to understand the world in which the text was written. After all, a text read out of context often results in misunderstanding. Worse, a text taken out of context is easily distorted and manipulated, which is often the fate of the New Testament today. Providing a context for informed reading is the primary goal of the essays assembled in this book. Together they offer an interpretive framework or constellation that will help the modern reader become more knowledgeable about the ancient Mediterranean world and thus better able to comprehend an all important text that sprang from it.

These essays take a common approach and share several basic assumptions. All acknowledge that the modern world is very different from the ancient one (similarly, Neufeld 2008b: 1–9). All rely on interpretive models from the social sciences, particularly cultural anthropology and ethnographical studies of non-western, traditional cultures, to bridge the gap between these two worlds. Cultural sensitivity and a cross-cultural perspective are guiding stars. Such an orientation has prompted the authors of these essays to seek out interpretive frameworks and models with the aim of shedding light on the world of the New Testament and thus the text itself.

The models introduced in the essays that follow can be usefully organized under two headings: (1) Identity and (2) Engagement and Social Interaction.

(Some chapters and their models may properly be listed under either heading.) Yet these essays are not meant to be read in isolation from each other. True, they deal with a variety of distinct topics. These topics bear on each other, however; they are inextricably interwoven. Moreover, they work together as a whole to illuminate the New Testament. The synergy among them will become evident when we turn to the biblical text.

The need for interpretive models and their interconnectedness becomes immediately clear once one reads the New Testament and tries to make sense of it. A deceptively straightforward account from the New Testament book mentioned above, the Acts of the Apostles, will provide a case study. The story of Stephen in chapters six and seven begins this way:

> 6:1 Now during those days, when the disciples were increasing in numbers, the Hellenists complained against the Hebrews because their widows were being neglected in the daily distribution of food. 2 And the twelve called together the whole community of the disciples and said, "It is not right that we should neglect the word of God in order to wait on tables (or keep accounts). 3 Therefore, friends (literally brothers), select from among yourselves seven men of good standing, full of the Spirit and of wisdom, whom we may appoint to this task, 4 while we, for our part, will devote ourselves to prayer and serving the word." 5 What they said pleased the whole community, and they chose Stephen, a man full of faith and the Holy Spirit, together with Philip, Prochorus, Nicanor, Timon, Parmenas, and Nicolaus, a proselyte of Antioch. 6 They had these men stand before the apostles, who prayed and laid their hands on them.
>
> 6:7 The word of God continued to spread; the number of the disciples increased greatly in Jerusalem, and a great many of the priests became obedient to the faith.
>
> 6:8 Stephen, full of grace and power, did great wonders and signs among the people. 9 Then some of those who belonged to the synagogue of the Freedmen (as it was called), Cyrenians, Alexandrians, and others of those from Cilicia and Asia, stood up and argued with Stephen. 10 But they could not withstand the wisdom and the Spirit with which he spoke. 11 Then they secretly instigated some men to say, "We have heard him speak blasphemous words against Moses and God." 12 They stirred up the people as well as the elders and the scribes; then they suddenly confronted him, seized him, and brought him before the council.
>
> (Acts 6:1–12)

At first glance, what the narrative conveys is clear. The circle of Jesus's disciples is growing rapidly, so much so that it has outgrown its organizational structure and, as a consequence, is no longer meeting the needs of its members. Realizing this, the group's leaders, "the twelve" or "apostles," add a new layer of leadership, with the aim of meeting the needs of the group and enhancing its efforts to increase adherents to it. The group quickly agrees to these steps and the new leaders are identified and appointed. Shortly thereafter we learn that the solution to the crisis works: problems within the community have evidently vanished, and we are informed that the circle of believers is now growing exponentially: "the number of the disciples increased greatly in Jerusalem." The story has a familiar ring: a consensus-based change in management structure has improved group morale and made it more effective in its primary task. This is how a successful enterprise negotiates change.

Yet the narrative continues, and the lines that follow show that what appears to be a reasonable interpretation of this story will not work (6:8–10). What we learn is that the new layer of leadership evidently headed by Stephen does not set about the task assigned to it (Witherington 1998: 240; Haenchen 1971: 256). Instead of undertaking the task of service within the community, Stephen adopts the very role that the twelve were determined to reserve for themselves: serving the word, that is, proclaiming the message about Jesus.[1] The text is not explicit about it, but it is nonetheless clear that Stephen is a missionary, carrying the message to a new audience and doing so very effectively: "Then some ... stood up and argued with Stephen. But they could not withstand the wisdom and the Spirit with which he spoke." [2]

So what is this story actually about, if not about organizational improvement and institutional development?[3] The opening sentence of the passage provides some hints that the modern reader may miss. It mentions Hellenists and Hebrews, evidently indicating ethnic difference among the believers. The Hellenists had very likely grown up speaking Greek but had a Judean heritage that encouraged their migration to Jerusalem, where this scene is set. The Hebrews were very likely native Judeans who spoke Aramaic, a common language of Judea at the time. If tension between ethnic groups sometimes threatens the unity of human communities even nowadays, in an era when ethnic origins have lost much of their significance, in the ancient world ethnic rivalry would have been endemic. The denizens of the Mediterranean were not only acutely aware of ethnic difference, they developed and perpetuated stereotypes of various ethnic groups and evaluated people based on those stereotypes.

Ethnicity is a complex matter and it was a pivotal issue for the movement around Jesus that grew into the ancient church, because it brought different ethnic groups together in the same community. Dennis C. Duling considers the central role ethnicity played in ancient perceptions about human identity and how it figured in the apostle Paul's thinking and writing in an essay titled "Ethnicity and Paul's Letter to the Romans." While his focus is Paul, his treatment of the topic is relevant to the entire New Testament. Family, territory, language, customs, religion, tribal affiliation, names, stories about common ancestry, and shared historical memories were the cultural markers of ethnic group identity. These markers were fiercely protected and hotly disputed. Thus, they were often the cause of tension between ethnic groups.

The second hint the narrative gives us as to what is going on is the mention of widows: "the Hellenists complained against the Hebrews because their widows were being neglected in the daily distribution of food." This complaint must be set next to an earlier passage in Acts, where we learn that the whole group of believers held everything in common and that a welfare system was in place: "There was not a needy person among them, for as many as owned lands or houses sold them and brought the proceeds of what was sold. They laid it at the apostles' feet, and it was distributed to each as any had need" (Acts 4:34–35). The breakdown of this redistribution system, and the resulting Hellenists' complaint, would naturally lead one to understand the passage as one about the lack of organization and efficiency. Yet attention to such matters may well reflect the modern preoccupation with those issues. Confirming this is the fact that Acts of the Apostles never mentions the system again.

More important in Acts 6:1 may be who is shortchanged: the widows. While it is quite right to think of this group as the most defenseless in the patriarchal society of the ancient Mediterranean, as is the case generally in human societies, it is also important to keep in mind the widows' gender: they were women. Carolyn Osiek and Jennifer Pouya's collaborative essay titled "Constructions of Gender in the Roman Imperial World," though it focuses on the apostle Paul's letters, helps us understand why the conflict that emerges in Acts between the Hellenists and Hebrews centered on women. Feminine qualities, as stereotypically enumerated in the ancient Mediterranean world, included susceptibility to deception, which may have been assumed in the story. More important, the female body was thought of as the site of male shame, for men demonstrated their honor (or lack of it) in the degree to which they controlled the women's bodies associated with them. In other words, women's bodies regularly served as the battleground on which the male struggle for honor was fought. So shortchanging the widows has immediate social ramifications for the male family members to whom the widows are connected. The (male) Hebrews are confronted by the (male) Hellenists on account of *their* widows.

Ethnicity and gender are important topics in their own right, but they take on added significance because they were also facets of a key cultural value that deeply colored all human interaction in the world of the New Testament: honor. Much like a credit rating in today's society—so important that the criminal activity that compromises it is called identity theft—

one's honor ranking determined one's place and potential in the ancient Mediterranean world. Richard L. Rohrbaugh's essay titled "Honor: Core Value in the Biblical World" describes it as the primary form of social evaluation in the Mediterranean world, and by that he means two things: (1) the public had to recognize any claim to honor; and (2) that reputation was continually subject to testing. If self-esteem is sought by moderns, the ancients treasured social esteem, which meant that any claim to worthiness had be publicly acknowledged. If moderns endure regular insults to their self-esteem, ancients faced daily threats to their honor ranking in the form of public challenges.

This all-encompassing interpretive frame or model provides a roadmap for following the twists and turns of the biblical narrative. In the story before us, if we focus on the social reputation of the Hellenists and their representatives—first the seven, then Stephen—what we find is a narrative that coheres around the establishment and confirmation of the Hellenists' high honor ranking through a series of challenges. Honor challenges and responses to them are complex phenomena and vary subtly across social locations and cultures, but when the Hellenists complain to the Hebrews about the treatment of their widows, what is at stake is the Hellenists' status in the circle of believers, not the improvement of the distribution system. What follows in the narrative is the very public working out of the Hellenists' status. As the appointment of the seven proceeds, we learn that they are "of good standing," "full of Spirit and wisdom," and that Stephen is "full of faith and Holy Spirit," honor-granting evaluations that are acknowledged by the whole group. Acts 6:1–7 constitutes an honor challenge that is positively resolved with Hellenists gaining full status in the community. We know this because their foremost representative, Stephen, assumes the same task as "the twelve," the leaders of the Hebrews, who enjoyed the highest honor ranking in the community.

In the next phase of the narrative, Acts 6:8–12, the playing field of honor expands outside the circle of believers. Stephen enjoys divine acknowledgment of his high honor status as the story begins: "Stephen, full of grace and power, did great wonders and signs among the people." Predictably, a new honor contest immediately ensues, because such a report cannot go unchallenged. Members of a local synagogue—probably fellow-Hellenists who did not follow Jesus—challenge Stephen verbally but are bested by him. When this honor challenge fails, Stephen's antagonists resort to deceit, crowd manipulation, and physical force against him, confirming what their failed honor challenge indicated: they are dishonorable. As Stephen's honor ranking climbs, theirs plummets.

A reading of Acts through the lens of honor brings three additional aspects of the narrative to the foreground, which we might otherwise overlook. Because of the public nature of honor contests, the narrative very soon introduces "the public" involved in the first honor challenge episode, the circle of disciples. The twelve address them as "brothers," a term the NRSV replaces with the more gender-neutral "friends." This is a reasonable substitution, for the circle of disciples obviously included women, but what is lost in the change is any sense that the circle of disciples is at some level a family. As Margaret Y. MacDonald in her essay "Kinship and Family in the New Testament World" points out, the extended family was foundational across all domains of ancient Mediterranean society, so it is not surprising that the circle of disciples would come to understand themselves as a family, albeit a fictive or symbolic one. This familial underpinning is probably also at work behind the earlier notice in the text, noted above, that the circle held possessions in common and met the needs of every member. While moderns typically read such reports as evidence of communalism—even communism!—among the first believers, we do well not to ignore the powerful influence of family on all organizations in the Mediterranean world.

Once "the family" is assembled to act as the Hellenists' public court of honor, we find a group whose uniformity in attitude and action are striking: all the disciples are immediately amenable to what their leaders say, and they act on their words in complete harmony. What kind of political organization is this that has achieved such unanimity? It looks like totalitarianism in the New Testament. Yet it is inappropriate to project a modern phenomenon back to ancient society. Instead, it is better to think about human cultures in which the honor contest would thrive. Since public acknowledgment is an essential feature of that contest, group consensus around the decision of group leaders becomes a prized virtue. Bruce J. Malina's essay, "Collectivism in Mediterranean Culture," reminds us that the ancient Mediterranean world was not populated by individualists. Because honor was *the* social value, people derived their identities from the group they belonged to. Hence, like-mindedness, co-dependence, and conformity were valued attributes, as our Acts narrative suggests.

A third salient feature of the Acts narrative, related like the others to the public nature of status evaluation, is ritual, a social action that alters and/or confirms social arrangements. By Acts 6:6 we have reached the conclusion of an episode that began with crisis and ends with consensus; the honor challenge has been positively resolved. Both components of the Jesus group, leaders (the twelve/the apostles) and non-leaders alike, have acted to resolve the crisis. Now comes a final step, a ritual act, which gesturally confirms the group solidarity that has been verbally expressed. It also enacts the group's decision by empowering the newly chosen seven: "They had these men stand before the apostles, who prayed and laid their hands on them." Ritual has great importance in honor-based cultures, and its importance to the Jesus movement should not be underestimated, as Risto Uro notes in his essay "Ritual and Christian Origins." In the case before us, ritual action has a dual aspect, confirming the solidarity of the disciples but also elevating, hence transforming, the seven from prominent Hellenists into group leaders and apostolic missionaries.

The ultimate confirmation of the seven's new status comes in the verses that follow, where we learn that evangelical activity has reached a new level of success, evidently energized by fresh blood in the missionary effort, and that Stephen's activity enjoys divine sanction: "The word of God continued to spread; the number of the disciples increased greatly in Jerusalem, and a great many of the priests became obedient to the faith. Stephen, full of grace and power, did great wonders and signs among the people" (Acts 6:7–8). Stephen has become the mediator of divine power—most scholars consider great wonders and signs as a reference to healing—which provides divine confirmation of the high honor that the circle of disciples gave him in the previous verses. Mention of signs and wonders confirms his apostleship, for this very language describes the apostles' activity earlier in the narrative (5:12).

As noted above, this bold honor claim triggers an immediate challenge, which redounds negatively on the challengers. Their failure to counteract Stephen verbally drives them down the path of shameful activity involving secrecy, false witnesses, trumped up charges, and, when Stephen once again demonstrates his verbal skills, deadly violence against him (Acts 6:11–7:58). Yet this is more than a narrative about a failed honor challenge.

While honor is at stake, Stephen's access to divine power sparks immediate opposition and increases the level of conflict that ensues. Though he focuses in his essay on Jesus, John Pilch's "Jesus's Healing Activity: Political Acts?" usefully explores the connection between healing activity and political authority in the Mediterranean world. The miraculous power mediated by Stephen implies that there is a new or alternative authority structure. Hence, Stephen draws opposition because he poses a threat to the existing authority structure. As contrived as the charges were against him, the ruling council of Jerusalem understood what was at risk. It took them seriously and demanded a response from Stephen to them. His rejoinder, however, infuriates them.

6:8 Stephen, full of grace and power, did great wonders and signs among the people. 9 Then some of those who belonged to the synagogue of the Freedmen (as it was called), Cyrenians, Alexandrians, and others of those from Cilicia and Asia, stood up and argued with Stephen. 10 But they could not withstand the wisdom and the Spirit with which he spoke. 11 Then they secretly instigated some men to say, "We have heard him speak blasphemous words against Moses and God." 12 They stirred up the people as well as the elders and the scribes; then they suddenly confronted him, seized him, and brought him before the council. 13 They set up false witnesses who said, "This man never stops saying things against this holy place and the law; 14 for we have heard him say that this Jesus of Nazareth will destroy this place and will change the customs that Moses handed on to us." 15 And all who sat in the council looked intently at him, and they saw that his face was like the face of an angel. 7:1 Then the high priest asked him, "Are these things so?"

(Acts 6: 8–7: 1)

Blasphemy against God? Words against Moses? Against this holy place, the Temple of Jerusalem? The narrative does not report the contents of Stephen's proclamation to the inhabitants of Jerusalem. Nor, oddly enough, does Stephen directly address these charges in his very lengthy response before the council (7:2–53). The reader's puzzlement at these apparent non sequiturs is shared by scholars who have debated why Moses and the Temple make an appearance at this point in the narrative and why Stephen fails to defend himself (Dibelius 1956: 167–9; Witherington 1998: 259; Conzelmann 1987: 44).

Essential for making sense of the narrative's logic are insights from the essays by Eric C. Stewart, "Social Stratification and Patronage in Ancient Mediterranean Societies" and by Alicia Batten, "Brokerage: Jesus as Social Entrepreneur." Stephen's opponents would have understood their relationship with the divine in terms of patronage, which Stewart defines as a social system of exchange for goods and services between parties that are not equals. A patron, in this case God, provided material support as well as power, protection, knowledge, and influence—in religious terms, blessings—to clients. Clients in turn gave praise to their patron—in religious terms, worship—thus enhancing the reputation of the patron.

Key to establishing and maintaining patron–client relations, Batten notes, are brokers, who enable exchanges between the two parties. Stephen's marshaling of divine power in the miracles he performs marks him as a broker between God and humankind and, by implication, raises questions about existing brokerage arrangements. Moses and the Temple make their appearance in the narrative at this point because they represent the established brokers of the day, the former being the quintessential broker of Judean traditions, and the latter being the concrete embodiment of divine–human brokerage in first-century Judea (at the time reflected in the narrative). The Judean leadership—elders, scribes, the council, the high priest—understandably keen to maintain the status quo, readily join in confronting (and ultimately rejecting) Stephen, the alternative broker. Not to do so would have undermined the authority and power they derived from their existing patron–client relationship with God.

Brokers figure prominently in the long speech that follows, which is not a speech in which Stephen defends himself, as we might expect (Chance 2007: 109). Rather, it asserts that the Judeans and their ancestors invariably rejected divinely-sanctioned brokers:

> 7:2 And Stephen replied: "Brothers and fathers, listen to me. ... 7:8 ... and Isaac became the father of Jacob, and Jacob of the twelve patriarchs. 9 The patriarchs, jealous of Joseph, sold him into Egypt; but God was with him, 10 and rescued him from all his afflictions, and enabled him to win favor and to show wisdom when he stood before Pharaoh, king of Egypt, who appointed him ruler over Egypt and over all his household. ... 7:20 At this time Moses was born, and he was beautiful before God. ... 22 So Moses was instructed in all the wisdom of the Egyptians and was powerful in his words and deeds ...
>
> 7:37 This is the Moses who said to the Israelites, "God will raise up a prophet for you from your own people as he raised me up." 38 He is the one who was in the congregation in the wilderness with the angel who spoke to him at Mount Sinai, and with our ancestors; and he received living oracles to give to us. 39 Our ancestors were unwilling to obey him; instead, they pushed him aside, and in their hearts they turned back to Egypt, 40 saying to Aaron, "Make gods for us who will lead the way for us; as for this Moses who led us out from the land of Egypt, we do not know what has happened to him." 41 At that time they made a calf, offered a sacrifice to the idol, and reveled in the works of their hands. ...
>
> 7:51 You stiff-necked people, uncircumcised in heart and ears, you are forever opposing the Holy Spirit, just as your ancestors used to do. 52 Which of the prophets did your ancestors not persecute? They killed those who foretold the coming of the Righteous One, and now you have become his betrayers and murderers. 53 You are the ones that received the law as ordained by angels, and yet you have not kept it.
>
> (Acts 7:2a, 8b–10, 20a, 22, 37–41, 51–53)

The speech informs us that Joseph, Moses, the prophets, and the Righteous One, that is, Jesus, all enjoyed divine authorization as brokers between God and the Judeans, past and present. Yet they all faced rejection. And Stephen, who exhibits the same power and wisdom as Moses, suffers the same fate at the conclusion of his speech.

Lest there be any doubt about Stephen's legitimacy as a broker, the narrative frames his speech with two visions that connect the divine and human worlds, much as Moses's vision of the burning bush reported in

Stephen's speech. First, the council members experience a Stephen who has been transfigured: "And all who sat in the council looked intently at him, and they saw that his face was like the face of an angel" (Acts 6:15). Second, Stephen himself reports a vision he has: "But filled with the Holy Spirit, he gazed into heaven and saw the glory of God and Jesus standing at the right hand of God. 'Look,' he said, 'I see the heavens opened and the Son of Man standing at the right hand of God!'" (7:55–56). Both the council and Stephen enter what anthropologists would call an altered state of consciousness, in which they encounter an alternative reality. Pieter F. Craffert explores the nature of this phenomenon in his essay titled "Altered States of Consciousness: Visions, Spirit Possession, Sky Journeys," and he notes the ubiquity of such states in the world described by the Bible. This is not window dressing in the New Testament that modern readers, who typically devalue or ignore altered states, can dismiss. In the narrative before us they serve an important function, confirming Stephen's connection to the divine world in the face of his rejection and execution.

Just as human agents can act as brokers or mediators between God and humankind, so do institutions. Consequently, the Temple figures prominently in the charges against Stephen and in his speech to the council. As the speech reaches its climax, Stephen takes the Judean's ancestors to task for seeking the patronage of the wrong gods and misapprehending the nature of their true patron, such that they built an earthly dwelling for God, namely, the Temple:

> 7:41 At that time they made a calf, offered a sacrifice to the idol, and reveled in the works of their hands. 42 But God turned away from them and handed them over to worship the host of heaven, as it is written in the book of the prophets: "Did you offer to me slain victims and sacrifices forty years in the wilderness, O house of Israel? 43 No; you took along the tent of Moloch, and the star of your god Rephan, the images that you made to worship; so I will remove you beyond Babylon." 44 Our ancestors had the tent of testimony in the wilderness, as God directed when he spoke to Moses, ordering him to make it according to the pattern he had seen. 45 Our ancestors in turn brought it in with Joshua when they dispossessed the nations that God drove out before our ancestors. And it was there until the time of David, 46 who found favor with God and asked that he might find a dwelling place for the house of Jacob. 47 But it was Solomon who built a house for him. 48 Yet the Most High does not dwell in houses made with human hands; as the prophet says, 49 "Heaven is my throne, and the earth is my footstool. What kind of house will you build for me, says the Lord, or what is the place of my rest? 50 Did not my hand make all these things?"
>
> (Acts 7:41–50)

It is understandable that the personnel of the Temple, like the high priest, and the Judean leaders in general were resistant to Stephen's words: "When they heard these things, they became enraged and ground their teeth at Stephen" (Acts 7:54). But their brutal execution of him seems excessive until one considers how centrally important the Temple was to their world. The Temple gave monumental expression to a sacrificial system that allowed the Judeans to maintain right relations with God by eliminating any unholiness that arose in daily life. That system was but one node in an elaborate network of beliefs and practices that organized the entire Judean worldview. Ritva H. Williams's essay, "Purity, Dirt, Anomalies, and Abominations," is essential reading for those wishing to understand how the binary of purity and impurity or holiness and unholiness allowed the Judeans to give order to the environment around them and thus make existence meaningful. An attack on the Temple, therefore, had deep reverberations: it threatened to topple the cosmos as the Judeans understood it.

For these reasons, the accusations against Stephen aroused the passions of his listeners. His accusations raised questions about an elaborate system that classified persons, places, things, times, activities, and experiences in ordered categories, so that everything had a proper place. These categories comprised a road map that both Stephen and his listeners had in their heads. It enabled them to discern whether something was acceptable or unacceptable, and how to deal with it if it was unacceptable. Stephen's accusations invalidated this road map and the ordered world in which they lived and moved. Hence, violence against Stephen and his death were predictable.

The contemporary counterpart to the Temple would be the global financial system, which is interwoven in many aspects of life today. Yet the Temple had an even wider reach. It was not only central to what moderns might label organized religion but, as noted above, played a central role in the Judean conceptual universe. Moreover, it was intricately tied into the ancient economy, because of the taxes and donations that flowed to it. David A. Fiensy's essay "Ancient Economy and the New Testament" focuses on Galilee, Jesus's home territory and some distance from Jerusalem by ancient standards. Yet any picture of the Galilean economy would be incomplete without reference to the Temple, which Fiensy makes clear in his contribution to this volume. Quite literally everything was in jeopardy when the Temple was threatened.

While much has already been said about Stephen's speech, more needs to be said. It is the longest speech in the Acts of the Apostles, a book noted for its lengthy speeches (Witherington 1998: 264; Aune 1987: 77–115; Johnson 1987). Besides being a speech about the ancestral brokers of the Judeans and their (misguided) institutionalization of brokerage in the form of the Temple, the speech evidently has a broader purpose, for it talks not only about ancestral brokers but the full sweep of Judean history. The names would have been quite familiar to the audience: Abraham (7:2, 8, 16, 17, 32), Isaac (7:8, 32), Jacob (7:8, 12, 14, 15, 32, 46), the twelve partriarchs (7:8, 9), Joseph (7:9, 13, 14, 18), Pharaoh (7:10, 13), Moses (7:20, 22, 27, 29, 31, 32, 35, 37, 40, 44), Pharaoh's daughter (7:21), Egyptian(s) (7:22, 24, 28), Israelites (7:23, 37), Aaron (7:40), Joshua (7:45), David (7:45), Solomon (7:47). The place names were familiar as well: Haran (7:2, 4), Egypt (7:9, 10, 11, 12, 15, 17, 18, 34, 39, 40), Canaan (7:11), Shechem (7:16), Midian (7:29), wilderness of Sinai (7:30, 38, 44), Red Sea (7:36), Israel (7:42), Babylon (7:43). But, as scholars have noted, Stephen weaves the names and places together in a novel way that departs from the version of the story the Judeans would have known, found in the Old Testament/ Hebrew Bible (Haenchen 1971: 289–90; Dibelius 1956; Aune 1987; Witherington 1998: 265).

The litany of persons and places the speech rehearses is best understood as an act of remembering and identity creation or, because it seeks to undermine and replace the Temple-centered world of the listeners, memory and identity *recreation*. It does so by reconfiguring the key figures and places from the Judean past into a story that disconnects them from the listeners, the Judean leaders who base their legitimacy on them. It reattaches the story to Stephen himself, as alternative broker and representative of the circle of believers around Jesus. The essays by Halvor Moxnes, "Landscape and Spatiality: Placing Jesus" and Alan Kirk "Memory Theory: Cultural and Cognitive Approaches to the Gospel Tradition," offer important insights in this regard. Moxnes explores the connection among place, identity, and memory, while Kirk examines the active role memory plays in forging identities and realities. Stephen's creative retelling of Judean history contests his audience's memory of these events and claims legitimacy for himself and his circle.

This is all too much for Stephen's audience, which acts aggressively and decisively in response: "Then they dragged him out of the city and began to stone him; and the witnesses laid their coats at the feet of a young man named Saul" (7:58). It bears noting that Stephen is not only executed but also expelled from the city. The modern reader might regard this detail as incidental, but it, along with the stoning, underscores the rejection of Stephen as alternative broker. The ancient city functioned as a hub of patron–client relations in the ancient Mediterranean world. Peter Oakes's essay, "Urban Structure and Patronage: Christ Followers in Corinth" examines this aspect of urban life as he looks at cities connected with the apostle Paul, but the integral connection between cityscape and patronage undoubtedly obtained in the case of Jerusalem, a temple-city that understood itself as a broker for God. Stephen's expulsion from the city, as much as his execution, signals his listeners' refusal to acknowledge his claim to be broker.

This concise introduction to the chapters that follow, prompted by the interpretive puzzles that emerge from reading Acts 6 and 7, should give the reader some idea how indispensable they are for understanding the New Testament. It is not surprising that such interpretive models form necessary companions to that task. For the New Testament comes from a world that is neither modern nor western. As a consequence, the literature that comes from it tells a story whose logic, flow, and contents are often perplexing. What the chapters that follow provide are insights into the social world of the New Testament, which will equip readers to understand the New Testament itself. While each essay in this book offers rich insights into that world, the ensemble of them will give the reader a full set of tools for making sense of a sometimes puzzling but always fascinating text.

Notes

1 Ernst Haenchen observes that Luke avoids the term deacon for these "relief officers" for good reason: they were in reality preachers and missionaries— Stephen in particular was quickly caught in the cleavage between the Hellenists and Hebrews because he may have led "a mission among his compatriots and erstwhile champions of the synagogue, the more so if that mission had been crowned with great success...consequently he did the best for Stephen and the Seven by creating for them an honourable place as guardians of the poor" (1971: 266–7).
2 These two rather different depictions of Stephen's role in Acts have long perplexed commentators and have been answered in a variety of ways (Witherington 1998: 252; Conzelmann 1987: 44; Bruce 1976: 132–3; Haenchen 1971: 266–7).
3 The interpretation that follows takes its inspiration from Pilch (2004) and the many excellent essays in Neyrey (1991).

Part I

Identity

1

Collectivism in Mediterranean Culture

Bruce J. Malina

Individualists and Collectivists
Common Erroneous Reading Perspectives
Reading with Collectivistic Lenses
Further Reading

Why is it that in the game of chess, if the piece called the King is captured, then the game is over—even if there are still many other same-colored chess pieces on the board? Why cannot some other piece take up the King's role and carry on? One might say, those are the rules of the game. Yet why are those the rules of the game? In what sort of social system does the capture of the King mark the end of the contest and the submission of the King's forces?

At the Beijing Olympic games in the summer of 2008, when hurdler Liu Xiang took to the track with a pronounced limp—he had an ankle injury— the announcement that this nationally admired athlete would not compete triggered an outburst of weeping both within the stadium and throughout the country. Such behavior is typical of collectivistic societies, and it is the rules of collectivism that are replicated in the game of chess and the national weeping of the Chinese.

Collectivism and its opposite, individualism, are somewhat technical terms to describe in general how people think of themselves and others. Collectivistic persons think of themselves primarily as part of a group, for example as a member of a family, an ethnic group, a team, a gang. In their "off the top of the head" judgments, group members come first, and what counts above all is the needs and concerns of group members. Single persons always represent the groups in which they are embedded. Collectivists take their clues for what to do and think from the values and attitudes of the members of the group in which they are embedded. They feel their best when their group and its members succeed in the face of competing groups. It is groups that are unique and distinctive, not individuals.

Individualistic persons, on the other hand, think of themselves as having to stand on their own two feet, as having to make it by themselves, on their own terms. They believe they have to think for themselves and make their own choices alone. They are willing to use other people who support their goals. Their parents are very happy with their successes on their own behalf. Individuals are unique and distinctive, not groups.

In general, some 80 percent of the people on our planet today are collectivistic. The far smaller percentage are individualists, mostly northern Europeans and northern European immigrants in the US, Canada, and Australia. The significant fact for those individualists who read the Bible is that biblical writers and the people they depict were collectivists, including Jesus. There are no statements in the Bible directed to individualists. This essay considers that state of affairs.

Individualists and Collectivists

Whenever we observe people interacting with each other, whether in a shopping mall, on the street, on TV shows, or in films, we invariably interpret what is going on in what we see. What sort of criteria or norms are available to us to judge what people are doing? I would presume that we invariably judge others in terms of what we have learned from our parents concerning the ways in which people interact in our society. What parents teach their children are the norms of behavior acceptable in our society. This parental socialization process would have us learn and live in terms of the norms and meanings of social interaction that prevail in our society. We learn literally thousands of "proper" ways of behaving in shopping malls and supermarkets, in crossing streets and respecting the space of our fellow pedestrians, ways of interpreting what is happening on TV shows or films, ways of understanding the various sections of newspapers, and the like. In each scene that confronts us, we invariably interpret what is going on in terms of the behaviors of single persons who, presumably, are much like ourselves. The same is true, of course, of the way we interpret the persons we encounter in reading, whether the sports pages or biblical books. We tend to believe that all individual selves are much like we ourselves are. And it is on the basis of our self-understanding that we empathize with the people depicted in the various scenarios that we observe on TV, for example, or that we imagine in our reading of the Bible, or novels, or newspapers.

The question I wish to pose here is whether our judgments in this regard are accurate or fair. To judge other persons in our own society according to the social norms we have learned is usually quite accurate and fair since without shared social norms, mutual understanding of language and other behaviors would be impossible. On the other hand, to judge other persons in alien societies according to the social norms of our own society would be quite unfair, pregnant with misunderstanding, and the source of much unnecessary conflict, to say the least. It would seem that there really is no entity like a neutral, universal "self." Rather every person we might meet or read about is a socialized or enculturated self. And since not all social systems or cultures are the same, it follows that not all individually socialized or enculturated persons are the same.

Even though all people on the planet, as far as we can verify, use the word "I" and equivalents, the meanings invested in that word in the various social systems of the world are often radically different. By "I" and equivalents, I refer to the "self."

> The self here is defined as all the statements a person makes that include the word "I," "me," "mine," and "myself." This definition means that all aspects of social motivation are included in the self. Attitudes (e.g., I like ...), beliefs (e.g., X has attribute X in my view), intentions (e.g., I plan to do ...), norms (my ingroup expects me to do ...), roles (my ingroup expects people who hold this position to do ...), and values (e.g., I feel that ... is very important), are aspects of the self.
>
> (Triandis 1990: 77)

The way people conceive of and deal with the self can be plotted on a line whose extreme points are individualism (awareness of a unique and totally independent "I") on the one hand, and collectivism (awareness of an "I" that has nearly everything in common with the kinship group and its spin-offs) on the other.

Individualistic cultures are a rather recent phenomenon in recorded history (sixteenth or seventeenth century CE at the earliest; see Duby 1988, for antiquity see Veyne 1989). Consequently, the Mediterranean selves we read about in the Bible could not be individualists. Rather, they were all group-oriented selves, very concerned to share the viewpoints of the group members whose fate they shared.

Individualists believe that single persons are unique and distinct relative to other persons. Collectivists on the other hand believe groups are unique and distinct relative to other groups. The unique and distinct groups to which persons belong through no choice of their own are groups into which a person is born and socialized: parents and family by birth, place by location of the kin group, gender by patriarchal gender roles. Genealogy, geography, and gender serve to define single groups as unique and distinct. It is group features that then define single group members.

For example, if ancient persons had family or second names as we do, it would be the family name that defined the group and all of its members as unique, such as all family members of the Williams family. If you meet one you meet them all, since they are really all the same. Furthermore, the family's location further defines the group. For example, all the members of the Chicago Williams family are quite the same. In their patriarchal system, the males of the Chicago Williams family would be all quite similar, as would the females of the Chicago Williams family. What is unique about them all is the group, its location, and gender, the patriarchal Williams family of Chicago. All members of this unique and distinct group form a primary ingroup. The term "ingroup" refers to a collection of individual persons who perceive themselves to be members of the same social category, sharing some emotional involvement in this common definition of themselves, and achieving some degree of social consensus about the evaluation of their group and of their membership in it. Single persons who realize that their values and attitudes are defined by their unique and distinct primary ingroup are said to be collectivistic persons.

There are additional features of this primary ingroup that can make it expand like a set of Russian dolls or Chinese boxes. Since the Williams of Chicago are located in Illinois, in turn located in the United States, the expanded group of all who live in Illinois and/or all who live in the US form a sort of expanded, if secondary, ingroup, for example, fellow Americans. These secondary ingroups come into play in contexts where ingroups of the same level of abstraction are set in comparative situations: state versus state, country versus country. Since the American government gratuitously attacked Iraq and killed nearly a million Iraqis, all of America and each of its citizens is the enemy of Iraq and worthy of revenge killing in the eyes of collectivist Iraqis.

Note that all these ingroups have their memberships determined by ascription. That is, people are situated into their groups by no choice of their own. As collectivists, they are not expected to have a choice about belonging to such birth-dependent groups. Birth-dependent groups are kin groups, immediate or expanded kin groups consisting of members whose situation has been determined by birth. Collectivists find it difficult, if not impossible, to leave such groups or to deny these ascribed features. To leave the group is much like divorcing family, or one's lands, or rejecting one's gender orientation—all the features that define a human being as a person. Since Jesus calls for a disciple's self-denial, the self that is denied is the group self. A person has to leave "house or brothers or sisters or mother or father or children or lands, for my [Jesus's] sake and for the gospel" (Mark 10:29–30). It is the household, kin group, and lands that constitute the self of the (male) person in question.

The birth-dependent House of Israel (literally: children of Jacob/Israel) at the highest level of abstraction consisted of people called Judeans, Galileans, and Pereans, places named after the groups and their members inhabiting them. For collectivists, groups give their name to places; wherever group members are, they always bear the name of their group/place of origin. Judeans are Judeans no matter where they are located in the Roman Empire, and no matter how long they have lived away from the original group birth locations. For individualists birthplaces do not give their name to individualists; in individualistic societies, wherever individualists are, they take on the name of their new place of residence. Chicagoans become New Yorkers by living and working in the new place for a prolonged period of time and the passing of time away from the original group birth location. In ancient collectivistic societies, exile from the group/place of origin is considered the most terrible of punishments. In individualistic societies, such "exile" from group birth location may simply mean searching for new opportunities.

In collectivistic societies, one might join a secondary group that is birth-dependent in a broader, mediate way. For example in the house of Israel, there were a number of secondary groups apart from the primary domestic birth and place related groups. Birth-dependent secondary groups include political groups such as the Herodians, political religious groups such as the Pharisees or Sadducees or Essenes, as well as groups founded by John the Baptist and Jesus of Nazareth. All the secondary groups form Israelite birth-dependent groups, open only to members of the House of Israel. The secondary group takes on a secondary identity based on some fictive birth rite, thus constituting a fictive kin group of brothers and sisters.

Individualists

American mainstream individualism is characterized by internal control and identity as well as internal responsibility and worth. Clifford Geertz tried to develop a somewhat precise and specific definition of the "individual" as found in current, mainstream US behavior. He tells us that the individual here is "a bounded, unique, more or less integrated motivational and cognitive universe, a dynamic center of awareness, emotion, judgment and action organized into a distinctive whole and set contrastively both against other such wholes and against its social and natural background." And he goes on to note that this way of being human is, "however incorrigible it may seem to us, a rather peculiar idea within the context of the world's cultures" (Geertz 1976: 225; see also Augsburger 1986: 85–7).

This sort of individualism seems rooted in a social contract of discrete individuals. Individualism as a lifestyle favors doing over being, actions over reflection, equality instead of hierarchy, informality rather than formality, and functional friendships above long-term loyalties or obligatory commitments to friends. Group membership is by renewable contract, with rights and duties defined by one's own goals. Achievement and competition are seen as motivational necessities and norms. The worth of a person is measured by objective, visible, social achievements (education, appointments, memberships, certifications) or material possessions (wealth, property, status symbols). Personal accomplishments are more important than birth, family prestige, heritage, or traditional prominence. Achieved status is valued over ascribed status.

Collectivists

Ancient Mediterraneans and nearly 80 percent of people today live in collectivistic cultures. Collectivism may be described as the belief that the groups in which a person is embedded are each and singly an end in themselves, and as such single persons in the group ought to realize distinctive group values notwithstanding the weight of one's personal drive in the direction of self-satisfaction. In collectivistic cultures most people's social behavior is largely determined by group goals that require the pursuit of achievements which improve the position of the group. The defining attributes of collectivistic cultures are family integrity, solidarity, and keeping the primary ingroup in "good health."

Individualism stands radically apart from traditional Mediterranean socio-centrism with its solidly rooted external control and worth, and range of responsibility and identity, from internal among elites to external for non-elites. This group-centeredness is founded on group solidarity of ingroup members, persons "committed" to their groups. To paraphrase Geertz, our first-century person "would perceive himself or herself as a distinctive whole *set in relation* to other such wholes and *set within* a given social and natural background; every individual is perceived as embedded in some other, in a sequence of embeddedness, so to say" (Malina 2001: 60–7). Such group solidarity ranks the division of ingroup versus outgroup as a primary perception.

Group membership derives from one's social and familial place in society, with one's behavior in the group dictated by the group's customs and sanctions or the authority of the leader. Unless for the benefit of the group, achievement and competition are seen as disruptive of social harmony. The worth of a person is measured by familial status, social position, class and caste; birth, family prestige, heritage, or traditional prominence are more important than personal accomplishments. Ascribed status is valued over achieved status. Collectivists favor hierarchical cultural groups in which the self is seen as good, valuable, of intrinsic worth; identity is conferred from family, ancestral place, and rank and role. The primary group participates in an individual's decision making. Lifestyle is dependent on the ingroup, and responsibility is rooted in a person's response to his/her obligations to others. Should a group member fall ill, the goal of an individual's healing is group well-being. Focus is on the ingroup, cooperation with ingroup members, maintenance of ascribed status, and group-centered values.

Common Erroneous Reading Perspectives

Most modern readers find it quite difficult to imagine Jesus as a collectivist. After all, if anyone was just like us in our individualistic features, it must have been Jesus. The fact is that in collectivistic societies, there were persons who had some individualistic traits. We might call such persons pseudo-individualists. Collectivistic societies are strongly hierarchical, with wide variations in status and rigid social stratification ("mind your own status"; 1 Cor 7:25). Yet such societies tend to produce pockets of individualistic-like behavior in otherwise collectivistic situations at the extremes of the societal hierarchy: the extremely wealthy and the extremely downtrodden. For example, elite members of otherwise collectivistic societies often evidence quasi-individualistic behavior, frequently motivated by pleasure, personal needs, or achievement aspirations. Harry Triandis cites Latin America as a contemporary example (Triandis 1990: 82). Elites indulge in all kinds of conspicuous consumption, carnivals, trade, luxury goods, and so on. The picture is not at all unlike that in ancient Rome (or Palestine). In Rome a similar quasi-individualism emerged among the urban elite who differed markedly from the collectivists that predominated elsewhere in the society.

At the other extreme, the lowest levels of hierarchically stratified societies, one finds people who cannot maintain their usual social status: beggars, prostitutes, disinherited sons, family-less widows, orphans or children that families cannot support who are abandoned to the streets to fend for themselves, are all obvious examples. These lowest levels of society, often called "the most marginalized," are persons who are cut off from the ingroups that guarantee survival in collectivistic cultures.

Beggars, orphans, prostitutes, and the like may not have conformed to the norms of the main-stream, but no one in that society, not even beggars and prostitutes, lived outside the social norms prescribed for those in their respective positions. Their behavior fit recognizable patterns. Thus the key fact about such persons is that they are isolated from groups and left to fend for themselves.

It is important to recognize, therefore, that the individualistic behavior of these people does not come from personal choice or enculturation. It is a response forced upon them by their circumstances in life. The result is that they are not modern individuals with a "definite view of him/herself." Instead they are collectivists living at the bottom of the hierarchy, experiencing a marginalized sense of isolation.

In summary, then, though the Mediterranean societies of antiquity were predominantly collectivist in outlook, two types of quasi-individualistic behavior existed there as well. There was, first, the narcissistic and hedonistic behavior of the urban elite, and, second, the solitary behavior of the low status, "marginalized," and degraded. The first was an outlook derived from privilege and choice, the second from isolation and despair. It is important to recognize that both types of individualistic behavior are mentioned in the Jesus traditions.

Reading with Collectivistic Lenses

As an example of reading with collectivistic lenses, I have chosen the passage Acts 16:11–40. What would a collectivistic person see/hear in his/her reading of the scenarios in this passage? In its literary structure, the book of Acts develops on two commands of the resurrected Jesus. The first command to the apostles sends them out to proclaim the gospel in Judea, Samaria, and the coastal Israelite cities (the ends of the land; Acts 1:7–9). The next command is directed to Paul (Acts 13:1). From this point Acts reports Paul's activities among Israelite minority populations in the northeastern Mediterranean (Acts 13:1–28:31). The story of Paul's travel opens with his Mediterranean expedition in Acts 13:1–16:5. What follows is an Aegean expedition (Acts 16:6–21:26). This is where Acts 16:1–40 fits, opening with a conclusion to the Mediterranean expedition (Acts 16:1–5), then continuing with the first events in the Aegean travels (to Troas [Acts 16:6–10]; in Philippi [Acts 16:11–40]).

The opening scenario (Acts 16:11–12) describes the travels of Paul and Silas from Troas to Philippi. A presumption among collectivists is that to name a city is to name all the persons constituting the city, the city residents. Traveling for collectivistic persons is moving through various groups of people. At this point, Paul and companions have been traveling among Jesus groups living in the region "to deliver to them for observance the decisions that had been reached by the apostles and elders who were in Jerusalem" (Acts 16:4).

This section of Acts 16:11–40 offers five different reports or episodes: a continuation of the travel narrative and meeting one Lydia (16:11–15); the exorcism of a slave girl, another of Paul's mighty deeds (16:16–18); the unhappy consequences of the exorcism for Paul and friends (16:19–24); rescue from prison by an earthquake (16:25–34); and reaction by Philippian leaders to Paul's complaints about the treatment accorded to him and his companions (16:35–40). The mention of Lydia at the beginning and end of the section forms an inclusion.

Episode 1

Paul and companions travel to the island occupied by Samothracians, in the northeastern Aegean, then on to the port serving the Philippians (located 10 miles inland): Neapolis. They eventually arrive among the Philippians and tarry for a while undoubtedly awaiting the Sabbath, when Israelites, Paul's audience, gather to pray. As noted in this the first of five episodes in the section, they go to "the river" (most likely the nearby creek named Crenides) on the Sabbath. Here they expected to find a place of prayer (not a synagogue, but a place where Israelites would gather as a group to pray). The ready availability of water for ritual ablutions makes the expectation plausible (see also Josephus, *Antiquities* 14.20.23). Indeed, Israelite women—the ones most likely to seek ablutions (see Lev 15:19–23)—are already gathered there.

Given the rigid separation of genders in ancient Mediterranean cultures, especially in public places, how is it that Paul and his companions were able to engage these women in conversation (see John 4:27)? The primary understanding and interpretation of space depend to a degree on the function it serves. In general, "public" space such as a riverside would be male. Yet some places can be used by males and females, but one gender generally has control over the space at any given time. If used for ablutions, the space could be under female control. If used by a teacher, women could gather there because that is where the (male) teacher sits and now controls the space.

In his Israelite audience, there is a woman named Lydia, called a "worshiper of God" (Greek: *sebomenos ton theon*; Acts 13:50; 16:14; 17:4, 17; 18:7; 19:27; cf. 18:13; 19:27), a term equivalent to the technical term "fearer of God" (Greek: *phoboumenos ton theon*; Acts 10:2, 22, 25; 13:16, 26). The Septuagint routinely uses this latter phrase to describe members of the house of Israel. The God in question, of course, is the God of Israel, indicating that the designation would include those assimilated Israelites who neglected circumcision and/or did not observe the Torah in its entirety. Lydia and (quite likely) her household are not fully observant Israelites. They were "Greeks," that is Israelites assimilated to Greek customs and language.

Lydia's place of origin, Thyatira, was in Asia Minor located near the Lycus River on the road from Pergamum to Sardis. The city was noted for purple goods, a luxury item in the ancient world. Hence, one might hypothesize that Lydia owned a business that catered to elites. However, since animal urine was used in purple dyeing, Lydia and her workers might well have lived outside the city for obvious reasons.

At Acts 16:15 we learn for the first time that part of the innovation proclaimed by Paul included the ritual of baptism. The fact that Lydia's entire household submits to baptism is typical of collectivistic societies (see Josh 24:14–15; also Acts 16:33). Everyone acts with a view toward harmony and promoting the common good. Individual choices and preferences simply do not factor into consideration. After the baptism, Lydia engages in the informal relation of reciprocity again typical of Mediterranean societies. She offers the trio hospitality. She phrases her invitation in a way that will redound to her honor: "If you have judged me to be faithful to the Lord … ." The word "prevail" accurately describes the Middle Eastern custom of insistently repeating an offer which the beneficiary is expected to refuse initially but to acquiesce only after the second or third offer (cf. Gen 19:3; 1 Sam 28:23; 2 Kgs 2:17).

Episode 2

The second episode associated with this place of prayer (Acts 16:16–18) is Paul's role of holy man, revealed in his exorcising a slave girl from a "python spirit" (correctly rendered by the NRSV "spirit of divination"). This is the only actual report of a disciple working an exorcism in the New Testament. It may be a Lukan creation intended to parallel the experience of Jesus (see Luke 4:33–34; 8:28–35). Through the slave girl the spirit world publicly testifies that these men serve the Most High God and offer "a way of salvation." That the girl shouts is an indication that she is in an alternate state of consciousness (see Pilch 2004: 111).

The reference to God as "Most High" is a typical Lukan way to refer to the God of Israel (Luke 1:32, 35, 76; 6:35; 8:28; Acts 7:48 and also very frequently in Judean writings such as 2 Esdras and Sirach; however, the name was also used in Hellenism). Paul and Silas are called slaves of the Most High God.

Slaves are people who are deprived of their freedom of decision and action with a view to the social utility of the enslaving agent, in this case, the God of Israel. Because Luke uncharacteristically does not use the definite article here with "way" as he does elsewhere (see Luke 9:57; 18:35; 19:36; 20:21; 24:32), it is plausible that Luke intentionally omitted the article here, allowing Paul to conclude that the girl was possessed by a deceptive spirit rather than one from the realm of the God of Israel. Hence the exorcism. What is clearly distressing to Luke/Paul is that the girl's owners (plausibly a man and a woman, a couple) were profiting financially from her soothsaying (16:16).

Episode 3

The third episode (Acts 16:19–24) reports the consequences of Paul's good deed. Though her mediumship abilities brought profit to her owners, the ancient world ridiculed such profit taking and considered the practice to be charlatanism (see Apuleius, *Metamorphoses* 8.26–30). Even so, Paul has infuriated her owners, who now seek revenge. The owners get some men to seize Paul and companions and bring them before the magistrates (*duoviri* of Philippi), charging that these Judeans are causing a disturbance by "advocating customs that are not lawful for us as Romans to adopt or observe" (16:21). The charge is false on its face (as were those against Jesus; see Luke 23:1–16). On the other hand, since Paul and his companions interacted only with Israelites and told them of the word of the God of Israel meant solely for Israelites, it is quite possible that the possessed girl was herself an Israelite slave. After all, the mention of the "Most High God" indicates her knowledge of Israelite practices. Yet her masters do not seem to have been Israelites, or they would not have put themselves at risk with their charges. Further, Israel's political religion was permitted in the empire.

In some of his letters Paul recounts his mistreatment and flogging at Philippi (1 Thess 1:1; Phil 1:30; 2 Cor 11:25). Of course, an obvious question arises: Why did Paul not invoke his Roman citizenship here as he does later in Acts 22:25? After the humiliation of the flogging, the traveling trio is locked up in some innermost prison cell with their feet secured to a stake.

Episode 4

The fourth episode (Acts 16:25–34) opens with the imprisoned group singing hymns to a "captive" audience at midnight just like the patriarch Joseph, when fettered in Pharaoh's prison "sang praise ... and rejoiced with cheerful voice, glorifying ... God" (*Testament of Joseph* 8:5). Then an earthquake occurs, enabling the prisoners to flee.

In the first-century Mediterranean world, earthquakes were said to be caused by celestial entities, often deities (see Acts 4:31). In accordance with this perception, Luke explains earthquakes as indications of divine intervention as throughout the Israelite tradition (see Acts 4:31; Exod 19:18; Judg 5:4; 1 Kgs 19:11; Matt 27:51, 54). God rescues his faithful agents. Impressed by the events as interpreted by Paul, the collectivistic jailer and his family become believers in the God of Israel (16:34).

In these contexts where entire households were baptized, some have wondered whether children were included. It would seem that those baptized had to be capable of attentively listening to and understanding Paul's instruction. Scholars think this would exclude children. On the other hand, while individuals were baptized, in collectivistic societies children were part and parcel of their parents and the whole collectivistic ingroup—hence the baptism of a family's adults sufficed for the ingroup children as well.

Just like Lydia, so too the jailer reciprocates his good fortune by hosting his benefactors in his house.

Episode 5

This fifth and final episode (Acts 16:35–40) shows how the Philippian authorities respond to Paul's complaints concerning the group's imprisonment. In Luke's storyline, it seems that the magistrates' experience of the earthquake and their associating it with "those men" prompted them to send officers to command the jailer to let them go.

Paul's response to the magistrates' order that he and his companions be released from prison is to refuse until the magistrates come personally to release them. Paul informs them that he and Silas ("us"; 16:37) are Roman citizens who have been totally dishonored by being publicly flogged without a trial to investigate the charges against them. Paul's claim to Roman citizenship (here and in Acts 22:28, but nowhere in his authentic letters) is either a Lukan presupposition (based on a datum that Paul was born in Tarsus) or a Pauline deception. It is honorable to lie to an outgroup person, but to be lied to is a challenge to honor.

In any event, Paul shames the magistrates into publicly apologizing. At the same time in Luke's story line, the magistrates ask them to leave the city. Paul and Silas head for Lydia's house (Acts 16:15), where they encourage those gathered and then proceed on their way. The identity of the "brothers" (NRSV's "and sisters" is not in the Greek text) is puzzling to scholars. So far, we have learned only that Lydia and household joined the Jesus followers. However, since in this culture males are the significant personages, even though Paul goes to Lydia's house the cultural custom would be to mention the men only, as Luke and Luke's Paul literally do.

The saga of Paul and Silas continues. After departing from Philippi, the duo make their way westward to Thessalonica. From that city, hostile Judeans force them to flee to Beroea, where the same scene repeats itself. Paul leaves his collectivistic companions behind as he wends his way southward to confront the Israelites among Athenians.

Further Reading

Malina, Bruce J. (2001) *The New Testament World: Insights from Cultural Anthropology*, 3rd edn, Louisville, KY: Westminster John Knox, pp. 62–8.

Malina, Bruce J. (2007) "Who Are We? Who Are They? Who Am I? Who are You (Sing.)?: Explaining Identity, Social and Individual," *Annali di storia dell'esegesi*, 24, no. 1: 103–9.

Taylor, Charles (1989) *Sources of the Self: The Making of the Modern Identity*, Cambridge, MA: Harvard University Press.

2

Kinship and Family in the New Testament World

Margaret Y. MacDonald

New Testament Household Codes and the
Classical Model of Family Organization
Marriage
Slaves and Masters
Parents and Children
Further Reading

Kinship and family are closely related concepts in the study of the New Testament, but they do not refer to exactly the same thing. Kinship refers to the imposition of "… cultural order over the biological universals of sexual relations and continuous human reproduction through birth" (Parkin 1997: 3). The study of kinship systems typically involves investigations of relations of filiation (links between parent and child), relations of siblingship (brothers and sisters), and relations of marriage. Social anthropologists have described a variety of kinship systems in many societies throughout the world which take account of the way individuals or groups of individuals are understood to be related to one another. For example, various societies emphasize patrilineal descent (that is, links through the father backwards into preceding generations and forward into future generations), while others are matrilineal, emphasizing links through the mother (Parkin 1997: 15).

In some societies kinship is the sole or primary structuring agent of family life (e.g., societies with clans or large intergenerational extended families), but this is not the case with the families of the Roman world. While kinship was central to family life in the Roman Empire, the inclusion of slaves in family life, and ongoing association of former slaves, clients, or dependent workers with some households means that we must think in broader terms than kinship (strictly speaking) when we discuss families in the New Testament world. The situation is further complicated by the fact that within ancient households slaves lived out their own kinship systems with a certain degree of independence from their owners. Slaves formed family groupings despite the fact that their owners could separate slave couples and parents and children on a whim. Slave families were not recognized in Law (see further below).

When thinking about the families of New Testament times, it may also be helpful to draw upon the insights of social scientists who have distinguished between families as defined by kinship and households as "task-oriented residence units" (Netting, Wilk, and Arnould 1984: xx; Moxnes 1997: 17). It is true that in many respects ancient households were akin to what we think of today as family businesses (Talbert 2007: 150–3). But even if this notion does capture the connection between family life and economics (Saller 2007: 87–8), it is important not to lose sight of the fact that relations between members of the household defined by an emphasis on production, such as those between masters and slaves, also sometimes revealed qualities associated with kinship. For example, slave children were frequently raised as the pseudo-siblings of freeborn children by the slave caregivers and sometimes even won the special affection of freeborn parents at the head of the household (Rawson 2003: 255–63). At least for a short period of time, such children shared the common ground of play despite the inequality that would ultimately define their existence.

The modern concept of family (husband and wife with one or more children) does not have a precise parallel in ancient terminology, and there is considerable overlap in the ancient terms with respect to what we normally consider as family, household (involving co-residence), and kinship. The Greek term *oikos/oikia* and the Latin term *domus* can refer to a physical dwelling, but more often refer to the household's property involving material goods and slaves as well as the blood family or kin (Moxnes 1997: 20–1; Osiek and Balch 1997: 6). Emphasis on property is especially striking in comparison to modern concepts of family. It is also central to the notion of *oikonomia* (household management) which is of particular importance for understanding the New Testament household codes (e.g., Col 3:18–4:1; see below). The Latin term *familia* usually refers to more than the nuclear family, emphasizing the authority of the *paterfamilias* (male head of the household) over the wife, children, and slaves—all persons and things under his legal power (*patria potestas*). Emphasis on household headship and control of property is so central to the concept of *paterfamilias* that in legal discussions the term is sometimes retained even in cases where the property owner is actually a woman (Osiek and MacDonald 2006: 154–5; Saller 1999: 184, 187).

It is important to recognize the diversity of families in the Roman world. Family life in ancient Palestine differed considerably from family life in cities such as Corinth, Rome, or Ephesus. For example, Mark 10:28–31 not only speaks of siblings, parents, children and their house, but also of fields; this underlines the close connection between residence and subsistence in the villages of Galilee (Moxnes 1997: 23; Guijarro 1997: 42–64). We know much more about the families of the elite in the ancient world than those of the non-elite peoples whose lives are reflected in the New Testament. In what follows we will concentrate primarily on Pauline literature which promulgates a moral vision which is tied to the life of house churches, but which nevertheless displays points of contact with family values of the well-to-do. This is especially true of the household codes (Col 3:18–4:1; Eph 5:21–6:9). Taking these as our starting point, we will seek to understand the nature of family relations in early church groups, including the way both conventional and counter-cultural elements shaped these relations. We will consider the interaction, and even tension, between the concrete realities of family life and the phenomenon revealed by the Pauline churches which anthropologists refer to as "fictive kinship" or "ritual kinship." This is when an idiom of kinship (e.g., brothers and sisters in Christ) is used "… to create or symbolize relationships between particular individuals or groups within the society who are not related by what the society normally regards as kinship" (Parkin 1997: 124).

New Testament Household Codes and the Classical Model of Family Organization

The classical expression of the organization of the household is found in Aristotle's *Politics* (see *Politica* 1.1253b–1260b26). It is immediately apparent that the discussions of household management from classical Greek times to the Roman era assumed the interdependence of household and civic welfare (including state, economy, and religion): "And now that it is clear what are the component parts of the state, we have first of all to discuss household management (*oikonomia*); for every state is composed of households" (*Pol.* 1.1253b; LCL; see also Xenophon, *Oeconomicus*). Aristotle examines the primary and smallest parts of the household in turn: master and slave, husband and wife, father and children, noting that some believe that "the art of getting wealth" also should be discussed when considering household management. Moreover, ancients did not distinguish between religion and politics the way moderns do. So when Jewish authors from the New Testament era such as Flavius Josephus and Philo of Alexandria sought to illustrate the respectability and civility of the Jewish population, they naturally turned to matters of household management. For example, in his apologetic work, *Against Apion*, marriage between Jews under the Law is identified as a key aspect of identity closely bound up with the Jewish conception of God and the Temple (*Contra Apionem* 2.190–203). Thus, Josephus naturally turns his attention from the wider political and religious sphere to the domestic sphere when he holds out women and other members of the household as communicators of the piety (*eusebia*, a term that links familial [including the obedience of children], political, and religious duties) of all their obligations in life (*C. Ap.* 2.181; Osiek and MacDonald 2006: 128).

Two elements are particularly striking when comparing discussions of household management in ancient literature to the New Testament evidence. The first is the presence of the same three pairs of relationships that we find in the households codes. Colossians and Ephesians are usually understood to offer the clearest examples of the household code genre (Col 3:18–4:1; Eph 5:21–6:9), with other New Testament works drawing on household management themes more loosely, sometimes lacking one or more pairs of the relationships or exhorting only one of the partners (e.g., 1 Pet 2:18–3:7; 1 Tim 2:8–15; 5:1–2; 6:1–2; Titus 2:1–10).

The second element is less obvious, but no less important. Like discussions of household management in the ancient world more generally, the household codes view familial relationships as determinative of wider social realities, even theological conceptualizations. This is made especially clear by the metaphorical comparison of marriage to the interaction between Christ and the church which runs through Ephesians 5:22–33; domestic relations here are used to articulate nothing less than the relationship between the human and the divine. It is often said that Aristotle's vision presents the household as the microcosm of the state. This connection between micro and macro is very interesting to consider in relation to Ephesians which interweaves concepts of citizenship with familial concepts to describe the nature of the church community: "So then you are no longer strangers and aliens, but you are citizens with the saints and also members of the household of God" (Eph 2:19; NRSV). This is a text that prepares the way for the celebration in Ephesians 3:15 of God as the great *pater* (father) from whom every family (*patria*, literally fatherhood) in heaven and on earth is named (Osiek and MacDonald 2006: 128–9). Using theological categories to profess a new identity, we have a clear example of what anthropologists call fictive kinship. Members of the church (in the period of the New Testament, usually new converts) have a new, ultimate Father and belong to a new family—an entity that seems both to subsume, and to stand in some critical tension with, their earthly family/kinship alliances (see further below).

In exploring parallels between the New Testament household codes and teachings concerning relations in the household in ancient works more generally, scholars have noted a dual tendency. On the one hand, there is general consensus that the codes draw their origins for traditional expositions of the household management theme discussed by philosophers, and various political and moral thinkers from Aristotle onward (Balch 1981; Dunn 1996: 243). In much the same way as the New Testament household codes, these traditional discussions emphasize hierarchy and harmony in the household and frame these priorities with a view to the good of the broader social unit as described above. What this tells us is that New Testament authors (and audiences) thought about family/kinship in largely conventional terms and even conceived of the behavior of their constituencies in light of family groupings, reflecting conventional values and expectations. Like their contemporaries, New Testament authors seem to have placed a high importance on the virginity, purity, and faithfulness of women as daughters and brides, reflecting the core values of honor and shame (Osiek 2002: 29–39). In the household code of Ephesians, such values are intertwined with the directives concerning the behavior of wives and the responsibilities of husbands (see further below).

On the other hand, in exploring parallels between the New Testament household codes and teachings concerning household relations in ancient literature, scholars have noted that the traditional teaching is not fully replicated. For example, interpreters have pointed to a pattern or schema in the way the material is organized—seen especially clearly in Colossians and Ephesians—with a direct address to the subordinate members (wives, slaves, and children) followed by the address to the members in positions of authority (husbands, masters, and parents), and certain stylistic and grammatical features such as the presence of motivational clauses (Verner 1983). By way of illustration we might consider the close parallel between Colossians 3:20 where children are to obey their parents "in all things" which contains almost identical language as that found in the *encomium* (a formal expression of praise) of Rome given by Dionysius of Halicarnassus (30–7 BCE; *Antiquitates romanae* 2.26.1–4), but Colossians adds the motivational clause tied to an early church context: "for this is your acceptable duty in the Lord."

In addition, New Testament commentators have highlighted differences in the way the traditional vision of family relations is incorporated within particular New Testament documents. For example, the household code material of 1 Peter 2:18–3:7 includes an explicit reference to women who are married to non-believers (1 Pet 3:1)—a very delicate situation in a context where wives were expected to adhere to the religion of their husbands (see further below). Given the document's concern with dealing with tense relations with outsiders involving some forms of suffering (e.g., 1 Pet 3:13–17), scholars have tended to ascribe an apologetic intent (an effort to explain and defend the group's position in relation to household and societal values and expectations) to the household code of 1 Peter; this orientation stands out especially clearly in comparison to the internal focus of Ephesians which contains no explicit reference to dealing with outsiders at all (cf. Col 4:5–6).

Finally, despite their highly conventional appearance, it is important to realize that the codes could even incorporate some countercultural elements

(Standhartinger 2000; Walsh and Keesmaat 2004: 201–19) which would have been more evident to their original audiences than to us. The promise that the slaves will receive "inheritance" in Colossians 3:24 has frequently been noted as especially significant as real inheritance was completely outside the realm of possibility for slaves. Does such a text offer a glimpse of new expectations within the community? The implication here seems to be that slaves will ultimately stand beside legitimate children in the new order created by being raised with Christ which is still unfolding (Col 3:1–4). There is much uncertainty about the way family members interacted with each other in early church groups. But as explored further below, because they ultimately place all family members under the authority of the Lord, household codes open up potential for considerable tension between authority of the Lord and authority of the heads of households: husbands (and presumably widows who were sometimes at the head of households), masters, and parents (Gundry-Volf 2001: 56).

Marriage

For both Jews and Gentiles in the period of the New Testament, marriage represents the foundation of the household and the anchor of kinship. The Gospel traditions often simply presume marriage as the cornerstone of family life (e.g., Mark 1:30; John 2:1–11). Because of the importance of marriage as a profound human commitment, marriage sometimes takes on a symbolic significance. Wedding ceremonies can serve to explain the nature of Jesus's mission (Matt 22:1–14) and his presence is cast as that of the bridegroom (Mark 2:18–20; Matt 25:1–13; cf. John 3:29). But it is undoubtedly Ephesians 5:22–33 where marriage is given the greatest symbolic significance in a metaphorical exploration of how it reflects the relationship between Christ and the church. In light of some New Testament evidence which qualifies the value of earthly marriage on the basis of the dawning of the kingdom of God (e.g., see 1 Cor 7; Mark 12:18–27; Matt 22:23–33; Luke 20:27–40), Ephesians 5:22–33 leaves no room for doubt that human marriage—especially between believers—has a central role to play in the life of the Christian community.

While marriage might sometimes have taken on new meaning, and in certain circumstances was treated as a less favorable choice than celibacy (1 Cor 7:1–9; Mark 10:29–30; Matt 19:10–12; Luke 14:26; 18:29–30), the evidence suggests that many followers of Jesus and members of the earliest Christian communities simply continued with the usual customs and practices with respect to marriage associated with their previous life. We should think of girls being very young by our standards when they married. Among the elite, girls married as early as twelve years old, but were probably a little older among the less well-to-do people we read about in the New Testament. Boys were considerably older, often in their late twenties. By New Testament times, the consent of both the bride and the groom for marriage as well as that of the *paterfamilias* was required, but one imagines that for adolescent girls in particular, it would be difficult to resist parental pressure (a situation that may be reflected in 1 Corinthians 7:36–38 which speaks of a man who is not behaving properly towards "his virgin" and which has sometimes been interpreted as referring to a father and daughter as opposed to an engaged couple).

The Romans had two types of legal marriage, marriage with or without *manus* (literally, "hand"). By the New Testament period, marriage without *manus*, where a father maintained legal and economic authority (*potestas*) over his married daughter, was much more common than the type of marriage where this authority was transferred directly from father to husband along with the woman's dowry. The popularity of marriage without *manus* was probably tied to the desire to keep family fortunes intact—the daughter was a potential inheritor from her father (a factor much more important for elite classes). Such arrangements kept links between daughters and their families very much alive and seemingly gave daughters allies in marriage disputes, but there could also be considerable tension between the authority of husbands over their wives and the authority of fathers over their married daughters.

We know much less about the particular arrangements of Jewish marriage in the Greco-Roman world of the first century CE (conclusions based on later rabbinic evidence must remain tentative; see Satlow 2001). Jews could certainly describe their marriages and family life as part of what set them apart from Gentiles (see further below), but in terms of practical arrangements, Jewish marriages seem to have shared many points in common with marriages in the ancient world generally, reflecting such practices as the payment of dowry, family-arranged marriages, and emphasis on the virginity of the bride.

Concepts of gender are closely related to the fundamental importance of marriage in the New Testament. In conducting their public affairs, there was an expectation that men interacted with each other as married heads of households. In household management ideals the husband's authority over his wife was closely tied to his ownership of property. He had exclusive sexual access to his wife, and the children born in the household belonged to him. The New Testament household codes recognize (though it is not unqualified, see further below) the formal authority of husbands.

Although subject to her husband's authority in the household, the wife played a crucial role in managing the daily affairs of the house, from overseeing slaves, to guiding the education of children, to directing the replenishing of storerooms, to continuing to influence the lives of married children. A matron in the Roman world had "… a certain status of respectability as mistress of the household, which was enhanced if she became a mother and further elevated if she became a widowed mother" (Dixon 1988: 44). By the first century, especially in Rome, but increasingly also in the eastern cities, widows and wives were demonstrating greater independence (sometimes free of male guardianship altogether) and public visibility (Winter 2003: 32–7; Saller 2007: 97–9). This meant that a wife shared the role of patron with her husband—often acting for him in his absence or even independently of him after his death—and was active in building the networks of relationships that were crucial to the worlds of business and politics in the Greco-Roman world. The poignant work by Plutarch, *A Consolation to His Wife*, written to his wife upon the death of their two-year-old daughter, provides interesting evidence of this very independence, where Plutarch acknowledges the ability of his wife to manage funerary and household affairs in his absence (Pomeroy 1999: 76).

All of this means that when one reads the New Testament household codes, one should be aware that there were unspoken expectations and conventions that might not be immediately apparent to us. These codes reinforce the formal authority of husbands, fathers, and masters but they must be understood in light of the informal authority and influence that many women exercised. This may explain why modern readers experience tension or even contradiction between teachings concerning women, kinship, and the family such as we witness in Colossians, a document that includes both hierarchical household teaching (Col 3:18–4:1) and instructions concerning real women such as Nympha and the church which meets in her house (Col 4:17); this text suggests that Nympha is a leader and patron of a house church community.

Even beyond authority structures and the organization of the household, the virtues and ideals associated with marriage in the New Testament reflect deep cultural roots. Unity and faithfulness (especially of the bride to her husband) were well-attested virtues in the Greco-Roman world. Marriage could be represented as an intimate union (see Plutarch's *Advice to the Bride and Groom* [142F–43A]). A famous funerary inscription from Rome, written for a woman named Turia (dating from the last decade of the first century BCE), known as the *Laudatio Turiae*, praises the harmony of a long marriage where the wife achieved the status *univira*: having only one husband in one's lifetime (cf. 1 Tim 3:2, 12; 5:9). The concord of the married couple was celebrated in art (especially funerary art) and in philosophical, moralistic, and political discourse about society. The symbolically rich imagery of Ephesians 5:22–33, with its emphasis on unity and faithfulness, is in keeping with much textual and visual interest in marriage as a means of encoding complex social messages (Osiek and MacDonald 2006: 118–43).

Marriage also appears as a prime sign of identity among Jews and as a prime indicator of a type of sexual morality that sets them apart from others in the ancient world. Thus, Josephus argues that the Law recognizes only the sexual union of husband and wife, and only for the procreation of children (*C. Ap.* 2.199). It is perhaps not very surprising that some of the most distinctive teaching in Ephesians 5:22–33 draws heavily on scriptural allusions (e.g., Eph 5:26 [Ezek 16:9]; Eph 5:28 [Lev 19:18]; Eph 5:31 [Gen 2:24]), reflecting the Jewish roots of the church. Generally speaking, Ephesians makes use of the recurring motif from ancient near eastern literature, the *hieros gamos* (sacred marriage), to emphasize the need for the community's dislocation from a corrupt society. It does so by highlighting the sexual purity of the bride and drawing upon notions of the preparation of the Jewish woman for marriage by washing (Eph 5:26)—here juxtaposed with symbols of baptism (Eph 5:26–28). Therefore, the text reflects ancient constructions of gender and ties the community's reputation symbolically to the sexual purity and concomitant shame of its brides. But once again, the household teaching is more complicated than it may first appear, for it forms part of a broader vision which is intended ultimately to draw the community apart from the standards of the Gentile world, "in the Lord" (see Eph 4:17–5:20).

One of the most distinctive in relation to both Jewish and Greco-Roman societies and well-attested teachings on family life in the New Testament is Jesus's teaching prohibiting (in the case of Matthew's Gospel, restricting) divorce (see Matt 5:31–32; 19:1–12; Mark 10:1–12; Luke 16:18; 1 Cor 7:10–16). While a prohibition against divorce is not made explicit in Ephesians 5:22–33, the virtue of permanency clearly undergirds the idealized image of marriage, revealing the nature of the relationship between Christ and the church. But despite this idealization, the reality of divorce surfaced early in church communities, as Paul's letters clearly demonstrate (1 Cor 7:10–16). Paul's language suggests that divorce could be initiated by either husband or wife, which fits with what is known about frequent divorce among Gentiles in the Roman world. Moreover, while the Hebrew Bible presupposes that only husbands may divorce their wives (Deut 24:1–4; cf. Deut 22:13–19), archaeological findings call for caution when interpreting the evidence. A number of second-century CE marriage contracts from the Dead Sea region (known as the Babatha Archive) and the marriage contracts from the Jewish military colony at Elephantine in Egypt (fifth century BCE) have led scholars to warn against assumptions that the right of women to divorce their husbands did not exist at all among Jews in this period. In reality, however, many Jewish and Gentile women must have had little control over the factors which determined their fate in divorce matters.

One situation is particularly relevant for understanding the tensions which could shape the family lives of the first Christians: marriage between believing wives and non-believing husbands. Paul views mixed marriage (he envisions both men and women as possible believing partners) as a situation where the believer might be forced into accepting divorce if the non-believer is no longer willing to live with him or her (1 Cor 7:12–16). But the household code of 1 Peter (1 Pet 3:1–2), like most subsequent early Christian evidence, presents the wife in the difficult circumstance of living with a non-believing and potentially non-supportive (in some later evidence, violent) husband (MacDonald 1990: 221–34). Even though they are not always singled out for teaching, it is important to leave open the very real possibility that audiences who heard the household codes were comprised of some people involved in mixed marriage. Some of these would end up divorced; in particular, wives might find themselves abandoned. While such women might return to their father's household after divorce, they would risk separation from their children because children remained under the legal authority of their father after divorce or their father's family after his death. We are very familiar with blended and complicated family scenarios in our world, but in the ancient world as well, frequent widowhood, death of both parents, divorce, and remarriage created the need to keep in contact with children living in someone else's house; families comprised not only siblings, but also half-siblings, step-siblings, and orphans (Saller 2007: 91).

Slaves and Masters

The separate pairs of relationships (wives–husbands, slaves–masters, children–parents) in the household codes mask the overlapping aspects of identity which in reality were part of family life in New Testament times. As a slave member of the audience hearing Colossians 3:18–4:1 for the first time, for example, one might have heard oneself addressed as a "married" member of the church community as well as a slave. While slaves lacked the legal capacity for marriage in the ancient world and might have been sold to anyone at any time without regard for personal alliances, we know from surviving funerary monuments that slaves formed familial groupings among themselves and made use of marriage terminology to refer to their partnerships (Martin 2003: 207–30). As the various agricultural handbooks from the ancient world illustrate, sometimes the preservation of slave families was viewed as a means of treating slaves humanely and fairly (e.g., Varro, *Agriculture* I.17.5; Columella, *Agriculture* I.8.5), but it was also a strategy of slave management (Harrill 2006: 85–7). The points of contact with traditional views on master–slave relations in household codes make it difficult to assess in what sense these relations were given new meaning in the Lord. Would early Christian slave-owners have heard an indirect acknowledgement of the need to preserve slave families and to respect their partnerships in the exhortation to treat their slaves justly and fairly (Col 4:1)? Scholars have recently highlighted the widespread use of male and female slaves (including child slaves) as sexual objects in the ancient world (e.g., Glancy 2002). Reservations about the sexual use of slaves are very rare in ancient literature and the New Testament does not address this issue directly (MacDonald 2007: 97–100). But the interest in sexual morality in Colossians 3:5–6 and new ethical standards for the community imply that "stripping off the old self with its practices" might include new expectations for the treatment of slaves in a community where ultimately there is no longer slave and free (Col 3:11).

Overlapping aspects of identity are also tied to the question of membership in a household with a believer as the *paterfamilias* versus membership in a household with a non-believer as the *paterfamilias*. The household code of Colossians 3:18–4:1 does not explicitly distinguish between the two scenarios as does the author of 1 Timothy (6:1–2; cf. 1 Pet 2:18–25), but neither is it stated explicitly that the masters whom the slaves should obey are brothers in Christ. The question of whether there were slaves in the community who were the property of non-believers must at least be left open, and given the persistent evidence for subordinate members of unbelieving households joining church groups, the presence of such slaves seems more likely than not. New Testament interpreters are faced with many unanswered questions with respect to how slaves may have interpreted the message of being subject to their masters in all things in light of the various circumstances of their lives (MacDonald 2007: 100–5).

Much of the treatment of the slave–master relationship in the New Testament household codes is potentially dangerous and unsatisfactory from a contemporary moral perspective, and in light of the use of scripture to justify the institution of slavery throughout history (on structures of domination see Schüssler Fiorenza 1999: ix). The parallel between fearing masters and fearing the Lord is especially problematic (Col 3:22–24). Yet it remains important to recognize that in Colossians, fictive kinship and the symbolic family is given priority over the concrete circumstances of family life. "Fearing the Lord" is unquestionably being presented as the ultimate priority of slaves. Masters are reminded that they have a Master/Lord (the term is the same in Greek, *kyrios*) in heaven. In a similar light, the promise that slaves will share inheritance (Col 3:24) reinforces their identity as brothers and sisters in the Lord with non-slaves. The countercultural resonances of this language stand out sharply when we keep in mind that in law slaves had no father and could not legitimately father a child—they stood completely outside the realm of inheritance, having no legal right to patrimony or even the passing down of a family name.

Given the nature of the ultimate commitment to God the Father (Col 3:17), it is not surprising that sibling terminology is such a prominent feature of Pauline communities (Aasgaard 2004). In Paul's letter to Philemon this language is used in a fascinating manner in a delicate circumstance involving the runaway slave Onesimus who Paul is now sending back to Philemon as a fellow-believer. Paul instructs Philemon to receive Onesimus "... no longer as a slave but more than a slave, a beloved brother—especially to me but how much more to you, both in the flesh and in the Lord" (Philem 16; NRSV). The institution of slavery was by no means eradicated in these early communities, but Paul's letter to Philemon in particular suggests that with respect to inter-believing relationships, the concept of a new family could significantly challenge the existing social norms within the context of the church. While recognizing Philemon's legal prerogatives as a master, Paul's strong suggestion appears to be that Onesimus be granted his freedom. Similarly, because fictive kinship and the symbolic family are given priority in these communities, this offered real potential for church communities to enter into conflict with the families of the neighborhoods where church communities developed. Slaves were welcomed into communities on the promise of having one true Lord who stood above both masters and slaves.

Parents and Children

Although Paul makes varied and extensive use of metaphors drawn from the world of children and parent–child relations, he makes only very rare references to real, living children (e.g., 1 Cor 7:16; Aasgaard 2008: 249). Thus, the household codes of Colossians and Ephesians are striking, for, despite their brevity, the exhortations in Colossians 3:20–21 and Ephesians 6:1–4 contain a direct appeal to children (still apparently young enough to be living with their parents, though a minority of scholars have seen here an appeal to adult children). These exhortations offer, arguably, the first explicit valuing of the parent–child relationship in early Christian texts (MacDonald 2008: 279).

As with the teachings concerning the slave–master relationship, the exhortations concerning the relationship between parents and children should be understood in light of multiple aspects of the identity of community members. Some parents and some children in the community no doubt were slaves. Due to the blending of families after divorce and widowhood as described above, some children did not live in the same house as one of their parents and, in the case of slave children, might have no parents living with them at all. Moreover, some children may have had one or perhaps even both (see further below) parents as non-believers.

Given the previous discussion of inheritance, the situation of slave children is particularly intriguing. In the households of the Roman world, it was very common for slave caregivers to raise their own children side by side with the children of their masters, and for the mixed group of children to share the same household spaces as playmates especially when they were very young. But in contrast to the realities of the early stages of childhood, ideological discourse reinforced the separation that would inevitably divide the adult slave from the freeborn adult (Seneca, *Epistulae morales* 12.3; MacDonald 2007: 106–7). Ancient texts present the slave as being in a perpetual state of childhood—never maturing and never participating in the familial/economic cycle of succession and transference of property. In contrast, freeborn children were viewed as essential for family continuity and were a source of comfort and protection in old age (Aasgaard 2008: 253; Parkin 2003: 205–15).

In using the same language, calling for obedience "in everything" from both slaves and children (Col 3:20, 22), the household code of Colossians reflects the traditional stance of the head of the household and slaveholder. In many respects, the teaching concerning the parent–child relationship is the most conventional aspect of the household codes of both Colossians and Ephesians. The concept of honoring parents (implicitly into old age) which is found in Ephesians 6:2 (citing Exod 20:12; Deut 5:16) was a basic value of the ancient Mediterranean person (Plevnik 1993: 97). Biblical tradition and Greco-Roman moral tradition agree that children are to honor and obey (Balch 1992: 403) and this is the ideal that we also find in the household codes. At the same time, the New Testament household codes seem to be in keeping with more moderate approaches with respect to the discipline of children, avoiding the articulation of harsh consequences for disobedience (e.g., Dionysius of Halicarnassus, *Ant. rom.* 2.26.1–4; 2.27.1) and warning parents against being overbearing and discouraging (Col 3:21; Eph 6:4). Moreover, the education of children emerges for the first time as community priority in Ephesians 6:4, which urges that children be brought up "in the discipline and instruction of the Lord." This is consistent with the focus on the education of children as a feature of Jewish identity (e.g., Josephus, *C. Ap.* 1.60; 2.173, 178, 204; cf. Philo *Hypothetica* 7.14; MacDonald 2008: 286–7) and marks the beginning of an interest in the Christian socialization of children that continues beyond the New Testament into the early Christian writings of the second century (cf. 1 *Clement* 21.6, 8; *Didache* 4.9; Polycarp, *Letter to the Philippians* 4.2).

Despite the many conventional overtones in the household codes of Colossians and Ephesians, however, we detect a certain resistance to equating parental authority with divine authority. In both Jewish and Greco-Roman literature the parallel between parents and God or the gods is well attested (e.g., Philo, *De specialibus legibus* 2.225–7; cf. 2.231; 4.184; Josephus, *C. Ap.* 2.206; Stobaeus, *Anthology* 4.25.53). There are certainly elements of Jesus's teaching in the Gospels (e.g., Matt 11:25) that could be interpreted as releasing children from the ultimate authority of parents and masters in certain circumstances (Gundry-Volf 2001: 56). Ephesians 6:4 points to the existence of the family context (and ultimately the house church setting) of the Christian education of children and it is difficult to avoid the impression that this fictive kinship group was risking upsetting real families and their hopes for the future. Asceticism and the recruitment of subordinate members of the household were potentially very threatening especially if combined into one uncompromising message. This is illustrated especially clearly by the second-century *Acts of Paul and Thecla* which tells the story of the virgin daughter Thecla's enchantment with the ascetic message of the apostle Paul.

The most detailed and sophisticated critique of early Christianity by a non-Christian author, Celsus, emphasized the recruitment of unsupervised and uneducated children along with slaves and women (Origen, *Contra Celsum* 3.44; 3.50; 3.55). Although clearly intended to cast early Christians in the worst possible light, the images that Celsus draws are by no means completely unbelievable. He speaks of the most reckless early Christians urging children to rebel against parental authority and teachers in favor of adopting a new way of life in disreputable places where they will find playmates: the wooldresser's shop or the cobbler's or the washerwoman's shop (Origen, *c. Cel.* 3.55). Such shops were closely connected to housing in the Roman world (Meeks 1983: 30), with houses sometimes incorporating shops facing the street; in more modest circumstances, families shared one or two rooms above a shop. In aligning itself so closely to the physical world of the family, early Christianity was able to capitalize on existing infrastructure and networks of relationships that no doubt facilitated the expansion of the movement. But as Celsus's comments illustrate so clearly, the family setting of early Christianity could appear as a source of danger to outsiders who understood their households as vital to their own welfare and to the welfare of their descendants.

Further Reading

Aasgaard, R. (2004) *"My Beloved Brothers and Sisters!" Christian Siblingship in Paul*, London: T & T Clark International.

Balch D. L. (1981) *Let Wives be Submissive: The Domestic Code in 1 Peter*, SBLMS 26, Chico, CA: Scholars.

Dixon, S. (1988) *The Roman Mother*, Norman, OK: University of Oklahoma Press.

Glancy, J. A. (2002) *Slavery in Early Christianity*, Oxford: Oxford University Press.

Gundry-Volf, J. M. (2001) "The Least and the Greatest: Children in the New Testament," in M. J. Bunge (ed.) *The Child in Christian Thought*, Grand Rapids, MI: Eerdmans, pp. 29–60.

Moxnes, H. (ed.) (1997) *Constructing Early Christian Families: Family as Social Reality and Metaphor*, London: Routledge.

Osiek, C., and D. L. Balch (1997) *Families in the New Testament World: Households and House Churches*, The Family, Religion, and Culture, Louisville, KY: Westminster John Knox.

Osiek, C., and M. Y. MacDonald, with J. H. Tulloch (2006) *A Woman's Place: House Churches in Earliest Christianity*, Minneapolis: Augsburg Fortress.

Parkin, R. (1997) *Kinship: An Introduction to the Basic Concept*, Oxford: Blackwell.

Rawson, B. (2003) *Children and Childhood in Roman Italy*, Oxford: Oxford University Press.

Saller, R. P. (1999) "*Pater Familias, Mater Familias*, and the Gendered Semantics of the Roman Household," *CP*, 94: 182–97.

Saller, R. P. (2007) "Household and Gender," in W. Sheidel, I. Morris, and R. Saller (eds) *The Cambridge Economic History of the Greco-Roman World*, Cambridge: Cambridge University, pp. 87–112.

Satlow, Michael L. (2001) *Jewish Marriage in Antiquity*, Princeton, NJ: Princeton University Press.

3

Constructions of Gender in the Roman Imperial World

Carolyn Osiek and Jennifer Pouya

After a series of Roman civil wars in the first century BCE that rocked the republic, one of the newly established imperial government's goals was to redefine itself as a community that was characterized by domestic values. The household was to be the central institution, around which Roman civic life was to be built. Augustus constantly focused on traditional family values—marriage, child raising, and women's domestic work—in speeches, in legislation, and in public art, bringing what was considered the private sphere into public discussion and legislation (Milnor 2005: 4, 27).

Beginning in 18 BCE, new laws were enacted to encourage marriage and procreation. One of them provided incentives for married couples who had children: a freeborn woman could be released from *tutela* (male legal guardianship) if she had three children, or a freedwoman for four. Other imperial laws were enacted to curb undesirable relationships and sexual relations; freeborn men were forbidden from marrying prostitutes, adultery was proscribed, and there were various restrictions placed on marriages between different classes (Dixon 1988: 73, 85; Langlands 2006: 20). These laws shed light on the sociohistorical background for the apostle Paul's writings about women and men.

Honor and Shame in the Imperial World

In crowded first-century Greco-Roman cities where genuine privacy was hard to come by and often considered suspect, people critically observed one another in the public sphere. Honor was a way of self-regarding as well as critically competing with the other. Honor codes applied to persons of different status in different ways. "The honor of the poor moved in delicate counterpoint to that of the aristocracy, the honor of the women to that of the men. Sometimes their strategies were mirrors, sometimes complements, sometimes alternatives, but they were always in relation" (Barton 2001: 13, 21–2; Langlands 2006: 20). Shame was sensitivity to one's honor in itself and in comparison with others. It is essential to be sensitive to Greco-Roman honor–shame protocols and language when reading Paul's letters.

How is Masculinity Constructed in Paul's World?

To appreciate ancient constructions of gender, we must recognize that the ancients did not think in our modern, dichotomous, biological terms that define male and female sexes. Rather, gender can be seen as a model of two dynamic, interacting frameworks: a cosmic hierarchy and a regulation of desire. Masculinity and femininity were located on two different poles of a spectrum, which inscribes the interrelation of masculinity or femininity as superior/inferior, societal status as more/less powerful, and sex role as penetrator/penetrated.

> Embodying the negative polarities, females represented both the weaknesses of, and dangers to, the social structure. Thus a Greek or Roman woman was by definition the penetrated, empty vessel that her husband filled (see 1 Thess. 4:4), while the male citizen was legally free and expected to penetrate inferior sex partners: his wife, slaves, prostitutes, and occasionally actors or dancers.
>
> (Swancutt 2004: 54–5)

Because of this single spectrum paradigm, gender was not a stable characteristic. Thus maleness was not a given, but an achieved, state (Swancutt 2004: 55). To be a man in the ancient world was to participate in a balancing act: he must appear masculine, but not *too* masculine. Still, as we shall see, it was far better for a man to err on the side of excessive masculinity than the opposite.

Men were driven to pursue honor and glory actively. In an honor–shame society, masculinity had to be constantly proven, typically by competing with other men. One might be born a male (Greek *arsēn*; Latin *mas*) or a human (*anthrōpos, homo*) and still not be a man (*anēr, vir*); one could only become a *vir* by energetically seeking honor, which was seen as a moral quality, denoting virtue and courage.

Interrelated with the framework of the cosmic hierarchical spectrum is the appropriate control of sexual desire. The most important characteristic an honorable man possessed was his self-mastery. He must prove he had control of his "passions," including anger, greed, desire, and self-indulgence. To exhibit this self-mastery he relied on the use of his reason, which was, naturally, a particularly masculine attribute. A man must also display mastery of women, children, and slaves within his household.

A certain, albeit limited, amount of physical deprivation was encouraged by ancient moralists: fasting, sleeping on the ground, and wearing rough clothing were prescribed. In his autobiography, Jewish historian Josephus described the physical privations he underwent voluntarily. After receiving intellectual training from Pharisees, Sadducees, and Essenes at age sixteen, he opted to live in the wilderness for three years, wearing clothing from trees and washing himself in cold water day and night for purification (*Life* 2.11).

Whereas being manly was always worthy, being effeminate was loathsome. The next worst thing to effeminacy in male thinking was to be a woman. Yet there were different and competing norms of masculinity operating in the Roman world. The cultivated might understand masculinity as character achievement, but others may have understood it as prowess.

How is Femininity Constructed in Paul's World?

We have seen how damaging it could be for a man to be effeminized. But a woman must characterize feminine qualities. A virtuous woman was above all a faithful, obedient wife, a good mother, and a good manager of her household. Even a "good woman" was understood to be emotional rather than rational, physically weak, gullible, and particularly susceptible to flattery and deception (Dixon 1988: 87). Interpreting Eve's susceptibility to deception by the serpent in Genesis 3, the first-century Jewish philosopher Philo writes that the serpent speaks to the woman rather than the man because woman is more susceptible to deceit than man, whose judgment like his body is masculine and rational, whereas woman's judgment is softer and more easily given to falsehood (*Questions in Genesis* 1.33).

The virtuous woman was continually concerned about her honor as reputation for properly controlled sexuality. A "bad woman" who did not evince proper concern for her honor was seen as sexually rapacious, unfaithful, and greedy. While it is difficult for many of us who live in contemporary western societies to understand, the deliberate and ubiquitous "overlooking" of women in literary sources in ancient Greco-Roman societies may well imply *honor* for women, or their male family members, rather than insult or lack of interest, for the woman of good reputation did not need to be spoken about (Barton 2002: 218–19).

Augustus's elite ideal Roman life of quiet domesticity was probably not a reality for poorer families, where female members could not afford to stay indoors. Poorer households lacked sufficient space and privacy; it was likely that children in these houses learned early about sex. The evidence that survives indicates that elite Roman girls married young, between the age of twelve and the late teens. Non-elite girls seem generally to have married slightly later, from late teens to early twenties. Marriage indicated a dramatic change in status for girls. Upon marriage, the young girl would move into the household of her husband's family and be expected to manage it, even though she would be quite a bit younger and less experienced than many of the household staff.

There remained a sharply differentiated gendered division of labor in the Roman world. Women were to supervise domestic work, care for children and other members of the household, and attend to their husbands' wishes, while men worked in the public sector and participated in intellectual and political discourse with other men. Even within this domestic context, a respectable wife, a matron, probably exerted significant control and moved about somewhat freely. She managed household slaves, arranged hospitality for her husband's guests, and attended social occasions with her husband. Although she was prohibited from entering into politics herself, she may have kept her husband apprised of political events through informal gossip channels. Also, because status was privileged over gender in the Roman Empire, women with a higher social status were often actively engaged at many levels of society. Many elite women were benefactors, property owners, builders, and patrons (Hemelrijk 1999: 9-10).

The honorable *matrona* was respected by all in the household and bore the deferential title *kyria* in Greek, *domina* in Latin, addressed to her by all in the household, including her husband, as a sign of mutual respect (Saller 1998: 86). A woman's status and authority increased when she became a mother, particularly a mother of sons. Some mothers exercised significant political power through their sons. Conversely, childlessness, resistance to child raising, and sexual behavior of women past childbearing age were regularly described as morally reprehensible (Langlands 2006: 132). Unfortunately there was another, dreadful limit on the authority of the matron: ultimately the *paterfamilias* had the authority to determine whether an infant was allowed to be reared or exposed to die.

One final, crucial point about gender must be made before we consider the Pauline writings on this topic. Some people were not seen as possessing gender. Men who were deemed not manly enough—male slaves, defeated enemies, and barbarians were stereotyped as lacking *andreia* (Greek), *virtus* (Latin), manliness (Ivarsson 2007: 165–6). Slaves, both male and female, were not seen to possess gender, which brought with it cultural attribution of defined characteristics and expectations. They were therefore unable to make claims for honor, status, rights, or protection based on their maleness or femaleness. Those in the household with no authority, who were the most marginalized, were female slaves, including children. Male and female slaves had no sexual privacy. They could be sexually used at any time by their owner or anyone else with their owner's permission.

1 Corinthians 11:2–16 and 14:34–35

Paul wrote 1 Corinthians from Ephesus, perhaps in the mid-fifties CE, in response to oral reports and a letter he had received from the Corinthian community, which was largely Gentile. Paul is deeply concerned about factionalism there, and he provides instruction on many points.

In 1 Corinthians 11:2–16, Paul issues directives on head coverings for women and men during worship. For centuries this passage has proven divisive for scholars, theologians, church members, and others. Some scholars posit that because it is different linguistically and thematically from Paul's other writings about women—particularly compared with Galatians 3:28— it must therefore be a later interpolation, though this is definitely a minority opinion among scholars. There are numerous questions that continue to be contentious, including what Paul really means by his use of *kephalē* (head) and "on account of the angels" (11:10), whether or not Paul is concerned primarily about *women's* decorum, and if he is referring to head coverings or hairstyles. A larger issue is whether or not Paul intended to subordinate women to men.

It is important to note the literary context of 11:2–16, which immediately follows Paul's argument about food offered to idols (8:1–11:1) and precedes his discussion of abuses at the Lord's Supper (11:17–34). In this much larger context, Paul is worried about a religious problem. Crucial in considering 1 Corinthians 11:2–16 is the recognition that Paul was responding in an ad hoc manner to specific concerns of a community. This passage is not a systematic, global statement from Paul about gender roles and behaviors.

In verse 2 Paul confers status by commending the Corinthians for following the traditions he has handed on to them. Although it is unclear to which traditions Paul refers, many scholars argue that it is "the eschatological inclusion of men and women as active participants in prayer and prophetic speech" (Thistelton 2000: 811). Paul introduces a "limited dress code" in verses 4 and 5 according to which women must cover their heads when they pray and prophesy. Believers are instructed to manifest a divinely ordained, hierarchical, and patriarchal order of creation with God as the head of Christ, Christ as the head of man, and man as the head of woman (Collins 1999: 401). Embedded in this ordering is Paul's own masculine role as a *paterfamilias* who mediates God's authority to these Corinthians.

In 11:4–6, Paul is concerned with honor and shame. He insists that men reflect the "glory" of God rather than the "image" of God, as in the original Genesis passages to which Paul alludes (Gen 1:27; 2:21–23). He is concerned about the respectability of the Corinthian congregation in the eyes of others. If they are seen as a group that does not observe a respectable manner of behavior, they would not be accepted in their social world, and thus be unable to live securely or evangelize others. Paul's concern to maintain social acceptability betrays deeper concerns, however. He wishes the Corinthian community to affirm publicly his ability to assert leadership and thus masculine honor. As we have seen, in antiquity men were expected to prove their honor publicly. Because the community reflects the household, the female body becomes the cultural and rhetorical battleground for Paul's and the community's honor. It is clear in 11:5 that women in the Corinthian community pray and prophesy. Through controlling the behavior of the women prophets, Paul asserts his control of the community as household, one of the primary contexts for the exertion of masculine power.

The Greek word for head (*kephalē*) is crucial for Paul's argument here. It occurs nine times in this passage (11:3, 4, 5, 7, 10). Although some scholars have argued that *kephalē* means source in this context, it more likely refers to the head. Yet the usage is problematic: while there are many other ancient contexts in which one person is "head," that is, authority over a group of others, there is little precedent for this meaning of one person as authority over one other person. There is probably a wordplay at work in verses 5 and 10 where Paul exhorts a woman to have authority over her head and not disgrace it. Not only is he concerned about the shame of her uncovered head, he is concerned about shame to her metaphorical head—to her husband or other males in the Corinthian assembly.

Paul justifies his requirement that women cover their heads from Scripture (verses 7–12), from nature (13–15), and, finally, from church custom (16). Drawing on the second creation account in Genesis 2, Paul argues in 11:7–9 that woman was created from man and for man. Yet in verses 11–12, he argues that men and women are interdependent, and acknowledges that men are born from women. Paul affirms gender differences in two distinct ways, hierarchical (11:7–9), but also complementary (11:11–12).

Finally, in verses 14–16, Paul further supports his argument about head coverings by appealing to nature (verses 14–15). The word he uses for "nature" (*physis*) was used in a variety of meanings, most having to do with what we would call cultural conditioning. This is how it functions here. Paul has just said in verse 13 that it is proper for women to cover their heads in worship. He is at pains to make sure this fledgling Corinthian community observes proper first-century social conventions in order to maintain their public honor.

1 Corinthians 14:33–35 is another passage that continues to vex scholars. Paul directs women to be silent in the assembly and to submit to men, asking questions of their husbands at home, not in worship. Again, some contend that these verses are an interpolation, and this time there is some slight manuscript evidence that may point in that direction. Why would Paul argue for women to be silent in worship when their praying (aloud) and prophesying is already a given (1 Cor 11:5; 14:31)? Others wonder if verses 34 and 35 are a Corinthian slogan Paul quotes before rejecting. Some maintain that Paul's concern is again merely proper decorum, and that women asking questions would disturb the assembly. But why would only women ask questions? Others argue that the word used here for speaking (*lalein*) sometimes (but not always) can refer to ecstatic utterances, which, again, would be disturbing. But Paul has already acknowledged that women prophesy (11:5).

In these verses we see again Paul's overriding concern about potential shame for the community. Paul claims that women's speech in worship is shameful (*aischron*). We should also remember that a man's honor was impacted by his wife's public comportment, as we saw in 11:2–16. Once again, the issue is public order so that the community (and ultimately Paul) will not be shamed by negative publicity.

1 Timothy 2:9–15

1 Timothy, one of three so-called Pastoral Epistles (with 2 Timothy and Titus), is a hortatory letter composed to persuade an early Christian community to observe certain behaviors and to assume distinct gendered societal roles, as well as to warn them against inauthentic teachers. There is no scholarly consensus on the letter's original date or setting, although it might have been written in the early second century, possibly in Ephesus. Most scholars argue that the letters are pseudonymous, written several generations after Paul's death. Differences between the undisputed letters of Paul and the Pastoral Epistles in style, vocabulary and theology support this. Little is known about the original recipients of the letter, though there may have been socioeconomic diversity if some female church members wore gold and pearls (2:9).

The author, likely an early second-century admirer of Paul eager to advance Paul's reputation, expresses grave concerns about the public appearance of this early Christian community in the Roman Empire. He is at pains to enforce traditional hierarchical, patriarchal codes. The Christian male is expected to exercise self-control and control over the behavior of all household members. Like most biblical writings, 1 Timothy is directed to men, perhaps male church leaders; women, children, and slaves are to be brought along by their instruction. Clear gendered roles and behaviors are indicated; the distinction between male and female roles is crucial throughout the letter in the author's construction of masculinity (D'Angelo 2003: 272–3). The author adapts traditional hierarchical household ideals and applies them to the whole community as an extended household.

The focus of 1 Timothy 2:9–15 is on women's proper dress and behavior, primarily in public but also in private settings. In this controversial passage, women are told to be submissive and silent and to refrain from teaching and exercising authority over a man. Since the time Eve was deceived and sinned (on her own, for the author of 1 Timothy!), women have been subordinate to men but may be saved through childbearing provided "they" (the antecedent is not clear) display appropriately modest and holy behavior. Many of the words used in the directive echo honor–shame language. The passage is framed by the Greek word *sophrosynē* (2:9, 15), translated variously as modesty, discretion, or self-control. In 2:9 women are told to dress themselves with *aidōs*, which approximates the English word modesty, and *sophrosynē*. These Christian women must manifest a positive sense of shame in their dress, avoiding an obvious display of wealth with gold ornaments, pearls, expensive attire, or braided hairstyles. It is rather their good works that should be displayed conspicuously (2:10). Male critique of female adornment was traditional, usually out of fear of the economic power in the hands of women that accompanied it. Use of this motif here may suggest the same. Also, by preventing women from displaying their status, the writer hoped to prevent male Christians from drawing public ridicule that might occur if outsiders thought that women were exercising control.

The author continues his exhortation by recommending silence and submission for women. They must not teach or exercise authority over men. Although the author makes a similar plea for silence in 2:2, his concern there is for a generally peaceful life for all. In 2:11–12 the picture shifts to become one of "verbal silence and social subordination" of women (Bassler 1996: 59). The prohibition in 2:12 differs markedly from references to women in the undisputed Pauline letters, where Paul refers to Junia as an apostle (Rom 16:7), to Phoebe as a minister or deacon (Rom 16:1), and to Prisca (1 Cor 16:3; Rom 16:3), Euodia and Syntyche (Phil 4:2) as his co-workers, all of whom might have been entrusted with teaching. For the writer of 1 Timothy, "The existence of autonomous females in the household of God signals that the householders, the male leaders of the church, have not mastered the congregation as the Pastor demands" (Glancy 2003: 254).

The author defends his regulations by providing two biblical proofs: first, from the order of creation in Genesis 2 where the first-born has superior status, and, second, from Genesis 3 where Adam and Eve are duped by the serpent. As we have already seen, in the ancient world there was a popular stereotype about women being easily deceived. Thus the author of 1 Timothy alerts male Christians to be attentive to women's propensity to be deceived (1 Tim 5:11–12, 15). 1 Timothy's male audience must be vigilant to guard these women against potential deceivers by exerting their masculine control (Heidebrecht 2004: 179).

The last verse of this passage is problematic. In 2:15 the author argues that "she" will be saved provided "they" abide in faith, love and holiness with self-control (*sophrosynē*). Does this mean childbearing is a condition of salvation for women? And who are "they"—women, men and women, or even children? Scholars have offered numerous interpretations of this verse. Given the likely second-century social context of the writer and audience, as well as the socially conservative leanings of the writer, this verse probably indicates that women must remain in their socially acceptable proper domestic roles.

Homoeroticism in Paul's World

Few New Testament writings are as contentious for Christians living in the twenty-first century as are Paul's purported writings about homosexuality. We will examine two passages from Paul's letters: 1 Corinthians 6:9 and Romans 1:26–27. Before doing so, however, we need to consider briefly Greco-Roman understandings of sexuality, as distinctive from gender, which we have already discussed. Sex was commonly regarded as a relationship of dominance and submission; gender, rank, and social status were crucial in determining power relations in sex. The ancients viewed sexual desire itself as necessary in moderation but dangerous in excess. According to medical theories, there were within the natural balance of the body hot and cold, dry and moist elements. Males were characterized as hot and dry (preferable, of course), females as cold and moist. Sexual desire was thought to originate from the body's natural heat. The heat produced by desire was essential for a man's production of semen, and for women's childbearing, but excess desire was regarded as an illness. A healthy man needed to strike a balance between excessive heat, associated with young men, and excessive cold, which was dangerously feminizing. A woman's desire was thought to be limited by her physical nature, of which the goal was procreation. Surprisingly, though, women were stereotyped as having more trouble than men resisting desire; it was thought that once women experienced sex, they developed an insatiable appetite for it. Because a woman's inappropriate sexual activity could dishonor the men in her family, male family members were to exert authority over female sexuality. Women were enjoined to have sex within marriage, solely for procreative purposes. It was generally considered acceptable for a married man to have sexual relations with his wife, slaves, and prostitutes. Yet inability to exert self-mastery led to the suspicion of effeminization, precisely because it was "womanish" not to be able to control oneself.

In the contemporary western world we have learned to think and speak in categories of heterosexuality and homosexuality, but the concept of sexual orientation was unknown in antiquity. There were no clear terms for "homosexual," "heterosexual," or "bisexual" in ancient Mediterranean languages. Greeks and Romans did not condemn homosexuality per se as we might conceive it. Rather, the moralists criticized inordinate desire, which they understood to be the reason for disordered heterosexual sex as well. Same-sex relations were seen as an extreme manifestation of *heterosexual* desire (Martin 2006: 137–8). Moralists also decried receptive anal intercourse by men, because they construed sexuality as a binary opposition between penetrator and penetrated. The real shame for a male was not necessarily involvement in a male homoerotic relationship—it was involvement as the penetrated partner. The true man must always play an active, not passive role, in sex as in everything else. Only women, slaves, and boys should be the penetrated. Sex was regarded as an intrinsically non-relational act in which participants "acted out the relevant hierarchical distinction between them in social status and sexual role" (Halperin 2002: 255).

As difficult as it is for us to understand, the practice of pederasty (adult male relationships with preadolescent boys) was widespread in the Greco-Roman world. When the practice emerged in ancient Greece, the older man was seen as a mentor to the boy through his period of initiation. Ancient moralists sometimes criticized pederastic relationships because they were concerned that young men might not mature into appropriately masculine men if they assumed the penetrated role too often (Swancutt 2004: 56–7).

The word lesbian originates from the Greek island Lesbos, where the Greek poetess Sappho wrote lyric poems in the late seventh and early sixth century BCE. While many of her poems articulate desire and love for girls and women, it is anachronistic to apply a modern understanding of lesbianism to ancient Greece or Rome. The earliest extant expression of same-sex female desire occurs in a fragment of an ode written by the male poet Alcman in the late seventh century BCE. It is notable that a male writer depicts female homoerotic expression. Sappho's writings were admired by male readers, and in fifth- and fourth-century BCE Athenian comedies she was depicted variously as a lover of men, and occasionally as a prostitute. Her writings about same-sex female desire were not seen as unusual. It was not until the late first century BCE and early first century CE that the Roman poets

Horace and Ovid first questioned Sappho's homoeroticism, and it was not until the second century CE that the people of Lesbos were first associated with female homosexuality (Halperin 2002: 230–1).

1 Corinthians 6:9

Although Paul sometimes spoke of sex in his letters, it does not seem to have been a primary concern occupying his thought. He said very little about sex in Romans, his most theologically sophisticated epistle (Hays 2004: 137). In 1 Corinthians, Paul addresses sexual matters out of his larger concern for unity and in order to regulate proper gendered behaviors. Even so, there has been no lack of attention over the millennia to Paul's views on sex and marriage.

1 Corinthians 6:9–10 has long been recognized by scholars as a vice list, used in antiquity for instruction in upright moral behavior. Vices corrupted men, adversely impacting their masculinity and ability to exert power; to be full of vices was to be like a woman. Effeminacy was commonly found in vice lists. The lists that Paul employs in 1 Corinthians 5:10, 5:11 and 6:9–10 are probably stereotypical. The language is not characteristic of Paul. The function of the vices in 1 Corinthians 6:9–10 was probably to contrast righteous and unrighteous persons, and the objects of the condemnation were outsiders, not insiders (Elliott 2004: 22).

With this in mind, we look at two words in 1 Corinthians 6:9–10 that have been used repeatedly to claim that Paul condemned homosexuality. The first is *malakoi*, of which a literal translation might be "soft males." As we have seen, it was not uncommon for the ancients to deride men as effeminate. It is poorly translated as "male prostitutes" in the New Revised Standard Version. A more difficult term to define is *arsenokoitai* (1 Cor 6:9), rendered "sodomites" in the NRSV. Unfortunately, there is little evidence for the use of this word in antiquity. Considering its order in the vice list immediately preceding *malakoi*, it may refer to the sexually active or dominant male partner, with *malakoi* referring to the passive male. Was Paul condemning outright homosexuality as it is understood today, as many modern theologians (and politicians) are wont to claim? This is unlikely.

Romans 1:26–27

Paul probably composed Romans in the mid to late-fifties CE to a community he did not found. Paul's last extant letter, Romans is his lengthiest and most theologically refined. In 1:16–17, Paul has stated that now all are saved through the Gospel. Romans 1:26–27 is located in Paul's first following argument that all people with or without the Law were able to know God and what God requires (1:18–32). In verse 26, Paul accuses women of exchanging natural sex for sex that is "beyond nature" (*physis*: the same word used in 1 Cor 11:15–16 for short hair on men, long hair on women). In verse 27 he says that in the same way, men abandoned natural use of women and burned with desire for each other. Paul derides men for this shame, which exceeds the proper limits of desire (Martin 2006: 136). Paul's censure of men who exhibit passive, feminine behavior would have been heard loud and clear by Paul's earliest audiences.

Conclusion

Questions about sexuality are always socially controversial. When we try to interpret what ancient authors were saying, we need to remember that they felt, thought, and spoke out of their own social context with its presuppositions and prejudices, and that we do the same.

Further Reading

Hjort, Birgitte Graakjaer (2001) "Gender Hierarchy or Religious Androgyny? Male-Female Interaction in the Corinthian Community—A Reading of 1 Cor. 11, 2–16," *Studia Theologica*, 55: 58–80.

Joshel, Sandra R. (1992) *Work, Identity and Legal Status at Rome: A Study of the Occupational Inscriptions*, Norman, OK: University of Oklahoma Press.

Joshel, Sandra R., and Sheila Murnaghan (1998) *Women and Slaves in Greco-Roman Culture: Differential Equations*, New York: Routledge.

Knust, Jennifer Wright (2006) *Abandoned to Lust: Sexual Slander and Ancient Christianity*, New York: Columbia University Press.

Martin, Dale B. (2006) "Heterosexism and the Interpretation of Romans 1:18–32" in Mathew Kuefler (ed.) *The Boswell Thesis: Essays on Christianity, Social Tolerance, and Homosexuality*, Chicago: University of Chicago Press.

Milnor, Kristina (2005) *Gender, Domesticity, and the Age of Augustus: Inventing Private Life,* New York: Oxford University Press.

Økland, J. (2004) *Women in their Place: Paul and the Corinthian Discourse of Gender and Sanctuary Space,* JSNTSup 269, London: T & T Clark.

Osiek, Carolyn (2005) "Family Matters" in Richard A. Horsley (ed.) *Christian Origins,* A People's History of Christianity, vol. 1, Minneapolis: Fortress Press, pp. 201–20.

Osiek, Carolyn, and Margaret Y. MacDonald with Janet H. Tulloch (2006) *A Woman's Place: House Churches in Earliest Christianity*, Minneapolis: Fortress Press.

Penner, Todd, and Caroline Vander Stichele (2005) "Unveiling Paul: Gendering Ethos in 1 Corinthians 11:2–16" in Thomas H. Olbricht and Anders Eriksson (eds) *Rhetoric, Ethic, and Moral Persuasion in Biblical Discourse*, New York: T & T Clark International, pp. 214–37.

Penner, Todd, and Caroline Vander Stichele (eds) (2007) *Mapping Gender in Ancient Religious Discourses*, Leiden: E. J. Brill.

Sawyer, Deborah F. (2002) *God, Gender and the Bible*, London: Routledge.

Skinner, Marilyn (2005) *Sexuality in Greek and Roman Culture*, Malden, MA: Blackwell.

Williams, Craig (1999) *Roman Sexualities: Ideologies of Masculinity in Classical Antiquity*, New York: Oxford University Press.

4

Memory Theory

Cultural and Cognitive Approaches to the Gospel Tradition

Alan Kirk

In the past two decades analytical approaches drawing upon memory theory have made major inroads into the social sciences and the humanities. They have been slow, however, to leave a mark upon New Testament scholarship. Their neglect is especially problematic when it comes to the origins and history of the gospel tradition, arguably the most basic issue in the study of early Christianity and its literature. In what follows we shall see that the phenomenon of the gospel tradition is closely bound up in the cognitive, social, and cultural operations of memory.

This cuts against the conventional wisdom. Gospels scholarship typically has regarded "memory" and "tradition" as incommensurable. This view derives from the form critics, who were active in the first half of the twentieth century. They understood memory narrowly as "reminiscence," personal recollections like those of an eyewitness trying to recall details of events. Obviously the gospel materials did not fit that profile at all, for they lacked the particularity of detail and idiosyncratic perspectives of the sort one finds in individual recollection. Instead, the gospel materials were formal and impersonal, they appeared in certain standardized "forms," or genres, and they gave expression to general community concerns. Moreover, the different versions of a story or saying found in the tradition often diverged from one another, sometimes quite dramatically. All this seemed proof that memory (so understood) had not been an important factor in the origins and history of the tradition, and, accordingly, that the tradition had developed independently of determinative connections to the past. Though ostensibly referring to Jesus and events of origin, in fact the tradition was largely the projection of the contemporary social realities and experiences of the early communities. Any "authentic" memory traces were residual and inert, increasingly buried under multiple layers of tradition, the latter for its part mostly the product of the developing interests, doctrines, and conflicts of the early churches.

Memory theory raises significant challenges to this view. It does not authorize any sharp distinction between memory and tradition. Maurice Halbwachs, the pioneer of social memory studies, showed that memory is not at all the isolated, individual faculty of personal recollection it is often taken to be. On the contrary, it is a thoroughly *social* phenomenon: it is in the framework of the social realities and communicative interactions within groups (family, village, church, voluntary associations) that the memories of the individuals belonging to those groups receive substance, coherence, and duration (Halbwachs 1980; 1992). Moreover, cognitive science is now showing that the neural processes of the human brain are highly "enculturated," tightly networked, that is, into the external matrix of cultural tradition, the latter constituting "an external memory field" indispensable for the brain's formation of memory in its conceptual and symbolic fullness (Donald 2001: 150, 311). This cognitive/cultural interface will direct our discussion.

The Nature of Human Memory

Human memory is not so much a passive faculty of storage and recall as it is an actively constructive cognitive faculty that condenses and compounds elements from the flux of experience into economical memory artifacts, creating cognitive scripts that give individuals and the groups to which they belong dispositional orientation to the world (Bartlett 1932: 126–7; Bonanno 1990: 177; Prager 1998: 207; Rubin 1995: 7; Squire and Kandel 1999: 46). This is more than just a matter of efficiency—shedding the massive amounts of detail that otherwise would paralyze memory's cognitive operations. Rather, from experiences memory abstracts patterns and concepts, and out of similar events it compounds generic memories with representational, emblematic functions. Larry R. Squire and Eric R. Kandel write:

> We are best at generalizing, abstracting, and assembling general knowledge, not at retaining a literal record of particular events. We forget the particulars, and by our forgetfulness gain the possibility of abstracting and retaining the main points. ... We can forget the details, and we can

therefore form concepts and gradually absorb knowledge by adding up the lessons from different kinds of experiences.

(Squire and Kandel 1999: 206; also Rubin 1995: 111; Sapir 1949: 14; Tattersall 2002: 153)

The corollary cognitive operation, likewise an element of this large-scale reduction in complexity, is the conforming of memories to genre types and narrative patterns that have achieved conventional status within a culture. Besides bestowing durability and mnemonic efficiency, this encoding in conventional forms renders memories *communicable*. Here we see with particular clarity the intersection of cognitive, social, and cultural aspects of memory. As Halbwachs showed, communicative interaction within groups is the medium in which persons form and absorb durable memories. It is to render memories communicable that memory work draws upon the cultural repertoire of communication genres and narrative schemata. This repertoire forms the bridge, accordingly, between the cognitive operations of memory and publicly shared tradition (Bruner and Feldman 1996: 293; also Bartlett 1932: 53–4; Fentress and Wickham 1992: 47–8, 72–4; Malkki 1995: 140; Namer 1987: 140–57; Rosenzweig and Thelen 1998: 196; Wagner-Pacifici 1996: 308).

This accounts for key features of the gospel tradition, for example, its existence in certain genres or forms, such as *chreias* and healing stories. While the emergence of a comprehensive, normative body of tradition (like the gospel tradition) entails a number of additional factors and circumstances, the operative memory dynamics are the same. An emergent community marks and commemorates certain elements of its past as being of constitutive significance to its existence and identity, typically events and persons foundational to its origins and embodying its constitutive values (Olick 1999: 342–4; Schwartz 1982: 377; Zerubavel 1997: 4–7). It fashions and cultivates its foundational memories collaboratively, in face-to-face communication, casting these in culturally shared narrative and instructional genres (Weldon and Bellinger 1997: 1167–73; Malkki 1995: 106; see Assmann 1992: 141–2).

Memory as Symbolic Representation

The next crucial step of our inquiry is to analyze memory as *symbolic representation* and to observe how this plays out in the formation and history of tradition. Memory's condensing, compounding, and encoding activity, we have seen, is geared toward distilling out the *meaning*, the *significance* of experienced events for the rememberers (Bruner and Feldman 1996: 291–3; Schwartz 2005: 251; Squire and Kandel 1999: 78). Memory artifacts, therefore, fit the classic definition of cultural symbols: they are "condensations" of meaning (Sapir 1949: 564), or in Clifford Geertz's fuller formulation, "vehicle[s] for a conception ... abstractions from experience fixed in perceptible forms, concrete embodiments of ideas, attitudes, judgments, longings, or beliefs" (Geertz 1973: 91). This cognitive impulse of the human faculty of memory towards symbolic representation is far more than just a neurobiological matter. Rather it occurs across the active interface of the neural processes of the mind with the "vast and diverse" external field of the symbolic artifacts of culture (epic narratives, texts, law codes, material objects, rituals, images) that constitute the accumulated cultural memory of a society (Donald 2001: 150).

A community's traditions form along this continuum. The master narratives and moral codes that coalesce as a community's deposit of tradition are distillations of essential meanings and norms perceived to be immanent in foundational events, with historical details receding to support the normative appropriation (Malkki 1995: 95; Farmer 1999: 29; Lowenthal 1985: 204). As with any symbolic artifact (linguistic, ritual, or material), the forms of the tradition into which memory material is transmuted render the community's norms "visible, permanent, and transmittable" (Assmann 2006: 70; also Geertz 1973: 443–4). As with the cognitive operations described above, this symbolic refinement of a community's memory materials nourishes itself upon all the resources of the established, more ancient cultural tradition.

Among other things, this accounts for the pronounced moral complexion of the gospel tradition, visible especially in its density in dominical sayings and pronouncement stories, its Christological focus, and also for its framing and deep tincturing by older biblical traditions. Jesus's own actions and words were, of course, "deeply symbolic" (Meyer 1979: 250). Before considering specific examples, however, we must enquire into the functional *autonomy* of the tradition vis-à-vis the empirical realities of the past that it purports to describe, its taking on what seems an independent, self-organizing, constantly morphing life of its own. This is what induced the gospel form critics to think that the tradition had more to do with present than past realities, but the real reasons for it should now be clear. Memory work, we have seen, is not concerned for exact redescription but for abstracting salient elements and patterns of meaning from the flux of raw experience and configuring these in symbolically concentrated tradition artifacts (see Geertz 1973: 91). The effect, as Terrence Deacon puts it, is an "increasingly indirect linkage between symbolic mental representation and its grounds of reference" (Deacon 1997: 454). The autonomy of the tradition is due to the fact that, as with any symbolic entity, tradition stands in a *representational* relationship to the past that Casey describes as "intensified remembering" (Casey 1987: 280; see also Tattersall 2002: 153; Deloache 2004: 66). So powerful are its representational effects that enacted tradition (as is the case with symbols) seems to participate in, even to mediate tangibility and reality to what it represents (Sapir 1949: 10–11; Donald 2001: 153–6). It is by virtue of its autonomy, moreover, its casting off of ties to the specifics of the concrete events that are its ultimate grounds, that tradition is able to operate, much like language itself, as an internally ordered, "superordinate" system of symbols, as a living cognitive system, the elements of which are capable of being brought into new combinations and new applications (Deacon 1997: 87–99, 451; also Tattersall 2002: 154; Fentress and Wickham 1992: 72).

This is what enables tradition to function as a memory system, as a dynamic, living basis for cultural identity. Though it seems paradoxical, it is the tradition's autonomy, its coalescing in mnemonically efficient, durable linguistic forms loosened from originating historical contexts, that makes it possible for the community to remember its normative past, to mobilize its tradition within ever-changing historical and social contexts. Tradition operates as a cultural symbol system, objectifying a community's axiomatic meanings and norms, thereby giving moral intelligibility and dispositional orientation to the world (Geertz 1973: 95–7, 363–7). In the gospel tradition, the past is marked and represented in such a way as to enable it to exercise this sort of culture-symbolic power for the Jesus communities. Their rehearsal of the tradition constantly reconstitutes them in their identity as moral communities. The resolving of the salient past into the symbolically dense, autonomous forms of the tradition also renders it—and hence cultural identity—*transmissible*, and thus *replicable* from one historical or social context to another, indeed, from one generation to another. Just as with language (likewise an external symbol system that grounds a specific cultural identity), it also enables the *inter-mnemonic* appropriation and transmission of the salient past, which is to say that all members of the community carry about mental representations of the tradition (Parks 1991: 57; Hurford 1998: 34; Donald 2001: 150).

Preservation of Traditions and Memory

We have seen that the gospel tradition, far from being a collection of museum pieces that statically preserves the past, in fact operates as an autonomous, and we can add, highly versatile system of symbols. This is what makes tradition so efficient in solving new problems of cultural identity that constantly arise out of the changes and crises in a community's social and historical realities. Like language, and like the faculty of memory itself, tradition as an autonomous, configurable symbol system makes possible higher-order cognitive reflection on present predicaments (Bartlett 1932: 225–7; Casey 1987: 286; Fentress and Wickham 1992: 48; Geertz 1973: 214). It makes available the conceptual and moral resources for comprehending and mastering present experiences.

Tradition and its contemporary social frameworks of reception, it must be emphasized, affect each other *reciprocally*.[1] "To remember," says Barry Schwartz," is to place a part of the past in the service of the needs and conceptions of the present" (Schwartz 1982: 374). Present realities constitute "the human context in which words about the past become meaningful" (Thatcher 2008: 11). Like memory, tradition is refracted through the contemporary social realities of the communities in which it is enacted, such that it comes in important respects to reflect, even to signify those realities. Tradition has the "intrinsic double aspect" of a cultural symbol system: it naturalizes itself to its social contexts of enactment in the course of exerting its normative power in those contexts (Geertz 1973: 93; see Thompson 1996: 103). On the one hand, tradition is "an expressive symbol—a language, as it were, for articulating present predicaments," and, on the other, "an orienting symbol—a map that gets us through these predicaments by relating where we are to where we have been" (Schwartz 1996: 910). This interactive relationship between the salient past and the exigencies of the present accounts for the rich *multiformity* of the tradition, its transformations in different social contexts, a dynamic that allows the community to anchor itself to its core identity and values in ever-changing circumstances and in the face of contemporary crises. As with any cultural object, tradition leads a cultural life of its own as it constantly reacts with the historical contingencies of its tradent communities. Representations of the past unengaged with contemporary realities fall into irrelevance, then into oblivion, and no living culture is formed and perpetuated.

This is where the older but still influential conceptions of the gospel tradition went off track. Memory for many gospels critics was a peripheral factor hardly worth mentioning, not the powerful cultural force that it truly is. Rightly observing the often close fit of the tradition with the social realities and preoccupations of the early churches, critics wrongly inferred that the tradition was mostly invention, the attempt by the early communities to legitimize their present practices and teachings by projecting them back into the sacred past. They erred in regarding culture as the "mere reflex" of social structure (Geertz 1973: 169). To the contrary, Geertz argues, cultural symbol systems and social structures are better understood as distinct, interdependent variables. More often than not, cultural tradition and social realities exist in some tension with each other (Geertz 1973: 143–4).

Paul and the Gospels as Memory Sites

An important memory site for the early Christians was the Eucharist, and in Paul's discussion of it in 1 Corinthians 10 and 11 we see memory not just articulated in gestural, linguistic, ritual, and material media, but also ramifying into questions of ethics and community life. But for our case studies we will turn to the gospels, where the tradition is concentrated and thus where the dynamics discussed above are most easily observed.

This chain of admonitions in Matthew 5:38–42 and Luke 6:27–30 (Figure 4.1) illustrates the heavy investment of the gospel tradition in inculcating moral norms. Of the numerous differences between the two versions, the one we will focus on is the reversed order in which one's garments are lost. Matthew describes first the confiscation of the inner garment (*chiton*), then the giving of the outer garment (*himation*). Luke describes first the loss of the outer garment (*himation*), then the inner garment (*chiton*).

We can account for these transformations by approaching the gospel tradition as a highly versatile symbol system, the activation of which makes possible the reproduction and dissemination of cultural identity, grounded in the normative past, in quite different social and cultural environments. When in class students are asked to point out some of the differences between the two, they quickly figure out that Luke appears to have in view a more general situation of robbery or confiscation, whereas Matthew depicts quite specifically a court setting where a poor man is being sued and forced to give up his *chiton*, probably for a bad debt. They also note that Luke's order seems more intelligible than Matthew's—when someone takes your outer garment, make him the gift of your inner garment as well (Luke). It seems curious that the inner garment would be taken first (Matthew).

In fact Matthew's version, and in particular the reverse order in which the items of clothing are stripped off, makes full sense only to an audience with

Matthew 5:38–42	*Luke 6:27–30*
38 You have heard that it was said, "An eye for an eye and a tooth for a tooth." 39 But I say unto you, Do not resist an evildoer. But if anyone strikes you on the right cheek, turn the other also; 40 and if anyone wants to sue you and take your coat (*chiton*), give your cloak (*himation*) as well; 41 and if anyone forces you to go one mile, go also the second mile. 42 Give to everyone who begs from you, and do not refuse anyone who wants to borrow from you.	27 But I say unto you that listen. Love your enemies, do good to those who hate you, 28 bless those who curse you, pray for those who abuse you. 29 If anyone strikes you on the cheek, offer the other also; and from anyone who takes away your coat (*himation*) do not withhold even your shirt (*chiton*). 30 Give to everyone who begs from you; and if anyone takes away your goods, do not ask for them again.

Figure 4.1 Matthew 5:38–42; Luke 6:27–30: the Cloak and the Shirt

knowledge of Jewish laws governing loans to the poor, spelled out in Exodus 22:25–27 and Deuteronomy 24:10–13. These stipulate that the cloak of a poor man, taken in pledge for a loan, be returned to the poor man every night so that he can stay warm. Seen in this light, Matthew's version emerges as a biting satire of the powerful, who conform to the letter of Torah by leaving the poor man with his cloak (*himation*), but use their control of the courts to confiscate, quite literally, the shirt (*chiton*) off the poor man's back. Matthew's Jesus, addressing the poor of Palestine suffering this and other degrading forms of oppression, tells the poor man to cast off his cloak in the court assembly, thereby provocatively exposing the hypocrisy of the powerful, their transgression of the Torah's demand that the poor be treated with justice (see Bruner 2004: 251; Luz 2007: 274; Wink 1992: 177–9).

These finer points would mostly be lost on the inhabitants of Luke's Greco-Roman, urban world. Luke transforms the tradition to render it more directly apprehensible to the people in his immediate social and cultural environment. Under his hand the Torah-defined framework of this tradition becomes a general situation of robbery and confiscation. What might seem the illogical order in which the garments are taken away (inner–outer) is rectified (outer–inner). While not unintelligible, the original tradition without these adaptations presents some difficulties for Luke's audience. It loses something of its forcefulness, and a specifically Christian moral identity takes root with greater difficulty outside the narrowly confined cultural environment of Jewish Palestine. Conversely, Luke's changes bring to light the rich symbolic potential of the tradition, its capacity to exert its normative force in fresh ways in new situations, to spring to life in different cultural environments.

Luke 10:38–42: Mary and Martha

The *Cloak and the Shirt* shows the symbolic range of a single unit of tradition invoked in different social and cultural contexts, and accordingly, how tradition functions as a "model for" and a "model of" the community that treasures it. *Mary and Martha* illustrates how the gospel tradition, taken in aggregate, functions as a *system* of autonomous symbols, configurable in all sorts of arrangements and patterns to advance context-specific projects of moral and cultural formation. This accounts for the freedom the gospel writers exercised in arranging the materials at their disposal.

The Mary–Martha episode (Luke 10:38–42) is located near the beginning of Luke's Journey Narrative. Luke gathers an enormous amount of Jesus's teaching material into this long section of his gospel (9:51–19:44), punctuating it with occasional references to Jesus's journeying "on the way" from Galilee to Jerusalem for the Passover.

Now as they went on their way, he entered a certain village, where a woman named Martha welcomed him into her home. She had a sister named Mary, who sat at the Lord's feet and listened to what he was saying. But Martha was distracted by her many tasks; so she came to him and asked, "Lord, do you not care that my sister has left me to do all the work by myself? Tell her then to help me." But the Lord answered her, "Martha, Martha, you are worried and distracted by many things; there is need of only one thing. Mary has chosen the better part, which will not be taken away from her."

(Luke 10:38–42)

What is curious about this episode is that Luke assigns it a geographical and chronological location early in Jesus's journey south from Galilee to Judea, identifying the village of Mary and Martha with studied vagueness as a "certain village." But according to John 11:1–7, 18, and 12:3, Mary and Martha are from *Bethany*, in Judea, on the outskirts of Jerusalem. John identifies Mary as "the one who anointed Jesus" (John 11:2), a detail that links John 11–12 to the Bethany of Mark 14:3, where the incident of anointing occurs at the home of Simon the Leper. Bethany was the last station on the pilgrim road from Jericho to Jerusalem, and nine chapters later Luke correctly depicts Jesus reaching Bethany (19:29).

What reason could Luke have had for substituting the vague "certain village" for what was quite possibly, in an earlier form of the tradition, a reference to Bethany, and positioning the episode in the early stages of Jesus's journey? To account for this, it is necessary to look at the *arrangement* of materials within which Luke places this episode. We observe the following sequence:

(1) Lawyer's Question and Answer (10:25–28)
    Love God
    Love Neighbor
(2) Parable of the Good Samaritan (10:29–37)
(3) Mary and Martha (10:38–42)

In the first unit a lawyer asks Jesus, "What must I do to inherit eternal life?" Responding to Jesus's counter-question about what the Law says, the lawyer cites what are known as the two great commandments of the Torah: "You shall love the Lord your God with all your heart ... and your neighbor as yourself." The lawyer then asks Jesus, "And who is my neighbor?" In response to this question, Jesus tells the Parable of the Good Samaritan, and in so doing he explains how a person fulfills the *second* of the two greatest commandments. But the Parable does not address how a person fulfills the *first* of the two greatest commandments.

Luke then has the Mary–Martha episode immediately follow the Parable of the Good Samaritan. In this position, it interprets the first of the two greatest commandments. Mary's devotion to Jesus and to Jesus's word is exemplary of how one fulfills the commandment to love God with all one's heart (Marshall 1978: 450). In both cases, moreover, Luke selects persons of lower status—a despised Samaritan, and a woman—to model fulfillment of the two greatest Torah commandments. In putting this sequence together compositionally, Luke takes up the two greatest commandments in reverse order. We can plot the symbolic relationships that Luke creates among the units of tradition as follows:

A^1 *Love God with all your heart*
    B^1 *Love your neighbor*
    B^2 *Parable of Good Samaritan*
A^2 *Mary sits at Jesus's feet listening to his word*

Luke's overriding concern, therefore, is for the moral formation of the community. To this end he moves this unit of tradition to this location in sequence following the Lawyer's Question and the Parable of the Good Samaritan. He depicts it as occurring long before Jesus reaches Judea (and Bethany), and to make the fit as smooth as possible, he gives it his vague geographical location: "a certain village."

Luke has another reason for his editorial placement of this episode. For Luke the Journey Narrative is a metaphor for following Jesus in the way of discipleship, and he signals this by placing three discipleship "call-stories" right at its beginning (9:57–62). Within this framework, the Good Samaritan and Mary provide vivid examples of what it means to be a disciple of Jesus. Mary's position "at the Lord's feet" is in fact the conventional posture of the disciple, sitting at the feet of the rabbi. Consistently with his symbolic usage of the journey motif, therefore, Luke places materials exemplifying discipleship, including the Mary–Martha episode, along the journey route.

Conclusions

This freedom in arrangement of traditional materials evident in Luke (and the other gospel writers) expresses the tradition's autonomy, its existence as a "superordinate" system of normative symbolic units capable of being brought into fresh combinations with one another in the furtherance of some project of moral formation and cultural identity. Yet it cannot be overstated that the gospel tradition is the artifact of memory, existing at the intersection of the cognitive and cultural operations of memory and retaining—in the Gospels at any rate—a historical and geographical frame of reference. This is the case even for the Gospel of John, with its bold exploration of the symbolic potential of the tradition. Itself the product of these memory forces, the tradition becomes in its turn the most important cultural memory resource for early Christianity and its literature.

Further Reading

Assmann, Jan (1992) *Das kulturelle Gedächtnis: Schrift, Erinnerung und politische Identität in frühen Hochkulturen*, Münich: Beck.

Assmann, Jan (2006) *Religion and Cultural Memory: Ten Studies,* trans. Rodney Livingstone, Stanford, CA: Stanford University Press.

Carruthers, Mary (1990) *The Book of Memory: A Study of Memory in Medieval Culture*, Cambridge: Cambridge University Press.

Connerton, Paul (1989) *How Societies Remember*, Cambridge: Cambridge University Press.

Farmer, Sarah Bennett (1999) *Martyred Village: Commemorating the 1944 Massacre at Oradour sur Glane*, Berkeley, CA: University of California Press.

Fentress, James, and Chris Wickham (1992) *Social Memory*, Maldan, MA: Blackwell.

Halbwachs, Maurice (1980) *The Collective Memory*, trans. Francis J. Ditter and Vida Yazdi Ditter, New York: Harper & Row.

Halbwachs, Maurice (1992) *On Collective Memory*, ed. trans. Lewis A. Coser, Chicago: University of Chicago Press.

Malkki, Liisa H. (1995) *Purity and Exile: Violence, Memory, and National Cosmology among Hutu Refugees in Tanzania*, Chicago: University of Chicago Press.

Olick, Jeffrey K., and Joyce Robbins (1998) "Social Memory Studies: From 'Collective Memory' to the Historical Sociology of Mnemonic Practices," *Annual Review of Sociology,* 24: 105–40.

Rubin, David C. (1995) *Memory in Oral Traditions: The Cognitive Psychology of Epic, Ballads, and Counting-out Rhymes*, Oxford: Oxford University Press.

Schwartz, Barry (1982) "The Social Context of Commemoration: A Study in Collective Memory," *Social Forces,* 61: 374–402.

Schwartz, Barry (1998) "Frame Image: Towards a Semiotics of Collective Memory," *Semiotica,* 121: 1–38.

Schwartz, Barry (2000) *Abraham Lincoln and the Forge of National Memory*, Chicago: University of Chicago Press.

Zerubavel, Yael (1997) *Recovered Roots: Collective Memory and the Making of Israeli National Tradition*, Chicago: University of Chicago Press.

Note

1   I increasingly take the view that the past is by far the more determinative variable.

5

Ethnicity and Paul's Letter to the Romans[1]

Dennis C. Duling

The Language and Theory of Ethnicity
Ethnic Features in Paul's Ancient Mediterranean Context
Examples of "Ethnic Reasoning" in Paul's Early Letters
Ethnicity and Paul's Letter to the Romans
Conclusions
Further Reading
Note

My brethren, my kinsmen according to the flesh … are Israelites, and to them belong the sonship, the glory, the covenants, the giving of the law, the worship, and the promises; to them belong the patriarchs, and from them according to the flesh is the Christ. God who is over all be blessed forever. Amen.

(Romans 9:3b–5)

For there is no distinction between Judean and Greek; the same Lord is Lord of all and bestows his riches upon all who call upon him.

(Romans 10:12)

In his Letter to the Romans, written from Corinth about the mid-fifties CE, the apostle Paul draws a contrast between "Greeks" and his people by kinship, the "Israelites" or "Judeans" (used here for the modern term "Jews"). The Israelites are described with great honor (Rom 9:3–5); yet he also says that Christ believers have God's riches—they are honorable—and that in this group there is no distinction between Judean and Greek (Rom 10:9–12).

Can Paul's comments be understood in terms of "ethnicity"? The present chapter addresses this question in four sections by: (1) exploring the language and social-scientific theory of ethnicity; (2) comparing ethnic features isolated in the social sciences to statements in ancient Mediterranean literature about personal and group identities; (3) looking at examples of "ethnic reasoning" in Paul's early letters; and (4) examining Paul's ethnicity in Paul's masterpiece, the Letter to the Romans, in light of ethnic conflict at Rome.

The Language and Theory of Ethnicity

The first task is to examine the ancient languages. The English terms "ethnicity," "ethnic," and "ethnocentrism" are derived from Greek *ethnos* (plural *ethnē*). This word for "group" could refer to almost any kind or size of collectivity, from swarms of bees and flocks of birds to bands of bandits, collections of males and females, trade associations, the inhabitants of a village, "citizens" of cities or regions, and migrants from a particular place (Saldarini 1994: 59, 68–83; Hall 1997: 34; Llewelyn 2002: 39; Kloppenborg 2003). In ancient Judean (Jewish) literature it often referred neutrally to the "peoples" of the world and Judeans even used it for themselves occasionally (e.g., 1 Macc 15:1–2; 2 Macc 11:27; Philo, *Decalogue* 96; Muthuraj 1997). However, *ethnos* and *ethnē* increasingly became designations for outsiders, often with negative associations; the preferred word for insiders was *genos* ("stock"; "people"), a descent term (Zech 12:9; cf. Zech 14:16; Tob 3:4; *IG* 2² 1283 [260/61 BCE]); an analogous development took place in Latin: *natio* for outsiders, *populus* for insiders. To illustrate, a Judean wrote that young Judean men who removed the marks of their circumcision (an operation called "epispasm") in order to look like the *ethnē* when they exercised nude at the gymnasium "sold themselves to do evil" (1 Macc 1:15; Hall 1988). Another writer says that the *ethnē* were "blasphemous and barbarous" (2 Macc 10:4; cf. 2:21).

In short, *ethnos/ethnē* gradually came to describe *other* peoples, often in a negative way: we are a *genos*, they are an *ethnos*. The original, broader meanings might suggest that the concept "ethnicity" is inappropriate to describe ancient groups (e.g., Denzey 2002). A present word, however, need not conform to its original meanings; to require it to do so is "the genetic fallacy."

Before turning to the social-scientific theory of ethnicity, three terms/ concepts in English that overlap need to be examined, that is, "race," "nationalism," and "ethnicity."

First, "race." In the eighteenth century, an old Medieval idea that there were three kinds of peoples, each descended from one of biblical Noah's three sons (Gen 10: *S[h]em*itic [= Asians], *Ham*itic [= Africans], and *Japhet[h]*ic [= Europeans]), took on a new look in the form of three "races": "Mongoloid" (= Asians), "Negroid" (= Africans), and "Caucasoid" (= Europeans). Behind this racial taxonomy was the widespread eighteenth-century biological evolutionary theory which claimed that various species of *homo sapiens* could be distinguished on the basis of inherited *physical traits* such as skull shape, hair texture, but especially skin color; that these traits evolved in distinct, more or less isolated, geographical regions; and that some races are more evolved than, and thus superior to, others. By the mid-twentieth century biologists and anthropologists in North America were abandoning this theory as pseudoscience (Montague 1942; UNESCO 1950; American Anthropological Association 1998; Angier 2000). Yet "race" is deeply rooted in US history, for example, the famous "one drop rule"—that one drop of African blood defines one as Negro (Hollinger 2003; White 1994)—and it has survived as a social, cultural, and political reality, even in official documents (US Census Bureau Race Data 2008).

A second English term, "nationalism," describes the deeply felt expression of identifying with one's own people on the basis of modern, geographically bounded "nation-states." Usually distinguished from "patriotism," or love of one's country, nationalism in the nineteenth century became a powerful political ideology associated with national language and emotionally laden symbols for national identity such as "blood," "soil," and the flag. Loyalty to the state was paramount; perceived traitors were often executed. Positively, nationalism represented the ideal of political and economic self-determination; negatively, it usually became aggressive, militant, and expansionist, as twentieth-century history so disastrously demonstrates (Armstrong 1982).

The third term is "ethnicity." When immigrants first came to North America in the early twentieth century they usually settled together in urban neighborhoods and identified themselves on the basis of language, homeland, customs, dress, religion, food preferences, and the like. Often they developed negative stereotypes and epithets of each other analogous to "racial" slurs (e.g., "wop," "kike") and physical features were sometimes important; nonetheless, biology was not the most important distinguishing mark. In 1942, sociologist W. Lloyd Warner, knowing that "race" was an inadequate concept to apply to these mostly "white" groups, coined the noun "ethnicity" from the then current adjective "ethnic" (Warner and Lunt 1942; cf. Huxley and Hadden 1935). The new term first appeared in the *Oxford English Dictionary* in 1953 and became a major social-scientific concept in the 1960s.

In summary, the three terms/concepts race, ethnicity, and nationalism clearly overlap, but can also be distinguished: "race" calls forth mainly *biologically inherited physical* ("phenotypical") identity; "ethnicity" refers mainly to *social and cultural* identity; and "nationalism" refers mainly to *national* identity and loyalty.

Did ancient Mediterranean persons such as Paul have a concept of "race"? This has recently been defended (Isaac 2004; Buell 2005; Buell and Johnson

Hodge 2004), but most historians say, "no" because evolutionary-biological theory, the basis for modern views of race, did not yet exist. Similarly, many say that there was no "nationalism" because nation-states did not yet exist. However one answers these questions—ancient peoples did have negative stereotypes of others based on physical differences and geographical locations—"ethnicity" is the most appropriate of the three related terms/concepts to describe attitudes toward the outside "other" in the ancient world. That decision will need some justification.

First, it will be important to refine the term/concept "ethnicity." Two of the most influential theories are "primordialism" and "constructionism"; there are modifications and combinations of them (Scott 1990; Jenkins 1994; 1996; 1997; 2001; Hutchinson and Smith 1996; Sollors 1996; Yang 2000; Buell 2000; Matlock 2007).

Primordialism

The English term "primordial" refers to what has always existed from the very beginning (Latin *primus*, "first," + *ordiri*, "beginning from"). Members of ethnic groups usually have powerful, deep-seated feelings for each other, feelings that they believe are natural, sometimes even sacred, and have been there from the very beginning. Such bonds of affection are especially potent in times of rapid social change and in such times groups sharply distinguish (draw "sharp social boundaries") between themselves and others. Two of the first social scientists to study ethnicity, Eduard Shils (1957) and Clifford Geertz (1963), identified five recurring features that characterize such groups: language, family, place (land) of origin, custom, and religion. These five features are emphasized by the groups themselves ("emic" description by "natives"). However, they are actually culturally generated; thus, this view might better be called "*cultural* primordialism."

An alternative to *cultural* primordialism is *sociobiological* primordialism. Sociobiologists observe that certain tendencies in human behavior—altruism, aggression, war, criminality—tend to run in families (Wilson 1978). These tendencies lead to the neo-Darwinian view that such traits are "naturally selected"—biologically inherited—because they contribute to adapting to the environment and benefit the species. Self-interested humans will seek to maximize their "fitness" by choosing mates from within their own kin group (Van den Berghe 1987). This view sounds similar to old pseudoscientific theories of "race," but sociobiological primordialists retort that the resemblance is superficial. Critics are not so sure (Harmon 2007).

Constructionism

In the 1960s a Norwegian sociologist named Fredrik Barth challenged the representatives of cultural primordialism (Barth 1969: 13–14; 1994; Jenkins 1997; 2001). Barth did not deny the importance of observable cultural features such as language, dress, and food—he called them "cultural stuff "—but he argued that they do not produce ethnic identity; rather, *groups use these features to describe themselves and thereby to differentiate and separate themselves from other groups in their immediate social environment*. The key for Barth is not the "cultural stuff," but "the *social organization* of cultural difference(s)." In other words, ethnicity is not natural, inherent, fixed, and unchangeable, but freely chosen, fluid, and changeable—continually constructed—in new contexts in relation to outsiders' views. It is *self-imposed* and dramatic events such as migration, oppression, or persecution intensify such social boundary marking. To be sure, certain cultural features remain; otherwise, there would be total assimilation and no separation. Ethnic identity features, however, can change; indeed, members of an ethnic group can change. This theory focuses on scholars' analyses of a group's self-perception ("etic" description by outside analysts), not the group's own point of view.

Instrumentalism, Social Psychology, Ethno-symbolism

Barth's constructionism has been modified, developed, and expanded. One approach, called *instrumentalism*, is that when an ethnic group constructs its identity, it is consciously attempting to advance its own socio-political self-interests (Varshney 1995). An example would be stressing one's ethnic identity to win a scholarship designed for students of a certain ethnic heritage. Another modification, developed in *Social Psychology*, stresses that in competition with other ethnic groups the one that is victorious tends to develop kinship myths about its own collective honor and to stereotype outsiders ethnocentrically as dishonorable (Horowitz 1985). A third modification, *ethno-symbolism*, examines an ethnic group's longing for its past "golden age," illustrated by its myths of origin and election and its capacity to endure, yet adapt (Armstrong 1982).

Criticisms of these various approaches exist (Scott 1990; Yang 2000: 47–56), but most scholars accept some form of constructionism as basic to theorizing. This means that while certain features of ethnic identity remain relatively constant—otherwise there would be no ethnic distinctions—ethnic identity changes over time. Some recent theorists call the alternation between primordial features and constructed ethnicity "fixity and fluidity" (Buell and Johnson Hodge 2004; Buell 2005: 6–8, 37–41; cf. Malkin 2001).

It is now time to develop a simplified, synthetic model of ethnic identity. As noted above, Shils and Geertz cited five cultural features typical of an ethnic group (sometimes called an *ethnie*): family, territory, language, custom, and religion. Subsequent scholars have added other features. The ethno-symbolist Schermerhorn added three more, "tribal affiliation," "nationality," and "phenotypical," that is, obvious physical features (1978: 12 [see no. 8 below]). Hutchinson and Smith added another three, namely, a common proper name; myths of common ancestry, including heroes and heroines, real or imagined; and shared "historical" memories, real or imagined (1996: 6).

Placing family, tribe, and nation in the same general "kinship" field, a socio-cultural model that stresses nine cultural features can be built.

Six significant points should be noted about this model. First, although it highlights the nine common cultural features, not every feature has to be present for ethnic identity to exist. Second, at least two features, kinship (no. 1) and myths of common ancestry (no. 2), are virtually universal; homeland (no. 3) runs a close third and is especially common in the ancient world (Buell 2000: 243–4; Esler 2003a: 60–1), more especially so among Roman Judeans (Walters 1993: 36). Third, the model contains three clouds marked Context A, B, and C. They represent three different social contexts for the same group, suggesting that a group's ethnic identity is not fixed, but fluid; it is open to progressive change (constructionism). As we shall see with respect to the Christ-believing community at Rome, it is likely that Judean ethnicity was a potent factor in the early stages of the community, that non-Judean ethnic identity became stronger when Christ-believing Judeans were

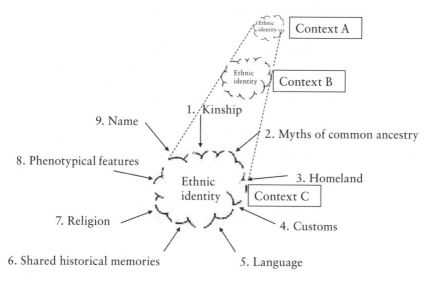

Figure 5.1 An ethnic identity model

expelled from Rome, and that ethnic conflict was probably intensified when they returned. Fourth, one aspect of fluidity is not in the model because it is difficult to represent, namely, a person can have several ethnic identities at once, one or more "nested" inside (an)other(s) (Esler 2003a: 60–1). For example, the New Testament book Acts of the Apostles tells about a Judean with the Greek name "Paul" who also has a Judean name "Saul" (Acts 13:9), who identifies himself as a citizen of the city of Tarsus, but is also said to be a citizen of the Roman Empire (Acts 22:28). Fifth, ethnic groups construct group boundaries in relation to those who are either like themselves (a "we" *aggregative* self-definition) or are different from themselves (a "we–they" *oppositional* self-definition; Hall 1997: 47), usually in relation to outsiders' views of them (social interaction). Sixth, in the ancient world "religion" (no. 7) was inseparable from/embedded in (part of) family and politics (Malina 1986: 86); it was often inseparable from customs, as well (no. 4). Yet it is also possible to distinguish them since ancient (emic) writers also sometimes distinguish what modern (etic) analysts would call "religion" (see Herodotus below).

In short, allowing for fluidity in ethnic identities, it is possible to present a model that highlights nine ethnic features that on occasion are more or less fixed.

Ethnic Features in Paul's Ancient Mediterranean Context

All nine ethnic features of the ethnicity model can be illustrated in ancient Mediterranean texts from various cultural and social contexts (Duling 2003b=2008a; 2005a; 2005b, 2006=2008b). Here is a quick survey.

1. *Kinship.* The most important indication of status was family (Malina 2001: ch 5). Except for certain magical texts, genealogies usually followed a single male line ("unilinear patrilineal descent"); the most common form of identity was "X *son of* Y (son of Z)," as in "James son of Zebedee" (Matt 4:21).
2. *Myths of common ancestry.* Herodotus wrote that "nations" traced their origins to their ancestral gods and heroes (Hall 1997: 41–3). Wealthy Greeks paid temple priests to fabricate family genealogies to enhance their social status (Hood 1961; Johnson Hodge 2007: 19–42). Biblical genealogies traced family origins to famous ancestors such as Abraham (Matt 1:1–17), or even back to the First Man (Adam), the "son of God" (Luke 3:23–38).
3. *Homeland.* The Greeks usually associated other peoples with their homeland (Hall 1997: 45; Esler 2003a: 58–9). The ancient Judean historian Josephus identified peoples by their lands (*Against Apion*) and

so did the New Testament (Mark 15:21; Luke 23:36). Ethnocentric stereotypes of others are usually related to land of origin. Judean burial inscriptions at Rome often identified persons in relation to their Judean homeland (Walters 1993: 36–7).

4. *Customs* (see *Religion*). The sixth-century BCE Greek poet, Anakreon, reports that Dorians were recognizable by their clothing (Hall 1997: 38). Religious customs—circumcision, kosher food, insider marriage, fasting, Sabbath laws, festivals, male beards—distinguished Judeans from other peoples, as did tassels (*tsitsit*) on rabbis' clothes and small boxes of scripture ("phylacteries," *tefillin*) on their heads (e.g., Exod 13:1–16; Matt 9:20–22; 23:5; Cohen 1999: 28).

5. *Language*. Greeks considered outsiders to be "babblers" (*barbaroi*, "barbarians"; Geary 1999). Egyptians called non-Egyptian speakers "other tongued." Judeans separated themselves by using sacred books written in antique Hebrew and by using insider language related to their sacred texts (Hamilton 1995).

6. *Shared historical memories*. The Greeks studied Homer's *Iliad*; Romans preserved accounts of the founding of Rome (Plutarch, *Lives of Romulus*). Greek and Latin historians wrote to reinforce ethnic identity. The Hebrew Bible contains stories about ancestors, the land, and the monarchy. In Paul's day, Josephus retold Judean history (*Antiquities*; *Wars*) and the New Testament contains many "historical" memories of ancient heroes, heroines, and events.

7. *Religion* (see *Customs*). Religion was inseparable from (embedded in) family (household shrines, etc.) and politics ("state" religion). Greeks were recognized by their myths, festivals, processions, and athletic contests (Neils 1992). Roman religion included ancestor veneration, myths, and vestal virgins, both in the household and in public ceremonies. Romans and Judeans considered themselves to be God's "chosen people" (Carter 2001: 22; Duling 2005a: 73–4).

8. *Phenotypical features*. Knowing nothing about the modern scientific view of "phenotypology" (Greek *phainein*, "to appear") in modern genetics (genes combined with environmental factors), the ancients explained physical features based on simple observation. It was said that Ethiopians had dark, curly beards and hair because they had been scorched by the sun and that Europeans had frosty skin and straight, yellow hair because they had been less exposed to the sun. The "physiognomic" literature ethnocentrically extends such features to character types: Corinthians and Leucadians, said to have small limbs, a small face, and small eyes, were judged to be small-minded (Pseudo-Aristotle, *Physiognomics* 808a, 30–33e; Malina and Neyrey 1996: ch 1)!

9. *Name.* Greeks ("Hellenes"), Romans, and Judeans identified ethnic groups by their names (Hall 1997: 47), especially as related to homeland, and often oppositionally. Herodotus labels Persians, Egyptians, Scythians, and Libyans "barbarians" (Greek *barbaroi*). Romans considered Greeks and Egyptians to be inferior. The Bible identifies many outsider groups (Canaanites, Midianites, Romans, and Samaritans). *Ioudaios*, "Judean," originally a non-Israelite's pejorative name, was adopted by Judeans for themselves (Von Rad, Kuhn, and Gutbrod 1965: 360–1; Kraemer 1989; Harvey 1989; Hanson and Oakman 2008; Cohen 1999: 70; Elliott 2007).

The following four quotations together contain all nine features of ethnicity in the above ethnicity model. Can you find them? Do you see any examples of ancients constructing their own social identity? Can you identify aggregative and oppositional social identity? Note what the ancient Greek historian Herodotus says.

For there are many great reasons why we [the Greeks] should not ... [desert to the Persians], even if we so desired; first and foremost, the burning and destruction of the adornments and temples of our gods, whom we are constrained to avenge to the utmost rather than make pacts with the perpetrator of these things, and next the kinship of all Greeks in blood and speech, and the shrines of gods and the sacrifices that we have in common, and the likeness of our way of life, to all of which it would not befit the Athenians to be false.

(Herodotus, *Histories* 8.144.2 [LCL]; Jones 1996)

The first-century historian Strabo observes similarly.

For the *ethnos* of the Armenians and that of the Syrians [Arimaeans] and Arabians [Erembians] betray a close affinity, not only in their language, but in their mode of life and in their bodily build, and particularly wherever they live as close neighbors... . And, too, the Assyrians, the Arians, and the Aramaeans display a certain likeness both to those just mentioned and to each other.

(Strabo, *Geography* 1.2.34)

From the biblical "table of *ethnē*" in the Hebrew Bible, take note of what is mentioned as the defining characteristics of ethnic identity.

These are the sons of Shem, by their families, their languages, their lands, and their nations.

(Gen 10:31)

Once more, reference is made to the assimilation of Judeans to customs of the *ethnē* in 1 Maccabees.

> In those days certain renegades came out from Israel and misled many saying, "Let us go and make a covenant with the *ethnē* around us, for since we separated from them many disasters have come upon us." This proposal pleased them, and some of the people eagerly went to the king, who authorized them to observe the ordinances of the *ethnē*. So they built a gymnasium in Jerusalem, according to custom of the *ethnē* and removed the marks of circumcision, and abandoned the holy covenant. They joined with the *ethnē* and sold themselves to do evil.
>
> (1 Macc 1:11–15)

Examples of "Ethnic Reasoning" in Paul's Early Letters

The first section of this chapter outlined the language and social-scientific theory of ethnicity and constructed a model of ethnic identity based on nine ethnic features found in social-scientific literature; the second section illustrated the model with ethnicity from ancient Mediterranean literature, including quotations. This third section begins to focus on Paul's view of his personal and group ethnic identity in more detail from his letters, especially the letter to the Romans. It will be important to observe that Paul stands on the boundary between ethnic and non-ethnic group mentalities (as also in "cultural marginality"; Duling 1995). Although he often attempts to transcend ethnic identity, he often retains ethnic terms and concepts. Thus, he cannot avoid "ethnic reasoning" (Buell 2005). On the one hand he denies the significance of ethnicity, especially kinship, for Christ believers, but on the other he defends himself against rival Judeans with his Judean ethnic heritage, co-opts the Judean archetypal ancestor Abraham as an example of faith for non-Judeans, and uses "father/brother/sister" language, or what social scientists call "pseudo-kin" or "fictive kin" language, for group relationships. All are critical for understanding Paul's constructing his personal and group ethnic identity.

In his earlier letters Paul sometimes appealed to his own ethnic heritage to defend himself against competing Torah-observant ethnic "brothers." When rival Judean missionaries at the town of Philippi (in northern Greece) wanted to circumcise his proselytes, Paul angrily wrote that these rivals "do evil" and labeled them "dogs" and "cutters" (Phil 3:2–3; Duling 2003b; 2008a). His self-defense included this:

Phil 3:4b If any other man thinks he has reason for confidence in the flesh, I have more:

3:5 circumcision on the eighth day,

of the ancestral stock (*genos*) of Israel,

of the tribe of Benjamin,

a Hebrew born of Hebrews;

as to the law a Pharisee,

3:6 as to zeal a persecutor of the church,

as to righteousness under the law blameless.

Paul's self-defense "in the flesh" stresses five well-known ethnic features from the model: (1) customs; (2) ancestors; (3) name; (4) perhaps a hint of language; and (5) especially his Torah-observant religion (Duling 2003b=2008a). He, however, claims that as a Christ believer this ethnicity is no longer of any significance. So he continues, "But whatever gain I had, I counted as loss for the sake of Christ" (Phil 3:7). Why loss? Because to be "in Christ" is to have a new social identity. On the one hand this new group consists of "brothers" and "sisters"—kinship language used for ethnic identity—but on the other this kinship is "fictive," that is, it is not based on actual lineage. Moreover, its norm is not family (ascribed) honor, but honor demonstrated (acquired) in faith and love for group members (Bartchy 1999: 68–78; Eisenbaum 2000: 136–41; Esler 2006).

In a second letter, Paul again defends his ethnic background against rival Judean missionaries at Corinth (southern Greece), 2 Corinthians 11:21b–23a (Duling 2006=2008b):

(21) ... But whatever any one dares to boast of—I am speaking as a fool—I also dare to boast of that. (22) Are they Hebrews? So am I. Are they Israelites? So am I. Are they descendants of Abraham? So am I. (23) Are they servants of Christ? I am a better one... .

Using ethnic names and his favorite ancestor Abraham (see below), Paul boasts like "the fool," a stock character of the ancient theater and banquet entertainment (Windisch 1924: 363–4; Welborn 1999). Paul is using rhetoric, including comparison and irony, to defeat his Judean rivals (Zmijewski 1978; Forbes 1986; Holland 1993; Lambrecht 2001; Duling 2006: 73–6; 2008b). His ethnic credentials, he claims, are equal to those of his opponents, but as the following verses state, his honor is not based on his ethnic heritage (ascribed honor), but rather on his sufferings as an apostle (acquired honor: suffering builds, and is a sign of, character).

A third example is found in Paul's Letter to the Galatians (Esler 1998; 2006). Paul does not defend himself with his ethnicity this time, but rather he lays a general ethnic foundation that paradoxically transcends ethnicity, one that will be refined in Romans. He is—again—extremely angry, this time because Torah-observant Judeans at Galatia (probably an ethnic region in central Turkey) want to circumcise his proselytes. "I wish that those who unsettle you would mutilate themselves" (Gal 5:12). He calls the Galatians "foolish" (3:1) and asserts that "there is neither Judean nor Greek ... for you are all one in Christ Jesus" (Gal 3:28; Stanley 1998). To support this theme he quotes Genesis 15:6: Abraham "believed and it was reckoned to him as righteousness" (Gal 3:6; cf. also Hab 2:4; 3:11b). Abraham's descendants are therefore those who believe, including the *ethnē*. He goes further: the "seed" of Abraham is not ethnic Israel, but rather Christ ("seed," a collective noun for many is grammatically singular; Gal 3:15–18; cf. Gal 4:30–5:1), and through Christ, those who believe have become the children of God by adoption (Gal 4:4–7). They are the free children of Abraham and Sarah, heirs to the promises to Abraham that all the *ethnē* of the earth will be blessed in him (Gen 12:3; 18:18). Paul uses harsh words: those who follow the Torah—ethnic Judeans—are under a curse (Gal 3:10 [Deut 27:26])! So, the sign that ethnic Israel is heir to God's covenant promises means nothing: "in Christ Jesus neither circumcision nor uncircumcision is of any avail, but faith working through love" (Gal 5:6; see Gal 6:15; Acts 21:21). One must live by the Spirit, not "the flesh" (Gal 5:16–25). Such severe language suggests that Abraham is the "father" of non-Judeans *at the expense of Judeans* (Tobin 1995: 442). In short, Paul has identified the "father of the Judeans" as the "father of the non-Judeans" by interpreting Torah promises about Abraham and the *ethnē*. Paul is constructing a new social identity, a new *ethnos* that to some extent is also a *genos* (Constructionism). This was not "good news" for his strict Torah-observant brothers and sisters.

Ethnicity and Paul's Letter to the Romans

In his Letter to the Romans, Paul used ethnic reasoning once again, this time, however, with more care, caution, and openness, and since he was no longer in the heat of battle, with a desire for ethnic peace and harmony (R. E. Brown 1982; Walters 1993; Esler 2003a; Johnson Hodge 2007). A little orientation toward the letter and ethnic conflict at Rome is in order.

Paul wrote his long, sophisticated "letter essay" (Stirewalt 1991: 147–71; Jewett 2007: 23–46) to the Romans from Corinth in the mid-fifties CE (Rom 15:19–29; Acts 20:2–3; Duling 2003a: 230–4). Literary and archaeological evidence shows that by this time there were many ethnic communities in Rome, most of them from the East. Most important, there were perhaps as many as 50,000 Judeans in the capital city, or about 5 percent of the total population, living mostly in the poor Judean quarter across the Tiber River, or Transtiberinum (Leon 1995: 11, 13, 257–8; Walters 1993: 7–18; Jewett 2007). The majority were of low status, mostly former slaves or "freedpersons" (so Philo, *Embassy* 156), Greek-speaking, and native born (Leon 1995: 148–9; Walters 1993: 31–3). They met in at least five independent "houses of prayer" (Leon 1995 [1960]: 166, 257–8, notes eleven synagogue buildings over three centuries; Wiefel 1991; Lampe 1991; Osiek 1995: xiv; Rutgers 1995; Richardson 1998: 29; for an artistic sketch of the not-so-poor synagogue at Rome's port city Ostia, see Esler 2003a: 97). It is likely that in contrast to Judeans at Alexandria, there was no central organizational council. There were also varying degrees of Judean assimilation and of non-Judean attitudes toward Judeans in the Diaspora; thus, careful analysis of each local situation is required (Walters 1993: 19–25).

No one knows for sure who introduced the belief that Jesus was a Judean Messiah at Rome, but it was not Paul. He had never been to Rome (Rom 1:10, 13–15; 11:13; 15:15–33).

Several reasons for Paul's writing to the Romans are possible. He says that he had long wanted to come to Rome (Rom 15:22–23) and that he desired to preach there (Rom 1:5–6, 11–12, 15). First, however, he needed to take a collection of money to the poor in Jerusalem; thus, he might have been thinking about his best defense against observant Judeans in Jerusalem (Rom

Figure 5.2 Remains of synagogue complex at Ostia (photo R. DeMaris)

15:25–28, 30–32). Most important, Paul wanted to launch a new mission further west in Spain and hoped that the Roman Christ believers would provide him a base of support (Rom 15:24, 28–32; Jewett 1988; 2007: 74–89).

Paul's plans were not without complications. He was a controversial figure whose reputation surely had preceded him. He had not founded the Roman congregations and his expressed principle was not to preach on other apostles' turf (Rom 15:20; 1 Cor 3:10; 2 Cor 10:13–17). Most important, as his earlier controversies show, Paul's attempt to deal with ethnic issues in the communities he had founded had the potential to offend Torah-observant ethnic Judeans—including Christ-believing ones.

It is also important for understanding ethnicity in Paul's Letter to the Romans to know that Rome had a considerable foreign population (Walters 1993: 7–11) and that ethnic conflict at Rome had a history. There had been expulsions of Judeans from Rome in 139 BCE and 19 CE, although the exact reasons for the latter are not clear (Rutgers 1998: 98–105). Some years later (according to the Roman historian Suetonius, ca. 121 CE) the emperor Claudius (37–54 CE) expelled the Judeans from Rome because of disturbances instigated by a certain "Chrestus" (*Chresto*) (Suetonius, *Claudius* 25.4). Inscriptions show that "Chrestus" was a common slave name (Bruce 1991: 178, n. 16) and could have referred to some otherwise unknown agitator, although certainly not to Jesus of Nazareth who had long since been executed in Judea. However, scholars suggest that Suetonius's comment probably reflects a misunderstanding of a conflict among Roman Judeans about whether Jesus was "the *Christus*" (e.g., Rutgers 1998: 105–6). Acts 18:2 mentions that Claudius expelled "*all* the Judeans." Given the thousands of Judeans at Rome, "all" is certainly a gross exaggeration. Since it is likely that the Romans in Paul's day would not have distinguished Judeans from Christ-believing Judeans, the comment is probably to be understood as Christ-believing Judeans (Wiefel 1991: 93; Donfried 1991a: 47–8; Walters 1993: 49–52; Leon 1995: 23–7; Duling 2003a: 231), although perhaps male non-Judean sympathizers, or "God-fearers," may have been included (see Walters 1993: 58–9, 63).

The Edict of Claudius is usually dated 49 CE. Five years later the new emperor Nero (54–68 CE) rescinded it. Returning Judean Christ believers (and perhaps non-Judean sympathizers) would likely have contributed to renewed ethnic tensions in the "house churches" (some prefer "tenement churches"; cf. Jewett 2007) that had become dominated by non-Judeans. Perhaps there was fallout in the Judean "houses of prayer" which contained "God-fearers" (Acts 14:1; 16:14; 17:4, 10–12; 18:4–7) and circumcised proselytes. An ethnic conflict context such as this is very plausible for interpreting the letter to the Romans, written about two or three years after Nero rescinded the Edict.

The following discussion of the letter may at first appear to be odd because it moves backwards, that is, from Romans 16, to Romans 14–15, to Romans 1–11 (slighting Romans 12–13). The reason for this sequence is that Romans 16 has the most concrete information about Judeans and non-Judeans at Rome, that Romans 14–15 takes up a conflict between "the strong" and "the weak," which might have been an ethnic conflict, and that Romans 1–11, which leads up to an "ethnic climax" in chapters 9–11, can be more readily understood in light of the most concrete passages. We proceed with the last chapter of Romans, Romans 16.

The argument has often been made that Romans 16 was not written to Rome, but rather to Ephesus in the Roman province of "Asia" (western Turkey) (e.g., Manson 1991 [1962]: 1–15; Koester 2000: 52). Yet many scholars have challenged this view (Gamble 1977; Meeks 1986: 16; Donfried 1991a: 48–9, 102–25; Lampe 1991: 216–30). The issue is not trivial since some of the best information capable of informing ethnicity is found in this chapter.

In Romans 16 Paul greeted twenty-six persons. This is an uncharacteristically high number, all the more so because Paul had never been to Rome. Most of those greeted did not have Judean names, but that is irrelevant because Judeans at Rome preferred Greek and especially Latin names (Leon 1960: 107–8, 121). Careful analysis shows that most were from the lower social strata; as many as two-thirds were slaves or former slaves (Lampe 1991: 226–30). Two of those mentioned, the wife-and-husband team Prisca (Priscilla) and Aquila (Rom 16:3), were Christ-believing Judeans who had been expelled by Claudius and had returned to Rome. Paul had previously known them at Corinth and Ephesus (Acts 18:1–3, 19–26; cf. 1 Cor 16:19). Paul called three others his "kins(wo)men" (*syngenēs*; Rom 16:7, 11) and also mentioned "fellow prisoners" and "fellow workers" (Rom 16:7, 8). Most scholars agree that the larger, dominant group of Christ believers consisted of non-Judeans (Lampe 1991: 225, n. 37 gives many passages). They probably had taken the Christ movement at Rome in a different direction after the expulsion of the Judeans (Gamble 1977: 136; Walters 1993: 56–66; 1998: 178).

A likely scenario, therefore, is that Paul knew about ethnic conflict between the non-Judean majority and the Judean minority in the Roman house churches, a conflict that might have spilled over into the Judean "houses of prayer" where there were also non-Judean "God-fearers" and proselytes. His addressing people he knew well would help him launch his new mission to Spain. Such a scenario will help to explain other parts of the letter.

Moving backwards, Romans 14–15 focuses on two mysterious groups, "the strong" and "the weak." Who are they? Is Paul generalizing from his previous experience of "the strong" and "the weak" at Corinth (Bornkamm 1991: 16–28; Meeks 1986: 133; Karris 1991: 65–84; cf. 1 Cor 8; 10)? It is more likely that Paul is speaking to a concrete situation at Rome (Karris 1991: 66, nn. 6, 7; Watson 1991; Sampley 1995; Nanos 1996: 85–165; Esler 2003a: 339–56).

The most obvious point in these two chapters is that the conflict centers on purity issues about food and sacred times (Rom 14:14). "The strong" think that they can "eat all things" (Rom 14:2, 21); drink wine (Rom 14:21); and consider "every day alike" (Rom 14:5). "The weak," called "weak in faith(fullness)" (Rom 13:1), are vegetarians (Rom 14:2, 21), do not drink wine, and celebrate certain days (Rom 14:3, 21). Paul speaks directly to "the strong"; he urges them to "welcome" "the weak" (Rom 14:1), whose practices are accepted by the Lord God (Rom 14:5–9); indeed, both sides should "welcome" each other, for God and Christ have "welcomed" both (Rom 14:3; 15:7). They should not judge each other, for the Master judges all (Rom 14:3–4, 10–13). They should live in peace and harmony (Rom 14:17–20; 15:5–6). If "the strong" lead a "brother" to stumble, they are not living according to love (Rom 14:13). Paul's purity principle is this: "In the Lord Jesus … nothing is unclean in itself… . Do not let what you eat cause the ruin of one for whom Christ died" (Rom 14:14, 15). He clearly places himself among "the strong" (Rom 15:1, 8).

Was the conflict between "the weak" and "the strong" simply one between ethnic Judeans and non-Judeans? Caution is in order since in the Diaspora some non-Judeans adopted Judean food practices (Josephus *Against Apion* 2.282 [39]) and some Judeans did not strictly observe dietary laws (see Collins 1986: 143). Yet it is most likely that the dietary and calendrical restrictions of "the weak" were based on the Torah, especially since observant Judeans often became vegetarians and avoided wine when dining with non-Judeans (Nanos 1996: 106–7; Gal 2:12; 4:10; Acts 10:9–16; 15:28–29).

A plausible scenario is that at least the *core* of "the strong" consisted of the law-free non-Judean Christ believers and *core* of "the weak" consisted of law-observant Judean Christ believers (Watson 1991: 203–15; Esler 2003a: 343–4). Indeed, some scholars think that the ethnic conflict was the primary reason that Paul wrote this letter (Marxsen 1964: 92–104; Minear 1971; Donfried 1991b: 102–27; cf. Esler 2003a: *passim*).

Romans 14–16 adds ethnic concreteness to the rest of the letter. In Romans 1–8 Paul opens with the tradition that God's Son is descended from the Judean King David (Rom 1:3–4), but he quickly adds that his message is for "*all* the *ethnē*, including yourselves [the Romans]" (Rom 1:5–6). He wants to impart some spiritual gift to strengthen them, but he then delicately rephrases to *mutual* encouragement "by each other's faith, both yours and mine" (Rom 11:12). He next stresses his special obligations to the "Greeks *and barbaroi* [of Spain?]" (Rom 1:14). Yet he seems to rank the Judeans *above* the non-Judeans since his gospel "is the power of God for salvation to everyone who has faith, to *the Judean first and also to the Greek*" (Rom 1:16; cf. 2:9–10; 3:1–2). In all this, Paul cautiously tiptoes on ethnic eggs: Jesus is a Judean and the Judeans are ranked first, but Paul's message is for "Greeks" and "barbarians."

Again, what is the position of non-Judeans vis-à-vis Judeans? In the Christ-believing communities, he declares, there is no distinction. "For God shows no partiality. All who have sinned without the law will also perish without the law, and all who have sinned under the law will be judged by the law" (Rom 2:11–12; cf. 3:22–25a). Monotheism, justification by faith, and Paul's view of ethnicity go together (Bassler 1982; Meeks 1987: 296; Walters 1993: 68–77).

> Is God the God of Judeans only? Is he not the God of the *ethnē* also? Yes, of *ethnē* also, since God is one; and he will justify the circumcised on the ground of their faith and the uncircumcised through their faith.
>
> (Rom 3:29–30)

Paul concludes the first four chapters of the letter by developing his familiar theme in Galatians that Abraham was justified by his faith (Cranford 1995), but in Romans Paul omits his Galatians statements that the true seed of Abraham is Christ himself (Gal 3:15–18) and that those who follow the law are under a curse (Gal 3:10 [Deut 27:26]). These omissions make his ethnic comments less oppositional, a revision that would help to unify Judeans and non-Judeans.

Ethnic themes are also developed in Romans 5–8. Briefly, members of the old humanity represented by the First Man (Adam) imagine that the solution to the human problem is to observe the Torah; members of the new humanity represented by the Last Man (Christ) realize that the solution is to live by "faith" (Rom 5:12–21; cf. 1 Cor 15:22–28). Members of the old humanity are so by birth and the sign of their inclusion is circumcision; members of the new humanity are so by faith and the sign of their inclusion is baptism (Rom 6:1–11). The law is "holy, just, and good" (Rom 7:12); it shows what one should not do. Yet the law is insufficient to deal with the power of Sin. So God had to do what the law, weakened by "the flesh," could not do: send his Son to condemn Sin "in the flesh" (Rom 8:3) for those who "walk in the Spirit" (Rom 8:4–8). In these comments, Paul wants to transcend ethnicity.

All this leads to the key ethnic question in Romans 9–11: if God justifies all believers by faith, including non-Judeans, has God broken his promise to ethnic Israelites that they are his chosen people?

Paul's initial comments betray sorrow and anguish that all his people have not yet come to believe in Christ (Cranford 1993). He even contemplates giving up his new-found identity on their behalf and wishes he were cursed and cut off from Christ (Rom 9:1–3). This attitude was hardly imaginable in Galatians. In the process, he describes the preeminence of ethnic Israel. They are:

(3) ... my brethren, my kinsmen according to the flesh. (4) They are Israelites, and to them belong the sonship, the glory, the covenants, the giving of the law, the worship, and the promises; (5) to them belong the patriarchs, and of their people according to the flesh, is the Christ. God who is over all be blessed forever. Amen.

(Rom 9:3b–5)

In this short passage Paul mentions seven of the nine features of ethnicity: (1) name; (2) kinship; (3) myths of common ancestry; (4) homeland; (5) customs; (6) shared historical memories; and (7) religion. Paul pays tribute to Israel with the usual ethnic categories.

Having duly honored ethnic Israel, however, Paul returns to his most fundamental theme: "... It is not the children of the flesh [ethnic Judeans] who are the children of God, but the children of the promise [those who have faith] are reckoned as descendants" (Rom 9:8). Who are these latter? As in Galatians, they are Abraham's children, to be sure, but not simply by physical descent. Recall that in the Torah God promised to Abraham that his elderly wife Sarah would bear a son; thereby, says the sacred text, Abraham would become father of the *ethnē* (Gen 12:2; 18:18). Miraculously, Sarah bore Isaac in her old age. So, Paul says, "Through Isaac (not Ishmael, Abraham's son by his slave/concubine Hagar) shall your descendants ("seed") be named" (Rom 9:17b). Isaac's direct heir was Jacob/Israel (not Jacob's older brother Esau). Paul seems to imply here an element of real descent, that is, that there had always been a remnant in Israel (see below). However, another point about Abraham intervenes: Abraham *believed*. That is the preeminent feature of the true children of promise, and *they include non-Judeans*. Paul quotes as evidence the prophet Hosea: "those who were not my people I will call 'my people,' ..."; those called "not my people" are the "sons of the living God" (Rom 9:25a [Hos 2:23; 2:1 LXX]). Later he quotes Isaiah: "I (God) have been found by those who did not seek me; I have shown myself to those who did not ask for me" (10:20 [Isa 65:1 LXX]). In Buell's terms, ethnic "fixity" shifts to ethnic "fluidity," and in this shift, Paul no longer relies exclusively on ethnic descent in the usual sense (Eisenbaum 2000: 136–41).

Still, is it fair to claim that ethnic Judeans who have worked so hard pursuing righteousness before God through careful Torah observance did not attain that righteousness, but that non-Judeans who did not pursue it have attained it? Yes, says Paul, because it cannot be obtained by observing the Torah (cf. Rom 2:21–24), but only by faith (Rom 9:30–35). "Christ is the end of the law, that every one who has faith may be justified" (Rom 10:4). Within the Christ-believing communities there is a new identity in which ethnicity is no longer important:

> The scripture says, "No one who believes in him will be put to shame" (Isa 28:16). For there is no distinction between Judean and Greek; the same Lord is Lord of all and bestows his riches upon all who call upon him.
>
> (Rom 10:11–12)

Again, has not God broken his promises to ethnic Israel? Paul responds with his famous, "By no means!" Again, he mentions his own "real" ethnicity: "I myself am an Israelite, a descendant of Abraham, a member of the tribe of Benjamin" (Rom 11:1; cf. Phil 2:4b–6; 2 Cor 11:21b–23a).

However, this serious question is not yet fully answered: if, unlike Paul, *some* are not accepted, has not God broken his promises to Israel *as a whole*, to *ethnic* Israel? This time Paul responds with a passage from Isaiah: "Though the number of the sons of Israel be as the sand of the sea, *only a remnant of them will be saved*; ..." (Rom 9:27 from Isa 10:23). He adds, "So ... *at the present time* there is *a remnant, chosen by grace*" (Rom 11:5), that is, *some* are chosen by God's free, merciful favor. "*The elect* obtained it, but the rest were hardened" (Rom 11:7). There is a reason: "... Through their trespass (refusing to accept Paul's gospel) salvation has come to the (non-Israelite) *ethnē* (who accept Paul's gospel) so as to make Israel jealous" (Rom 11:11). Paul also argues that God's rejection of ethnic Israelites is only *temporary*. He hopes that they will ultimately be included. "Now if their trespass means riches for the world, and if their failure means riches for the [non-Judean] *ethnē*, how much more will their full inclusion mean!" (Rom 11:12).

Paul's comment about non-Israelites' inclusion making Israelites "jealous" would not have impressed his non-believing Judean "brothers" and "sisters." As if to level the playing field, however, Paul turns to the non-Judean Christ believers because they are in danger of becoming arrogant. He addresses them directly (Rom 11:13) and offers two "arguments" about the Judeans and non-Judeans. The first, based on ancient sacrifice (Num 15:17–21), anticipates the second; it contains an argument from the part to the whole. "If the *part* of the dough offered [to God] as first fruits [like first fruits of the barley harvest] is holy, then the *whole batch* of dough is holy" (Rom 11:16). The second is based on a horticultural metaphor: "if the *root* is holy then *the branches* are also holy." Paul explains that Judeans who do *not* accept his gospel in faith are the branches that have been broken off a cultivated olive tree. The non-Judean *ethnē* who *do* accept it, who believe, are the shoots of a wild olive shoot grafted in their place. They share the rich root (Abraham?) of the cultivated olive tree. As Esler argues, this metaphor does not follow olive tree pruning practices (oleiculture) of the western Mediterranean known from the ancient writer Theophrastus (*De causis plantarum* 1.6.1–10) and practiced in Greece and Israel today. In such practices branches from mature, cultivated trees that bear fine fruit are grafted onto non-fruit-bearing wild olive saplings dug up from the mountains and replanted, the reason being that the old branches can draw nutrients from the new, extensive root systems of the wild trees. Rather, the metaphor follows the inverse practice known generally from the East and mentioned by the ancient writer Columella (*De re rustica; De arboribus*), namely, wild olive shoots are grafted onto cultivated trees so that the trees will bear more fruit (Esler 2003a: 298–305; 2003b; cf. Davies 1984: 160; Baxter and Ziesler 1985; Johnson Hodge 2008). Paul thereby honors the cultivated tree, which is "rooted" in ethnic Israel, but now there are two kinds of branches. To underscore the point, he adds that non-Judean believers should not boast; the root supports the branches, not the reverse: "So do not become proud, but stand in awe. For if God did not spare the natural branches (non-believing Judeans), perhaps he will not spare 'you' (believing non-Judeans)!" (Rom 11:20b–21). His "argument" complete, Paul says that it is a profound mystery. He concludes that as soon as the full number of *ethnē* come in, *all Israel will be saved*. As God has shown mercy to the non-Israelite *ethnē*, so he will show mercy to Israel.

Conclusions

In his earlier letters to the Philippians and Corinthians, Paul the Judean drew on his ethnic heritage to defend himself against rival Judean missionaries. In constructing his ethnic profile, he drew on all the nine ethnicity features except phenotypology: (1) kinship; (2) myths of common ancestry; (3) homeland; (4) customs; (5) shared historical memories; (6) religion; (7) name; and, perhaps by implication, (8) language. This was part of his defense rhetoric. Otherwise, he emphasized that his ethnic identity in the usual sense had been replaced by a new, more inclusive surrogate family of "fictive" brothers and sisters. His most extreme position is found in his angry Letter to the Galatians. Here he claimed that the true seed of Abraham and his wife Sarah were not only the community of believers "in Christ Jesus," but Christ himself; that within the new community the ethnic boundary marker circumcision was of no consequence; that historical memories, especially Abraham, belonged to the new family; and that the law was not enough for salvation. His principle was: there is neither Judean nor non-Judean, for all are one in Christ Jesus (Gal 3:28).

At first this sounds like a "universal religion" that has abandoned all "ethnic reasoning." This is not precise enough because Paul retains fictive kinship language and its rootedness in the archetypal father Abraham. As I have suggested elsewhere with respect to Philippians,

> ... Paul believed that he had entered another *ethnos,* which had its own boundaries, its own values, and its own symbols. This *ethnos,* however, was not specified as rooted in *genos* from Israel, the *phylē* of Benjamin, the Hebrew language and culture, the norms of Torah, and the rite of circumcision. It was a different sort of *ethnos.* This was the true *genos* from Abraham, a *sōma* of the new life of Christ, a more inclusive language and culture, the norms of a different kind of *gnōsis,* the model of suffering slavery, and the rite of baptism. This was a new family. While the boundaries were still somewhat fluid—the goal had not been attained—they were sharp enough to know who was in and out.
>
> (Duling 2003b: 240)

Paul's Letter to the Romans continues to emphasize this new *ethnos* as a true *genos* theme, but in contrast to Philippians and especially Galatians, Paul emphasizes reconciliation between Judeans and non-Judeans. Writing to the capital of the Empire, a city he had never visited, to house (or tenement) churches he had not founded, he was faced with communicating his gospel once again, this time to Christ believers familiar with Judean/non-Judean ethnic conflict. There was a very large and influential Judean community at Rome, and there had been an earlier expulsion of Judean Christ believers because of "Christus," a return, and a non-Judean majority that had filled the void in the several Christ-believing communities in the interim. This time Paul tempered his earlier ethnic comments and urged peace and harmony. This was an ethnic shift, a strategic ethnic construction, perhaps even an instrumental one. After all, Paul had said to the Corinthians,

> To the Judeans I became as a Judean, in order to win Judeans; to those under the law I became as one under the law—though not being myself under the law—that I might win those under the law. To those outside the law I became as one outside the law—not being without law toward God but under the law of Christ—that I might win those outside the law. To the weak I became weak, that I might win the weak. I have become all things to all people, that I might by all means save some. I do it all for the sake of the gospel, that I may share in its blessings.
>
> (1 Cor 9:20–23)

When speaking to the Romans, then, Paul reconstructs his hard-line ethnicity position. The "strong," the core non-Judean *ethnē*, were to "welcome" "the weak," the core Judean group; indeed, they were to "welcome" each other. Moreover, faithful Abraham was just the "father" of Christ and by adoption those who believe in him, but also—and always—the father of Isaac and Jacob. A Judean remnant had always existed and existed still. Although some branches of the cultivated olive tree were broken off (non-believing Judeans) and wild olive branches were grafted on (believing non-Judeans), ethnic Judeans were still the root of the cultivated tree. The message to the non-Judeans at Rome was that God could break them off, too. Paul's final ethnic answer, therefore, was to insist on ethnic unity and harmony between Judeans and non-Judeans. "May the God of steadfastness and encouragement grant you to love in such harmony with one another, in accord with Christ Jesus, that together you may with one voice glorify the God and Father of our Lord Jesus Christ. Welcome one another, therefore, as Christ has welcomed you, for the glory of God" (Rom 15:5–7).

Further Reading

Brett, M. G. (ed.) (1998) *Ethnicity and the Bible,* Biblical Interpretation Series 19, Leiden: Brill.

Buell, D. K. (2000) "Ethnicity and Religion in Mediterranean Antiquity and Beyond," *RelSRev,* 26: 243–9.

Buell, D. K. (2005) *Why This New Race? Ethnic Reasoning in Early Christianity,* New York: Columbia University Press.

Buell, D. K., and C. Johnson Hodge (2004) "The Politics of Interpretation: The Rhetoric of Race and Ethnicity in Paul," *JBL,* 123: 235–51.

Duling, D. C. (2003b=2008a) "'Whatever Gain I Had …': Ethnicity and Paul's Self-Identification in Phil. 3:5–6," in D. B. Gowler, G. Bloomquist, and D. F. Watson (eds) *Fabrics of Discourse. Essays in Honor of Vernon K. Robbins,* Harrisburg, PA: Trinity Press International, pp. 222–41. Reprinted in (2008) *HvTSt,* 64, no. 2 (2008): 799–818.

Elliott, J. H. (2007) "Jesus the Israelite was neither a 'Jew' nor a 'Christian': On Correcting Misleading Nomenclature," *Journal for the Study of the Historical Jesus,* 5, no. 2: 119–55.

Esler, P. F. (2003a) *Conflict and Identity in Romans: The Social Setting of Paul's Letter,* Minneapolis, MN: Fortress Press.

Note

1   Thanks to Dr. Charles Lamb for reading an early draft, to Dr. Philip F. Esler who offered a careful critique of a second, and to Dr. Eric Stewart and the Context Group for comments on the third.

6

Landscape and Spatiality

Placing Jesus

Halvor Moxnes

In his day, Jesus was known as "Jesus of Nazareth." To name people after their home area was a common practice at the time. From the Greek historian Homer we know the practice of asking people one encountered for the first time: "Where do you come from?" In small and isolated communities where strangers were looked upon with suspicion this was a way to locate people, to identify them and to associate them with something recognizable. Moreover, it was a common assumption that there was a relationship between place and people, so that from knowing the place and landscape one could know something about the character of the person.

This relation between place and identity also comes to the fore in a saying attributed to Jesus. In Mark 10:29–30 Jesus responds to a question from Peter about the compensation for disciples who had left everything to follow Jesus: "There is no one who has left house or brothers or sisters or mother or father or children or lands for my sake and the gospel, who will not receive a hundredfold now in this time … ." This saying illustrates the main issue discussed in this chapter: identity is always placed. There are three aspects of identity that come to the fore in this text from Mark's gospel. Identity is first and foremost connected to a place, and that to the closest place, the home place. "House" indicates the social and physical place of the household, and "lands" the fields that provide livelihood for the household. Second, a person is not a single individual, but located in the social group of a three-generational household. Finally, there is also a time element involved, of "leaving" the household. It is easy for us to think that identity is primarily related to time, since "leaving" indicates a break with the past, choosing a new present, with hopes for the future. But here the time aspect is related to place; it is about leaving the home place, and the promise of a future reward speaks of a new home place with land and social relations.

Return to Place

Taking its clue from this saying ascribed to Jesus, this chapter will focus on the importance of place in descriptions of identities. Until recently this perspective was overlooked in studies of identities in areas like philosophy, literature, and historical studies with their main focus upon time and history. Since methods and perspective in biblical studies to a large extent are shaped through interaction with these disciplines, biblical studies have followed the same trends. In the last generation the understanding of identity has been broadened as the importance of social relations for understanding identity, community formations, and communications has come to the fore. Biblical scholars have started to make use of perspectives and methods from sociology, social anthropology, and social psychology. This has made it possible to describe Judaism and the earliest Christianity not just as ideas, but in terms of communities within the social patterns, political structures, and value systems of the Greco-Roman world in Jewish Palestine and in the larger Mediterranean area.

Even with this emphasis on social relations there was little awareness of the importance of the place of the communities, their physical and symbolic spaces. The recent "spatial turn" has many reasons, both in intellectual trends like postmodernism that emphasize space over time, and in social and political trends with a growing importance of local communities. As a result there is now much more of an awareness of the importance of place, and interest in how it can be studied (Casey 1993). Theoretical perspectives developed in disciplines like geography, philosophy, and political science have become part of a common vocabulary that is also useful in biblical studies. One set of perspectives concerns *landscape* and is mainly developed by geographers working with historical and cultural studies (Butlin 1993). This perspective is especially helpful to study how texts speak of landscape and include it as part of their narrative plots. J. Z. Smith's influential book with the suggestive title *To Take Place* (Smith 1987) used perspectives from humanist geography to investigate relations between ritual and place. The other perspective, *space*, has been developed in geographical studies that use theories from social sciences and philosophy. This perspective represents more of a challenge to modern authors and the perspectives that we use. The purpose of engaging with these studies of landscape and spatiality is to find ways to study identity formation in New Testament texts by integrating the previous well-known perspectives of time and social relations with the more recent ones related to place.

Landscape

We shall start with landscape. Landscape is not a natural "fact." Both in studies of present communities and in studies of historical texts, like the New Testament, we are dealing with the perceptions people have of time and place. We may therefore speak of time in terms of the memory of the community, attached to the place where they live, for instance their home place, which is set within a landscape. Landscape makes up a contextual horizon for the places which are the meaningful spaces where people live. This landscape is molded by human actions or human perceptions, and we should therefore think of it as a process more than as a static concept (Stewart and Strathern 2003).

Since the term "landscape" entered the English language at the end of the sixteenth century it has had changing meanings, but it has always implied a place of human habitation and environmental interaction (Olwig 1996: 631). This unity between land and human life has been perceived in different ways. The term "cultural landscape" has been introduced to emphasize the human influence on landscape, in distinction from just "landscape" (Jones 2003). However, there is a growing awareness that even "landscape" is not independent of human influence. Instead of a distinction between the two terms it is now more common to see both as expressions of a complex interaction between human ideas, social structures, and the physical features of the human environment (Jones 2003: 33–6). I shall point to two aspects of this interaction: landscape and community identity and landscape and memory.

Landscape and Community Identity

Social structures are always placed. Families and households are located in a home place; larger communities are associated with landscapes. In the pre-modern period some Northern European languages used the term landscape to designate a certain territory. "Landscape" indicated that the people living in that territory had more self-determination and rights to political participation than in other areas that were ruled directly by state officials or princes (Olwig 1996: 633). Therefore, the local landscape expressed a collective socio-spatial attachment for people stronger than attachments to larger political units. Individual and group identity was associated with the local landscape. With the development of modern territorial states this local meaning of landscape changed in nineteenth-century Europe. Now language and landscapes were used as means to establish the nation state with its claims to a larger territory.

These pre-nineteenth-century understandings of landscape are relevant for modern scholars when they describe the topographical and political units in Israel/Palestine in the first century CE. Some scholars have recently argued that in the nineteenth century biblical scholars built on the presuppositions of the emerging nation states when they described ancient Israel as a nation (Whitelam 1996). Instead of the nineteenth-century idea of the nation state, earlier ideas of the relationship between landscape and community may provide a better model for descriptions of Israel/Palestine. We should not imagine the Herodian family state, subordinate to the Roman emperor, in terms of a modern nation state, but more like a feudal system where a prince ruled over often disparate areas (Hanson and Oakman 1998). Moreover, we should not envisage Judea, Galilee, and Samaria as subunits within a nation, but rather as separate landscapes with local communities, although with strong common (religious) elements in Torah observance and the temple in Jerusalem.

Landscape and Memory

If we focus on the perception of landscape, the relationship between landscape and time can best be expressed in terms of landscape and memory. Studies of how landscapes have been represented in history make us aware of how landscapes, which we often consider as "natural," are shaped and constructed. It is useful to know that the word "landscape" was first used in English as a technical term for paintings (Stewart and Strathern 2003: 2–3). Landscape paintings became a popular art form in Northern Europe in the early modern period and have remained so for centuries. This art form, which found parallel expressions in literature, plays, and music, was used for many purposes related to identity, e.g., to express local attachment to the land, to create ideal representations of the local community, to show historical traditions. Especially in the nineteenth and early twentieth centuries landscape paintings, in the US for instance paintings of the Rocky Mountains, became expressions of national identity.

These examples should make us aware that what we find in these art forms are not "place itself" but representations of places. This holds true also of our experiences of the landscapes that surround us. Landscape is shaped by and participates in memories associated with groups, communities, and even nations. In some instances this rich landscape tradition is focused on one single place that becomes an iconic site (Gray 2003). We may think of Mount Sinai, Philadelphia, and the Berlin Wall as places where topographical place, history, and cultural memories are united and inseparable. This meaning of landscape intertwined with myths and memories is very enduring and also has a strong power to shape institutions (Schama 1995: 15). Most nations have sacred centers or iconic sites that represent the uniqueness or special characteristic of the nation or community. They may commemorate significant episodes in history, symbolize official and symbolic power. Even if such places are enduring and part of the heritage of a community and a nation, they are also susceptible to changes. Some places may (gradually) lose importance, and important events may create new, iconic place, for instance "Ground Zero" after the destruction of the World Trade Center in New York on 9/11 in 2001.

Not only the iconic site in itself but also the journey to the site is important. Journeys undertaken to sacred centers for religious cults and veneration of saints are called pilgrimages. They may be undertaken out of piety, out of curiosity, or as part of belonging to a group. There have been many competing scholarly views on pilgrimages. E. Durkheim's (2001) functionalist view saw them as a way to build community and solidarity in societies under pressure. V. Turner studied pilgrimage as a liminal stage in traditional rites of passage as a journey away from society and its structures in order to create an alternative, unstructured community. More recent perspectives have emphasized the importance of the process of pilgrimage itself. A pilgrimage is a ritual journey, it involves going to a sacred place in a sacralized way, where the journey itself with the people involved becomes a sacred space (Gray 2001: 91–2).

Spatiality: Thinking with Space

The previous sections on historical and cultural geography have pointed out that landscape is not a "given" that determines human identities, but is always culturally shaped by people, both directly historically present or involved in descriptions and memorializations of landscapes through literature, paintings, and other media. This insight provides a link to approaches to geography and space from the perspective of social sciences and philosophy. In these disciplines the focus is even more upon the modern constructions of space and upon the models and presuppositions underlying these constructions.

This is part of the so-called "spatial turn" in postmodernity, that is, a new situation where the importance of place for identity is emphasized. From this viewpoint space is an interpretative category, a concept to "think with," that can be applied to many areas, not just geography. Here we will present two aspects: the introduction of "Thirdspace" and gendered space.

The introduction of the spatial turn in philosophy and sociology was the result of the works by the French philosophers Henri Lefebvre (1991) and Michel Foucault (1980), and developed by two North Americans in the areas of sociology, geography, and architecture: David Harvey (1989) and Edward W. Soja (1996; 1999). They wanted to achieve a break with the dualism of geographical imagination with its opposition between material and mental, real and imagined. It was Soja who coined the term "Thirdspace" for this effort (Soja 1996: 53–82). First space, as the concept was developed by Lefebvre, includes the material spatial practices ("perceived space"). In Palestinian society as described in the Gospels, material practices include the agricultural production of the peasants, but also the taxation and required tithing that is part of the control of this production by the elite and the Temple. Thus, there is a contrast between the material practice for use in the household and local community and the practice represented by the power of the elite. Second space is the representations of space or "conceived space," that is, the images and representations of spatiality, the thought processes and ideology that govern the material spatial practices. In Palestinian society reflected in the Gospels we may think of this ideology as the Torah regulations as well as oral traditions that provided legitimation of the material practices and made them appear as "natural" (Moxnes 2003: 13–14).

These two forms of spaces have defined the geographical or spatial imagination; they represent the generally accepted order. It is this order that is challenged by scholars like Lefebvre and Soja when they introduce "an-Other," a third possibility that breaks with the logic of dualism. Thus, Lefebvre speaks of this alternative as "lived spaces" or spaces of representation, Soja as Thirdspace (1996). For Lefebvre the images and thought structures of second space represented an elite perspective. His category "lived space" is associated with the non-elite and represents a critical perspective from the underground or from the margins (Lefebvre 1991: 33). For Soja it is important that Thirdspace represents a way to think differently. This makes it impossible to give a clear definition of the concept within our traditional categories. Soja uses terms like "seek," "explore," and he speaks of "'other spaces'—that are both similar to and significantly different from the real and imagined spaces we already recognize" (Soja 1999: 269). Obviously it is difficult to find fixed models to use for Thirdspace. But if we recognize that first space and second space are part of a spatial system that keeps people in place according to their class, race, and gender, we may recognize similarities between Thirdspace and other approaches that try to break with oppressive systems, like post-colonialism, feminist, and queer studies. If we attempt to relate the perspectives of Lefebvre and Soja to the Gospels, we might say that Jesus and the Jesus movement represented a spatial imagination from the margins. "Kingdom of God" in the proclamation of Jesus was a spatial symbol that was both well known and sufficiently vague to represent a challenge to the first space practice and the second space ideology that governed the life of the first audiences of Jesus and the gospels.

Gendered Space

It is one of the insights that feminist studies have brought to biblical studies that all structures of human life and all scholarly interpretations of texts and reconstructions of social life are gendered. Space is no exception; it is always

Figure 6.1 Interior scene from the Fullonica Stephani, a residence and workshop (laundry) in Pompeii (photo R. DeMaris)

gendered. This holds true of actual physical spaces, some spaces have been typically men's or women's spaces (for example pubs versus kitchens), and even more of the symbolic or value aspects of places (thrones and altars were for a long time reserved for men). The gender system with the dichotomy male/female corresponds to other dichotomies that represent spatial divisions, e.g., inside/outside, home/work, private/public (McDowell 1999: 8–13). These dichotomies also represent values and power; they are part of hierarchical and patriarchal structures. Therefore, many feminist historical studies analyse and expose the oppressive character of these structures. A good number of these views have been generally accepted and are part of social-science models of ancient societies, applicable also to the period of Jesus and the first Jesus followers. There are several problems, however, with these divisions and dichotomies. First, they represent dichotomies that received their meanings in later periods. For example, the distinction between women at "home" and men in the "work-place" and the gendered value systems associated with the two places is mostly a result of the industrial revolution. Even if ancient societies made distinctions between "men's place" and "women's place" they were not based on the same structures and values. For instance, in Palestinian society at the time of Jesus the house as "home" was not "private," it was the workplace for the household and its members, men and women. Therefore, to apply modern models of gender to Palestinian society at the time of Jesus can become a straitjacket, and hide the differences, ambiguities, and pluralities that existed.

Ancient Landscape

This last observation points to the necessity of using recent theories to investigate the material from antiquity, not to draw antiquity in our image, but to find out what characterizes the views of ancient writers on space, geography, and landscape. Eric C. Stewart has recently written an excellent study of how space in Greco-Roman and Jewish antiquity was understood and uses these understandings as the context for an "alternative spatial practice in the Gospel of Mark" (subtitle to Stewart 2009). Ancient writers had a vision of the totality of the inhabited world (*oikoumene*) and how it was divided into territorial regions. The characters of these regions defined the essence of the people living in them, their personalities, and their way of life, often described by way of ethnic and regional stereotypes (Stewart 2009: 62–127).

Within this larger picture of the inhabited world there were local geographic areas, defined by topographical and architectural stereotypes that expressed power relations and value judgments. One important example is the distinction between cities and villages. Most historians of ancient economy hold that in an economy based on land and agriculture, the city elites extracted their wealth from the production of the peasants in the villages. This power imbalance was reflected in geographical descriptions where "city" and "countryside" were presented as spatial expressions of values (Stewart 2009: 129–33). Since this literature was written by the elite, conceptualizations like "urban" and "rustic" reflected a value judgment that looked down upon peasants living in villages (Rosen and Sluiter 2006). In contrast, the Gospel writers in their presentation of Jesus's travels never mention any visits to the Galilean cities of Tiberias and Sepphoris, important centers for the Herodian elite, which might express a value judgment from a rural, peasant perspective.

Another important distinction made by ancient writers was between civilized areas, cities, and villages with buildings and people, and non-civilized areas. These non-civilized areas included borderlands and wilderness, that part of the *oikoumene* that was uninhabited. Therefore, because they were outside control, normal rules of spatial practices did not apply, and they were ambiguous places (Stewart 2009: 142–54). The interaction between geography and human presence is reflected in Stewart's description of people as geographic centers (Stewart 2009: 171–7). The Roman emperor, when in Rome but especially when he was travelling, represented in his person the geographic center of the empire. But also philosophers and holy men could be geographical centers in two ways. First, people travelled to see and hear them, and second, they themselves moved around to learn or to talk to people. We will use this last example in our discussion of Jesus's journey to Jerusalem in Luke's gospel.

Luke's Landscape of Jesus

After outlining some aspects of recent discussions of landscape, let us turn to Luke's gospel. Luke, the author or redactor of the gospel and Acts, uses landscape to shape the plot of his story. I suggest that Luke reveals the identity of Jesus and of his followers through their movement in space. Jesus is not just placed in a landscape; rather, following Jonathan Z. Smith's famous saying, "People are not placed, they put place into being," we shall see how Luke uses the figure of Jesus to shape the landscape and to reinterpret its meaning.

To speak of the landscape in Luke's gospel may have different meanings (Green 1995: 1–21). First, it may refer to the geographical context of Jesus in its historical sense. It has often been noticed that Luke does not appear to have an accurate knowledge of the geography of Palestine. For instance, as a topographical description his ten-chapters-long narrative of Jesus's journey from Galilee to Jerusalem (Luke 9:51–19:28) is both confused and confusing. Therefore, it is more helpful to consider what landscape it is that Luke presents and what meaning he ascribes to it. Luke seems to be engaged in a conscious effort to transform the landscape, to create new meanings associated with it. Luke describes the landscape of the Mediterranean world, but it is represented in such a way that it presents Luke's ideas and ideals. The journey from Galilee to Jerusalem is not described with attention to topographical accuracy, but to the teaching of Jesus that takes place along the route. Thus, the landscape of that journey becomes a moral or spiritual landscape.

The Memory of Iconic Sites

Luke starts his gospel by establishing three iconic sites or symbolic centers that determine the landscape of Jesus and his identity. The first is the temple. Jerusalem and the temple make up the most important iconic site in Luke's gospel. The gospel starts in the temple in Jerusalem (Luke 1:8–23), and that is also where it ends (Luke 24:52–53), so that Jerusalem and temple become almost synonymous. It is the temple as a place for cult and worship that is Luke's focus, and in this respect he reflects a "common Judaism" with the temple as the center for Israel's identity. The temple as a place of heritage, with memories from the history of the Jews, is central to the presentation of Jesus. From the perspective of Jewish tradition one might say that Luke placed the baby Jesus in the temple (Luke 2:22–38). Viewed from the course of Luke's narrative, however, he is concerned to present the temple as a place determined by Jesus. He is the salvation, a light of revelation and glory (Luke 2:30–32), and he speaks of the temple as "my Father's house" (Luke 2:49). Thus, the relation between Jesus and the temple in the infancy narrative prepares the transformation of the temple and Jerusalem that follows later in the story.

The second iconic site is Bethlehem, where the memory of David fills the birthplace of Jesus with significant meaning of a royal future. It is the tradition of this place, and his father Joseph as a descendant of David, that secure Jesus's position as "son of David" (Luke 1:32; 18:38, 39). But the memory and meaning of Bethlehem is not only based on ancient traditions. Luke presents the town in contrast to Caesar Augustus in Rome. It was his edict that brought Joseph to Bethlehem, where Jesus was born as the savior who would bring peace to the world (Luke 2:14), even more than the *Pax Romana* of Augustus. Thus, Bethlehem as the birthplace of Jesus is contrasted with Augustus in Rome as the real center for peace in the world.

Finally, Luke creates a new iconic site. In contrast to Jerusalem and Bethlehem, Nazareth was not linked to ancient memories. Matthew in his gospel had to make a forced argument when he tried to find a link to the

Scriptures for Nazareth (Matt 2:23). Luke is more creative when he refers to a new, memorable event that happened in Nazareth. He makes the angel Gabriel be sent "from God to a city of Galilee named Nazareth" (Luke 1:26). In this way Luke's gospel is in continuity with the Holy Scriptures in that the Jesus event is represented in memory and place. Moreover, Nazareth is the home place for a family that is obedient to God, and from it Jesus received his name, Jesus from Nazareth. But Nazareth itself and its inhabitants do not get a positive portrayal. Luke makes it the scene for Jesus's first, programmatic speech of his mission, but the scene ends with the rejection of Jesus by his co-villagers (Luke 4:16–30).

Luke makes an explicit link between landscape and memory: the history that creates the meaning of the landscape must be preserved in the memory of the listeners. In the infancy narrative it is Mary, the mother of Jesus, who preserves the significance of the event in "her heart" (Luke 2:19, 51). This landscape of memory is gendered; it is a woman who guarantees the preservation of Bethlehem, Jerusalem, and Galilee as iconic sites. Thus, Luke reshapes iconic sites of Jewish tradition and even configures a new site, and brings to the landscapes new memories that transform their meanings.

The Moral Landscape of Village and Wilderness

In the elite literature of Greek antiquity, city and city life represented a higher value than the rustic countryside. In Luke the opposite appears to be the case. This is not just based on a contrast between Galilee and Jerusalem that has played a large role in New Testament studies. This contrast is first and foremost based on Mark's gospel, and does not play the same role in Luke. Galilee does not have a dominant and unquestionable positive place in Luke's story. Instead, we find a more general contrast between village scenes and the city in terms of moral landscapes (Moxnes 1988: 48–74). Images of villages and village life play an important part in the narratives about Jesus and his disciples, but in particular in the parables that are unique to Luke. Here we find the large and dangerous landscape of the road from Jericho to Jerusalem (Luke 10:29–37); the fruitful fields of the rich fool at harvest time (Luke 12:16–20); the village surrounded by sheep pastures (Luke 15:3–7); the woman in her village house (Luke 15:8–10); and, in contrast, the city mansion of the rich man with poor Lazarus at his gate (Luke 16:19–31) and the feast with doors open to the beggars and the outcasts coming from the "highways and hedges" (Luke 14:16–24). With a few strokes Luke paints pictures that make the villages and cities come alive as landscapes filled with people. And Luke's concern is with human relations and interactions in the landscape; it is the moral landscape he will paint. In an almost stereotypical fashion he works with binary patterns: the priest and Levite versus the Samaritan, the rich city dwellers versus the beggars, or the solitary rich man who hoards his goods for himself versus the villagers who gather their community to share their joy. It is the village with its solidarity and its sharing that represents the moral landscape. And it is people who live on the outskirts and in marginal places who find themselves lifted into the festive banquet, the place that in Luke symbolizes the Kingdom (Luke 14:16–24). Thus, the landscapes in Luke are not permanently fixed—as moral landscape they participate in Luke's re-creation of the world through God's reversal of values, powers, and places (Luke 1:51–53).

This affects also Luke's use of the wilderness—a place that lies not only beyond the city but also beyond the rural habitable landscape. In the Greek tradition that was part of Luke's cultural context, the wilderness was beyond the human place—it was the counterpoint to civilization represented by the *polis*. But Luke presents a different picture of the wilderness. Luke 3:1–2 places the story of John the Baptist within the political landscape of power and authority, outlining who, in the reign of emperor Tiberius, ruled the various landscapes of Judea, Galilee Iturea, Trachonitis, and Abilene. This list is contrasted with the description of how the word of God came to John "in the wilderness" (Luke 3:3). The contrast indicates that this is a location at the margins. With the introduction of the memory of the prophetic voice that was "crying in the wilderness" (Luke 3:4), however, this becomes a place of revelation and therefore of true authority. Thus, the contrast between the centers of civilization and wilderness as margin is reversed, the moral and divine authority is now found in the wilderness. This reversal is made explicit in the contrast between the king's court and the prophet in the wilderness in Jesus's words about John in 7:24–27. The cityscape of the king's court is associated with systems of lordship and benefactions (22:25), in contrast to the message about sharing and justice from John in the wilderness (3:10–14).

Luke's Travel Journey: Following Jesus in a Pilgrimage Landscape

A characteristic element in Luke's gospel is the long travel journey that is introduced between Jesus's activity in Galilee (Luke 9:51) and his arrival in Jerusalem (Luke 19:28). This is clearly a Lukan construction. Instead of a journey of one chapter in Mark's gospel, Luke has a journey that covers ten chapters, two-fifths of the whole gospel story. The purpose is obviously not to describe the geographical journey, as the descriptions are quite unclear and the route difficult to place on the map. I suggest, therefore, reading Luke's presentation of the journey through the landscapes of Galilee, Samaria, and Judea as a pilgrimage journey to Jerusalem (Luke 9:31, 51, 53; 13:22, 17:11; 19:28). In light of recent studies of pilgrimage and how pilgrimage may create a temporary sacred space (Gray 2001: 91–2) we might see how Luke transforms the geographical landscape into a moral or spiritual landscape with the purpose to create a community of followers of Jesus.

The landscape where they travel is first and foremost shaped by their being on the way to Jerusalem together with Jesus. The journey is prepared by the first two predictions of Jesus's suffering and death (Luke 9:22, 44) and Luke's comment in the revelation on the mountain, that Jesus spoke "of his departure, which he was to accomplish in Jerusalem" (Luke 9:31). This sets the scene for the introduction of Jerusalem as the goal of the travel journey (Luke 9:51, 53). Luke presents the journey as willed by Jesus with a clear focus on the end of the journey. The main goal for the parables, speeches of Jesus, and the stories told of him and his disciples is to prepare them for the "way" of following Jesus, even after his death (Acts 9:2). It is the symbolic location of being "on the way" and "following Jesus" that is important, not where they are in the topography of Galilee, Samaria, or Judea.

At critical points throughout the journey Luke makes references to Jerusalem as the goal for the journey; the readers/hearers are reminded that he and his disciples are on their way to Jerusalem (Luke 13:22; 17:11; 19:11). Thus, on this way Jerusalem determines the horizon of the landscape. But as in *Pilgrim's Progress* it is not topographical distance that is the issue, it is the response of Jesus and his disciples to the challenge that Jerusalem represents. Jerusalem starts out as the place of power that represents judgment (Luke 9:22, 31, 44) and the narrative presents Jesus and his disciples as going towards destruction. The response of Jesus, repeated in his calls to his disciples and possible followers, is to leave home place and to enter into a new community following him (Luke 9:57–62). By portraying what it means to follow Jesus in service and suffering Luke creates a moral landscape that subverts the hegemony of Jerusalem. Jerusalem may still be a towering presence that dominates the traditional landscape, but an alternative landscape takes shape in the community around Jesus. This is the same perspective that Stewart has identified in Mark's gospel, when he describes the "alternative spatial practice" in that gospel in the title of his book, *Gathered around Jesus* (Stewart 2009).

From the beginning of the journey this alternative landscape was gendered male (Moxnes 2007). Those who follow Jesus are all men, his disciples who from the beginning of the gospel were called to "leave" and "to follow" him (Luke 5:27–28; 9:57–62; 18:28–30). The portrait of male disciples in Luke follows a stereotype of a pilgrim as one who experiences a spatial dislocation from his stable place and who is transformed "by the experience of not having a stable home or by the encounter with holy places and people" (Valantasis 1995: 809). In Luke's description of the journey to Jerusalem the ideal for his followers becomes increasingly clear, but also the inadequacy of the male disciples as followers. Women are never called to "leave" and "to follow" in Luke's gospel (Moxnes 2007). From the beginning of the gospel they represent not the pilgrim type, but what Valantasis terms the "integrative model" of ascetic life: somebody who stays in the same place, but who achieves a transformation of life within that place (Valantasis 1995: 803). Women who encountered Jesus or experienced healings are described as remaining in their homes or as continuing their typical roles as "serving" (Luke 4:38–39; 8:2–3). Although Luke has many and positive descriptions of women, he does not allow them to enter into the male roles of disciples and teachers. There is a significant change, however, in the portrayal of women in the last period in Jerusalem. Women lamented Jesus on his way to the cross (Luke 23:27–31), and at the end, the women who are witnesses to his death and burial are described as "women who had followed him from Galilee" (Luke 23:49, 55). At the empty tomb they are encouraged to "remember" the words of Jesus "while he was still in Galilee" (Luke 24:6, 8). As witnesses to Jesus's death and his place of burial, they are transformed to followers and as witnesses who can remember what Jesus said in Galilee. Thus, women fulfill the requirements for the new apostle to take the place of Judas (Acts 1:21–22), although only men were considered.

This is one of the transformations that happens at the end of the pilgrimage to Jerusalem. Not only the role of the followers, but also the role of Jerusalem itself is transformed. At the very moment when Jerusalem and Herod threaten Jesus with their power, Jesus reshapes the memory and the meaning associated with Jerusalem. It is now Jerusalem that is threatened, that faces destruction because it rejects Jesus (Luke 13:34–35; 19:41–44). Luke's travel narrative links Jesus to Jerusalem, but the long journey through the various landscapes of Galilee, Samaria, and Judea changes the relationship. It turns out in the end that the memories to be associated with Jerusalem are not those of power and triumph but of judgment upon the city (Luke 19:41–44). And when Jesus comes near to Jerusalem the landscape is dominated by the hope of a new Realm, the "Kingdom of God" (Luke 19:11). This kingdom is also the central spatial metaphor in the last meal of Jesus and his disciples (Luke 22:15–18, 28–30) and reappears at the crucifixion (Luke 23:42). In the midst of Jerusalem, as a landscape of terror, an alternative landscape takes place with a vision of a Kingdom characterized by service and suffering. In the narrative of the last supper, Luke makes Jesus address the readers/hearers of the gospel with "do this in memory of me" (Luke 22:19). Thus, the text, repeated at community meals, becomes performative. The Kingdom in Jesus's words establishes a visionary landscape for the community in its present place. The new space that is established through the words and acts of Jesus becomes a space of memory.

Kingdom as Thirdspace

The text of the last supper points to the continuation of this gathering in space in the life of the Lukan communities. Underlying the narrative lies a deeper structure that gives meaning to the listeners of the story when they created their Kingdom space through a repetition of the words of Jesus in their own meals (1 Cor 11:23–26). I shall attempt an interpretation of other Kingdom sayings in Luke in light of the Thirdspace perspective of Soja (1996). The Kingdom sayings of Jesus have traditionally been interpreted in a time perspective: "When will these things happen?" A space perspective will focus on what is often overlooked in a time perspective: what is the character of the Kingdom, what are the images and relations used to describe it (Moxnes 2001)? It is here that Thirdspace challenges the generally accepted order of things, known spatial practices and their ideological representations. I suggest that one of the ways this happens in the proclamation of Jesus is with his combination of the term "Kingdom of God" with images from ordinary households, especially the image of the father (Moxnes 2003: 113–21). The combination of the images of king and father used of God is found in many religions in antiquity, also in biblical texts. But Jewish texts very seldom speak of the Kingdom of God. In Jesus's sayings we find the opposite picture. He rarely uses the term "king," but speaks frequently of God as father and links that to the term "Kingdom of God." In this way, Jesus moves away from a political terminology of God that might serve to identify God with the ruling powers of the day—the Roman emperor and the vassal kings in Galilee and Perea. The meaning of the term "Kingdom of God" is never discussed; it is introduced without explanation as something that the listeners should know. It is a term that has associations to royal rule, but combined with images of household and fatherly care it moves from a symbol of power into the ambiguous place of Thirdspace; it questions the link between God and kingly power.

Many of the Kingdom sayings are preserved in Q, an early source of Jesus sayings used by Luke and Matthew. They most likely go back to some of the earliest groups of followers of Jesus, some of whom appear to have left their households and therefore were without social and economic support. The combination of images of kingdom and God as a caring father in the household in the Q texts in Luke 11:1–4 and 12:22–31 creates an "imagined place" (Moxnes 2003: 108–10). The hearers of the stories are so to speak moved into the Kingdom of God imagined as a household with God as the father and the listeners as his children. Viewed against their experiences of being displaced from their previous social location of household and family, this "fictive household" with God as father may have provided an alternative to despair. Different from the passage from Mark 10:29–30 that we started with, the Q texts do not describe their hope in terms of a return to home and household. The image of the Kingdom as God's fatherly household remains unspecified, more as a Thirdspace challenge to present structures than an established alternative.

We find a similar break with expectation if we raise the question of *who* enters into the Kingdom. The break with the first space and second space definitions of a man's place offers the best example of how Kingdom as Thirdspace questions gender roles. The Gospels portray Jesus's exhortations to follow him, invariably addressed to men, as a questioning of the male place and responsibility towards the household. To "leave the dead to bury the dead" (Luke 9:60) for a man who had the responsibility for the burial of his father meant to leave behind his place, authority, and respect not only in the household, but in the village and larger society as well. For men this move would imply to go into an identity in "no-place" together with Jesus, who described himself in these categories (Luke 9:58). In terms of the relationship between place and identity this would mean a dislocation of identity and of the male role. The eunuch saying in Matthew 19:12 "eunuchs for the sake of the kingdom" exemplified the implications; the eunuch represented a different type of place, breaking with the organization of space into male and female, pure and impure, sacred and profane. In modern categories we might speak of this as queer place, i.e., twisting the categories (Moxnes 2003: 88–90). Other sayings of Jesus follow up this perspective: those who belong in the Kingdom are barren women, children and those who live like angels, i.e., asexually (Matt 19:13–15; *Gospel of Thomas* 22:1–3; Luke 23:29; *Gospel of Thomas* 79; Moxnes 2003: 91–107). The blessing of barren women breaks with the image of the woman with many children as the ideal of a woman in the household, and Jesus welcoming of little children into the Kingdom breaks with prerogatives of the adults. With his sayings, Jesus pointed to a life in the Kingdom that was far from the ideal patriarchal household. When peopled with persons who did not correspond to the traditional gender roles, Kingdom appears as a Thirdspace.

Jesus as the Spatial Center in Luke's Gospel

Luke's narrative illustrates what is at stake in descriptions of landscape: the connections between landscape and community identity, and how landscapes are shaped by the memories of this community. His descriptions of the landscapes of Palestine should not be measured by geographical correctness, but understood from Luke's main purpose, to present the landscape as shaped by Jesus and his message. Luke sees his gospel in terms of God's spatial reversal of positions and structures of power (Luke 1:51–52), and that determines his geographical perspective as well and the spatial expressions of his value judgments. Not the city, but the villages represent the moral landscape. Luke partly changes the value and relevance of old iconic sites, like Jerusalem, and introduces or transforms other sites, like Bethlehem and Nazareth. The point of the travel narrative, the important middle section of Luke's gospel, is to portray Jesus, not Jerusalem, as the main geographical center in the land. And the journey is a pilgrimage, through which the followers are formed into a community expecting and being shaped by the Kingdom of God. In the deep structure of the narrative the Kingdom is a Thirdspace, challenging the power structures of the land. A still unresolved issue is how Luke's geography is gendered, whether the changes that took place in the end of his gospel, with women becoming "followers," gave them a new place, or whether they quickly were sent back into a "woman's place" again (Luke 24:10–11).

Further Reading

Davies, W. D. (1974) *The Gospel and the Land*. Berkeley: California University Press.
Freyne, S. (1980) *Galilee from Alexander the Great to Hadrian, 323 B.C.E. to 135 C.E.*, Wilmington, DE: Glazier.
Freyne, S. (1995) "Jesus and the Urban Culture of Galilee," in T. Fornberg and D. Hellholm (eds) *Texts and Contexts: Biblical texts and their Textual and Situational Contexts*, Oslo: Scandinavian University Press, pp. 596–622.
Freyne, S. (2004) *Jesus a Jewish Galilean*, New York: Continuum.
Lightfoot, R. H. (1938) *Locality and Doctrine in the Gospels*, London: Hodder and Stoughton.
Lohmeyer, E. (1936) *Galiläa und Jerusalem*, Göttingen: Vandenhoeck & Ruprecht.
Malbon, E. S. (1986) *Narrative Space and Mythic Meaning in Mark*, San Francisco: Harper & Row.
Moxnes, Halvor (2003) *Putting Jesus in His Place: A Radical Vision of Household and Kingdom*, Louisville: WestminsterKnox.
Økland, J. (2004) *Women in their Place: Paul and the Corinthian Discourse of Gender and Sanctuary Space*, JSNTSup 269, London: T & T Clark.
Stewart, Eric C. (2009) *Gathered Around Jesus. An Alternative Spatial Practice in the Gospel of Mark*, Eugene, OR: Cascade.

Part II

Interaction and Social Engagement

7

Honor

Core Value in the Biblical World

Richard L. Rohrbaugh

Honor, understood as one's reputation in the eyes of the public, was the core value of the ancient Mediterranean world. It was the goal, the passion, the hope of all who aspired to excel. To many, but especially to the elite of ancient society, it was dear as life itself. Moreover, even at the level of everyday living, honor status determined nearly everything in life: how one behaved, interacted with others, dressed, ate, married, even what happened at the time of death. Public rights and responsibilities, public speech, approved gestures, friends, associates, and even the guests one could invite to a meal were all determined by one's place on the scale of honor. It even determined which seat you could occupy at the dinner table in a friend's home (Matt 23:6; Luke 14:7–11; Seneca, *Epistulae morales* I.37.4).

Honor: A Universal Value

We are not surprised, therefore, to find that comment on honor and shame is pervasive in the literature of antiquity. Xenophon, for example, tells us that

In this man differs from other animals—I mean in this craving for honor. In meat and drink and sleep and sex all creatures alike seem to take pleasure; but love of honor is rooted in neither the brute beasts nor in every human being. But in them in whom is planted a passion for honor and praise, these are those who differ most from beasts of the field, these are accounted men and not mere human beings.

(*Hiero* 7.3)

Elsewhere he proudly proclaims, "Athenians excel all others not so much in singing or in stature or in strength, as in love of honor, which is the strongest incentive to deeds of honor and renown" (Xenophon, *Memorabilia* 3.3.13). In the *Nichomachean Ethics* Aristotle calls honor "the greatest of all external goods" (*Eth. nic.* 4.10), and even claims that being loved is "akin to being honored" (8.8.2). People of "superior refinement," he asserts, "identify happiness with honor" (1.4.4). Another ancient author, Aulus Gellius, claims that serious punishment is justified in order to protect the honor of an offended party (*Attic Nights* 7.14.2–4). Plutarch acknowledges that the want of honor is a deeply painful experience (*Non posse suaviter vivi secundum* 1100).

In the Judean world, Philo speaks often of honor, glory, fame, high reputations, being adorned with honors and public offices, noble birth, the desire for glory, honor in the present, and a good name for the future (*De migratione Abrahami* 172; *Legum allegoriae* 3.87; *Quod deterius potiori insidari soleat* 33, 157; *De posteritate Caini* 112; *De Abrahamo* 185, 263). He believes that "Wealth, fame, official posts, honors and everything of that sort are that with which the majority of mankind are busy" (*Det.* 122). He even claims that in Israel the title "elder" goes not to the aged but to the honorable (*De sobrietate* 16). The body itself, he says, is protected by honor (*De confusione linguarum* 18) and claims that people will sacrifice the well-being of their own children in order to gain it (*Abr.* 184). Of course he also believes that "Fame and honor are a most precarious possession, tossed about on the reckless tempers and flighty words of careless men" (*Abr.* 264).

The first-century Judean historian Josephus speaks of honors bestowed by Caesar, Vespasian, David, Saul, Jonathan, Augustus, Claudius, and the city of Athens (*Bellum judaicum* 1.194; 1.199; 1.358; 1.396; 1.607; 3.408; *Vita* 423; *Antiquitates judaicae* 7.117; 6.168; 6.251; 13.102; 14.152; 19.292). He tells of the honor that belongs to consuls, governors, priests, village judges and prophets (*B.J.* 4.149; 7.82; *A.J.* 4.215; 10.92; 11.309; 15.217). Even the Christian theologian Augustine, looking back over the long centuries of Roman domination, asserted that

the glory that the Romans burned to possess … is the favorable judgment of men who think well of other men. For [God] granted supremacy to men who for the sake of honor, praise and glory served the country. Thus for one vice, that is, love of praise, they overcame the love of money and many other vices.

(*De civitate Dei* 5.12.13)

The language of honor is likewise pervasive in the New Testament: honor (Greek *timē*) (John 4:44; Rom 2:7; 2:10; 9:21; 12:10; 1 Cor 12:23; 1 Thess 4:4; 1 Tim 1:17; 5:17; 6:1; 2 Tim 2:20; Heb 2:7; 3:3; 1 Pet 1:7; 2 Pet 1:17; Rev 4:9; 4:11; 5:12; 19:1; 21:26); to honor (*timaō*) (Matt 15:8; John 5:23; Acts 28:10); esteemed (*entimos*), place of honor (*prōtoklisia*) (Luke 14:8); glory (*doxa*) (John 5:41; 2 Cor 6:8; Rev 19:7); glorify (*doxazō*) (John 8:54; 1 Cor 12:26); honored (*endoxos*) (1 Cor 4:10); held in honor (*timios*) (Heb. 13:4); dishonor (*atimos*) (Matt 13:57; 1 Cor 12:23). Note especially Romans 12:10 where Paul admonishes Christians to outdo one another in showing honor. Suffice it to say that such comment from antiquity could be multiplied many times over.[1]

Honor Defined

Put very simply, honor is the status one claimed in the community, together with the all-important public recognition of that claim. Honor claimed, but without public recognition, was the boast of fools. Honor acknowledged by one's peers was of value beyond measure. It meant access to power and privilege that could be gained no other way.

It was important to know exactly where one fit on the social scale of the community. Says Plutarch, "Whenever, then, you are lost in admiration of a man borne in his litter as being superior to yourself, lower your eyes and gaze upon the litter-bearers also" (Plutarch, *Moralia* VI.201). That is, in relation to each type of man, the man on the litter and the litter bearers, you can find your proper place in the scheme of things.

Legitimate honor, honor that was publicly recognized, determined your life prospects. It provided access to power, opened doors to patrons, conferred the right to exercise authority and, above all, accorded one an audience and the right to speak in public. Aristotle is quite specific:

The tokens of honor are: sacrifices; commemoration, in verse or prose; privileges; grants of land; front seats at civic celebrations; state burial; statues; public maintenance; among foreigners, obeisances and giving place; and such presents as are among various bodies of men regarded as marks of honor. For a present is not only a bestowal of a piece of property, but also a token of honor.

(Aristotle, *Rhetorica* I.1361a.25–1361b.2)

Honor was likewise a relative matter in which one claimed to excel over others, to be superior. It thus implied a claim to rights on the basis of social precedence. This means that honor and shame are forms of social evaluation in which both men and women are constantly compelled to assess their own conduct and that of their fellows in relation to each other. As a result, expressions of praise and blame could function as public sanctions on moral behavior. Such sanctions were perpetuated by a pervasive network of public evaluation, the gossip network, which created an informal but effective mechanism of social control.[2]

It is also worth noting that honor is a limited good—similar to scarce resources such as land, crops, livestock, political clout, and female sexuality. There was not enough to go around and what there was, was already all distributed. This meant that honor gained was always honor taken from another person. The result was an intense competition and envy that characterized such agonistic societies.

Of special importance is the sexual honor of a woman. While male honor is flexible and can sometimes be regained, female honor is absolute and once lost is forever gone. It is the emotional-conceptual counterpart of virginity. Any sexual offense on a woman's part, however slight, would destroy not only her own honor, but that of all males in her paternal kin group as well. Significantly, the order of those expected to defend (to the death) the honor of younger women, even married ones, runs as follows: brother(s), husband, father. For older married women, the son(s) is the primary defender of honor.

Shame

If honor was a positive good, being shamed was a social catastrophe, especially since shame for one member of a family meant shame for all. But it is important to understand the notion of shame correctly. One can be shamed, meaning a loss of "face," a public loss of honor. This is negative shame. As Philo puts it, "Shame is a sign that one feels his conduct to be disgraceful, for only disgraceful actions are followed by shame" (Philo, *De specialibus legibus* IV.6). Being "thrown into outer darkness, where there will be weeping and gnashing of teeth" (Matt 8:12; 13:42, 50; 22:12; 24:51; 25:30; Luke 13:28; see Acts 7:54) describes the reaction of persons who have been publicly shamed or dishonored.

By contrast, having shame is positive. It means to have a proper concern for one's honor and to know what can bring about its gain or loss. Aristotle speaks of the "fear of dishonor" and likens it to fear of death—both make one go pale. However, he thinks having shame is unnecessary for older men to worry about because by that age they should know how to act and have no need of this kind of fear (*Eth. nic.* 4.9). Having shame is thus a form of wisdom: "For the wise man takes pleasure in what is honorable, but the fool is not vexed by shamefulness" (Plutarch, *Mor.* VI. 51). It is also a quality women are said to have in abundance precisely because of the widespread Mediterranean stereotype of women as wise.[3]

Unfortunate boys who do not have this wisdom naturally are taught shame by women (mothers, sisters, aunts, grandmothers) who have it naturally. Of course the patriarchal Plutarch thinks boys can learn it via the masculine pursuit of philosophy:

> For through philosophy ... it is possible to attain knowledge of what is honorable and what is shameful, what is just and what is unjust, what, in brief, is to be chosen and what is to be avoided, how a man must bear himself in his relations with the gods, with his parents, with his elders, with the laws, with strangers, with those in authority, with friends, with women, with children, with servants ...
>
> (Plutarch, *Mor.* 1.7.10)

People without shame, without this needed sensitivity to what is going on, make fools of themselves in public. Note the lament in Job 14:21 that a family's "... children come to honor and they do not know it, they are brought low, and it goes unnoticed."

In antiquity most people believed that persons such as prostitutes, innkeepers, sailors, tax collectors and actors, among others, were irreversibly shameless because their occupations loudly announced they did not possess the needed sensitivity for their own honor. They did not respect the boundaries or norms of the community's honor system and thus threatened social chaos.

It is also important to be clear that shame is not the same thing as guilt—a dominant concern in contemporary western societies. Guilt is triggered in an individual who is confronted with wrongdoing by the internal voice of conscience. But in the collectivist societies of the Mediterranean world, conscience existed in the community rather than the individual. Thus it is the community that accuses, not an internal voice. And what community accusation produces is public shame.

Challenge–Riposte

Because honor is a limited good, competition for it could be intense. Moreover, challenging the honor of another offered a means of gaining honor for oneself. The result was that the game of challenge–riposte became a central and very public phenomenon. The game consists of (1) a challenge (almost any word, gesture, action) that seeks to undermine the honor of another person and (2) a response that answers in equal measure or ups the ante (and thereby challenges in return). Both positive (gifts, compliments) and negative (insults, dares, public questioning) challenges had to be answered to avoid a serious loss of face. The game occurred in every area of life and every person in a village watched to see how each family defended and maintained its public reputation.

In situations of challenge–riposte, however, things could sometimes go too far. Because the honor of a whole family was at stake in the honor of any one of its members, a whole family's honor could be damaged by a situation that got out of control. The offended family would feel honor-bound to retaliate, which in turn would cause retaliation in response. The resulting feuds could escalate into violence and disrupt the stability of an entire village. This danger meant that a family or group would normally restrain its own more volatile members in order to avoid dangerous disputes because it was in everyone's interests to keep violence under control.

Moreover, an over-quick resort to violence in a challenge–riposte situation was frequently an unintended public admission of failure in the game of wits. It was an inadvertent admission that one had lost control of the challenge situation. Wits have failed and bully tactics have taken over.

The story in Luke 4:16–30 provides a good illustration. After the insulting question in 4:22 (reminding Jesus of his low birth-status), Jesus engages the crowd in dangerously escalating repartee. They insulted him once (4:22). He insulted them twice (4:25–26, 27). Unable to respond appropriately, the crowd then resorts to violence (4:29). Luke's ancient readers would have known immediately that the crowd had lost the exchange.[4]

In the Synoptic Gospels Jesus evidences considerable skill at challenge–riposte and thereby shows himself to be an honorable and authoritative prophet. A stirring (to ancient audiences) example is found in Matthew 4:1–11 (see also the parallel passage in Luke 4:1–13). It describes the ultimate honor challenge, coming as it does at the fearsome cosmic level. Note that it comes immediately after the opening of Jesus's career in which he has been acclaimed God's "beloved son." It is precisely that ascription (and the honor it implied) that is challenged by the Devil: "If you are the son of God …" (verses 3, 6). Moreover, everything in the rest of the story depends on Jesus passing this challenge with his honor vindicated. Of course, in this scene, it is not only Jesus who is being tested. God's honor is at stake as well because it was God who declared Jesus to be his "son." Hence it is with the word of God, offered in riposte, that Jesus defeats the Devil's challenge.[5]

It is also interesting to see how often in the Gospels questions are put to Jesus in public (Matt 19:17; 21:24; 22:46; Mark 11:29; 12:34; Luke 6:9; 20:40; *et al.*). Public questions are always honor challenges. Look at the exchange in Matthew 21:23–27. The chief priests and elders ask Jesus a question. But instead of answering, he turns it around and asks them one in return. Since they very publicly fail to answer his question, he is under no obligation to answer theirs. In this simple exchange, he gained honor and they lost it.

Perhaps an even better example comes a chapter later in Matthew (22:41–46). In a very public gathering Jesus asks the Pharisees who they think the Messiah is: "Whose son is he?" They reply that he is the son of David. Jesus reminds them that David calls the Messiah "Lord," so how can the Messiah be David's son? Very pointedly the narrator then tells us that when the opponents could not provide an answer to the riddle (public shame), the possibility of subsequent attacks on Jesus was gone: "nor from that day did anyone dare to ask him any more questions." By losing the exchange and demonstrating their own inferiority, the Pharisees no longer had the stature to challenge Jesus (their superior) publicly.

Honor: A Guide to Social Interaction

In a very pervasive way, then, honor served as the prime indicator of social place (precedence). As such it also provided the essential map showing people how to interact with superiors, inferiors, and equals in socially prescribed or appropriate ways.

For example, the challenge–riposte game is ideally played among social equals. To challenge those beneath you on the social scale is to be a bully. To challenge those above you is a failure to know your proper place. Ancient comment makes that clear: "We must, therefore, refrain from anger, whether he be an equal or a superior or an inferior who provokes its power. A contest with one's equal is hazardous, with a superior mad, with an inferior degrading" (*Ep.* I, 4.34.1). Later Seneca adds, "The man who has offended you is either stronger or weaker than you: if he is weaker, spare him; if he is stronger, spare yourself" (*Ep.* I, 5.5.8). Plutarch even offers a humorous example: "The maxim 'Keep to your own place' is wise, since those who take to wife women far above themselves unwittingly become not the husbands of their wives, but the slaves of their wives' dowries" (Plutarch, *Mor.* I.13–14.19). Of course many times inferiors were given gifts or compliments or offered some other positive challenge by their superiors. So what should one do when challenged in this way? Aristotle explains:

> This, then, is how we should treat unequals. If we are benefited in virtue or in money, we should return honor, and thereby make what return we can. For friendship seeks what is possible, not what corresponds to worth, since that is impossible in some cases, e.g., with honor to gods and parents. For no one could ever make a return corresponding to their

worth, but someone who attends to them as far as he is able seems to be
a decent person.

(Eth. nic. 1163b:13–18)

What about hostile challenges from inferiors to superiors? They did in
fact occur, thereby violating social expectations. Note that though Jesus's
opponents think he is a prime example of an uppity peasant challenging
his social betters, the Gospel writers go to great length to assert that the
opponents have seriously misunderstood his honor status. Matthew claims
he is son of Abraham, son of David. For Luke he is no less than son of God.
In either case, his status easily justifies the challenges he hurls at his elite
opponents.

Among the rights conferred by high status was the right to speak in public
(Plutarch, *Mor.* I.58.15). But note how Jesus's right to speak and act in
public was challenged by the elite authorities in Jerusalem (Luke 20:1ff).
Assuming that his rank provided no justification whatsoever for what he
was doing, they ask who "gave" him the right to speak. They considered his
behavior out of keeping with his honor status. But their inability to answer
his return challenge settled the matter. Moreover, observe how the question
about John the Baptist that Jesus poses in response plays on the fact that
public reputation provided unassailable cover for what John was doing.

Another interesting example of the way honor rank could determine how
one interacted with others is described by the ancient historian Herodotus. It
has remarkable implications for understanding the New Testament:

When they meet each other in the streets, you may know if the persons
meeting are of equal rank by the following token: if they are, instead of
speaking, they kiss each other on the lips. In the case where one is a little
inferior to the other, the kiss is given on the cheek; where the difference
of rank is great, the inferior prostrates himself upon the ground.

(Herodotus, *Historiae* 1.134)

In light of this, think about all of the times in the New Testament people
kneel or fall down in front of Jesus (Matt 17:14; 27:29; Mark 1:40; 3:11;
7:25; 10:17; 15:19; Rev 4:10; *et al.*) or God (Luke 22:41; Acts 7:60; 9:40;
20:36; 21:5; Rom 14:11; Eph 3:14, Phil 2:10; *et al.*), thereby indicating
their inferiority on the scale of honor.

The Content of the Honor Code

While the concept of honor and the desire to obtain it were nearly universal, it is important to point out that the content of the honor code was not the same in every locale or among every group. It all depended on local custom:

> ... not all peoples look upon the same acts as honorable or base, but that they judge them all in the light of the usage of their forefathers, they will not be surprised that I, in giving an account of the merits of Greeks, have borne in mind the usage of that nation. For example, it was no disgrace to Cimon, an eminent citizen of Athens, to have his own sister to wife, inasmuch as his countrymen followed that same custom; but according to our standards such a union is considered impious. In Crete it is thought praiseworthy for young men to have had the greatest possible number of love affairs. At Lacedaemon no woman without a husband, however distinguished she may be, refuses to go to a dinner-party as a hired entertainer. Almost everywhere in Greece it is deemed a high honor to be proclaimed victor at Olympia; even to appear on stage and exhibit oneself to the people was never regarded as shameful by those nations. With us, however, all those acts are classed either as disgraceful, or as low and unworthy of respectable conduct.
>
> On the other hand, many actions are seemly according to our code which the Greeks look upon as shameful. For instance, what Roman would blush to take his wife to a dinner-party? What matron does not frequent the front rooms of her dwelling and show herself in public? But it is very different in Greece; for there a woman is not admitted to a dinner-party, unless relatives only are present, and she keeps to the more retired part of the house called "the women's apartments" to which no man has access who is not near of kin.
>
> (Cornelius Nepos, *Great Generals of Foreign Nations*, Preface, 4–7)

Once we know that ancient people recognized the way the content of the honor code could vary from place to place and group to group, it becomes much easier to understand what Matthew's Jesus is doing at the beginning of the Sermon on the Mount (Matt 5–7).

Recent studies of the so-called "beatitudes" with which the "sermon" begins have shown that the Greek term there, *makarios* (usually translated blessed), is actually part of the ancient vocabulary of honor and praise (Hanson 1996: 87–93). The first beatitude (Matt 5:3) may thus be translated, "How honorable are the poor in spirit ... ." Similarly the Greek term *ouai*, used in Matthew 23:13–36 to heap reproach on the scribes and Pharisees, is usually translated "woe." But it is actually part of the language of shame.

Matthew 23:13 can thus be translated, "Shame on you, scribes and Pharisees
... ." In other words, what Jesus seems to be doing in these texts is rejecting
the content of the honor code that was prevalent in the dominant society and
asserting a new code that should characterize his own group. The contrast
between the two codes could hardly be more dramatic.

Two Types of Honor

In thinking carefully about all this it is important to distinguish between two
types of honor: ascribed and acquired. Ascribed honor comes primarily from
one's family, one's ancestry. Those born into great families share an indelible
mark of honor, while those born to families of no account will forever bear
the dishonorable stain. Honor status is thus given or ascribed at birth, which
meant that all members of the family, both male and female, were at roughly
the same honor level.

By contrast, acquired honor was a matter of the way one lived. It was the
product of virtue—a publicly acknowledged worthiness. Most gains or losses
of acquired honor were rather small and came as a result of normal daily
interaction with others. Moreover, whatever behavior one hoped would
offer honor gains had to take place in public because the whole community
had to acknowledge a gain in order to validate it. Private virtue was not the
basis for keeping score.

Ascribed Honor

Before we illustrate these two types of honor in texts from the New
Testament, let us look at each in a bit more detail. First, consider ascribed
honor, which we will illustrate from the Gospel of Matthew below. Ancient
authors explain it at length. Here is Plutarch:

> For those who are not well-born, whether on the father's or on the mother's
> side, have an indelible disgrace in their low birth, which accompanies
> them throughout their lives, and offers anyone desiring to use it a ready
> subject of reproach and insult. Wise was the poet who declares:
> > The home's foundation being wrongly laid,
> > The offspring needs must be unfortunate.
>
> (Mor. I.1.2)

Seneca agrees:

> So-and-so was the father of great men: whatever he may be, he is worthy
> of our benefits; he has given us worthy sons. So-and-so is descended from

glorious ancestors: whatever he may be, let him find refuge under the shadow of his ancestry. As filthy places become bright from the radiance of the sun, so let the degenerate shine in the light of their forefathers.

(*Ep.* III, 4.30.4)

He goes even further than we would expect: "In the competition for public office some of the most disreputable men are preferred to others who are industrious, but of no family, by reason of their noble birth and not without reason" (Seneca, *Ep*. III, 4.30.1). In other words, those born to great families were accorded high rank simply because of an honored ancestry.

For precisely this reason genealogies were of critical importance in antiquity.[6] Genealogies are honor claims, pure and simple. They are claims to superiority, to rights. Indeed, Romans loved to display their genealogies on tablets in their homes, often at the entrance to their houses. Entrance hallways were sometimes lined with busts of famous ancestors as a way of letting guests take the measure of their hosts as soon as they walked in the door. Seneca complains about making too much of a show of it:

Those who display ancestral busts in their halls, and place in the entrance of their houses the names of their family, arranged in a long row and entwined in the multiple ramifications of a genealogical tree—are these not notable rather than noble.

(*Ep.* III, 3.28.1)

Fictive genealogies, sometimes purchased from professional genealogists, even became a common means of attempting to climb the social ladder or to rehabilitate a damaged reputation. The genealogies of Jesus in Matthew and Luke, constructed from lists of the kings of Israel no less, should be understood in exactly this light.

Acquired Honor

The other type of honor we noted above is acquired honor, which we will illustrate below from the Gospel of Luke. It is the honor one accrues in the course of daily living and is the reward for public virtue. Because behavioral standards in the collectivist societies of the ancient Mediterranean world were dictated by community consensus, those who conformed to community expectations were considered virtuous and gained (acquired) honor accordingly. Plutarch says it clearly: "and the pleasure you will take in acts which are right will make the perseverance of your judgment more firm, inasmuch as your acts will win approval before spectators, so to speak, who are honorable and devoted to virtue" (*Mor.* VI. 247). So does Aristotle:

"Honor is the prize of virtue" (*Eth. nic.* 8.14). Demonstration of this type of honor for Jesus was just as important to the rhetorical strategy of Matthew and Luke as asserting the ascribed honor that came from birth.

Moving Jesus up the Scale

It is safe to say that in telling the story of Jesus both the ascribed and acquired honor of Jesus were of first priority on the agendas of Matthew and Luke. Both of them wrote for literate, urban audiences who expected to read a story of an honorific person. So how were they to gain a hearing when their story is actually one about a lowly village artisan (Mark 6:3)? Moreover, the actual circumstances of Jesus's birth were potentially embarrassing. In the audiences of Matthew and Luke a carpenter's son from a village like Nazareth was the kind of person who should be listening, not speaking.

The strategy both Matthew and Luke follow is to move Jesus as far up the honor scale as possible. Moreover, in attempting to do this they each had two basic options. One would be to address the ascribed honor of Jesus, the other to address his acquired honor. Matthew and Luke actually make bold use of both options, but given the limits of space we cannot describe these strategies comprehensively. Instead, we shall concentrate on illustrating one option with each author. We shall describe Matthew's arguments about Jesus's ascribed honor and then later Luke's regarding his acquired honor. Each is key in the respective author's rhetorical strategy.

Matthew and the Ascribed Honor of Jesus

As indicated above, one of Matthew's key strategies for commending Jesus to his audience is to move him up the scale of ascribed honor. But in order to catch the import of this strategy we must first take a brief look at the instructions offered in the ancient rhetorical schools for those learning to write in Greek.

Greek handbooks called *progymnasmata* provided exercises in which students were taught to organize their remarks around a series of conventional topics (Kennedy 1994: *passim*). For example, when writing an encomium (a speech or work in praise of someone), the rhetorician Hermogenes instructs his students to begin with the subject's origin and birth. They are told to speak of "race, as the Greek, a city, as Athens, a family as the Alcmaeonidae." Next, they are told to describe "what marvelous things befell at birth, as dreams or signs or the like" (*Rhetores graeci* II.14.8–15.5).

This of course is exactly what Matthew does in his story of Jesus's origins. First, he gives Jesus a royal genealogy, harking back to the most honored ancestors of Israel: Abraham and David. Since ascribed honor comes from lineage, this is a brazen honor claim indeed. Matthew has just moved Jesus from one end of the social spectrum to the other.

As recommended by Hermogenes, Matthew next tells of the "marvelous things" which occurred at Jesus's birth. There are dreams (Matt 1:20; 2:12, 13, 19), astronomical phenomena (2:2, 10), angelic appearances (1:20), and even attending astrologers with wonderful gifts (2:1, 11). Another teacher of rhetoric, Quintilian, tells students to note things that happened prior to the birth such as prophecies "foretelling future greatness" (*Inst. orat.* 3.7.10–18). Matthew provides these as well (Matt 1:23; 2:6).

According to the *progymnasmata* of Menander Rhetor, one of the first things the writer of an encomium should do is praise the city from which the subject comes because honor is ascribed to those born in an honorable city (*Treatise* II 369.17–370.10). To pull this one off, however, Matthew had to resort to some deft literary gymnastics. When he quotes the prophet Micah regarding Bethlehem, he turns Micah's meaning around completely. Micah had called Bethlehem "one of the little clans of Judah" (Micah 5:1; MT). In Matthew that becomes, "And you, Bethlehem, in the land of Judah, are by no means least among the *rulers* of Judah; for from you shall come a ruler who will govern my people Israel" (Matt 2:6; italics added).[7] In this way Matthew tells of a Jesus who comes from a royal city, has royal ancestors, and is to be a ruler of Israel. For the Jesus who started as a village artisan in Mark, the entire social spectrum has been traversed and the honor of Jesus has been boldly proclaimed at the very outset of the story.

Luke and the Acquired Honor of Jesus

Having illustrated ascribed honor in the Gospel of Matthew, let us now turn to the matter of acquired honor in the Gospel of Luke. In doing so it should be remembered that a critical part of acquired honor is public recognition or, as Plutarch puts it, winning "approval before spectators." Thus we are not surprised that Luke's strategy for moving Jesus up the honor scale is very conscious of this requirement.

Note that in the preface to both his Gospel and the book of Acts, Luke addresses his work to "most excellent" Theophilus (Luke 1:3, Acts 1:1). This is the way an ancient author addressed an elite patron.[8] So how does Luke make Jesus compelling to readers like Theophilus? As we noted above, his genealogy offers an even more exaggerated claim of ascribed honor for Jesus than does the genealogy of Matthew. He claims that Jesus is no less than the son of God—a common title for the Roman emperor. But Luke does not stop there. He repeatedly records the growing public reputation of Jesus.

The number of times Luke reports public praise of Jesus is truly amazing. Simeon praises the child in the temple (Luke 2:25–35). Anna does the same to all who will listen (2:38). His parents are amazed at his understanding (2:47). Luke tells us he increased in (divine and) human favor (2:52). John the Baptist publicly places Jesus higher than himself on the honor scale (3:16). A divine voice praises him and acknowledges his genealogy (3:22). The gossip network spreads his fame in the surrounding country and he is praised by everyone (4:14–15). All are amazed at him in the synagogue of Nazareth (4:22). In Capernaum they are astounded at his teaching (4:32) and his power over demons (4:36). Reports of him reach every place in the region (4:37). Word of his healing spreads abroad (5:15). He amazes onlookers by healing a paralytic and everyone is filled with awe (5:26). His reputation even reaches a high ranking Roman officer (7:3). After raising the son of the widow of Nain, Jesus is praised as a prophet (7:16) and his fame spreads throughout the region (7:17).

In Luke 7:18 the reputation of Jesus reaches John the Baptist who sends disciples to inquire about him. They are asked to report what they have seen and heard (Luke 7:22). After Jesus forgives a woman of the city, those at the table with him are taken aback by what they have witnessed (7:49). His disciples acknowledge that he commands even the wind and water (8:25). When Jesus heals a demoniac in the country of the Gerasenes, the swineherds tell everyone and the report spreads fear in the area (8:37). Jairus, a member of the elite, falls at Jesus's feet (a gesture of inferiority) to beg for his daughter's life. When she is healed he is "astounded" (8:56).

Luke reports that the reputation of Jesus even reaches the royal court (Luke 9:9). The crowds near Bethsaida also hear of him (9:11). Divine approval in the hearing of his disciples is again given to Jesus on the mountain (9:35). A great crowd is astounded at the healing of an epileptic boy, and indeed at everything he was doing (9:43). In Luke 10:17 even demons submit to his name (honor, reputation). Later, when Jesus is casting a demon out of a mute person, the crowd is again amazed (11:14), though opponents look for an alternate explanation for what is happening (11:15). In 11:27 a woman publicly praises Jesus's mother (hence Jesus by implication) by calling her "honored."

Luke's hyperbole in 12:1 ("thousands," "trampled one another") implies a growing reputation as well. Later in 13:17 we are told that Jesus's enemies have been "put to shame" while the entire crowd rejoices at what he does. "All" the people praise him when he heals a beggar in 18:43. When Jesus rides into Jerusalem to the praise of the disciples, Pharisees ask Jesus to quiet them. But Jesus replies that even the stones would cry out if the crowd did not (19:40). Later, when he teaches in the temple, we are told that the people were "spellbound" by what they heard (19:48). Having decisively confounded those who publicly challenge him over payment of taxes, the narrator reports that even his opponents were amazed (20:26). And finally, in 21:38 we are told that people will even get up early in the morning just to listen to him in the temple.

Given the fact that *all* of these notices are constructed by the narrator, it is safe to say that concern for acquired honor, for public reputation, is critical to Luke's rhetorical strategy (of the thirty-seven examples cited above, Luke added twenty-two to the story he inherited from Mark). Would a modern writer write this way? Unlikely. Would an ancient Mediterranean writer? Yes, indeed, if writing for someone above himself in the social order, someone he knows will view public reputation as the justification for any claims the story makes. By stressing the acquired honor of Jesus, Luke makes him worthy of Theophilus's attention.

Conclusion

Examples of concern for both ascribed and acquired honor can readily be found throughout the New Testament. So also can examples of patterned behavior based on the honor ranking of the participants. Especially prominent in the Gospels are attempts to assert or vindicate the honor of Jesus. His opponents keep trying to bring him down, but lose nearly every challenge–riposte in which they are involved. Even in orchestrating his death they do not succeed because the resurrected Jesus is exalted at the right hand of God—the most honored position in the cosmos. Elsewhere in the New Testament, concern for the honor of Paul, Peter, and other key figures in the early Christian movement is evident as well. That is especially true in Luke's second volume, the book of Acts.

Given the centrality of honor as a core value of the ancient Mediterranean world, none of this should surprise us. In that cultural setting there would be no other way for an author to gain an audience or be persuasive. While it is a cultural idiom with which persons in the contemporary western world are not much familiar, it remains the single most prominent characteristic of the New Testament attempt to communicate with its first-century Mediterranean audience. There simply was no other way.

Further Reading

Campbell, John K. (1964) *Honour, Family and Patronage*, Oxford: Oxford University Press.

Delany, Carol (1987) "Seeds of Honor, Fields of Shame," in D. Gilmore (ed.) *Honor and Shame and the Unity of the Mediterranean*, Special Publication of the American Anthropological Association 22, Washington, DC: American Anthropological Association.

Fisher, N. R. E. (1992) *Hybris: A Study in the Values of Honor and Shame in Ancient Greece,* Warminster: Aris and Phillips.

Gilmore, David D. (ed.) (1987) *Honor and Shame and the Unity of the Mediterranean,* Special Publication of the American Anthropological Association 22, Washington, DC: American Anthropological Association.

Hanson, K. C. (1996) "'How Honorable! How Shameful!' A Cultural Analysis of Matthew's Makarisms and Reproaches," *Semeia,* 68: 81–111.

"Honor" (1968–79) in D. Sills (ed.) *International Encyclopedia of the Social Sciences,* 18 vols, New York: Free Press, vol. 6, pp. 503–11.

Malina, Bruce J., and Jerome H. Neyrey (1991) "Honor and Shame in Luke-Acts: Pivotal Values of the Mediterranean World," in J. Neyrey (ed.) *The Social World of Luke-Acts: Models for Interpretation,* Peabody, MA: Hendrickson.

Malina, Bruce J., and Rohrbaugh, Richard L. (2003) *Social Science Commentary on the Synoptic Gospels,* 2nd edn, Minneapolis: Fortress.

Marshall, P. (1983) "A Metaphor of Social Shame: *Thriambevein,*" *NovT,* 25: 302–17.

Neyrey, Jerome (1998) *Honor and Shame in the Gospel of Matthew,* Louisville, KY: Westminster John Knox.

Peristiany, J. G. (1966) *Honour and Shame: The Values of Mediterranean Society,* Chicago: Chicago University Press.

Peristiany, J. G., and Pitt-Rivers, J. (1992) *Honor and Grace in Anthropology,* Cambridge: Cambridge University Press.

Pitt-Rivers, Julian (1966) "Honour and Social Status," in J. G. Peristiany (ed.) *Honour and Shame: The Values of Mediterranean Society,* Chicago: Chicago University Press.

Rohrbaugh, Richard L. (1995) "Legitimating Sonship—A Test of Honour: A Social-Scientific Study of Luke 4:1–30," in P. Esler (ed.) *Modelling Early Christianity: Social-scientific Studies of the New Testament in its Context,* London: Routledge.

Rohrbaugh, Richard L. (2000) "Gossip in the New Testament," in John J. Pilch (ed.) *Social Scientific Models for Interpreting the Bible: Essays by The Context Group in Honor of Bruce J. Malina,* Leiden: Brill.

Rohrbaugh, Richard L. (2007) *The New Testament in Cross-Cultural Perspective,* Matrix: The Bible in Mediterranean Context, Eugene, OR: Cascade Books.

Schneider, J. (1971) "Of Vigilance and Virgins: Honor, Shame and Access to Resources in Mediterranean Societies," *Ethnology,* 10: 1–24.

Wikan, U. (1990) "Shame and Honour: A Contestable Pair," *Man,* 19: 635–52.

Notes

1 Plutarch makes a modest attempt at exploring the semantic field of honor by commenting on Greek equivalents for the Latin term *honor*. He suggests *doxa* and *timē* as appropriate substitutes for his Greek readers (*Mor.* IV, 266).

2 Extended comment on the scope and function of gossip networks in honor–shame societies can be found in Rohrbaugh (2000).

3 Note that in the book of Proverbs wisdom is personified as a woman: Prov 1:25–6; 8:1ff.; *et al.*

4 See Rohrbaugh (1995: 195).

5 Rohrbaugh (1995: 188–92).

6   The importance of genealogies is easy for modern readers to underestimate. In an excellent study of genealogies in antiquity, Rodney Hood points out that in antiquity lineage was not only a source of pride, but also a device for self-aggrandizement (Hood 1961: 3–8). Plutarch tells of a group of writers ingratiating themselves with noble Roman families by producing fictitious genealogies showing descent from Numa Pompilius (*Numa* 21.2). To have a written pedigree, and especially a long one, was a mark of honor. Luke's genealogy of Jesus is, of course, the longest one possible.

7   The Matthew quotation matches neither the Hebrew (MT) nor the Greek (LXX) texts of the Old Testament, both of which are making a point about the insignificance of Bethlehem. The few attempts to argue for textual variants rather than deliberate change are somewhat tortured and not widely accepted. What none of the discussions of this quotation to date have recognized is the *social* significance of the Matthean changes.

8   Josephus, for example, addresses his efforts to his patron, "most excellent" Epaphroditus (preface to *A.J.* 1.8; *Vita* 430; *Contra Apionem* 1.1).

8

Altered States of Consciousness

Visions, Spirit Possession, Sky Journeys

Pieter F. Craffert

Defining Altered States of Consciousness
Listing Altered States of Consciousness
The Constituting Components of Altered States of Consciousness
Scholarship and ASCs
Altered States of Consciousness and New Testament Research
Further Reading
Notes

At the beginning of the twentieth century, William James noted that

> our normal waking consciousness, rational consciousness as we call it, is
> but one special type of consciousness, whilst all about it, parted by it from
> the filmiest of screens, there lie potential forms of consciousness entirely
> different. We may go through life without suspecting their existence; but
> apply the requisite stimulus, and at a touch they are all there in all their
> completeness, definite types of mentality which probably somewhere have
> their fields of application and adaptation. No account of the universe in
> its totality can be final which leaves these other forms of consciousness
> quite disregarded. How to regard them is the question—for they are so
> discontinuous with ordinary consciousness.
>
> (James [1902] 1994: 422)

Altered states of consciousness (ASCs) have been known to humankind
across cultures for centuries. The world's cultural and religious traditions
are filled with such experiences as the basis of cultural and religious
practices. For example, shamanism as a psychobiological adaptation
of the neurobiological capacity for such states of consciousness was a
central institution at the dawn of modern humans some 40,000 years ago
(Winkelman 2004: 145).

Religiously induced and interpreted ASCs are one of the best known and documented features of human societies. Anthropologists and scholars of religion have primary access to a vast repository of accumulated human experiences of alteration of consciousness (Locke and Kelly 1985: 4). Cross-cultural research shows that approximately 90 percent of societies in a worldwide sample have institutionalized ASCs (Bourguignon 1979: 245; Walsh 2007: 182). Furthermore, there is an almost universal drive among humans to seek and explore alternate states of consciousness (Laughlin, McManus, and d'Aquili 1990: 150) and in traditional societies these states are usually sacred. Besides supporting the hypothesis of ASCs as biologically based modes of consciousness (Winkelman 2000: 117), the above figure points towards the great diversity in appearances of ASCs.

Anthropologists divide cultures into *monophasic* and *polyphasic*. Cultures in which ASCs are regularly activated and employed in interaction with the world are referred to as polyphasic cultures. They value and cultivate these states, honor those who master them, and derive much of their understanding from them of the mind, humankind, and the cosmos. Such cultures also provide the rituals and prescriptions for the how, when, and who of these experiences. In contrast, a pattern of monophasic consciousness refers to the enculturation of people in Western cultures which give dominance to ego-consciousness (Laughlin, McManus, and d'Aquili 1990: 155). They recognize, Roger Walsh points out, "very few healthy ASCs and derive their view of reality almost exclusively from the usual waking condition. These societies give little credence to alternate states and may denigrate those who explore them, especially if they involve drug use" (Walsh 2007: 179).

Not only are ASCs "among nature's most fascinating enigmas" as Watkins and Watkins (1986: 156) remind us, but the study of ASCs, as Locke and Kelly (1985: 3) point out "involves some of the most enduring and vexing conceptual and methodological problems within the social and behavioral sciences." Therefore, to this day the question remains, as James noted, how to regard (altered) states of consciousness.

Defining Altered States of Consciousness

Some sixty years after James, the same sentiment is echoed in Arnold Ludwig's definition (1968: 69) when he remarked that beneath the thin veneer of consciousness lies a relatively uncharted realm of mental activity, the nature and function of which have been neither systematically explored nor adequately conceptualized. For many, however, Ludwig's definition remains the starting point for understanding what an ASC is:

I shall regard "altered states of consciousness"—as those mental states, induced by various physiological, psychological, or pharmacological maneuvers or agents, which can be recognized subjectively by the individual himself (or by an objective observer of the individual) as representing a sufficient deviation, in terms of subjective experience or psychological functioning, from certain general norms as determined by the subjective experience and psychological functioning of that individual during alert, waking consciousness.

(Ludwig 1968: 69–70)

Both definitions focus on mental states which are explained in the concise definition of Bourguignon: *"altered states of consciousness are conditions in which sensations, perceptions, cognition, and emotions are altered.* They are characterized by changes in sensing, perceiving, thinking, and feeling. They modify the relation of the individual to self, body, sense of identity, and the environment of time, space, and the other" (1979: 236, emphasis in original).

These definitions conceal as much as they reveal. For one, their binary structure is remarkable. Their common assumption is that our ordinary state of consciousness is somehow "natural" and "normal" (Tart 1980: 244) and ASCs are everything that does not belong to "waking" or "baseline" consciousness (Crapanzano 2001: 631). The problem is that ordinary consciousness itself is not stable but subject to many different definitions and descriptions.

Listing Altered States of Consciousness

Charles Tart, widely acknowledged as one of *the* experts in ASC research, remarks: "I have been repeatedly impressed with the incredible range of phenomena encompassed by the term and with the high degree of unrelatedness of most of these phenomena" (1980: 243). This followed on an earlier remark that the "number of discrete states of consciousness subsumed under the general heading of ASCs is very large: exactly how large is unknown" (1969: 7). A random selection of lists will confirm his observation that the term is used to designate an innumerable number of phenomena, many merely local designations of common human conditions.

The first two lists are induction-based. Ludwig (1968: 71–5) mentions at least seventy-five different forms of ASCs that are induced by means of five kinds of conditions:

1. Reduction of exteroceptive stimulation and/or motor activity (such as highway hypnosis, mental aberration while at sea, in the Arctic or in a

desert, alteration of consciousness during solitary confinement, hypnotic trance).

2. Sensory overload or bombardment (such as drumming or chanting).
3. Increased alertness (such as with radar screen operators).
4. Relaxation of critical faculties (such as during meditation).
5. Alteration in body chemistry or neurophysiology (using pharmacological agents).

A group of fifteen European researchers (Vaitl *et al.* 2005: 100) identify five methods of origin or induction of ASCs with many instances in each case:

1. Spontaneously occurring ASCs include states of drowsiness, daydreaming, hypnagogic states (drowsiness before sleep), sleep and dreaming and near-death experiences.
2. Physically and physiologically induced ASCs result from extreme environmental conditions (pressure, temperature), starvation and diet, sexual activity and orgasm and respiratory maneuvers (hyperventilating).
3. Psychologically induced ASCs are the result of sensory deprivation, homogenization, and overload, of rhythm-induced trance (such as drumming and dancing), relaxation, meditation, hypnosis, and biofeedback.
4. Disease-induced ASCs include psychotic disorders, coma and vegetative states and epilepsy.
5. Pharmacologically induced ASCs are the fifth category but not reviewed by them.

The following two are random lists. Krippner (1972: 1–5) identifies twenty states of consciousness: dreaming, sleeping, hypnagogic (drowsiness before sleep), hypnopompic (semi-consciousness preceding waking), hyperalert, lethargic, rapture, hysteria, fragmentation, regressive, meditative, trance, reverie, daydreaming, internal scanning, stupor, coma, stored memory, expanded consciousness, and "normal" consciousness. While excluding distortions of consciousness due to illness or trauma, Crapanzano (2001: 632) compiles a partial list of thirty-three ASCs while acknowledging that a host of drug-induced states are excluded: dreams, daydreams, nightmares, incubation dreams, hallucinations, illusions, visions, depersonalization, derealization, sexual ecstasy, mystical ecstasy, prayerfulness, *Ergriffenheit* (being seized), being charmed, transported, entranced, hypnotic trance, possession trance, television trance, distraction, soul loss, soul flight, shamanistic trance, and near-death experiences.

The map of White (1997: 98–100) which mentions nearly a hundred states of consciousness classified into five major categories is experience-based.

1. The first are *psychical experiences* and cover the phenomena usually referred to as parapsychological. These include extrasensory perception (ESP), telepathy, clairvoyance, and precognition.
2. The second are *mystical experiences* which refer to the sense of unity with aspects of the world or consciousness such as animals, plants, non-human beings, or divinities.
3. *Encounter experiences* refer to the spectrum of experiences where an object or being whose existence cannot be explained normally, is encountered. These include visitations by angels, aliens, the Virgin Mary, or some deity and UFO encounters which often include experiences of alien abduction.
4. *Death-related experiences* include near-death experiences (NDEs), apparitions of postmortem figures or ancestors, and experiences of reincarnation.
5. The fifth and potentially the largest category are *exceptional normal experiences*. These are all those experiences at the tip of everyday activities and exceptional experiences or performances in sports or adventure or of creativity in arts and literature.

And these experiences are only those that have been given specific names because of their repetitive occurrence.

Bourguignon (1979: 245) offers a map that distinguishes culturally interpreted alteration of states of consciousness as either possession trance or trance. The first entail the experience of possession by a foreign spirit entity while the second consist of the experience of one's own soul or spirit. Prominent in her list are soul absence, experience of powers or spirits, communication with spirits and the shaman's voyage—all with super-naturalistic explanations while ASCs in Western cultures are excluded.

Familiarity with instances of ASCs does not necessarily illuminate how they should be regarded. While some of these states are clearly related to pathologies or illness conditions, others are normal and natural features of any healthy human being. While some are brought about in the context of religious rituals, others belong to the realm of recreational activities. While dreaming and sleep are normal and everyday experiences of almost every human being, the same cannot be said about hysteria, trance, or coma. It is remarkable that many of the lists do not make a distinction between states associated with illness conditions, the intake of drugs, states related to ritual activities, or those that occur spontaneously (Bourguignon 1979: 244).

There is no reason to think that any of these lists are exhaustive; in fact, most are culture—disciplinary and/or experience—bound. More important, they are merely lists! It is apparent that when covering such a variety of states under a single banner, the category is unlikely to have any explanatory or even heuristic value. While they show the kind of things called ASCs, they do not clarify on what basis something is included or excluded. Put differently, besides knowing that something is an ASC, it is not yet clear what being an ASC implies. Therefore, the question remains how to regard them.

The Constituting Components of Altered States of Consciousness

To be explored here are the components and ingredients present in the scientific study of ASCs. Since the concepts *ASC/ASCs* are scientific terms for a variety of complex biopsychosocial phenomena consisting of the cultural manifestation of induced states of consciousness by specific means and methods and within particular cultural settings that in many (most?) instances have certain neurobiological correlates, this exploration will illuminate each of these elements.

ASCs Are in the First Instance *States of Consciousness*

The above definitions and lists of ASCs assume what *consciousness* is and normal or baseline consciousness is taken for granted as a yardstick to identify altered states of consciousness. But consciousness, Susan Blackmore recently remarked, "is at once the most obvious and the most difficult thing we can investigate" (2005a: 1). She points out that there is no generally agreed definition of what consciousness is (2005a: 6–8; Kallio and Revonsuo 2003: 112). If consciousness itself is not fixed but subject to its own circular definitions (consciousness is to be conscious of things), how to regard ASCs faces huge challenges.

Of the many issues in understanding consciousness, only two will briefly be considered. The one is to state the obvious, namely, that ASCs are in the very first instance states of consciousness and the second is to reflect about the status of what is called ordinary or baseline consciousness.

Consciousness is obvious because nothing is more obvious than our subjective conscious experiences. Therefore, definitions of consciousness often are circular in stating that consciousness is being conscious of something (Carter 2002: 49).1 But the contents of consciousness is different from consciousness itself; a state of consciousness is not identical with what is in the mind at a particular moment but refers to "far-ranging, radical, important changes in mental functioning" (Tart 1980: 249). Such states are made up from the spectrum of human potentialities for awareness plus the physical and cultural forces that impact on consciousness. Awareness of something or *sensations of the world* (the other concept used to refer to consciousness) do not explain what consciousness is because they do not explain the reality of non-material phenomena in a material universe (Kriel 2000: 84). The question of consciousness is: How can something as material as the human brain produce something as ephemeral as consciousness? Or, how can the firing of millions of synapses in the cells of the brain produce subjective, conscious experiences (Blackmore 2005a: 1)?

Traditionally, two solutions have been offered. Dualist theories have suggested the existence of a non-material, objective entity, a soul, spirit, or divine self inside the body that is responsible for subjective conscious experiences (Kriel 2000: 85; Blackmore 2005a: 3–4). Dualism, however, cannot explain how the mind (consciousness) arises out of and interacts with the body (or brain) in ordinary human behavior (Kriel 2000: 88). It also cannot account for the total dependence of consciousness on a normally functional brain.

The alternative is a dominant view in modern scientific and medical traditions, known as *materialistic monism* which reduces consciousness to brain processes (Kriel 2000: 87–8). This is found in attempts to identify the neural or physiological correlates of particular states of consciousness, such as the physiological indicators of hypnosis or dissociation.

Based on a systems view of reality and expressed in terms of a biopsychosocial conceptualization, consciousness is not something inside the body. It is a manner of existence of certain highly complex animals, "a manner of being-in-the-world of certain animal species ... Consciousness is a non-spatial aspect of biological reality" (Kriel 2000: 93–4). Since humans possess a certain kind of body and nervous system, there is a very large number of potentials that can, given specific cultural constraints, develop within each of us. In the words of Tart:

> Simply by being born human beings, we possess a certain kind of body and nervous system operating in accordance with physical laws governing us and our environment. Thus, there are a very large (although certainly less than infinite) number of potentials, thousands of potentials, which *could* be developed in us.
>
> (Tart 1980: 245)

According to a systems viewpoint, consciousness is neither a property of the brain nor a separate phenomenon but a manner of biopsychosocial existence in the world. In the human evolutionary process, "flesh became mindful flesh" (Kriel 2000: 112). Consciousness is not simply a by-product of neural activity but the mode of existence of the developed nervous system:

"Our nervous system is now conceived of as a complex affair, structured at multiple, hierarchically functioning levels" (Laughlin, McManus and d'Aquili 1990: 82).

An analytical distinction can be made between ordinary or baseline and altered states of consciousness but there is no room for the idea of *an* or *the* ordinary state of consciousness. Within the consensus reality of a particular group, a pattern of ordinary consciousness can develop (Tart 1980: 247). Such a mode of human consciousness, Winkelman (2000: 118) points out, is "a biologically based functional system of organismic operation that reflects conditions of homeostatic balance among brain subsystems to meet global organismic needs." "Normal" or "ordinary" consciousness is characterized by the habitual patterning of mental (and consequently behavioral) functioning that adapts an individual to function properly within their culture's consensus reality. Consequently, "our ordinary state of consciousness is a *construction*, not a given, and a *specialized* construction that in many ways is quite arbitrary" (Tart 1980: 245).

It should already be apparent that the word *altered* in ASCs should be used with caution, if not always be placed in italics. As Tart (1980: 256) emphasizes: "It is important to note that the adjective *altered* is only descriptive for scientific purposes." ASC is an analytical tool to make sense of diverse states of consciousness and they cannot easily be reified. Both the history of the term *altered* and its implicit pejorative (ethnocentric) connotation (these states represent a deviation from the way consciousness should be) discredit its continued use.2 The terms *alternate* or *discrete* states of consciousness should rather be used (Tart 1980: 255; Austin 1998: 306).3

ASCs Are Complex Multifaceted Phenomena

Given the above discussion, it is not surprising that Ward (1989c: 23) refers to ASCs as "multidimensional and complex phenomena." How complex and multidimensional only become visible once the components or ingredients making up consciousness, and consequently ASCs, are considered.

The Major Subsystems of Consciousness

Two terms that are often used to describe consciousness are *awareness* and *sensation* (Tart 1980: 244; Kriel 2002: 147–50). These can again be broken down into at least eleven major subsystems that constitute consciousness or awareness. Included are exteroception (the classical sensory systems for perceiving the physical environment), interoception (sensory receptors for perceiving what is happening inside our bodies), such as pain, memory, a sense of identity, emotions, the unconscious, and a sense of time and space

(Tart 1980: 258–60). Together these subsystems operate in order to create and maintain whatever is experienced as ordinary or baseline consciousness (Hobson 2007: 436).

Consciousness can be altered not only by interventions in these subsystems, for example, by a variety of induction procedures (drugs), but also by removing certain stabilizing mechanisms. For example, without a constant stream of sensory input, the orientation of the self in space (the world) is lost. One of the essential conditions for the creation of a self-perception is the ability to distinguish the embodied self from the outside environment and at least a limited level of sensory input of touch, hearing, and seeing is essential for maintaining this orientation in space (Ludwig 1968: 70; Huxley 1972: 40; Tart 1980: 260; Zangwill 1987; Newberg, d'Aquili, and Rause 2001: 86–7, 150–1). In a series of studies on the induction of out-of-body experiences (OBEs) in laboratory circumstances, it was found that visual perceptive and coordination between senses of vision and touch are essential for the sensation of being in the body or of self-consciousness. An illusionary visual perceptive was used to create a dissociation or OBE from the body. Not only exteroceptive stimulation but also an "in-body experience" is essential for self-consciousness (see Ehrsson 2007; Lenggenhager *et al.* 2007). This example illustrates how a single aspect of consciousness depends on a normal functioning brain that can easily be disrupted.

The Neural Ecology of Consciousness

ASCs found cross-culturally involve similar integrative brain-wave patterns (Winkelman 2000: 114). Together with the psychobiological effects of ASC agents and procedures as well as the common manifestations of certain general patterns, this confirms the biological basis of ASCs. It is today widely accepted that the brain is hugely involved in consciousness because changes in the brain cause changes in consciousness (Blackmore 2005a: 17). In addition, the structural and cross-cultural patterns and similarities in states of consciousness have been linked to the neurophysiological basis of consciousness (Laughlin, McManus, and d'Aquili 1990: 12–15; Winkelman 2000: 23–34).

Human consciousness as awareness of the world not only differs from that of other conscious animals but also is characterized by very specific physiological features which are products of evolution. Unlike insects with their compound eyes that can detect ultraviolet light and their acute sense of smell to pick up the chemical clues of decomposing food and unlike many birds with a four-color vision system and the ability to see ultraviolet light, humans inhabit an entirely different natural sensory world (Blackmore 2005a: 117–18). Consciousness as such and the particular features of human consciousness are totally dependent on the kind and structure of the human brain and central nervous system (Tart 1980: 247). It is the autonomous nervous system that constructs the world of everyday experience. In fact, Laughlin argues that "neuroscience can demonstrate that every thought, every image, and every feeling and action are demonstrably mediated by the human brain" (Laughlin 1997: 471–488).

> The brain is functionally and anatomically one with the peripheral sensory and motor systems, the proprioceptive system and the autonomic nervous system. These (sub)systems are not only required for the proper functioning of the body, but the outflow and inflow of impulses (information) to and from the body is necessary for brain functioning.
>
> (Kriel 2002: 144)

Most of the structures mediating consciousness are located in the brain—produced by the nervous system, with or without stimulation from events occurring in the external world (Laughlin, McManus, and d'Aquili 1990: 43). Despite the fact that all kinds of divisions or sections of the brain and nervous system can be identified, the nervous system does not neatly divide into parts like a Lego toy (Laughlin, McManus and d'Aquili 1990: 72). It is rather the case that each moment of consciousness is mediated by a field of neural connections that involve millions of neural cells and their support structures (Laughlin, McManus and d'Aquili 1990: 102).

The Induction of ASCs

As the induction-based lists of ASCs above show, ordinary waking consciousness can be disrupted in numerous ways. In addition to those methods already listed, it is necessary to emphasize that a "(near) universal of human culture is the existence of institutionalized procedures for altering consciousness" (Winkelman 2000: 115). Polyphasic cultures are those that employ a variety of methods and techniques in order to induce such institutionalized and culturally approved states of consciousness. While induction within a particular setting can normally be brought about by drugs or ritual procedures (such as drumming), it is possible that subjects discover the psychological pathways to an ASC, resulting in future induction without the help of any substance or ritual (Locke and Kelly 1985: 7; Alvarado 2000: 184).

Much is today known about the neurological processes in inducing ASCs: "Key physiological mechanisms underlying ASCs and integrative forms of consciousness are found in activation of the paleomammalian brain, specifically the hippocampal–septal circuits, the hypothalamus, and related areas that regulate emotions and the balance in the autonomic nervous system" (Winkelman 2000: 128). Furthermore, the *autonomic nervous system* (ANS) is divided into two complementary systems: the *sympathetic system* and the *parasympathetic system* (Laughlin, McManus, and d'Aquili 1990: 146). These manifest as ergotropic and trophotropic systems (Laughlin, McManus, and d'Aquili 1990: 313ff; Wulff 1997: 109; Fischer 1971: 898). In this model, both ritually and meditatively induced ASCs can be placed on a unitary continuum (Newberg, d'Aquili, and Rause 2001: 115). A unitary state of the self can be obtained by means of (religious or cultural) rituals. This is the result of the effect of rhythmic ritualized behavior upon the hypothalamus and the autonomic nervous system and eventually in the rest of the brain. Rhythmic behavior subtly alters the autonomic response and consequently the body's quiescent and arousal systems. Thus, physical activities affect the mind in a bottom-up fashion. But, the same neurological mechanism can be triggered by the mind working in top-down fashion—that is, "the mind can set this mechanism in motion, starting with nothing more substantial than a thought" (Newberg, d'Aquili, and Rause 2001: 97, 115; see also Winkelman 2000: 148).

The Sociocultural Shaping of Consciousness

States of consciousness are also shaped by culture. This is well put by Tart:

> Each of us is, however, born into a particular culture, and the culture may be viewed as a group of people who recognize the existence of only some of these potentials and have decided that some of those they recognize are "good" and thus to be developed, while others are "bad" and thus to be discouraged.
>
> (Tart 1980: 245)

Locke and Kelly distinguish three sets of factors in the cultural shaping or induction of ASCs. The first set, ethnoepistemology and cultural signs, symbols and metaphors, refer to the culturally framed concepts, language, habits, and world views that are responsible for any particular shaping of ASCs. What they say about possession trance in Haiti is equally true of all other instances in different cultural settings:

> Possession trance is learned and rehearsed from early childhood through play, mimicry, and observation of adult performances. Knowledge of possession is primarily expressed in the differences perceived and conventionally acknowledged between the habitual body of expression and the body invested with an "otherness".... . Understanding possession

trance as an ASC within Haitian culture requires this ethnoepistemological perspective.

(Locke and Kelly 1985: 13–14)

The second set of factors contains six major overlapping categories of predisposing factors. These are stress, personality type and socialization, diet and nutrition, social organization, ethnopharmacology, and ecological factors. While stress is instrumental in the human organisms adaptational make-up, the psychic style of dealing with it is shaped by culture. A growing body of research also indicates a connection between certain personality structures or types and susceptibility to various kinds of ASCs (Alvarado 2000: 185), while nutrition, and most often malnutrition, has to be considered as a source for shaping consciousness. The connection between dietary deficiencies and some forms of trance or possession states is well known while the correlation between socio-economic status and nutritional deficiency is clear. The overall environmental situation often contributes in particular societies to the social prevalence of ASCs (Locke and Kelly 1985: 20–7).

The third set of factors refers to situational conditions and particular ritual settings and techniques that are used for the production of ASCs. These could be procedures disrupting the distinct baseline state of consciousness, specific driving forces, such as singing, rhythmic dancing, or drumming, or pharmacological factors (Locke and Kelly 1985: 29–33). All three sets play a role in particular ASCs and are to be considered when comparing ASCs cross-culturally.

Modes and States of Consciousness

ASCs as biopsychosocial phenomena have been explored in the previous sections. A map based on the neurobiology of human beings goes beyond previous definitions and lists in clarifying how ASCs could be regarded.

All people, Austin (1998: 306) says, commonly experience at least *ordinary consciousness* (that which is waking awareness for them in everyday reality), ordinary discrete states of consciousness (such as sleep and dream states) and *extraordinary discrete alternate states of consciousness* that are possible and available if desirable and induced. Winkelman offers a refined version of such a map by distinguishing first between modes and states of consciousness, then identifies four biologically based modes of consciousness (waking consciousness, deep-sleep consciousness, REM [rapid eye movement] sleep [dreaming] and integrative consciousness) and then situates ASCs as states of consciousness within the latter mode.

Modes of consciousness are biologically based, and their functions are related to organismic needs and homeostatic balance. States of consciousness reflect sociocultural learning and psychosocial needs. States operate within modes, and states' functions are determined by the social, cultural, and psychological functions rather than by the strictly biological needs ... Different cultures produce different types of stable states of consciousness within the integrative mode of consciousness; these are referred to here as ASCs.

(Winkelman 2000: 124)

The biological base of these modes of consciousness is reflected in cross-cultural and cross-species commonalities in all four classes or modes. It should be noted that while cultures provide the specific states and content of consciousness within these modes, individuals are bound to certain cycles of biologically based alterations in consciousness (Winkelman 2000: 118–19).

From the point of view of the biological and neurophysiological make-up of the human organism, the waking mode is the "biological frame of reference for relating to the world and the system within which organisms function behaviorally and humans function egoically" (Winkelman 2000: 123). This mode is characterized by different activities, such as eating, having sex, reading a book, and depends on the above-mentioned bodily (sub)systems to maintain ordinary consciousness.

Within the necessary sleep mode of the human organism, two modes of sleep and dreaming are generally identified: deep sleep and dream sleep (or REM sleep). During deep sleep a number of discrete states of consciousness can emerge, some of them pathological. These include nightmares, somnambulism (sleep walking), nocturnal automatism, and sleep drunkenness. The dream mode of consciousness (REM sleep) also contains a number of identifiable states, such as sleep terrors, hypnagogic states, and lucid dreams. An often frightening state of consciousness experienced in this mode is sleep paralysis. Most cultures have their sleep paralysis myths such as the Old Hag, and Blackmore suggests that alien abduction might be a modern version of it (2005a: 102–3).

What Winkelman calls the *integrative* mode of consciousness refers to a wide spectrum of potential states of consciousness and represents the terrain where ASCs are found. This group is also referred to as *transpersonal, mystical,* or *transcendental* states of consciousness but should, according to Winkelman, rather be seen as "infrapersonal" because they are found "within all individuals, representing psychobiological factors that structure human experience" (2000: 128). ASCs, as the term referring to this category of culturally determined states of consciousness, represent universal but diverse manifestation among the world's populations as attested by cross-cultural data.

In order to offer a more complete picture of human consciousness experiences, it is necessary to include anomalous and abnormal experiences in this map.

> We define an *anomalous experience* as an uncommon experience (e.g., synesthesia) or one that, although it may be experienced by a substantial amount of the population (e.g., experiences interpreted as telepathic), is believed to deviate from ordinary experience or from the usually accepted explanations of reality ... Although there is some overlap, we distinguish anomalous experiences from altered state of consciousness ... We also contrast *anomalous*, a term that does not have any necessary implications of psychopathology, with *abnormal*, a term that usually denotes pathology.
> (Cardeña, Lynn, and Krippner 2000: 4)

Anomalous experiences include the following: hallucinatory experiences—that is, sense perceptions without external stimulation of which auditory hallucinations are the most common (Bentall 2000: 86); synesthesia—the curious phenomenon of perception where sensory images or qualities of one modality find themselves transferred to another: some people hear shapes, see noises, and feel sounds—such people literally taste a shape or see a color in a sound or a number such as musical notes that are heard in colors (Marks 2000; Ramachandran 2004: 18–20, 60ff; Blackmore 2005a: 20); out-of-body experience (OBEs)—those experiences where persons seem to have left their bodies and view the world from a location outside the body (Alvarado 2000; Blackmore 2005b); and near-death experiences (NDEs)—a complex of experiences of people who have experienced close encounters with clinical death or have been in emotionally stressful situations where they believed their lives were endangered (Greyson 2000).

Within the above description, anomalous experiences may be part of the ordinary state of consciousness of an individual (such as synesthesia) or happen to normal functioning individuals at unexpected moments (NDEs or OBEs) and in some instances overlap with culturally approved states of consciousness. The complexity of this map is supported by the fact that in some cultures visions and auditory hallucinations are not signs of psychopathology but culturally approved means of obtaining knowledge from ancestors (Brenenbaum, Kerns, and Raghaven 2000: 34).

Scholarship and ASCs

Despite their ubiquitous spread among the world's cultures, ASCs remain some of the most "complex human phenomena to analyze and understand" (Ward 1989c: 23). The complexity in scholarly traditions will be presented by means of two perspectives only: a brief historical picture and the interdisciplinary nature of current ASC-research.

The Checkered History of ASC-Research: Demonized—Demystified—Divinized

If the study of consciousness has a checkered history in psychological research, as Kihlstrom (1984: 149) suggests, the same applies to ASC-research in general. It can be presented by means of three descriptions: ASCs have been demonized, demystified, and divinized by scholarship.

Because of the Western world's belief that altered states are impossible or pathological, there are "widespread biases against ASCs and cultural resistance to ASC experiences in Western society and cultures" (Walsh 2007: 180). Indo-European societies and scholarship generally ignore these forms of consciousness or subject those who seek them to "pathologization, social marginalization, or persecution" (Winkelman 2000: 116; Ward 1989c: 22, 24; Laughlin, McManus, and d'Aquili 1990: 155; White 1997: 95; Krippner 1997b: 338; Walsh 2007: 179).

Scientific study, however, did not only demonize ASCs, but is also to be credited with their demystification. Due to the efforts of scholars like James, Ludwig, and Bourguignon, ASCs have been rehabilitated as a topic of research and a respectable field of investigation. In doing that they often succeeded in confirming that specific instances of ASCs, such as shamanism and certain forms of possession, are not pathological but natural cultural phenomena. ASCs were first explored by scholars in anthropology and cross-cultural psychology and more recently in the neurosciences (Vaitl *et al.* 2005) and in the space between anthropology and the neurosciences and in all of these they are demystified (Laughlin, McManus, and d'Aquili 1990; Newberg, d'Aquili, and Rause 2001; Throop and Laughlin 2007).

But the ethnocentric practice of demonizing ASCs as pathological can also be inversed in "divinizing" them as privileged states of consciousness. While it is sobering to remember that all our scientific models of ASCs are partisan if not outright ethnocentric ("our psychological categories are very much the product of our historical and cultural moment" Crapanzano 2001: 633), it is true of all cultural categorizations and constructions of ASCs. ASCs by whichever local name have no epistemological privilege. Therefore, they do not provide superior knowledge or access to realms of reality concealed from people in monophasic cultures. If visions and possession in traditional societies should not be discredited as pathologies, neither can they be elevated in an inverse ethnocentric way to reveal the "true" state of reality or "alternative reality" (Pilch 2005: 110). Reality or realities are constructed and presented by consciousness and if waking consciousness is not a yardstick, neither is any other state of consciousness.

Different states of consciousness, Crapanzano (2001: 646) points out, "has enormous power and can lead to social and political policies that alter the life of the individual and the polity." States of consciousness play an equally important role in creating and maintaining cultural beliefs and practices over a wide spectrum of cultures and societies. Visions, such as reason in waking consciousness, have played a role in establishing saints but also in starting wars.

ASCs are Complex Biopsychosocial Phenomena

Most research on ASCs has moved beyond the demonizing or divinizing and even demystifying attempts. Today ASC is a scientific term employed to analyze, categorize, and understand the variety of alterations of states of consciousness, both modern and ancient. As a scientific term it is no replacement for local terms but a way of understanding and illuminating local terms and phenomena. As biopsychosocial phenomena they are, on the one hand, grounded in neurobiology with the implication that the nervous system constructs the world of everyday experience and, on the other hand, the bodily potentialities manifest only as human experiences or as cultural realities. Most ASC-researchers acknowledge the biopsychosocial complexity of the phenomenon and that on a theoretical level they can probably be situated on a continuum between cultural relativism and universalism.

While interdisciplinary research acknowledges the multidimensionality of ASCs, it remains perspectivistic in that they pendulate between what Ward (1989a: 12) calls the "universalists" and the "cultural relativists" position. The universalist position emphasizes cross-cultural similarities in the experience and appearance of ASCs (Ward 1989c: 27–9) while the latter argues that in matters of culture, "the lowest common denominator cannot tell us very much" (Lambek 1989: 37). This is not merely a choice between emic (local) and etic (outsider) terminologies but between biopsychosocial phenomena as culturally constructed and experienced entities and as universal human manifestations. For example, at the one extreme it is maintained that instances of possession and trance (common forms of ASCs in anthropological data) cannot be isolated from their sociocultural construction and reality. Culture is not merely a layer placed onto a biological phenomenon but the manifestation of ASCs in any specific context is no more "natural" than the cultural model that guides it (Lambek 1989: 38). In arguing against a layer-cake model of humanity, he suggests we cannot peel back culture in order to reveal the *biological* layer of any particular ASC (vision, possession, or the like). There is no purely biological or neurophysiological core of such experiences. Instead, they must be understood as fully human, and therefore, cultural (1989: 46–7).

At the other end, cross-cultural study of ASCs from a universalist viewpoint "aspire to keep one foot in each world and understand and interpret altered states of consciousness in terms that have both culture-specific and culture-general relevance" (Ward 1989b: 63). The cross-cultural commonalities and cross-species neurobiological similarities in structures and patterns point towards similar adaptations and manifestations of certain evolutionarily determined potentialities. Within this approach spirit possessions could be interpreted as instances of dissociative phenomena (Krippner 1997b: 346).

Within the realm of interdisciplinary research such biopsychosocial phenomena are then also no longer separated into physical or biological and social or cultural components, but as unitary phenomena analyzed as ways of being. Spirit possessions can be treated as goal-directed phenomena (Spanos 1989: 108) or like hypnosis, various forms of dissociation can be seen as role-enacted states of consciousness where those affected are often socialized into the roles and socially expected goal-directed behavior (Spanos 1989; Chandra Shekar 1989). Or, dissociation in its various manifestations can be seen similar to imagination as a basic skill or capacity of humans employing them (Krippner 1997a: 33).

Altered States of Consciousness and New Testament Research

New Testament ASC-Reports

Potentially ASC-research can become one of the most powerful tools for understanding large parts of the biblical tradition, texts, and phenomena. The Christian Bible is filled with reports about visions, revelations, dream experiences, and other events, such as sky journeys or soul travel experiences that all strike the modern reader socialized into a monophasic culture as extraordinary.

God often spoke to the patriarchs in dreams and visions (e.g., Gen 12:7; 18:1; 26:3; 28:11–17). The story about the beginning of the Israelite nation in the land of Israel is filled with visionary and epiphanic experiences of Moses (Exod 19; Num 12:7–8). It was normal for Old Testament prophets to go into trance for receiving a vision or hearing the words of God (e.g., Isa 6:1–2; Jer 1:1, 13; Ezek 3:14, 22; 8:1) while Israel's first two kings were both involved in several such activities or experiences (e.g., 1 Sam 9–10; 19:9–24).

All of this continues in the New Testament. From the story about Jesus's baptism and the transfiguration to the resurrection appearances, the gospels are filled with ASCs. Pilch (2002b: 691) points out that Luke reports more than twenty such experiences in Acts, and others in his gospel too. Paul's own testimony is that he was attracted to this new movement on the basis of a revelation or a vision (Gal 1:11; 2:1) while the language of mystical experiences and spirit possession in his letters is overwhelming (Ashton 2000: 113–42).

Demystifying New Testament ASC-Reports

No one has done more than John Pilch to show that the above reports can be seen as ASC-reports. He points out that

> altered states of consciousness experiences fill the Bible beginning with Genesis when God puts the first creature into a deep sleep in order to create Eve, his helpmate (Gen 2:21) and ending with Revelation where John the Revealer repeats four times that what he reports is the result of experiences in trance (*en pneumati*: Rev 1:10; 4:2; 17:3; 21:10).
>
> (Pilch 2002b: 691)

The story of Jesus's transfiguration (Luke 9:28–36 par) is an instance of an experience in alternate reality (Pilch 1995: 63) while Jesus's contemporaries "truly experienced the risen Jesus in an ASC" (Pilch 1998: 59). The accounts of Paul's so-called call or conversion experience which Acts (9:1–19; 22:3–21; 26:9–18) describes as a vision with an auditory soundtrack and Paul himself describes as a revelation (Gal 1:12) from Jesus or an "appearance" (1 Cor 15:6), is seen as "Paul's encounter in an altered state of consciousness with the Risen Jesus in alternate reality" (Pilch 2002b: 697). The visions in Revelation (1:10; 4:2; 17:3; 21:10), Pilch shows, can be "properly understood as real, ecstatic experiences and spirit-guided journeys" (1993: 242)—in other words, as ASCs.

In contrast to traditional historical critics who often see such reports as literary constructions, Pilch (1993: 231; 2002a: 113), based on the argument that ASCs are common human phenomena and well established cross-culturally, points out that the study of ASCs provides the biblical interpreter with a set of tools to appreciate the cultural reality of such experiences. He shows that "cultural information interpreted by social-scientific methods strongly argues that these ASC experiences did occur in the life of Jesus and his followers" (2002a: 113). Demystification of ASCs indeed results in the establishment of their historical and cultural plausibility. In a similar way, Richard DeMaris convincingly shows that the "implications of anthropological research on altered states of consciousness for historical Jesus research is clear: this widespread and well-attested phenomenon, which usually comes to expression in Mediterranean societies as possession trance, provides the basis for keeping Jesus's baptism and baptismal vision together and treating the whole episode as a historically plausible account" (2002: 151).

Although his understanding of ASCs is much closer to the universalist position, Stevan Davies (1995: 207) offers a similar argument regarding the historical Jesus. While seeing the demon possessions accounts as reports about dissociative phenomena, his aim is to show that Jesus's healings could have been plausible and thus historical. In an extensive study of the historical Jesus, Pieter Craffert (2008) argues that seen as a Galilean shamanic figure, a large part of the Jesus traditions can be considered culturally plausible as phenomena that could have belonged to and have been attributed to the life of a shamanic figure. Thus, not only are the baptism, transfiguration, and resurrection stories treated as historically plausible, but it is suggested that Jesus's teaching about the son of man and kingdom of God could be taken as belonging to the life of someone often touched by ASCs. The study of the historical Jesus has taken a new turn, based on ASC-research. Finally, ASCs provide the background for Bruce Malina's (1995) interpretation of the genre and message of Revelation.

The demystification of these reports and texts is a first and very important step in the employment of ASC-research. However, reclassifying the visions, spirit possessions, sky journeys, and other related phenomena as ASCs and thus culturally plausible, is like adding them to the lists. The question remains how to regard such events if they were indeed ASCs.

Invoking Interdisciplinary Research of ASCs

What does the study of ASCs contribute to biblical interpretation? What is implied if the Bible is filled with ASC-reports? More concretely: What is invoked by, for example, calling the resurrection visions ASCs?

I want to suggest that the interdisciplinary research of ASCs offers a whole new dimension to be explored in biblical interpretation. Interdisciplinary ASC-research is not a way to rename biblical phenomena but to reassign them as human phenomena. In other words, it is not only a different label but an explanatory category for understanding certain phenomena. Affirming the cultural reality of particular ASCs (such as the visionary resurrection experiences) is neither endorsing the understanding of literal-minded scholars nor ratifying the claim of the natives. For literal-minded people, as for participants of ASCs themselves, things happen precisely as written: a *revelation* is a communication from a deity, a vision is an optical experience mediated by a god, being *in the spirit* is a condition where a known and identifiable entity entered someone's body and being *caught up to the third heaven* is a genuine sky travel. Renaming these as ASCs is not affirming them as literally true or as real in contrast to mere hallucinations. States of consciousness are not divided between real and non-real versions of reality but all are equally real and consequently equally vulnerable as representations and constructions of reality.

Being assigned to this category does not guarantee any reality status to these ASCs but situates them within the world of cultural realities. Claiming that a vision can be seen as plausible and historical is as ethnocentric as calling it a hallucination if it is not immediately made clear what the status of cultural realities are.

Furthermore, it is precisely as culturally real phenomena, as truly human phenomena, that these ASCs can also be considered as goal-directed or culturally determined role-played experiences or as neurobiological phenomena.

Figure 8.1 "St. John at Patmos" by Gustave Doré (courtesy of www.creationism.org)

Calling something an ASC is not a concealed way of affirming local claims of visions, revelations, sky travels, and the like but a way of making known in a culturally sensitive way what such experiences and phenomena entail as biopsychosocial phenomena. ASC-language reveals the nature of a whole range of phenomena that is concealed and inextractable from any of the local terms or descriptions. Therefore, the study of ASCs reveals events and phenomena not only as culturally plausible but also as truly biopsychosocial human phenomena.

Further Reading

Bourguignon, E. (1979) *Psychological Anthropology: An Introduction to Human Nature and Cultural Differences*, New York: Holt, Rinehart and Winston.

Carter, R. (2002) *Exploring Consciousness*, Berkeley, CA: University of California Press.

Craffert, P. F. (2008) *The Life of a Galilean Shaman: Jesus of Nazareth in Anthropological-Historical Perspective*, Eugene, OR: Cascade Books.

Greyson, B. (2000) "Near-Death Experiences," in E. Cardeña, S. J. Lynn, and S. Krippner (eds) *Varieties of Anomalous Experience: Examining the Scientific Evidence*, Washington, DC: American Psychological Association.

Neufeld, Dietmar (2000) "Jesus's Eating Transgressions and Social Impropriety in the Gospel of Mark: A Social-Scientific Approach," *BTB*, 30: 106–11.

Pilch, John J. (2002a) "Alternate State of Consciousness in the Synoptics," in Wolfgang Stegemann, Bruce. J. Malina, and G. Theissen (eds), *The Social Setting of Jesus and the Gospels*, Minneapolis: Fortress.

Pilch, John J. (2002b) "Paul's Ecstatic Trance Experience Near Damascus in Acts of the Apostles," *HvTSt* 58, no. 2: 690–707.

Pilch, John J. (2005) "Holy Men and Their Sky Journeys: A Cross-Cultural Model," *BTB*, 35: 106–11.

Notes

1   "Consciousness may be defined as our awareness of our environments, our bodies, and ourselves" (Hobson 2007: 435).

2   It was first used in the context of describing the states brought about by psychedelic drugs (Austin 1998: 309–10).

3   The term alternate makes it clear that "different states of consciousness prevail at different times for different reasons and that no one state is considered standard" (Zinberg 1977: 1, no. 1).

9

Jesus's Healing Activity

Political Acts?

John J. Pilch

Power
Healing as Political Activity
Jesus's Healing Activity as Treason
Conclusion
Further Reading

For many years now a number of biblical scholars have utilized medical anthropology to interpret healing reports in the Bible, especially the healing activity of Jesus (Pilch 1981; 1989). Medical anthropology is the study of "health care delivery systems" in a number of different societies and in a comparative way. To interpret sickness around the world in terms of our analysis of various sickness phenomena is called medicocentrism, which amounts to judging all medical systems in terms of our own. Fortunately, explanatory concepts like sickness, disease, illness, curing, and healing have eliminated or at least minimized the risks of falling into medicocentric interpretations (Pilch 2000).

The study of sickness and healing in the New Testament has to make do with the slim evidence at hand (mainly texts!). Consequently it is virtually impossible to identify with confidence the actual maladies presented to Jesus. For example, it is practically certain that in Palestine there were no first-century cases of Hansen's disease (the modern name for leprosy), since the earliest evidence of it in bones found in that region dates from second-century CE Egypt. Without the aid of something like "before and after" laboratory tests, it is impossible to determine exactly what physical condition existed, and how that condition might have changed (Pilch 2007a: 135–40).

However, if one recognizes the effectiveness of "meaning response" in human sickness conditions (Moerman 2002), it is fair to claim that some real physical changes did occur (Pilch 2008a; 2007b). Yet much more important to the sick person was the fact that meaning was restored to her or his life along with some experienced or imagined change in the given condition.

Jesus and others such as his disciples were recognized as folk healers, ordinary people who had power to heal. We owe these insights to medical anthropology, a cross-cultural discipline perfectly suited to the challenge of understanding healing reports from a non-western culture.

In a recent article applying the meaning response concept to Matthew's gospel, I briefly mentioned the power of the healer (Pilch 2008b: 106). The Greek word, *exousia*, is sometimes translated as authority (e.g., Matt 7:29, Jesus teaches with authority) and other times as power (e.g., Matt 9:8, Jesus has power to forgive sin and heal a paralytic; Matt 10:1, the disciples are empowered to heal and exorcize). Louw and Nida admit that both translations are possible because it is difficult to determine whether the focus is on the person's power or the person's authorization to do something, which implies power (Louw and Nida 1988: 1:681).

In the social-scientific register, however, the English words must be distinguished. "Authority" is the socially acknowledged right to command, direct, or order people (Lewellen 1983: 93). This aptly describes Jesus's teaching (Matt 7:29). On the other hand, "power" over adult persons is the ability to have effect with the sanction of force for non-compliance. Jesus and his disciples have power over spirits who are other-than-human persons. Power over things and children is the same as force. Jesus exhibits such power over the roiling sea (Matt 8:27, the word *exousia* does not occur but the reality is certainly implied). Since the notion of power is integral to politics (Lewellen 1983: 93–6), it would be useful to analyze the healing activity of Jesus from this perspective. Such a scenario is suggested by the question of the chief priests and elders to Jesus: "By what *exousia* are you doing these things, and who gave you this *exousia*?" (Matt 21:23; Mark 11:28; Luke 20:2). Though the question could pertain to Jesus's action in the Temple (Matt 21:12–13), or his entry into it, very likely it pertains to his entire ministry: teaching but especially healing (Foerster 1964: 568).

Power

Political anthropology helps to place Jesus's healing activity in a new light. Others have reflected on the political aspects of Jesus's healing activity, but without the use of political anthropology (Hollenbach 1982). This discipline seeks chiefly to study the processes involved in the competition for power and the way group goals are implemented by those who have power (Lewellen 1983: 89; see also Malina 1986). Process theorists view political activity as a play in which the same actors and groups are involved, but the action shifts over time, from act to act. In this play, the drama sometimes focuses on two or a few actors. The entire play would be called the "political field," the behavior of the few actors would be the "arena" (Lewellen 1983: 91).

Thus we might consider first-century Palestine as the political field in which health, sickness, and related issues are common concerns, and different groups compete for power, for dominance in each instance. Sirach reflects the ambivalence of Israelites toward human healers (especially from the Greek tradition) in the face of the community belief that "healing comes from the Most High" (38:1–15; see Exod 15:26 "I am the LORD, your healer"). The woman who spent all she had on many healers (Mark 5:26) quite likely approached some such as described by Sirach out of sheer despair. This wide picture is the political field. With their focus on Jesus, his followers, and opponents, the Gospels describe an arena, such as this story of the woman just mentioned (Matt 9:20–22).

In this arena, people both pursue and exercise power. It is important to distinguish between private and public power. Private power is typically exercised by a patriarch over the family (Sirach 30:1–13). Public power is that exercised in the political arena, the wider picture. This pursuit and exercise of power would definitely include healing, for "symbols of healing are simultaneously symbols of power" (Young 1982: 271; see also Freidson 1970). Health and well-being are culturally specific explanatory concepts of reality which reflect specific desirable views of the social order. Sickness thus is as much a social problem as it is an individual experience, because the social order is disturbed. Beliefs about the causes of sickness and the sources of healing power are also shaped by the social order.

Power can also be independent or dependent. Independent power derives from a person's capabilities such as specialized training, effective skills, or even personal appeal (charisma). Everyone possesses some sort of independent power, and "... everyone is constantly assessing the 'power' of those with whom they come into contact and adjusting their behavior accordingly, either through simple deference or through obedience to elaborate social rituals" (Lewellen 1983: 93–4). Dependent power is that which is delegated by someone with independent power to another. The delegation can be from one individual to another, from a group to an individual, or from a group or individual to a number of other people.

Like every human being, Jesus too had independent power, that is, the power of his personality, his rhetorical abilities (Matt 7:29; Mark 1:22, 27; Luke 4:32), the power of a holy man (Mark 1:24) learned in apprenticeship with John the Baptist and the like (John 3:22). But he has dependent power given by the Father (Matt 28:18), power to heal and forgive sins (Matt 9:6, 8; Mark 2:10; Luke 5:24). Jesus in turn delegated his power to his disciples (Matt 10:1; Mark 3:15; Luke 9:1; 10:19).

The competition for power relative to healing becomes explicit toward the end of Jesus's career. The chief priests and the elders of the people challenge him: "By what *exousia* are you doing these things, and who gave you this *exousia*?" (Matt 21:23). All English translations render *exousia* with the word authority. Polish language translations report, "By what power (*jaką mocą*) are you doing these things? Who gave you this authority (*władza*)?" The Polish versions are more appropriate translations (Kowalski 1957; Wujek 1963). As Louw and Nida noted, distinguishing the two notions in the concept of *exousia* is difficult (see also BDAG: 35, meaning 3). The question thus is about permission or approval (*exousia*) to use the power (*exousia*).

Healing as Political Activity

Theories of sickness are clues to what a group values, disvalues, and preoccupies itself with (Fabrega 1974: 257–301; see also Freidson 1970). Biblical "leprosy" is certainly not Hansen's disease and may be no disease at all (Pilch 2008a). Leviticus 13–14 and the New Testament reports of Jesus cleansing lepers (Mark 1:40–45; Luke 17:11–19) are concerned with being unclean. They concern ritual purity. It is not the physical problem that concerns this society, but the state of pollution or impurity which makes one incapable of approaching God in worship or even living in the holy community (see Lev 13:45–46; Pilch 2000). What healers do is first diagnose the problem, then make a prognosis, which if accepted by the petitioner, allows the healer to initiate therapy. Thus, "a blind and dumb demoniac was brought to [Jesus]" (Matt 12:22a). This is the diagnosis

Table 9.2 Exousia in Matthew (and synoptic parallels)

Matt 7:29	Mark 1:22, 27; Luke 4:32	Taught as one having *exousia*
Matt 8:9	Luke 7:8	Centurion - man under *exousia*
Matt 9:6	Mark 2:10; Luke 5:24	Son of Man has *exousia* on earth to forgive sins
Matt 9:8		marveled that God gave such *exousia* to human beings (to heal and forgive sins)
Matt 10:1	Mark 3:15; Luke 9:1 (*dynamis* [power] and *exousia*); 10:19	gave the twelve *exousia* over unclean spirits, to cast them out, and to heal every disease and infirmity
Matt 21:23	Mark 11:28; Luke 20:2	chief priests and elders: By what *exousia*? Who gave it to you?
Matt 21:24	Mark 11:29	I will tell you by what *exousia* I do these things, if …
Matt 21:27	Mark 11:33; Luke 20:8	Neither will I tell you by what *exousia* I am doing these things.
Matt 28:18		All *exousia* in heaven and on earth has been given to me.

offered by the evangelist. Presumably those who led this person to Jesus reported the condition. Surely Jesus himself could discern that the man was blind and mute. In addition the diagnosis affirms demon possession. Notice that the diagnosis is reported briefly, only half a verse. In all the reports of Jesus's healing activity, the diagnosis is very brief. "And [Jesus] healed him, so that the dumb man spoke and saw" (Matt 12:22b). This is the therapy, the healing. The report does not explain how; no details are given. The reality is that the man's ability to see and speak returned. And he was also liberated from demonic possession (Pilch 2008b: 102).

The prognosis is presented in Matthew 12:43–45. The exorcized spirit decides to return and possess his original victim. But the victim is in such an improved state, the demon recruits seven other even more evil spirits and they overpower him, possessing him once again. This high-context report requires that the non-Middle Eastern reader fill in the cultural gaps. The diagnosis brought to Jesus is clearly stated at the outset. It is possible that Jesus then gave the prognosis that appears in Matthew 12:43–45. If I heal you, you must mend your life. If you do not mend your life, the demon and misfortune will return. It is also possible that the intervening narrative (Matt 12:23–42) served to sketch out the prognosis for the healed man before Jesus finally made it explicit in Matthew 12:43 and following.

The intervening narrative (verses 23–42) reports the typical response to a healing deed of Jesus: some were favorable and some disapproving. In this case, the discussion is about power: some conclude that Jesus has healing power because he is the Son of David (Duling 1992: 112–13), others claim the power is from Beelzebul. They agree that Jesus's power is dependent but disagree on the identity of the independent source. Jesus identifies the independent source when he attributes his effectiveness as healer to the Spirit of God, a phrase that always describes God's power in the Bible.

The three stages in the healing process (diagnosis, prognosis, therapy) correlate with three stages in the political process: explain, predict, control (Fabrega 1974). In the United States during elections each candidate offers his or her explanation of the problem: the economy, security, etc. (diagnosis). This is followed by the prognosis: if you vote for my opponent, you will get more of the same, or my inexperienced opponent is totally incapable of understanding and thus treating the pressing problem (prognosis). Whoever is elected then strives to control the problem (therapy). Thus it should be clear how the healing process is a political process.

The chart in Table 9.3 analyzes the healing reports in Matthew (and parallels) using this model. Of the fourteen healing reports listed, only five contain an explicit prognosis. That lacuna does not invalidate the model. Many social-scientific models are comprehensive as constructed. When applied to specific cases, parts of the model might be missing for one reason

Table 9.3 Healing reports in Matthew (and parallels)

Sick person	Diagnosis	Prognosis	Therapy
1. Matt 8:1-4 (Mark 1:40-44//Luke 5:12-14) "Leper"	v. 1 unclean (emic) = "leper" (etic)	None	v. 3 "be made clean"
2. Matt 8:5-13 (Luke 7:1-10//John 4:46-63) Paralyzed servant	v. 6 paralysis, terrible distress	None	v. 13 "servant was healed."
3. Matt 8:14-17 (Mark 1:29-31//Luke 4:38-39) Peter's mother-in-law	v. 14 "fever"	None	v. 3 "fever left her"
4. Matt 8:28-34 (Mark 5:1-20) Gerasene demoniac	v. 27 demon possession	None	v. 32 to the demon: "Go!"
5. Matt 9:1-18 (Mark 2:1-12// Luke 5:17-26) paralyzed man	v. 2 paralytic	None	vv. 6-7 "Rise, take up your bed and go home. He rose and went home."
6. Matt 9:18-19, 23-26 (Mark 5:21-24, 35-43//Luke 8:40-42a, 49-56) daughter of Jairus	v. 18 ruler: daughter just died v. 24: Jesus: not dead but sleeping	v. 18 ruler: "lay your hand on her, and she will live"	v. 25 "took her by the hand, and the girl arose."
7. Matt 9:20-22 (Mark 5:25-34//Luke 8:42b-48) hemorrhaging woman	v. 20 twelve year hemorrhage (severe menstrual irregularity)	None	v. 22 instantly made well.
8. Matt 9:27-31 two blind men	v. 27 blindness	v. 28 do you believe I can do this? Yes.	29 touched eyes, according to your faith let it be done; eyes were opened.
9. Matt 9:32-33 mute demoniac	v. 32 mute demoniac	None	v. 33 exorcism, mute man spoke
10. Matt 12:9-14 (Mark 3:1-6//Luke 6:1-11) withered hand	v. 10 withered hand	None	v. 13 hand restored, whole like the other
11. Matt 12:22-37, 43-45 (Luke11:14, 24-26) blind and mute demoniac	v. 22 blind and mute demoniac	vv. 43-45 seven worse demons will return.	v. 22 he healed him, so he spoke and saw.
12. Matt 15:21-28 (Mark 7:24-30) demoniac daughter	v. 22 severe demon possession	v. 28 "Let it be done for you as you desire."	v. 28 daughter was healed instantly.
13. Matt 17:14-20 (Mark 9:14-29) moonstruck boy	v. 15 moonstruck; lunatic; not epileptic v. 18 demon possessed	v. 17 faithless and perverse generation; v. 20 healers' little faith	v. 18 exorcism, boy was healed instantly.
14. Matt 20:29-34 (Mark 10:46-52//Luke18:35-43) blindness	v.30 two blind men	None	v. 34 Jesus touched eyes and immediately they saw.

or another. In this case, a prognosis may seldom be mentioned because the Gospel (like the entire Bible) is high-context literature reflecting high-context culture. In other words, those in need of healing would know how to try to maintain well-being once it is restored. The healer would not have to spell that out. To illustrate, while one unclean skin condition mentioned in Matthew 8:1–4 might be remedied, it might recur at another time, or another form of uncleanness might be contracted. Remember that this is not a biomedical problem but rather a sociocultural problem. It is not a disease but rather an illness. The same might be said of vision problems. A couched cataract (proposed by medicocentric interpreters of the healing of blindness in Matthew 20:29–34) could be replaced by a newly developed cataract. In antiquity, no one—neither healer nor client—expected healing to be permanent. Testimonies of sick pilgrims to healing shrines who returned annually seeking help for the same illness confirm this.

The diagnoses also must be explored from a sociocultural perspective. For instance, the diagnosis of the sick person in Matthew 8:1–4 is given in first-century terms, from the native's point of view (i.e., emic "unclean"), along with a modern, medicocentric (etic) interpretation ("biblical leprosy," definitely not Hansen's disease). The reader must question each diagnosis. Even if the translation is accurate (blind, blindness), the actual condition experienced must be viewed more from the Middle Eastern cultural viewpoint than the twenty-first century biomedical perspective.

Particularly noteworthy is the diagnosis of a condition most often translated ethnocentrically as epilepsy, or epileptic (Matt 4:24; 17:15). This is an irresponsible and grossly unfair translation. The Greek word in both instances literally should be translated as "moonstruck." The ancients believed that objects in the sky were not simply inert rocks but living beings (Dan 12:3 "stars"; Psalm 121:6) who had an impact on human beings on earth. Again, a reader must avoid making biomedical diagnoses in search of a disease or organic irregularity but rather seek instead the sociocultural construct of an illness, a temporary loss of meaning in life. Uncleanness removes one from the holy community (Lev 13:45–46) which is tantamount to a death sentence for a member of a collectivistic culture.

Notice the verbs in the passive voice in the therapy column. This is known as the "divine passive" or the "theological passive." It was the common strategy for referring to God as the agent of the activity without mentioning God's name. God is the healer, Jesus is the broker between God and the needy petitioner.

Jesus's Healing Activity as Treason

The question posed to Jesus by the chief priests and elders (Matt 21:23) concerning his power and its source is a serious challenge. The chief priests and elders are the authorities; they are in charge. They authorize or permit collectivistic individuals to function for the benefit of the group, to achieve the group's goals. They did not authorize Jesus to teach or to heal, that is, to use the power he had which no one ever denied in the Gospels. Worse, Jesus never asked them for permission. Who therefore is the source of his dependent power? In that episode Jesus sidesteps the question. He poses a dilemma to them on either of whose horns they will be impaled. When they refused to answer the dilemma he posed, Jesus does the same. "Neither will I tell you by what *exousia* I do these things" (Matt 21:27).

This of course infuriated the authorities. Throughout Matthew, Jesus has insulted the Pharisees, his most frequent opponents, by calling them "actors" (*hypokrites*). "They preach, but do not practice" (Matt 23:3). Scripture may well be the lines these actors recite, but it is not the script by which they live. And to the very same chief priests and elders who question his power and authorization, he asks insultingly: "Have you never read in the scriptures … ?" (Matt 21:42). The insult was understood by the chief priests and the Pharisees (verse 45), but they hesitated to move against him for fear of the multitudes who viewed Jesus as a prophet (verse 46). Finally as Passover approached, the chief priests and elders plotted how to arrest Jesus by stealth and kill him. But they hesitated to do this during the feast lest the people react (Matt 26:3–5). Still, it happened. Jesus had to be removed from society for his treasonous political behavior.

Conclusion

Building on previous analyses of New Testament reports of Jesus's healing activities with insights from medical anthropology, this chapter added political anthropology to the social-scientific hermeneutical tool-box. This tool helped to focus on the power Jesus wielded, the source of this power, and the interpretation of Jesus's healing deeds as political acts. Since authorities did not authorize this use of power, Jesus was given the death penalty for his treasonous activity.

Further Reading

Fabrega, Horacio (1974) *Disease and Social Behavior: An Interdisciplinary Perspective*, Cambridge, MA: MIT Press.
Hollenbach, Paul W. (1982) "Jesus, Demoniacs, and Public Authorities: A Socio-Historical Study," *JAAR*, 49: 567–88.

Moerman, Daniel E. (2002) *Meaning, Medicine and the "Placebo Effect,"* Cambridge: Cambridge University Press.

Pilch, John J. (1981) "Biblical Leprosy and Body Symbolism," *BTB*, 11: 119–33.

Pilch, John J. (1989) "Reading Matthew Anthropologically: Healing in Cultural Perspective," *List*, 24: 278–89.

Pilch, John J. (2000) *Healing in the New Testament: Insights from Medical and Mediterranean Anthropology*, Minneapolis: Fortress Press.

Young, Allan (1982) "The Anthropology of Illness and Sickness," *Annual Review of Anthropology*, 11: 257–85.

10

Social Stratification and Patronage in Ancient Mediterranean Societies

Eric C. Stewart

Characteristics of Patrons and Clients
Patronage Systems
The Institution of Patronage: An Ideal View
New Testament Examples
Conclusion
Further Reading

A high degree of social stratification characterized the social world(s) of the New Testament (Lenski 1984: 242–96; Oakman 1986; Stegemann and Stegemann 1999; Hanson and Oakman 2008). These societies were characterized by a small elite group, serviced by a somewhat larger group of retainers. The vast majority of the population consisted of a rather large group of peasants and artisans, a small but substantial group of slaves, and a group of those unable to work or to support themselves due to illness or some other misfortune. Due to this stratification of society, there were large distances between the social status of elites and those of most of the population. The elites controlled most of the land, extracted much of the food through rents and taxes, and held most of the wealth. Furthermore, elites controlled the armies and the administration of the cities (Stewart 2007).

The fact of vast social and material differences between individuals at different strata of society necessitated the procurement of patronage for those individuals that lacked key provisions for maintaining their status or livelihood. Patronage, above all, is a system of exchange for goods and services between people who are not social equals. It is important to note that not all exchanges involve "economic" elements. Oftentimes patronage involved material support, but it also frequently involved power, protection and influence. Good patrons promote their clients' interests. Clients, correspondingly, offer praise for their patrons, advertising their "grace" to all who would hear. In an honor-based society, such public praise is particularly significant for enhancing the reputation of the patron. Clients might provide other things as well, notably information and service to their patrons. Clients function in the social networks of patrons to promote the interests of the patrons with those outside of the patronage network.

Patronage falls under the broader category of reciprocity. Reciprocity is as much a social relationship as it is a material one. "A specific social relation may constrain a given movement of goods ... If friends make gifts, gifts make friends" (Sahlins 1972: 186). It is in this context that patronage is operative. According to Sahlins, there are three types of reciprocity: negative, balanced and generalized. Negative reciprocity is characterized by a high amount of self-interest and the desire to obtain something for nothing from the other party in the transaction (Sahlins 1972: 193–6). It is characterized by an attempt to get more than one gives up in a transaction: "to get something for nothing with impunity" (Sahlins 1972: 195). In balanced reciprocity the parties exchange goods or services in equal amounts. Nearly universally, such exchanges do not involve material goods of the same kinds coming from the different parties, for that would defeat the purpose of the exchange. Parties trade items to which they do not have equal access or for which they do not have equal need, but which nevertheless have roughly equal value to each of them. Generalized reciprocity "refers to transactions that are putatively altruistic, transactions on the line of assistance given and, if possible and necessary, assistance returned" (Sahlins 1972: 193–4). Generalized reciprocity is the type most frequently found among kin groups. It is characterized by a lack of definite accounting and the fact that the expectation of reciprocation is indefinite. In other words, there is no expectation of immediate repayment.

Of the three types of reciprocity, generalized has the most potential for continuing for an indeterminate length of time. When reciprocity is balanced it does not eliminate the relationship, but it does "even the score" in such a way that the parties are not obligated to one another any longer until they attempt to enter into some other interaction. Negative reciprocity is mostly practiced only toward those with whom one has no ongoing social relationship. This type of reciprocity assumes that the relationship, even if it is ongoing, is not friendly. Finally, generalized reciprocity, due to the fact that frequently there is no immediate reciprocation for benefaction, entails an ongoing relationship in which one party is always obligated to the other party. Here Sahlins uses the example of a mother breastfeeding her child. The child is not able to repay the benefaction in kind, nor is he or she expected to do so. Ideally, however, the child will always be an advocate for the mother's interests and understand that he or she can never balance the score. Along with kinship relations, patronage is a type of generalized reciprocity (Crook 2004a: 58).

Characteristics of Patrons and Clients

Richard P. Saller's important work on personal patronage in ancient Rome suggests three criteria that distinguish patron–client bonds from other types of relationships: (1) "the *reciprocal* exchange of goods and services" and (2) "a personal [relationship] one of some duration" that is (3) "asymmetrical, in the sense that the two parties are of unequal status and offer different kinds of goods and services in the exchange—a quality that sets patronage off from friendship between equals" (Saller 1982: 1). To these three characteristics have been added a fourth by others working in the area of patronage in the Roman empire: these relationships are entered voluntarily (Garnsey and Woolf 1989: 154; Drummond 1989: 101). Both patrons and clients are free to enter into and exit from the patronage relationship, though there are costs associated with doing so. S. N. Eisenstadt and Louis Roniger, discussing characteristics of patronage in broader cross-cultural comparison, stress again the personal, voluntary, unequal, and reciprocal elements of the relationship, but they add to these that such relationships are frequently extra-legal and they involve elements of trust and solidarity, stressing the continuation of the relationships, at least in ideal terms, for entire lifetimes (1984: 48–9).

The types of goods and services exchanged between patrons and clients can vary significantly from one patronage relationship to the next. Patrons might supply their clients with any number of items of support: land, money, protection, support in legal cases, food, access to other patrons, and any other provision that might be necessary for their overall well-being. What characterizes patrons is their control over access to the resources needed by clients. The resources might involve things like political positions or letters of recommendation for high-status clients or basic necessities of life in the form of food or protection from foreign armies or enemies. Clients, in return, might also provide money to support their patrons' interests, military service, and, above all, honor to their patrons. The most important thing that clients can provide their patrons is honor and loyalty or fidelity (Eisenstadt and Roniger 1984; Malina 1988: Crook 2004a).

Patronage Systems

What is sometimes lost in discussions of personal patronage is how a system of patronage operates at multiple levels in a society. While individual clients could and did find personal patrons for any number of things, patronage as a system is ignored frequently by historians dealing with patronage in the Roman world. Andrew Wallace-Hadrill discusses the relationship between the specificity of patronage in a Roman context (which he argues differs fundamentally from Greek contexts), but acknowledges that the difficulty in discussing patronage lies in the relationship between cultural specificity and patronage as a cross-cultural phenomenon (1989b: 65–8). Wallace-Hadrill notes that there are those social historians who argue that even where the language of patron–client might not be present, the phenomena of patron–client relationships sometimes occur.

T. Johnson and C. Dandeker, two sociologists, argue concerning the Roman world that historians frequently assume a "market" context in which patronage performs a deviant, problematic, or sometimes safeguarding function (1989: 234–40). Further, historians of Roman patronage usually assume a distinction between the "state" and patronage and assume the "normal" structure of society exercised through the state (1989: 234–6). They argue that patronage, rather than being a "fill-in" when the market breaks down is actually the structural system of the Roman state; "for much of its history Rome was a society in which public agencies and official functions were mediated by the private personal ties of patronage" (1989: 236). These relationships "play a dominant (not exclusive) role in the organization of the economy, polity and society" (1989: 223). To sum up the kind of patronage system that they are describing it can be said that this system is not merely an aggregation of numerous patron–client relationships, but is in fact "the prime mechanism in the allocation of scarce resources and the dominant means of legitimizing the social order" (1989: 223). In other words, the Roman Empire was not a market economy in which more people "fell through the cracks" than in modern industrial market economies. The Roman economy itself was structured largely through patronage.

Johnson and Dandeker note that two developments in the Roman change from Republic to Empire signal the beginning of the end for patronage as it was practiced in the period of the Republic. The first of these developments is the reduction in the "competitive pluralism of the system" that the emperor brought with him due to the concentration of more resources in fewer hands. This development limited to a great extent the availability of multiple patrons with access to goods. This element brought much more brokerage (see Batten in this volume) into the system, making access to the imperial household and its benefaction that much more important. The second development that caused adaptation in the patronage system was, in large part, due to the first. Patronage toward communities, towns, and regions weaken patronage as a system since it undermines the personal connection between patrons and their clients. As a result, "patron–client bonds necessarily became less diffuse and all-encompassing" and tended to reduce the reciprocal relationship to "the exchange of benefaction and honor alone" (1989: 239). As the imperial household monopolized more and more of the resources of the Roman empire, collective clients increased in number. These collective clients, whether villages, cities, ethnic groups or other types of associations, repaid the benefactors who were at a much greater remove from them personally by erecting honorary inscriptions, statues, and buildings, among other items to praise patrons to whom they had no direct relationship. The personal nature of patronage was severed in this practice, and a move toward "state" control of resources was well underway.

It is unclear, however, to what extent either of these developments would have changed things for lower-status clients. Clearly those who had access to multiple senatorial sources of patronage might have ultimately had their choices limited by the concentration of resources under imperial control. Poorer clients, however, those not directly connected to the high-status patrons of Rome, likely worked through several layers of brokers or mediators if they needed benefaction that could only be provided from that level. C. H. Landé, speaking of the dyadic alliances that form the basis for patron–client relationships, has argued that "persons who own or have access to substantial resources have many would-be allies," while those of lower status and fewer means "may have few willing allies to choose from" (1977: xvi). Those who lack the resources to provide as patrons would have fewer clients from which to choose, and those who lack the means or abilities to provide any meaningful return to patrons lack selection in securing patrons.

The Institution of Patronage: An Ideal View

Dionysius of Halicarnassus, a Greek historian who composed a history of early Rome, the *Antiquitates romanae*, noted that it was the founder of Rome, Romulus himself, that established both the hierarchical nature of the society and the practice of patronage at Rome. His description of Roman patronage is clearly idealized and written in order to indict the practice as it existed in his own lifetime and its "deterioration" in his contemporary Rome. His account, however, is useful in as much as it sets out the description of what the patron–client relationship could be in ideal terms.

Dionysius describes the manner in which Romulus organized the newly formed society at Rome in *Antiquitates romanae* 2.9–11. After being made king of Rome, Romulus divided the people into two classes: patricians and plebians. Since the patricians were "by nature" more fit for ruling, these were placed above the plebians. The patricians were given the tasks involved in aiding Romulus in the public exercise of running Rome. They were to be the priests, the rulers or leaders, and the judges. The plebians, on the other hand, were given other tasks necessary to the maintenance of society, such as farming, trade, and rearing animals, but not those of ruling Rome. This fact is due to their lack of acquaintance with public affairs and their lacking the amount of leisure time to pursue such acquaintance (*Ant. rom.*

2.9.1). Romulus understood that is was necessary for the better to rule the lesser, and he allowed the plebians to choose for themselves patrons from the patrician class (*Ant. rom.* 2.9.2).

Dionysius goes on to relate the duties of clients and patrons to one another.

It was the duty of the patricians to explain to their clients the laws, of which they were ignorant; to take the same care of them when absent as present, doing everything for them that fathers do for their sons with regard both to money and to the contracts that related to money; to bring suit on behalf of their clients when they were wronged in connexion [*sic*] with contracts, and to defend them against any who brought charges against them; and, to put the matter briefly, to secure for them both in private and in public affairs all that tranquillity [*sic*] of which they particularly stood in need. It was the duty of the clients to assist their patrons in providing dowries for their daughters upon their marriage if the fathers had not sufficient means; to pay their ransom to the enemy if any of them or of their children were taken prisoner; to discharge out of their own purses their patrons' losses in private suits and the pecuniary fines which they were condemned to pay to the State, making these contributions to them not as loans but as thank-offerings; and to share with their patrons the costs incurred in their magistracies and dignities and other public expenditures, in the same manner as if they were their relations. For both patrons and clients alike it was impious and unlawful to accuse each other in law-suits or to bear witness or to give their votes against each other or to be found in the number of each other's enemies; and whoever was convicted of doing any of these things was guilty of treason by virtue of the law sanctioned by Romulus, and might lawfully be put to death by any man who so wished as a victim devoted to Jupiter of the infernal regions.

(Dionysius of Halicarnassus, *Ant. rom.* 2.10.1–3)

Dionysius goes on to explain that the Romans exported this type of patron–client relationship to all the places colonized by Rome. In fact, those places did not have such an arrangement forced upon them, but rather chose this type of social order for themselves (*Ant. rom.* 2.11.1). This type of patronage relationship, Dionysius insists, prevented bloodshed among Romans for 630 years (*Ant. rom.* 2.11.2)!

It is important to note that the relations between patrons and their clients are idealized in Dionysius' account. In actual practice, of course, patronage could roam far from this ideal kind of practice. Dionysius, however, notes two elements that likely did keep the relationships between patrons and clients from breaking into open hostility in many cases. The first is that such bonds could exist over many generations due to a kind of filial piety. Sons of patrons were obligated to fulfill the demands made upon the patron, not through legal requirements, but due to an ongoing competition for honor since "it was a matter of great praise" (*mega epanion*) to maximize the number of one's family's clients (*Ant. rom.* 2.10.4). For clients, as well, there was the expectation to uphold the relationship with patrons, but, as noted above, there was certainly the possibility of frequenting more than one patron. A second element that held the relationship together was the expectation of the desire for honor on the part of patrons. Patrons, according to Dionysius, competed for honor among one another by trying to maximize the number of clients. Clients might have occasion to provide material aid to their patrons (see the list of circumstances under which clients might provide monetary loans or gifts to their patrons), but more than that they provide status enhancement. The more clients a patron had at his or her disposal, the greater that patron's reputation might be among his or her peers. Finally, it should be noted that at least in ideal terms, patrons and clients are to treat one another as if they were members of their own kin group (*Ant. rom.* 2.10.1). This type of reciprocity is generalized reciprocity, the ideal to which patrons and clients ought to be compared.

Divine Patronage

Deities could also be patrons (Neyrey 2004; Malina 1988; Crook 2004a). For the early followers of Jesus (and perhaps for Jesus himself), to claim the God of Israel as patron meant that there were no other patrons to whom one could turn and expect access to all of the same goods and services. The God of Israel controlled all resources. This claim should be read as a counter to the imperial claims to provide patronage to all the residents of the Roman empire. It was God, rather than Caesar, who controlled all resources, including land, status, victory, salvation, and the kingdom.

Image of Divine Patronage

Unlike most people in the Roman Empire, Judeans, including those who aligned themselves with Jesus, did not have access to multiple heavenly patrons. Jesus is perhaps best understood, in reading the Gospels this way, as a broker for God who provides access to God for the clients (Malina 1988; Williams 2006: 42–7). The clients are those who obligate themselves to God by receiving his benefaction. It is, of course, an open question whether God's benefaction extends to all irrespective of whether people join the patronage network (Matt 5:45).

New Testament Examples

There are numerous examples in the New Testament of patron–client relationships at work. The remainder of this chapter will be devoted to exploring several different examples of the phenomenon in the Gospels and in Paul's first letter to the Corinthians.

Jesus and Patronage: Healing the Centurion's Son

Perhaps one of the clearest New Testament examples of patronage and patronage networks comes in Luke's Gospel. Jesus heals the slave of a Roman centurion (Luke 7:1–10). The centurion is a patron of a certain community of Judeans. He is able to ask of his clients, in this case the Judean elders, a favor of Jesus on his behalf. They do so, suggesting to Jesus that he is "worthy" because of his previous patronage to the Judean community due to his love of their people (7:4–5). Their indication that he is worthy of Jesus's benefaction is an indication that they are faithful clients to their patron. He is not like other Roman soldiers who are not friends to the Judeans. Rather he is a builder on their behalf. Here the clients of the centurion appeal to Jesus, functioning as brokers because of their ethnicity as Judeans. Jesus does, in fact, heal the centurion's servant, indicating that the brokerage of the elders of the Judeans was successful in providing access for their patron.

It is significant to note who is and is not a patron or client in this episode. Even if we assume that Jesus's role is best described as broker for the kingdom of God (Malina 1988), here, through the power of his patron God, he provides the benefaction of healing for the slave of the centurion. The centurion, however, describes himself as someone who is subject to authority (Luke 7:8). He commands those under him, including both soldiers and slaves. He is patron neither to the soldiers nor to the slaves, but he is a patron to the Judeans. The Roman soldiers and the slaves (of unknown ethnicity) do not have a choice in the matter of service to the centurion. One presumes they have not entered into the relationship with him voluntarily, and they are certainly not free to leave. The Judeans, however, have entered into the relationship more freely. Even where they are bound to accept Roman rule over themselves, they do not have to accept the centurion's building efforts on their behalf. Having done so, however, they are obligated to provide what assistance they can in his time of need. To that end, they approach Jesus, their compatriot, to provide benefaction for their patron. The centurion himself greets Jesus with a characteristic description of his unworthiness in order to show his deference (7:6). Despite the fact that he is a Roman officer, he does not claim equality with Jesus but insists on his own lack of standing in relation to Jesus. The centurion's willingness to acknowledge Jesus's superiority to himself, to place himself in the position of client, occasions Jesus's remark regarding the centurion's faithfulness (Luke 7:9). Here *pistis*, the Greek word most frequently translated as "faith," is better conceived of as an acknowledgement of the centurion's indebtedness and corresponding loyalty toward Jesus (Crook 2004b: 174–5).

1 Corinthians

J. K. Chow (1992) has analyzed 1 Corinthians through a lens of patronage. He attempts to read behind the text of 1 Corinthians to address some of the circumstances with which Paul was dealing in Corinth. Chow is certainly correct in arguing that patronage is a significant feature of any Roman colony in the first century CE. He discusses the status incongruities present among the Corinthian community by means of network analysis and the role that patronage played in Corinthian networks (1992: 83–112). Chow argues that three factors predominant in Corinth led to a problem with patrons in the Jesus group there. These problems involve (1) varying degrees of status inequality in Corinth, (2) a difficulty accepting Paul's apostleship, not least because he was unwilling to accept money and indebt himself to the rich patrons of Corinth, and (3) those who were patrons within the community there maintained ties to non-members of the group in order to advance their own interests. In other words, powerful (in Chow's discussion this basically equates to wealthy) patrons dominated the community at Corinth, and these patrons were those people who opposed Paul's apostleship and vision for the group.

Chow's understanding of patronage is important and interesting. It is, however, burdened by his neglecting to consider Paul in the light of divine patronage. Paul is also involved within patronage systems, even if he is unwilling to take money from the Corinthians. Part of the difficulties Paul seems to be having with the Corinthians is that he understands them to be a single group indebted to the benefaction of God. Crook (2008) has recently argued that the language of *charis* (grace, goodwill) in the New Testament is best understood as "benefaction" because it is a word whose cultural meaning is linked to the concept of patronage. In the case of 1 Corinthians, without disputing Chow's (1992) analysis of the difficulties patronage may have caused for the community at Corinth, Paul is working to bring the Corinthians to understand themselves as a single community which has received benefaction from God. As Paul has received such benefaction (1 Cor 3:10; 15:10), so also the Corinthians have received benefaction from God (1 Cor 1:4; 2:12; 7:7).

Such benefaction, then, would make all members of the group clients of the God of Israel, whose patronage is brokered through Christ and also through

Paul. If all of the Corinthians are clients of God, then divisions among them cause dishonor to God. Perhaps nowhere will this fact be seen more clearly than in the case of members of the Corinthian community taking one another to court (1 Cor 6:1–8). Chow (1992: 123–30) is certainly correct to note that the Roman legal system produced situations in which rich, powerful persons could easily take advantage of those without the same means. Even if we assume this to be the case here, however, Paul considers their going to court against one another as already being defeated (1 Cor 6:7). The reason he gives for this point is their status as siblings (1 Cor 6:8). As noted above, patrons and clients frequently invoked the language of kinship among themselves. Paul argues that it is preferable to be wronged than to be exposed as having insurmountable disagreements over matters pertaining to the legal system (1 Cor 6:7–8). Clients and patrons, or in this case patrons of the same client, taking one another to court would no doubt cause grievous injury to the reputation of the patron. As Dionysius wrote in his idealized account of the origins of Roman patronage, taking one another to court is impious and unlawful and amounted to treasonous behavior. It is the reputation, or honor, of the God of Israel and his broker Jesus that is imperiled by behaving in a manner that Dionysius labels "sanctioned by neither divine nor human law" (2.10.3). To go to court before the unrighteous (1 Cor 6:1) is to be defeated (1 Cor 6:7).

Paul's concerns about the patronage of God extend beyond their behavior in court. Chow (1992: 141–57) rightly notes that the context of eating meat offered to idols is related to social elements of the Corinthian situation. He argues that the context for some of the Corinthian Jesus group's participation in eating in temples dedicated to Roman or Greek gods (1 Cor 8:1–6) is likely due to the influence of the imperial cult in Corinth. He basically assigns as motivation for their participation the maintenance of key social connections to prominent people who governed Corinth and had connections to the household of Caesar. While all of this is certainly possible, and perhaps even likely, Paul is concerned for another reason. Certainly one of the major reasons for attending festivals (of whatever sort) at the temple of a Roman deity would be to seek the divine benefaction of that deity. This matter is precisely Paul's concern. He does not seem to have a difficulty with the eating of meat offered to idols generally (1 Cor 10:27–30), but it is the context in which one eats that causes the difficulty. Paul does not even seem to mind the Jesus group engaging in sharing meals with those outside the group (1 Cor 10:27), so that the maintenance of ties with former patrons or clients does not seem to be the issue. For Paul, the issue is that the God of Israel will not continue to provide patronage to those who seek it from other gods as well. Paul does not accept the positions of the Corinthian "strong" that "there is no idol in the cosmos" and that "no one is God except one"

(1 Cor 8:4). These beings do exist as alternative patrons to the "one God" and "one Lord" that are benefactors "for us" (1 Cor 8:6). These other beings, however, far from being benevolent patrons, are demons (1 Cor 10:20). God is a jealous patron who does not sit idly by while his clients appeal to other patrons (1 Cor 10:21–22). To seek benefaction from other divine patrons is to lose the patronage of the God of Israel. Paul's rhetorical aim in 1 Corinthians, then, is to cause the Corinthians to understand themselves as a single group based on fictive kinship that has but one patron and one broker (Bartchy 1999; 2008).

Conclusion

There are certainly many other New Testament texts that could be profitably analyzed using the model of patronage and clientage. Throughout the New Testament God is understood as a patron to his followers (Neyrey 2004). Jesus is a broker for God's benefaction in the Synoptic Gospels (Malina 1988). Paul's conversion to the Jesus movement is best read against the background of benefaction, patronage, and loyalty (Crook 2004a; 2008). Prayer is frequently a call for a patron to provide benefaction or thanksgiving for benefaction provided (Neyrey 2001; Crook 2007). Patronage, though it was changing during the period of the Roman empire, was still alive and well. The sheer volume of dedicatory inscriptions, statues, and buildings we have from the first-century Roman world attest to the practice of honoring patrons publicly for their benefactions to individuals, communities, and ethnic groups. Patronage remained a significant factor in the social world(s) of the New Testament.

Further Reading

Bowditch, P. L. (2001) *Horace and the Gift Economy of Patronage*, Berkeley, CA: University of California Press.

Damon, C. (1997) *The Mask of the Parasite: A Pathology of Roman Patronage*, Ann Arbor: University of Michigan Press.

Eilers, C. (2002) *Roman Patrons of Greek Cities*, Oxford: Oxford University Press.

Lomas, K., and T. Cornell (2003) *'Bread and Circuses': Euergetism and Municipal Patronage in Roman Italy*, London: Routledge.

Sahlins, M. (1972) *Stone Age Economics*, Chicago: Aldine-Atherton.

Saller, Richard P. (1982) *Personal Patronage Under the Early Roman Empire*, Cambridge: Cambridge University Press.

Verboven, Koenraad (2002) *The Economy of Friends: Economic Aspects of Amicitia and Patronage in the Late Republic*, Collection Latomus 269. Bruxelles: Éditions Latomus.

11

Brokerage

Jesus as Social Entrepreneur

Alicia Batten

Today the first image that might emerge in the mind of a North American upon hearing the word "broker" or "brokerage" is that of a real estate agent or stock broker, and the characteristics of this broker may not be terribly flattering given that such persons are sometimes perceived as making large amounts of money for relatively little work! Yet many people who rely on the services of brokers are usually appreciative of the contacts, skills, and knowledge that these agents provide—they make life much easier when certain complicated transactions need to be made. Likewise in the ancient world, brokers were go-betweens or people who linked one individual or group with another using particular strategic means. Such activities not only served the interests of the separate parties, but also those of the broker, whose gain from the interaction motivated him or her to provide such services in the first place. In particular, the broker played a central role within the patron–client relationship. As patronage and clientage are the subjects of another chapter in this volume, I shall not describe them in detail here, but provide a brief review of these phenomena as brokerage cannot be understood apart from this larger framework. Subsequently, this chapter will explore some of the general characteristics of brokerage including some discussion of how this phenomenon could function within the context of ancient religions. Finally, the chapter discusses some specific passages in the New Testament in order to examine how the brokerage model can shed light on the interpretation of these texts.

Patron–Client Model

Since the late 1960s, the patron–client model as a tool for understanding types of social exchange has flourished among anthropologists, sociologists and political scientists. Studies of patronage and clientage have focused both on interpersonal dyadic (two-person) relationships between a single patron and his or her client and on more institutionalized and social interactions between associations (Eisenstadt and Roniger 1980: 42–3). As intimated above, the patron–client interaction provides a structure for providing various kinds of resources or favors (economic, political, legal, etc.) in exchange for honor, loyalty, and other forms of support. This type of reciprocity presupposes a strong power and wealth differential between the patron and client(s). As S. N. Eisenstadt and Louis Roniger point out, "the crucial element of this inequality is the monopolization by the patrons of certain positions that are of vital importance to the clients" (1980: 50). Thus, one can appreciate how the patron–client relationship effectively undermines "horizontal group organization and solidarity" (1980: 50), especially given the fact that such exchanges are not performed within contractual or legal relationships and thus the client, who is obviously the more vulnerable party, does not have institutions to turn to when facing exploitation by the patron.

The weakness of the client is particularly relevant for the study of patronage and clientage in the Greco-Roman world. Thomas Carney's classic study of the use of models in antiquity, *The Shape of the Past*, explains how for the peasant, the establishment of a client relationship with a patron provided some measure of security yet it could simultaneously develop into overt exploitation such that peasants were "reduced to amoral familism by destitution" (1975: 200). The fact that most ancients viewed all goods— whether they be land, money, honor, protection, or food—to be in fixed quantities and in short supply, that is, to be "limited goods," meant that one person's or family's gain would be perceived to be at the expense of others.[1] Such perceptions contributed to the agonistic dimension of society in the sense that there was a constant struggle and suspiciousness among people, especially among the vast majority who were in want (Carney 1975: 199). These features made the poor all the more dependent upon alliances of some duration with patrons (Saller 1982: 1), and all the more susceptible to patronal manipulations. In Greco-Roman antiquity, chronic indebtedness was seemingly the norm for the poor, and such a state of affairs subjected them to "brutal compulsion and oppression" (Oakman 2008: 13). In Palestine, for example, with rising debt came greater landlessness, and thus tenancy and control centered on fewer and fewer wealthy landowners (Oakman 2008: 25). The estimates for the overall elite population of the Roman empire in the first century range between 1 and 5 percent of the population and thus the vast majority of people were poor and dependent upon some sort of patron for their survival (Stegemann and Stegemann 1999: 77).

Brokers

The person who enables and manoeuvres patron–client exchanges is thus the broker. Brokers are types of social entrepreneurs—their role is to bring people together for the purpose of exchange, and in doing so they must be innovative in order that the entire enterprise not only serves the interests of each party but also procures a benefit for the broker. One of the key anthropologists who has studied brokerage in a variety of contexts, including those of the Mediterranean, is Jeremy Boissevain on whom I rely considerably here. Boissevain points out that unlike the patron who distributes first order resources such as land, money, food, and protection to clients in exchange for labor and/or honors, the broker manages second order resources— essentially "strategic contacts with other people who control such resources directly or who have access to such persons" (Boissevain 1974: 147). This means that brokers must be proficient at networking: they must be expert at bringing people together, and they must be willing to "manipulate ... social relations for a profit" (Boissevain 1974: 154). Whether in a highly industrialized city or a rural peasant village, the broker must also possess the ability to bridge different social levels, cultures, or localities, he or she must have the time to do so, and have a significant degree of power that enables him or her to convince the patron and/or client to engage in a particular type of exchange in the first place (Boissevain 1974: 158).

Moreover, rarely does the broker receive a payment (which is usually not money, but status, favors, information, or some other service) at the moment of the exchange; rather, the broker acquires credit which "consists of what others think [the broker's] capital to be" (Boissevain 1974: 159), capital being the perceived contacts the broker has with potential parties of interest, or the second order resources that were referred to above. Thus, expectations and hope play key roles in the broker's work as the interested clients *do not know* the extent of the broker's contacts whereas they may be familiar with the limitations of a specific patron's resources (Boissevain 1974: 160–1). A broker can manipulate people through promises that first order resources will be provided, and as people become more and more indebted to a broker, he or she increases a credit that can then be turned into profit, consisting of privileges, increased status, property, or other resources.

A broker, however, must be careful not to convert his or her credit into profit too hastily, for in such a situation brokers become patrons in that they can now distribute first order resources of which they become obligated, as patrons, to provide. They are no longer dealing in promises but in concrete material resources that their clients will expect them to supply and if they do not deliver, the brokers now turned patrons will lose their credit as both patrons and brokers (Boissevain 1974: 162).

In addition to the possibility of losing credit, brokers were often viewed suspiciously. For example, in pre-modern Arabia, "the whole range of public criticism against the brokers centered in the premise that they were unscrupulous and deceitful" (Beg 1977: 88). Although in this Arabian context everyone admitted that people needed capital, the capital of brokers was perceived to be lying (Beg 1977: 89). Moreover, brokers could hold somewhat isolated positions in that once they began serving the interests of the ruling class, providing fewer benefits to their group of origin, they might be shunned by their own group while at the same time remaining an outsider for those people whose interests they were serving (Zenner 1990: 142–3). Thus, becoming a bridge between different cultural and social and/or religious groups could mean that ultimately one was an outsider to all of them.

In some cases, however, this outsider status enabled brokers to become cultural innovators. If brokers managed to maintain membership in their community of origin, be it ethnic and/or economic, they could become voices for that community and channel communication back and forth between their group and the ruling elites, as Walter P. Zenner has illustrated with regard to various Jewish retainer figures at different points in history (1990: 143). In copying the customs and practices of the elites, such brokers could bring about cultural innovation within their primary group. In doing so, Zenner writes that

> the minority retainers were cultural brokers who mediated and reinterpreted both the cultures of the minority and of the ruling elite. While their role as manipulators may be more apparent, their role as cultural innovators was of consequence in its own right. It could wean the minority from its traditional role in the economy.
>
> (Zenner 1990: 149)

This notion of cultural brokerage is important to remain cognizant of, for although brokers were distrusted in many contexts by those on the bottom, they might also be agents of change that actually improved conditions for the client group.

Primary and Secondary Resources

The distinction between primary and secondary resources, or *beneficia,* was apparent within the Greco-Roman world. The first-century Jewish historian, Josephus, brokers on behalf of a range of people including family members (Josephus, *Vita* 75–76; Hanson and Oakman 1998: 80). The Roman orator Cicero makes a distinction in Latin between *facultas*, or resources that could be immediately distributed, and *gratia* or influence that brokers had over other people, that is, their social networking power (*Epistulae familiares* 13.6.2).[2] Letters of recommendation from ancient Rome reveal the complicated systems of social networks in which brokers played a key role. As the broker built a reputation as an influential person who could procure *facultas*, the more credit and eventual profit the broker would receive. But as Koenraad Verboven illustrates with regard to these Roman recommendations, just as a broker could quickly create a name as a person with important contacts, this name could become blacklisted if the broker failed to fulfill promises to people, illustrating Jeremy Boissevain's point above (Verboven 2002: 321–9).

Divine Brokers

The models of patronage, clientage and brokerage applied as equally to ancient forms of religion as they did to social interactions among people. A god was often perceived as a patron or benefactor[3] and the worshippers as the clients. Thus, priests and priestesses within temple precincts, parents within the domestic religion of the household, and other religious officials functioned as brokers who mediated the favors of the gods "in exchange for human gratitude and praise" (Williams 1999: 120). Within ancient forms of Judaism, God could be understood as a patron in addition to other roles, such as king or father, and numerous scholars have examined the patronage imagery used for God in both the Hebrew Bible and the New Testament (Malina 1996: 150–1; Scott 1989: 207). Moreover, within the Hebrew Bible, various figures, especially prophets, play the role of broker for they mediate God the patron's wishes to the worshippers and likewise express the cries and demands of humans to the deity (Green 1989). Some have argued that the figures of Abraham and especially Moses conform to the brokerage model (Brown 2003: 56; Neyrey 2007: 277).

When we turn to early Christian writings we observe that the models of patron, broker, and client apply to a variety of figures found therein. What is particularly interesting is how the ancient writers use the model in ways that both conform to but sometimes alter the expectations for how a broker should behave. In the next section we shall thus examine a few of these texts.

Jesus as Broker in the Gospels

Probably the most well-known application of the model of broker is to the figure of Jesus. If God is understood as a divine patron or benefactor, then Jesus, in many texts, functions as God's broker, who mediates God's grace, that is, God's favors or benefits, to believers in exchange for their trust or faith. The New Testament is littered with the language of benefaction (see Danker 1982); God is the father and benefactor who provides for humans. Bruce J. Malina, therefore, argues that to enter the kingdom of God would be to enter into God's patronage or benefaction and as Jesus proclaims this kingdom, Jesus effectively functions as a broker for God (Malina 1996: 147–50). Jesus is a social broker who puts people in touch with the divine patron who can provide primary benefits to those willing to enter a "dyadic alliance" with such a patron. In Malina's view, this work "was the chief occupation of the last period of Jesus's career" (1996: 154).

Boissevain's model of the broker applies itself easily to the figure of Jesus as depicted in the gospels. The network of people around Jesus was his capital and he seems to have had little difficulty creating this system. For example, in Mark 1:16–20 he calls various people to leave their occupations and follow him, which they do immediately, no questions asked. The gospels also indicate that at points Jesus had a spectacular credit rating given what others' expectations were of what favors he could guarantee (Malina 1996: 154). Early on Mark's gospel makes it clear that Jesus has difficulty finding "alone time" as people constantly crowd in on him and search for him, seeking the benefactions, such as healings, exorcisms and teachings, that they think he can mediate (Mark 1:28, 33, 37, 45). Indeed Jesus usually fulfills their expectations and thus he incurs a tremendous debt of gratitude from people which serves to increase his credit rating even more (Malina 1996: 155). Jesus himself gained "tariffs" from people who were in his debt in the form of invitations to people's dining tables, loyalty, and honor but as Malina says, these tariffs are never paid in full, for if they were, the open-ended relationship would cease, all accounts would be settled and closed and there would be no more need for a broker (1996: 154). Yet, in the Gospel of Mark, the ultimate benefactor is God who unlike human benefactors has a limitless supply of favors to grant to humans. Jesus is "a broker of God's riches" (Neufeld 2008a: 61) in Mark, and due to this limitless supply of divine wealth, human beings obviously and unsurprisingly want to maintain an ongoing relationship with God's agent, Jesus. Hence, Jesus conforms in many ways to the broker model, but he differs somewhat in that the benefits from God that he can promise are without end, unlike those of human patrons.

Matthew and Luke, the two other synoptic gospels, share many of Mark's stories but even in many instances in which there is no parallel with Mark, they present Jesus as God's broker. For example, in Matthew 8:5–13 and Luke 7:1–10 we read of the famous centurion of Capernaum, who because of Jesus's credit rating, asks Jesus to come and heal his servant, which Jesus obliges. Jesus thus provides the first order resources of God to this centurion's slave (Malina and Rohrbaugh 1992: 75). What is also noteworthy here is the fact that Jesus is mediating benefits to people who—unlike himself and his immediate followers—are Gentiles, thus illustrating Zenner's point that brokers are potential sources of cultural innovation for they can bridge differences between cultural and religious groups. Likewise the risen Jesus in Matthew commands his network to go out to all nations, not just to the house of Israel (Malina and Rohrbaugh 1992: 166), indicating that God's benefits are potentially available to all, regardless of ethnic or cultural origin and that the networking continues to expand (Malina 1995: 155). A similar situation arises in Luke's account of the resurrected Jesus, who tells the disciples that the message of repentance and forgiveness of sins should be proclaimed in God's name to "all nations" (Luke 24:47) and that Jesus, God's broker, is indeed sending upon the disciples God's benefits, which is what God promised (Luke 24:48).

Although the Gospel of John reflects a higher Christology than that of the synoptic gospels, Jesus remains a broker in this narrative as well. Jerome H. Neyrey has argued persuasively that Jesus resides in two worlds in this gospel: that of God the patron and that of the disciples who are clients. Jesus is the mediator whom God sends to provide "knowledge, power, loyalty and material benefaction [and who] correspondingly ... brokers the interests of the clients by praying for them and urging them to 'pray in [his] name'" (Neyrey 2007: 272). Jesus becomes a broker in John's gospel because God has sent (10:36) and authorized him (6:27) to do so; his brokerage is successful for a variety of reasons, including the fact that he mediates God's wondrous benefactions such as all of the "signs" that he performs, and maintains a lasting relationship with both the patron, God, and the clients, or disciples; he "remains" with both and they "remain" with him (John 14:10; 2:10; 4:40; Neyrey 2007: 283–5). Indeed, many reject Jesus as broker, but this does not affect Jesus's relationship with either the followers, who maintain their loyalty to him, or with God, to whom Jesus ascends at the end of the gospel.

Jesus's brokerage work in John, however, departs somewhat from the standard model of brokers who manage second order goods. Rather, the Jesus of John's gospel can make first order goods available to people. God has placed all things in Jesus's hands (3:35) and shows Jesus all that God is doing (5:20). Neyrey notes, however, that Jesus can only broker what God has bestowed upon him even though he functions as a "superior broker" in this gospel, or a broker *par excellence* (2007: 286). Indeed, Neyrey argues that although the model of Jesus as a broker is consistent throughout the gospels[4] and in other sections of the Christian scriptures as well, it is "the Fourth Gospel that uses this model most extensively" (2007: 291).

Despite the fact that the gospels present Jesus as a broker for God, one cannot say whether the historical Jesus understood himself to be occupying this role.[5] Some scholars, however, who attempt to determine what were the historical Jesus's authentic teachings and actions do address the issue of brokerage. Most notable is John Dominic Crossan, who concludes that Jesus proclaimed a "brokerless kingdom" (Crossan 1991; 1994). By this Crossan means that Jesus challenged the pervasive patterns of patronage and clientage within the ancient Roman empire by practicing a radical itinerancy. Rather than settling down in Nazareth and becoming a patron to many, Jesus traveled about and healed those whom he met along the way. He rejected the patron–client structure and the concomitant brokerage that went with this system. Therefore, one of the reasons, argues Crossan, why Jesus's family is presented as not believing in him (Mark 6:4) was because he was behaving in this strange manner and repudiating the structures and systems that the vast majority simply took for granted (Neufeld 2000). It was this behavior that disturbed the family, but this is not to say that they did not have faith in his significance and power (Crossan 1994: 99). Such itinerancy was the "programmatic symbolization" of the radical egalitarianism of Jesus, which manifested itself through the sharing of material and spiritual gifts, through eating and drinking together at a common table. If Jesus had remained in one specific place, such settlement would have bred centralization and with it, the reestablishment of patronage, brokerage, and clientage, all of which contradict Jesus's understanding of the Kingdom of God (Crossan 1994: 101). For Crossan, Jesus's message and activity rejected this whole notion of brokerage, for it advocated an equality in which people were in "direct contact with one another and with God, unmediated by established brokers or fixed locations" (Crossan 1994: 101).

We observe, therefore, that when it comes to Jesus, he is portrayed as a broker by the gospel writers but perhaps he himself was opposed to the notion of brokerage and its attendant larger framework.[6] Certainly not all historical Jesus scholars would agree with the latter interpretation of Jesus, but I refer to it here in order to provide a concrete example of the many distinctions between the Jesus of history and the ways in which he was portrayed within the gospels. It may be said with certainty, however, that as the Christian church changed both institutionally and theologically, Jesus's identity as a broker in the gospels shifted dramatically such that he became the one to whom believers prayed for first order resources. In other words,

Jesus gains a big promotion in that he goes from being a broker for God in the gospels to the position of chief executive officer itself,[7] or as one scholar has put it, "when Jesus becomes the church's Lord (*kyrios* is both master and lord) or returning Son of man, he becomes their patron" (Scott 1989: 207).

Other Brokers in the New Testament

Other figures throughout the New Testament appear as brokers as well. Sometimes the disciples play this role, such as Andrew in the Gospel of John. Andrew does not broker for God, but for Jesus, in that he facilitates meetings between Jesus and Andrew's brother, Simon Peter (John 1:40–42); he brings a young boy in possession of loaves and fishes to Jesus such that Jesus can feed the multitude (John 6:1–14); and arranges a meeting between Jesus and some Greeks (John 12:20–22). As K. C. Hanson and Douglas E. Oakman (1998: 80) point out, Andrew fulfills all the roles of an effective broker for he recruits (meeting with Simon Peter), he manages resources (feeding of the multitude), and brings people from differing cultural backgrounds together (meeting with the Greeks).

The fourth gospel's depiction of the spirit, or Paraclete, can be compared to that of a broker. Like Neyrey, Tricia Gates Brown argues that Jesus is a broker for God in John but that once Jesus ascends to God, the Paraclete brokers access to Jesus. The Paraclete and Jesus are not equal; rather, the Paraclete is subordinate to Jesus and does not speak on its own authority, as is evident in John 16:13–15 (Brown 2003: 233). In fulfilling this role, the Paraclete reminds the disciples of all that Jesus had taught them (John 14:26); it testifies on behalf of Jesus (John 15:26); furthers Jesus's work in the world concerning sin, righteousness, and judgment (John 16:8–11); and offers guidance in the truth to the disciples (John 16:12–15). Thus, the Paraclete is the figure that allows for access to the glorified Jesus just as Jesus provided access to God (Brown 2003: 232–3). In these senses then, the Paraclete functions very much according to the model of a broker.

Paul and Brokerage

Thus far, the examples of brokerage have been taken from the gospels, but it is important to point out that the apostle Paul, likewise emerging from a world in which patronage, clientage, and brokerage were endemic, uses the image of broker. Like the gospel writers, God was the patron *par excellence* for Paul, and God's agent or broker was Jesus. Although Paul, as a Jew, would have always thought of God as his patron, with perhaps Moses or the Torah functioning as the broker (Crook 2004a: 194), his transition to becoming an apostle proclaiming the significance of Jesus was motivated by his reception of a revelation of Jesus Christ (Gal 1:12; 1 Cor 15:8). This appearance was received as a benefaction (Gal 1:15–16; 1 Cor 15:10) by Paul. God the benefactor had bestowed a revelation of Jesus the broker to Paul such that Paul felt impelled to go out and proclaim the gospel. Zeba Crook argues that Galatians 1:15–16 is Paul's "clearest acknowledgement yet that God was the actual benefactor and Jesus 'only' the broker" (Crook 2004a: 171). Paul was called by God through what was a well-known act of benefaction: that of the appearance of a divine being, and this caused his "conversion" to spread the message about Jesus Christ. It leads Paul, as Crook argues, "to alter behavior he had thought was honoring of God, as well as alter his understanding of certain issues having to do with the relationship of God with non-Jews" (Crook 2004a: 177). Jesus's brokerage thus facilitated a unity of peoples of diverse backgrounds—Jew and non-Jew—which could often be, as we have observed, a function of brokerage. This is cultural innovation. Moreover, despite the fact that in Crook's estimation, the revelation of Jesus as God's broker was the key motivation for Paul's conversion, as in the gospels, Jesus never displaces or finds equal footing with God in Paul's letters. For Paul, "Jesus as broker is always subordinate to God as divine patron. The confusion of the two for one is a later theological development that, from the perspective of patronage and benefaction, would have appeared foreign to Paul" (Crook 2004a: 195–6).

Conclusion

We have observed that the brokerage model is directly relevant to a number of passages from the New Testament, especially those focusing upon the figure of Jesus, whether they are in the gospels or the letters of Paul. One could explore many other texts of early Christianity, both canonical and extra-canonical, and find brokers in the form of Jesus (e.g. 1 Tim 2:5; Heb 9:15), the apostles (Acts 3:5–10), the Holy Spirit (Acts 4:31), or a variety of other figures. As the church became more of an institution, moreover, the brokerage role increasingly shifted to specific leaders, especially clergy (Williams 1999) and holy people (P. Brown 1982) who mediate goods and services between believers and the heavenly realm, of which God and eventually Jesus, were the ultimate patrons. Although some have argued that Jesus may have proclaimed a brokerless kingdom, brokers did not disappear from the Christian tradition, either in the early church and certainly not in the world of post-Constantine Christianity, and if the notion of a brokerless kingdom is authentic to Jesus's message then it is indeed ironic that he himself came to be perceived as a broker and, eventually, a patron (Williams 1999: 119). Continuing discussion of these issues needs to occur, but it is thanks, in part, to the integration of social-scientific models into biblical studies that we are better able to observe these shifts and transformations within the texts themselves, which in turn enables us to further understand how and why this ancient religion developed.

Further Reading

Boissevain, Jeremy (1974) *Friends of Friends. Networks, Manipulators and Coalitions*, Oxford: Basil Blackwell.

Green, John T. (1989) *The Role of the Messenger and Message in the Ancient Near East*, BJS 169, Atlanta: Scholars.

Malina, Bruce J. (1996) *The Social World of Jesus and the Gospels*, London: Routledge.

Neyrey, Jerome H. (2007) "`I am the Door' (John 10:7, 9): Jesus the Broker in the Fourth Gospel" *CBQ*, 69: 271–91.

Schmidt, Steffen W., Laura Guasti, Carl H. Landé, and James C. Scott (eds) (1977) *Friends, Followers, and Factions: A Reader in Political Clientelism*, Berkeley, CA: University of California Press.

Notes

1 On the notion of Limited Good, see George Foster (1965: 293–315; 1972: 57–64).

2 Koenraad Verboven (2002: 318–19) points to these references in Cicero.

3 I have argued elsewhere (Batten 2004) that prior to the emergence of the late imperial age, ancient Greeks in particular made distinctions between patrons and benefactors and that in the letter of James, at least, God is understood more as a benefactor than a patron.

4 Ritva Williams (1999: 121) indicates how in the Gospel of Thomas Jesus is the broker of heavenly, secret knowledge.

5 Indeed, as a first-century Mediterranean person Jesus probably did not contemplate his "interior" identity, but was more concerned with how he was perceived by others. See Richard L. Rohrbaugh (2007: 61–76).

6 Bernard Brandon Scott's (1989: 205–15) work on Jesus's parables, for example, explores how these short stories often challenge the assumed roles and identities of patrons and their clients.

7 As Bruce J. Malina (1996: 151) states, "certainly after Constantine" Jesus became a patron.

12

Urban Structure and Patronage

Christ Followers in Corinth

Peter Oakes

A Patronage Model of First-Century Urban Layout
The Patronage Model and Various Types of City
Corinthian Followers of Christ and a Patronage Model of Urban
Structure
Further Reading
Notes

> To stand at the door of an upper-class Roman house of the late republic or
> early empire is already to glimpse something of the centrality of patronage
> in Roman society ... The way the Roman house invites the viewer from
> the front door, unparalleled in the Greek world, flows from the patronal
> rituals so often described in the Roman sources: the opening of the doors
> at dawn to the crowd of callers, the accessibility of the dominus to the
> public, his clients and his friends. Patronage was at all periods for which
> we have information central to the way the Roman upper class wished to
> present itself to the world.
>
> (Wallace-Hadrill 1989a and b: 63–4)

Patronage was indeed central to the way the Roman elite presented
itself to the world. This went beyond what the Romans would have
called *patrocinium*. As is shown elsewhere in this volume, from a social-
scientific viewpoint, patronage was a social relationship central to behavior
throughout the preindustrial world (and, of course, it still lives today). A full
social-scientific definition of patronage is complex but its core characteristics
are that it is a non-market relationship between socially unequal people in
which dissimilar benefits are exchanged (Eisenstadt and Roniger 1984: 48–
9). The most characteristic exchange involves the patron providing access to
resources normally unavailable to the client, and the client providing honor
to the patron. This relationship went beyond Romans to other groups in the

Empire. Patterns of Roman elite behavior are replicated in many non-Roman cities. It went beyond the elite. The house of a cabinet-maker in Pompeii has a stone bench outside, a structure that archaeologists have often taken as a sign of exercise of patronage. Irrespective of that, the size and style of the cabinet-maker's house suggest that, although he himself was almost certainly someone else's client, he probably did exercise some patronage to people further down the scale.[1] Patronage also went beyond affecting just the design of individual houses. It provides a key to understanding many features of the structure of towns and cities in the New Testament period.

The places where most New Testament texts were written and first read out were Greco-Roman urban centers such as Ephesus, Corinth, Antioch, and Rome. We shall consider how the layout of such towns reflected the exercise of patronage. We shall think about how the structure of various particular types of town related to variations in forms of patronage. We shall then

Figure 12.1 Interior of large villa (House of Pansa) at Pompeii (photo R. DeMaris)

reflect on texts from Romans 16 and 1 Corinthians by considering how first-century Corinthian followers of Christ related to their urban environment.

A Patronage Model of First-Century Urban Layout

Andrew Wallace-Hadrill walks his reader into a Roman house. If we did the same for a Greco-Roman town, such as Pompeii, what would we see? Before we reached the town gate we would walk past dozens of elaborate funerary monuments, proclaiming the status and achievements of the town's wealthier families. We would then walk through a substantial gate in an impressive wall, once needed for defense but now lending weight to the impression of the town's status and also enabling some control of activities. Then on into a street lined with shops, bars, and domestic doorways, all mixed together—bakers, shoe-makers, bars selling food, grand house entrances, humble doors to upstairs apartments. Graffiti and *dipinti* (painted rather than scratched into the plaster) covered the walls—scurrilous abuse, advertising for house-rental, wine or prostitutes, and election propaganda. As we walked into town along the street we would see other streets opening off ours, generally in a grid pattern. Then, suddenly we would reach the end of the street and come out into a dazzling main square—the shaded relative narrowness of the street being replaced by an area bathed in sunlight. This main square was surrounded by impressive buildings, many of them temples, and filled with statues and other honorific monuments. There were practical facilities around the square—usually a market here or nearby—but the main planning of the space was for show.

A basic element of the layout of first-century towns (including large cities) was the presence of a central space, the most obvious feature of which was elite display.[2] Alternatives to a Roman forum, such as a Greek *agora*, would, at this period, also function in this way. In the central space, members of the civic or more distant elite were honored by statues and inscriptions in return for benefaction to the town, especially by provision of buildings and festivals, or by representing the interests of the town in Rome (Saller 1989: 54–6; Braund 1989: 137–9). The design of the forum, and its prominence in the town, proclaimed that the town operated under a patronage system. The statues and inscriptions in the forum showed who the town's main patrons were.

A patronage model of urban structure first sees the town as a central display area for the elite (the patrons) surrounded by the rest of the town (the clients). The civic elite were patrons in three ways. Individually, they each had a network of clients. Collectively, they operated a rotating system of individual patronage of the town as a whole. Particularly when each held a magistracy, they paid for public buildings and events such as games at the

Figure 12.2 Graffiti (*dipinti*), Pompeii (photo R. DeMaris)

amphitheater. Third, the civic elite acted as brokers, on the town's behalf, in dealings with higher, external patrons such as senators and emperors. Many forum inscriptions honor such patrons. Implicitly, they also honor the civic elite that brought the town such patronage.

Ancient writers did not, as far as I know, use patronage language to describe the benefactions made by magistrates in office. It is also controversial, sociologically, to argue that such benefactions constituted patronage (it would be a form with a collective client: see Eisenstadt and Roniger 1984: 221–2, 245–6). The broad argument, however, seems hard to resist, that the centering of a town on a space designed for display of benefaction by, and honoring of, the civic elite represents a patronage system (for a definition of which, see Johnson and Dandeker 1989: 220–1). It proclaims the message, "We are the patrons in this town. Everything good that is done for it is by our favor. Moreover, we act as the brokers that give the town access to these excellent external benefactors who you see also honored here." The elite domination of the town is ideologically supported by the presentation of the relation between the elite and the town as being a mutually beneficial interchange in which the elite provide benefactions and the town responds with honor.

The center of a typical modern town is not like this. There may be the occasional statue to someone such as a key founding figure but there is no pervasive honoring of the town's elite. Instead, the pervasive image is of shops (in most of the world and in some US cities, such as New York and Philadelphia, in which downtown shopping remains prominent) and other businesses. There is status display to be seen in the impressiveness of shop frontages and corporate headquarters. The function of the status display, however, is primarily advertising. This reflects the difference between modern and ancient societies in distribution of wealth. The modern non-elite customer is the main source of wealth for companies, so the town center is given over to advertising to, and catering for, the customer. In the ancient town, the elite, who controlled the town center, gained most of their income from agricultural rents and production, so their priorities for use of the town center were not the modern ones.

A glance at the pattern of housing in Pompeii reveals that, although some areas have a higher concentration of large houses than others, large houses are generally scattered across the whole town. This suggests a second level of a patronage model of a Greco-Roman town: that, at local level, the town is made up of a set of small patronage networks, each controlled by a member of the elite (or, for very small networks, by someone non-elite but reasonably well-off). The classic cross-cultural point of comparison for this would be Jacques Heers's study of the division of medieval Italian towns into neighborhoods persistently dominated by the houses of heads of clans (Heers 1977: 146–54). Dominic Perring uses Heers's evidence as suggesting the likely link between "the clan-like ties of *familia* and *clientele*" and the common mixing of rich and poor housing in Roman towns (Perring 1991: 284). The comparison can actually be made more securely, without the risky analogy between clan and *clientela*. The elite domination and patronage that Heers demonstrates covers the people in the neighborhood generally, not just the members of the clan that controls it.

Particular evidence in favor of the existence of local patronage networks within towns is provided by Henrik Mouritsen's study of the thousands of *programmata*, endorsements of candidates for local elections, found on walls in Pompeii. He maps their locations and finds two patterns for where *programmata* for particular pairs of candidates were situated. The strongest pattern is a preference for main roads, where the *programmata* would be seen most often. There is also a clear secondary pattern that some candidates are represented more heavily in particular parts of the town. In some cases the candidates' actual houses are known. There is a fairly clear pattern of those candidates being especially well represented in the vicinity (Mouritsen 1988: 50–6, 69, figs 4–8). As Mouritsen says, it is hard to be sure of the motives behind the placements of all the *programmata* (Mouritsen 1988: 52). Local patronal influence, however, does seem an especially likely explanation for preferential use of walls in particular areas for particular candidates.

Our patronage model of urban layout of a Greco-Roman town operates at two levels. At town level, the patronage model sees the basic layout as being an elite display center, which represents the honoring of the town's patrons, surrounded by the rest of the town, whose population forms the client-base for these patrons. Even people who are not, individually, clients to particular elite patrons form part of the town as a client group. The town receives benefactions, such as the provision of games, from various members of the elite in turn. In return the town puts up honorific inscriptions (and, in an ironic social twist, this means, in practice, the elite town-councilors putting up inscriptions for each other). At a local level, the patronage model sees the detailed layout of the town as an agglomeration of small patronage networks, typically dominated by a large house or apartment.

Like any model, this one picks out a few key features of the environment and seeks to conceptualize them. Greco-Roman towns had many other features, some of which can usefully be thought of in patronage terms and some of which cannot. Temples are a good example of features that relate closely to patronage. They fit into a patronage model in two ways. First, they act as large honorific monuments for the human patrons who pay for their erection and maintenance. The patron confers both the benefit of provision of the building itself and, by paying for the cult, the benefit of brokerage in relation to the deities as external patrons. Second, temples represent the influence of the divine patrons themselves, who are honored at the temples in return for their favor. The temple precinct reminds people of the patronage of both the gods and the elite.

The Patronage Model and Various Types of City

As well as offering an explanation for some features of the layout of a typical Greco-Roman town, a patronage model offers some suggestions for differences in layout between major types of town.

Rome, from Aristocratic Republican City to Palace City

When Nero built the gargantuan *domus aurea*, sprawling across the center of Rome, we might see it as an attempt to change Rome, in patronage terms, from one type of city to another. Traditionally, the center of Rome—the Forum and its surroundings—had been an area of display for the city's elite as a whole. In patronage terms one might call Rome an *aristocratic republican city*. This is effectively the model that we have been describing so far as the typical Greco-Roman one. The aristocratic elite paid for buildings and games, and received honor in the Forum. The aristocratic elite were the patrons of the city.

This republican urban structure had been eroded by the building programs of the early Caesars but it was still significantly present. Nero, however, by replacing much of the center of Rome with a vast complex of magnificent buildings dedicated to the Emperor, could be seen as turning Rome into a *palace city*. In a palace city, instead of a central display area for the elite in general, it is for display by a single ruler. A large palace dominates the central area. Other forms of honoring are also focused on the ruler. In patronage terms, the urban layout represents the message that *the ruler is patron*.

After Nero's death, the Flavian emperors demolished much of Nero's building, returning Rome to a shape more in tune with its republican ideology. Having said this, the longer Rome was under emperors, the more strongly the central area reflected the patronage of them alone.

Athens, the Classical Greek City

The *classical Greek city* had an ideology of independence. In terms of urban layout, this was represented especially by possession of city walls and an acropolis. This was a fortified hill top, within the city walls. Its ability to provide safety under external attack was warrant of the city's autonomy. The presence of walls and an acropolis in a city layout represent the message, *we have no external patron*. Athens, Thessalonica, and many other Greek cities fall into this category.[3] The classical Greek city is probably one key source for the grid layout that characterized many first-century towns. As well as giving a general signal about ability to "civilize" the environment, this also possibly represented something of a democratic ethos: *there are no patrons here*. The urban structure is developed rationally, rather than growing up around a palace or other buildings of the elite. (For both avoidance and occurrence of patronage in Greece, see Millett 1989.)

The Roman Colony

One particular form of grid layout was the specifically Roman one, laid out around the crossroads of the *decumanus maximus* and the *cardo maximus*. This pattern, especially prevalent in Roman colonies, had military overtones, originating in the layout of legionary camps. The layout was part of a broader pattern of specifically Roman elements that came to be used in other towns as well as colonies. Many of these elements imitated the city of Rome. The most striking was the presence of a forum, especially when it evoked the position of the Capitoline Hill. At Rome, the temples of the three greatest Roman gods, Jupiter, Juno, and Minerva, stood on this hill at the head of the

Forum. At Philippi, the temple of this Capitoline Triad of gods overlooked the forum from the hillside just above it. At Ostia there was no hill available, but the temple was set on a raised platform, built at the head of the forum. The message of such a layout in Roman colonies or their imitators was, *Rome is our patron*.

The Temple City

A final type of town was a *temple city*. In such a city, a large temple dominates the central display area or another prominent location. This urban layout represents the message, *this deity is our patron*. Such a message implicitly carries a further one, which would be central to the city's status and economy: *we are the brokers for this deity*. The elite of the city controlled access to the benefits that the deity could bring. In the case of a major cult center such as Ephesus or Jerusalem, people would come from distant cities to the central temple, bringing substantial honor and income.

Figure 12.3 Temple to Jupiter, Juno, and Minerva in Forum, Ostia (photo R. DeMaris)

Sjoberg's Preindustrial City

This analysis of types of city allows us also to comment, in patronage terms, on Gideon Sjoberg's classic model of the *preindustrial city*, known to New Testament scholars particularly through Richard Rohrbaugh's innovative use of it in relation to Luke's Gospel (Rohrbaugh 1991). Sjoberg studied urban patterns across a range of preindustrial cultures. He found a frequent pattern in which a central area of elite residence, with a palace and temple, was separated by a wall from the surrounding city, which was itself physically separated into several sections, with particular areas often relating to particular trades (Sjoberg 1960: 91–103). In terms of our patronage model of urban structure this is a very sharply marked form of *palace city* (with the temple presumably subordinate to the palace). The ruler is the sole patron. Moreover, his or her patronage mainly extends only to the elite, who live with the ruler in the central area. Unlike the Greco-Roman model, the elite do not themselves exercise patronage over groups of people around the town.

The strong physical barriers testify to the weakness of patronage links with the non-elite and, conversely, the weakness of non-elite allegiance to the ruler and the rest of the elite. The physical barriers between groups of the non-elite replace one of the subtle functions of a patronage system. The barriers put a limit on the ability of the non-elite to form a coherent group—and thus maybe threaten the elite. Patronage does the same thing. It builds a social system in which vertical social links, between rich and poor, are more important than links between the poor. In a strongly patronal system, the poor tend not to act together as a class. This shape of social system is characteristic of E. Gellner's model of the "agro-literate state," in which the hierarchical elite rule "laterally insulated communities of agricultural producers" (Gellner 2006: 9–10, fig. 1; applied to cities in Morris 1991: 46–7 and fig. 6).

The Sjoberg model is rooted in a range of cultures so it is interesting that typical Greco-Roman towns differ sharply from it. In historic cultural terms, Greco-Roman towns may be rather unusual. Such towns were the main centers of production of New Testament texts. There are New Testament texts, however, where we do find cities more like the Sjoberg model. They probably appear in several of Jesus's parables, in which powerful rulers hold sway over their populations. Richard Rohrbaugh's study shows how Sjoberg's model can fruitfully be put to work on these texts.

Corinthian Followers of Christ and a Patronage Model of Urban Structure

In Romans 16, three Corinthians are named and something is indicated about each of their social situations. A range of social circumstances are also discussed in 1 Corinthians. Several scholars, most notably John Chow (1992), have considered this letter in relation to patronage issues. If we, however, take texts in 1 Corinthians that, explicitly or implicitly, put the Corinthian Christ-followers at various places in the city, and then consider these in relation to our patronage model of urban structure, some further interpretative possibilities emerge.

We will apply our general patronage model for the structure of a Greco-Roman city to Corinth. Corinth was also a Roman colony and, to an extent, it fits our more specific *Roman colony* patronage model, in which elements of the urban structure (especially the grid pattern, laid out at the colonial foundation in 44 BCE, and prominent buildings such as the Julian Basilica) testify to the whole city, including the elite, being client to Rome as patron. Consideration of this model will affect our handling of one scenario for the eating of idol-meat in 1 Corinthians 8–10. We must, however, not overstate the significance of this model for understanding Corinth. The effect of Corinth's colonial identity on its urban structure is rather ambiguous. Most notably, although the forum occupies a space formed by the grid laid out at colonization, the buildings in the forum are aligned differently. Some monumental Greek constructions in the forum survived from classical Corinth (sacked by Romans in 146 BCE). Moreover, even the new Roman buildings are more closely aligned to some of the Greek structures than to the colonial street grid (Romano 2005). In layout terms, there is some qualifying effect on the sense of Rome as the city's sole patron. Greek cultural reference points are also given some honor. In many ways, Corinth is more like a general Greco-Roman city than like a typical, overwhelmingly Roman colony such as Philippi or the many colonial foundations in the west of the Empire.

The Corinthians of Romans 16

Three of the Corinthians named in Romans 16 can be related fairly confidently to our patronage model. Phoebe, a *diakonos* (deacon) of the church in Cenchreae, and a *prostatis* (benefactor) to many, including Paul (Rom 16:1–2), is presumably a local patron in an area of the eastern port settlement of Corinth, about 10 km from the city center. Similarly, Gaius, "the host to me and to the whole church" (Rom 16:23), must have a fair-sized house and reasonable financial resources. He seems likely to be a local patron in an area of Corinth.

As we have seen, this does not mean that Phoebe and Gaius were necessarily (or even probably) elite, in the sense of being at the social level of civic patrons of Corinth. The Pompeian cabinet-maker probably exercised some low-level patronage and could rent a house of sufficient size to host a meeting of a few dozen, which was conceivably the extent of the Corinthian "whole church." Having said this, his patronage would have to have been rather limited. It could not have made the cabinet-maker the patron of the local area. His house is right next to the vast House of the Menander, whose owner was of senatorial level and was probably landlord and patron to the cabinet-maker. If there are cases where someone at the upper end of the social range of craft workers acted as a local patron, this would probably be "local" in the sense of being a network that included a number of people from a particular area, rather than the craft worker being the area's main patron. In fact, one of the main patronal functions of such a low-level patron would be as broker for access to an elite patron to whom the craft worker was client.

Romans 16 does not show that Phoebe and Gaius were elite, although it does suggest that they were each at the center of some local patronage network. Paul's indication of their social status could function for the Roman hearers as an indication of the success of the gospel in Corinth in making inroads into society in some parts of the city.

Erastus, the *oikonomos* (steward) of the city (Rom 16:23), has been subject of long debate: whether he was of high or low status; whether he is the archaeologically attested Erastus the aedile, who dedicated a pavement in Corinth in the first century CE (for the two sides, see Clarke 1993: 46–56 and Meggitt 1998: 135–41). Irrespective of the answer to these questions, we can think about the Erastus of Romans 16 in relation to urban layout. Whereas Phoebe and Gaius are probably local patrons, Paul asserts that Erastus relates to the urban center. A follower of Christ is presented as having some sort of responsibility for the city as a whole. The Christ movement has penetrated to the heart of the city. It is curious that Paul points this out. Possible analogies are his assurances to the Philippians that the gospel has spread "among all the praetorium" (Phil 1:13) and that there are followers of Christ in Caesar's household (Phil 4:22)—the imperial slaves and freed slaves. A likely intended function of these assurances is to encourage the Philippians as they undergo suffering: the gospel can survive and prosper even in the Empire's central places. The reference to Erastus's position could be intended to offer some encouragement to the hearers of Romans.

Taking Cases to the Judges of Corinth (1 Cor 6:1–11)

In 1 Corinthians 6:1–11, Paul criticizes the Corinthians about lawsuits. Very surprisingly, the main focus of the criticism is not on the fact of lawsuits between believers. He writes, "Does one of you dare, having a grievance against another, to take it to be judged by the unrighteous and not by the holy ones?" (1 Cor 6:1, author's trans.). The key issue is about who is judging. In terms of urban layout, the Corinthians are going into the elite display center, where the matter will be judged in one of the basilicas or other spaces around the forum. This is the zone of elite urban patronage. By coming here for resolution of disputes, the followers of Christ put themselves under the patronage of the city's elite, as judges, advocates, or juries.

Paul rejects the structural implication. Even the lowest-status follower of Christ is more suitable than an outsider to adopt the patronal position of resolving a dispute (1 Cor 6:4–5). Paul trumps the city's social structure by appeal to a larger structure, that of the universe. In the law-courts of the universe as a whole, the assembly of Christ's followers lie at the heart of the system. They, and not the first-century social elite, will act as judges of the world and even of angels (1 Cor 6:2–3).

Places where People Eat Idol-Meat (1 Cor 8–10)

In 1 Corinthians 8–10, Paul deals with an issue raised by the Corinthians about food offered to idols. Geographically, he considers three scenarios. First, there are people who are "reclining in an idol-temple" (1 Cor 8:10). This is probably the same situation as is characterized in 1 Corinthians 10:21 as "sharing in the table of demons." Second, there are people buying meat in the meat-market, presumably to eat at home (1 Cor 10:25). Third, there are people who are invited by a non-believer to eat with them, presumably at their home (1 Cor 10:27).

The first scenario worries Paul most. He is concerned about people who are participating in meals held in Greco-Roman temples (1 Cor 8:1, 7, 10; 10:19–22). In terms of our patronage model of urban layout, one of two possible events is happening. Either the people are going to the forum and its vicinity, to take part in religious meals sponsored at a civic level, or they are taking part in meals in temple areas away from the center, such as the slopes of the hill of the Acrocorinth or individual locations around the town (for temples in Corinth, see Bookidis 2005). In both cases there is a double patronage at work, although the specific shapes differ somewhat.

The double patronage is of human sponsor and sponsoring deity. For a cultic meal in the urban center, the participants implicitly put themselves under the patronage of the civic elite. There will usually have been one

Figure 12.4 Temple of Isis at Pompeii (photo R. DeMaris)

person who has paid for the particular festival. This, however, will often have been done as part of his holding of a municipal office, so there was also a sense of the meal as a civic function. For a cultic meal in the urban center, the deity who was viewed as divine patron of the event would tend to be one strongly tied to the city's identity. For the Roman colony of Corinth, this especially meant the imperial family or the definitively Roman gods such as the Capitoline Triad or Roma herself. As participants put themselves under the patronage of such a deity, they were not only expressing allegiance to a god, they were also expressing allegiance to Rome as a divine superintending power. Clearly, we must not overstate the commitment expressed by eating a meal, but to go to the urban center and participate in one of the civic religious meals did carry at least a symbolic commitment to patronage of the local elite, the deities in question, and Rome as a divine governing force (cf. Chow 1992: 147–57).

The other possibility is that the criticized group is dining at one of the local temples around the city. In this case we should think in terms of local patronage networks. Human patronage of a temple could be a key public element of patronage of a local area. The deity who, in a sense, was viewed as host of the meal, might also be seen as patron of the area. It could be useful to think of the area around a local temple as being like a *temple city*, writ small.

In either situation, followers of Jesus who participated in cultic meals in Corinth placed themselves, at least symbolically, under both human and divine patronage. Paul was bound to disapprove of the latter. His reaction to the issue of lawsuits in chapter 6 means that he was also likely to have concerns about the former.

Eating a meal at home, using meat bought at the market, raised none of these issues of patronage. Although market buildings often carried dedicatory inscriptions celebrating the person who paid for the building, it would be going too far to say that people would see goods bought in the market as being bought under that person's patronage. Similarly, the meat itself was presumably not advertised as coming from the temple of a particular deity, even if some was the surplus from a festival meal that involved a sacrifice. Away from the temple, the meat was not provided under the deity's patronage. In fact, Paul may make a counter-assertion to any such idea: "The Earth belongs to the Lord—and everything in it" (1 Cor 10:26, citing Ps. 24:1). If there is any patron for the general providing of meat, it is God, not a Greco-Roman deity to whom it may have been offered.

For some types of Corinthian followers of Christ, one of the most likely occasions for being invited to someone's house to eat (1 Cor 10:27) would have been if they had a patron. The invitation would then be a patronal benefit to the client. This practice was an element of traditional Roman patronage. Clients in that kind of relationship might tend to be at the upper end of the non-elite. This means that most Christ-followers would be excluded, as being too poor. Eating at the house of a local patron would not have an obvious link to issues of idol-meat. Paul is relaxed about such meals (1 Cor 10:27). This may also mean that he is happy for Christ-followers to continue to accept local patronage from non-believers. In the Gospel accounts, Jesus and his followers accept invitations to meals from all sorts of people. His one caveat occurs when the host draws attention to the temple origins of some meat. The follower of Christ should then decline it (1 Cor 10:28). There is, however, no patronage issue here, as far as I can see.

When You Gather Together as an Assembly (1 Cor 11:17–34)

Our final example is the problem about communal meals, criticized by Paul in 1 Corinthians 11:17–34. Since the ground-breaking work of Jerome Murphy-O'Connor, scholars have given much thought to the possible concrete realities of this situation, as it would work out in a Roman domestic setting (Murphy-O'Connor 2002; Horrell 2004). This work is very valuable, revealing a wide range of points at which the norms of Greco-Roman household structure and behavior would raise difficult issues for a socially mixed community that ate together.

Our model suggests that we may be able to take this one stage further. The implicit geographical note here is the gathering together (1 Cor 11:18). The group of Christ-followers from across the city comes to a single place. The host of this meal clearly has accommodation of some size. This makes it rather likely that he or she will be patron of a local network. If that is the case, then the behavior that Paul criticizes becomes quite easily explicable. Although patronage involved transfer of benefits—such as provision of a meal—between patron and clients, the relationship was founded on structural inequality. If a patron participated in a meal with clients we would expect the meal to reflect the structural inequality. Patrons stop being patrons if they do not generally eat more food, and more expensive food, than clients. This is sharpened by the fact that the patron's need to project his or her status goes beyond the people gathered at the meal. The patronal network might extend across several blocks of houses. Maintenance of the patron's position required maintenance of appropriate status relationships. Paul's challenge to social differentiation in provision of communal meals could cause difficulties for maintenance of patronal relationships, both with fellow believers and with other people in the local area. Paul's instructions would stop the meetings of the assembly from being occasions for demonstration of structural inequality—the structural inequality that was, and is, inherent in patronage.

Further Reading

Bookidis, Nancy (2005) "Religion in Corinth: 146 B.C.E to 100 C.E.," in D. Schowalter and S. J. Friesen (eds) *Urban Religion in Roman Corinth: Interdisciplinary Approaches*, Cambridge, MA: Harvard University Press, pp. 141–64.

Horrell, David G. (2004) "Domestic Space and Christian Meetings at Corinth: Imagining New Contexts and the Buildings East of the Theatre," *NTS*, 50: 349–69.

Oakes, Peter (2009) *Reading Romans in Pompeii: Paul's Letter at Ground Level*, London: SPCK/Minneapolis: Fortress.

Rich, John, and A. Wallace-Hadrill (eds) (1991) *City and Country in the Ancient World*, London: Routledge.

Saller, R. (1989) "Patronage and Friendship in Early Imperial Rome: Drawing the Distinction," in A. Wallace-Hadrill (ed.) *Patronage in Ancient Society*, London: Routledge, pp. 49–62.

Notes

1   Patronage defined social-scientifically not classically—elite Roman writers would not have talked about patronage operating at such a level. For discussion of this house see Oakes (2009).

2   Elsewhere in the town, there would also be subsidiary elite display areas at other points of particular benefaction, such as temples and theaters.

3   In Thessalonica's case this was ironic, because the walls and acropolis were built by a Hellenistic king. However, such exceptions prove the ideological rule. The Macedonian kings were strongly hellenized, wanting to engage in Greek life as Greeks. Their equipping of towns with the appurtenances of an independent Greek city was a strong expression of their Hellenistic ideology.

13

Ancient Economy and the New Testament

David A. Fiensy

The Ancient Economy in General
Lower Galilee
Conclusions
Further Reading
Note

Why is there a chapter about the ancient economy in a book about the New Testament? It is because the economy affects every other aspect of life (family, religion, community, work, health, and politics). Further, there are numerous direct references and allusions to economic issues in the New Testament. Scholars are now realizing that we cannot understand the New Testament without some attention to the subject.

Yet the subject would be too broad for a general survey through the entire New Testament. One could with profit write about the economic teachings in the epistles or the Apocalypse (book of Revelation). But for the purposes of this chapter, we shall focus on the ministry of Jesus in Lower Galilee. Such a focus will give our treatment more unity and at the same time handle what has been a growing debate. Was the ancient economic system like that of modern, western, capitalist societies? Were the economic conditions driving the peasants toward starvation? Or was Lower Galilee so prosperous that the economic boom "floated all boats" so to speak? Did Jesus criticize the ancient economic system? We cannot answer these questions fully but perhaps we can give some of the information upon which conclusions should be based. We shall return to these three questions at the end of the chapter.

We will divide the inquiry into two parts. First, we shall describe the ancient economy generally. That is, we shall describe the economy for the Mediterranean world and Palestine (including Idumea, Judea, Samaria, and Galilee) as a whole. Second, we shall turn specifically to Lower Galilee and there we shall present and explain our economic model.

The Ancient Economy in General

The study of economics has to do with, "... the production of goods and services, the distribution of these among members of society, and the consumption of goods and services" (Beals and Hoijer 1965: 450). The economy includes then not only the farm crops and handcrafted goods (pottery for example) but also human labor and who gets to make the most use of these items. Was one group privileged and another deprived? If so, which was the favored one?

There are three descriptors in the main that one should discuss in reference to the ancient economy. It was agrarian, it was aristocratic (ruled by a dominant political group), and it was a peasant society. We shall take each of these in order.

Agrarian

The first thing we should say about the ancient economy of the Mediterranean and Middle Eastern regions is that it was agrarian. This observation is so common as to be beyond dispute (Rostovtzeff 1957: 270; Lenski 1966; Finley 1973; Bedford 2005; Malina and Rohrbaugh 1992: 3–6; Oakman 2008; Davies 2008: 77). An agrarian economy was based on land ownership and farm production. This fact implies two corollaries. First, agrarian economies were one step up from horticultural economies. The latter were capable of supporting small communities of gardeners who used primitive tools such as the hoe. Agrarian economies saw much more land cultivated (by the plow) and could support large cities. Second, the way to acquire wealth in an agrarian economy was to acquire more land. There was not much else a person could do with wealth but buy land. One could invest in trading/shipping but it was risky. The culturally acceptable and economically less risky investment was land. People wanted land and the more the better. A fair-sized estate of 200 acres could make the owner very wealthy.

An agrarian economy was marked by certain common features. Lenski (1966: 192–210) lists twelve main characteristics but we might summarize these into three: First, agrarian societies were controlled by monarchs who gained and held power by their military. They imposed their will on their subjects (and enriched themselves) usually by brute force. Thus, the economy almost always produced a certain political reality as well. Second, due to technological advances, diversity of labor, and improved trade, there was a collective surplus of food beyond what was needed merely to subsist. Most of the surplus, however, was siphoned off by the rulers. Third, since there was a surplus, urban communities could exist and the population in general could increase. In most agrarian societies about one tenth of the population lived in urban centers, the rest in small villages which worked the land (Lenski 1966: 200; Mann 1986: 264; Saller 2005: 236; Fiensy 1997: 235; Malina and Rohrbaugh 1992: 7).

Aristocratic

Ancient agrarian societies tended to be structured around two groups: the takers and the givers. These societies, then, were mostly empires ruled by an aristocratic class. J. H. Kautsky defined the aristocracy as those persons who, while not laboring on the farms themselves, benefit from the farm produce by controlling the peasants' surplus (1982: 79–80). The aristocrats did not engage in physical work and usually did not even live on the farms. Rather, as absentee landlords, they lived in the cities and demanded rents and taxes from the peasants. Jesus reflected this system in his parable of Mark 12:1–8. In this parable an absentee landlord has planted a vineyard and left tenant farmers to take care of the crop and harvest the grapes. At harvest time, he sends his servants to collect his share (usually one third to one half of the crop). The tenants are surly and angry toward the landlord and beat the servants. They evidently thought their lives were too miserable to pay the rent.

The number of these aristocrats was always small in agrarian societies. Most historians estimate that only about 1 percent of the population was in this class (MacMullen 1974: 89). The surplus was simply not large enough to support a greater number of wealthy persons. That percentage would mean that Lower Galilee with a total population of around 175,000 had between 1,500 and 2,000 aristocrats. Most, if not all, of these persons lived in one of the two main cities: Sepphoris or Tiberias. Some of their houses in Sepphoris have been excavated (Fiensy 2007: 39–40).

Some of the aristocrats in the Roman empire controlled huge tracts of farmland. We read of farms comprising, for example, 75,000 acres in Egypt and one whopping estate of 270,000 acres in Spain (Finley 1973: 99; MacMullen 1974: 38; Hitchner 2005: 213). Such farms required a large labor force and must have produced huge harvests for the owners/ controllers of the land. Of course most of the elites had somewhat smaller farms of a few hundred acres.

There certainly were large estates in Palestine as well (Fiensy 1991: 21–73). But were there such large farms specifically in Lower Galilee (the area from Nazareth on the south to the northern tip of the Sea of Galilee) where Jesus came from? So far the archaeological evidence says no (Fiensy 2007: 43). Yet, on the Great Plain, just south of Nazareth, there is both literary and archaeological evidence that large estates had been in existence already for 300 years by the time Jesus was born. Jesus had only to look over the Great Plain from the edge of the Nazareth ridge to view some of these vast farms.

Perhaps Jesus's observation of these estates furnished material for many of his parables. As mentioned above Mark 12:1–8, the Parable of the Tenants, refers to a vineyard with tenant farmers, an absentee landlord, and several slaves who were sent to collect the rent. In order to support several tenant farmers, the vineyard must have been quite large (Hengel 1968: 1–39). Luke 16:1–12 speaks of debts of 100 measures of oil and 100 measures of wheat which would have required at least a medium-sized estate to produce (Herz 1928: 98–113). The same conclusion can be made with respect to the Parable of the Talents (Matt 25:14–30; Luke 19:11–27), the Parable of the Debtors (Luke 7:41–43; Matt 18:23–34), and the Parable of the Unforgiving Servant (Matt 18:21–35). These parables speak of large sums of money which imply great wealth. In the ancient economy one could possibly become wealthy as a merchant but the overwhelming majority of wealthy people acquired their wealth through land. Thus great wealth implies large estates.

Still other parables depict scenes on a large estate. The Parable of the Rich Fool (Luke 12:16–21), for instance, describes an estate owner hoarding grain in a manner reminiscent of accounts in Josephus (*Vita* 71–72, 119) about the granaries "of Caesar" in Upper Galilee and of the granary of Queen Berenice on the Great Plain. Luke 17:7 refers to a man's servant plowing his field for him. Matthew 20:1–15 narrates about a large landowner who has so much land he must hire day laborers to work it. Luke 12:42–43 alludes to a wealthy man who has a bailiff to run his estate. Matthew 13:24–30 describes a farm which requires several slaves to work it. Finally, Luke 15:11–32 pictures an estate with day laborers and slaves. Clearly Jesus was familiar with what happened on these huge farms but archaeologists have not found evidence for their existence in Lower Galilee itself.

Peasant

Another way of describing agrarian societies, instead of in terms of empire and the elite class, is from the perspective of the largest number (90 percent) of their inhabitants: the peasants. Peasants were "… rural cultivators whose surpluses are transferred to a dominant group of rulers that uses the surpluses both to underwrite its own standard of living and to distribute the remainder to groups in society that do not farm …" (Wolf 1966: 3–4). The peasants and the ruling elites viewed the land and its labor in a very different way. The ruling class regarded their land and the peasants as income for themselves (Wolf 1966: 13); the peasant saw his land and work as the means of feeding his family and not as a business for profit (de Ste. Croix 1981: 210–11;

Redfield 1956: 27–8). Peasants worked for subsistence. They were not trying to become wealthy or even comfortable. They wanted to feed themselves.

Peasants labored on their land as family units (when they were freeholders or tenant farmers). Those bound to a piece of land also were bound to their families. But when they became landless—a dreadful plight in an agrarian society unless one knew a craft—they also tended to lose family bonds. Day laborers and agricultural slaves, then, were at most risk for loss of subsistence. Land means, to a peasant, family-bonding in addition to guarantee of subsistence.

All peasant societies have been and still are marked by a radical bifurcation in which a small group of aristocrats stands over against the mass of agriculturalists. The aristocrats see their taxes and rents as their due; the peasants see them as one more burden placed on their labor and their land (Fiensy 1991: vii). Consequently, peasant protests were common. In Egypt, for example, the papyri attest to peasants frequently going on strike and threatening to move to another location because of unfair treatment and, thus, being beaten and coerced to stay on the landowner's estate (Rostovtzeff 1922: 76, 80, 85). In Syria, the inscriptions witness to about the same: the tenant farmers are forced to pay more rent than the agreement had stipulated; they file a complaint with an official; and they are beaten and tortured for filing the complaint (de Ste. Croix 1981: 214ff).

The peasant surpluses, extracted in rents and taxes, kept the wealthy in their accustomed style of living and also fed the landless merchants, craftsmen, and day laborers, many of whom lived in the cities. From the point of view of peasants, life was a continual challenge to juggle the demands of the powerful on their farm produce with the subsistence needs of their families (Wolf 1966: 15). Improved technology and farming methods gave them a small surplus, but the surplus was gobbled up by the powerful and ruthless ruling class.

Lower Galilee

To assist us in visualizing the ancient economy with special reference to Lower Galilee in the first half of the first century CE, we will present a model. The model we will use as an heuristic visualization of the economic system is based on that of John K. Davies (2005: 150). Davies's model stresses the flow of goods and services as the key to understanding how the economy worked. The direction of the flows and the relative size of the flows (see the arrows in Figure 13.1) quickly inform us as to what the economy was doing. Especially telling is when we see the unidirectional (one-way) flow or uneven reciprocity. For example, note the one-way flow from the villages to the Temple in Jerusalem and the uneven flow (uneven reciprocity) between

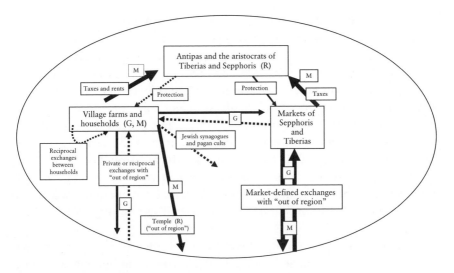

Figure 13.1 Flowchart of resource movement, Lower Galilee, first century CE (after Davies 2005: 150)

the villages and Antipas, the Tetrarch or ruler of Galilee. In other words, the village peasants received nothing economic in return for their tithes to the Temple in Judea. Likewise for their rents and taxes, paid to Antipas and other aristocrats, the peasants received certain government services, such as protection, which probably did not seem like an equal exchange to them.

The Model

The reader will notice that the oval shape of the flowchart is intended to represent the economic unit of Lower Galilee. Lower Galilee formed an economic system because of politics and geography. Politically, Lower Galilee was under the control of the Tetrarch, Antipas. In the ancient world, economics were not divorced from politics since the political leader was personally enriched by and held dominance over the economy. Therefore, sociologists often use the term "political economy" in describing ancient economies (Hanson and Oakman 2008: 99–129).

Geographically and topographically Lower Galilee is differentiated from Upper Galilee (the region from the northern tip of the Sea of Galilee to Lebanon). Upper Galilee is more mountainous and remote and, therefore, was more isolated in antiquity. Lower Galilee is more open to travel and thus in antiquity saw more vigorous trading activity.

Secondly, note the multitude of economic relationships the average village peasants had. They might trade with other family members or with fellow villagers ("Reciprocal exchanges between households"). These would be equal exchanges of goods and/or services. They would trade, for example, a basket of figs for a basket of grain or a jar of olive oil for a handcrafted tool.

They might also trade outside the village ("Private or reciprocal exchanges with 'out of region'") or at the "Markets of Sepphoris and Tiberias" whether trading surplus farm produce or handmade crafts. Two villages from Lower Galilee are now becoming, because of archaeological excavations, known as major exporters of common pottery. Likewise, two other villages produced and marketed a significant number of stoneware vessels. These exchanges might have been made at the market centers in the two largest cities of Lower Galilee, Sepphoris and Tiberias, or they might have been done in market centers outside of Lower Galilee. For example, the pottery manufactured in Kefar Hananya has been found in towns and villages in the Golan (Fiensy 2007: 51).

Peasant villagers were also obligated to send tithes, wave offerings, and temple taxes to the Temple in Jerusalem. They received nothing economic (in the physical sense) in return for this flow of goods. But as Davies points out (2005: 142) there are "non-physical flows" that play a role in the economy. For example, a person who donated a sum of money to a village might receive back only the non-physical flow of increased honor. Yet the honor made the act of charity entirely worth it. Therefore, it is probably incorrect (even ethnocentric!) to maintain that the Galileans resented having to send tithes to the Judean Temple. It ignores the value of sacred space in ancient culture (Fiensy 2007: 189–91; Eliade 1959: 28) and, thus, misses the value of the non-physical flow of "blessing" which returned to the village peasant. Nevertheless, I have chosen not to represent non-physical flows in the model.

Finally, peasants were compelled to pay a portion of their farm produce to the tetrarch or the absentee landlord. The amount of the tax paid to Antipas is debated but if we assume that it was at least 12 percent, we will not be too far off. The amount of rent the tenant farmers paid to the landlords ranged from one quarter to one half of the crops (Fiensy 1991: 81, 99). In return (notice the difference in the width of the arrows) the village peasant received from their tetrarch and other aristocratic overlords what I have abbreviated "protection" (Davies's term, 2005: 150). By this term, I mean the various government services such as laws, peace, rituals, ceremonies, and even medical advice (Edwards 1992: 62). Was it a fair trade? I doubt that the village residents thought that it was but they were helpless to change anything (cf. Lenski 1966: 206).

Four features in the model need explanation. First, note the different width of the arrows. The greater the width, the higher the volume of the flow of goods and services. The different "bandwidths" (Davies's term), thus, illustrate uneven exchanges such as the exchange between the villagers and the aristocracy just described. The fattest widths represent the greatest flow (to markets, to aristocrats); the thinner solid arrows represent somewhat less flow (to, for example, the Temple); the thinnest solid arrows represent private exchanges; and the broken lines represent the least amount of flow.

Second, the points labeled "M" represent what Davies calls "motors." Motors are impulses or motivations that keep the flow going. I can think of four: First, there was the drive to accumulate wealth that propelled the aristocracy. They wanted more land, more surplus, bigger houses, and more luxury goods. The Parable of the Talents/Minas found in Matthew 25:14–30 and Luke 19:12–27 illustrates this motor very well. In the story (the details of which are somewhat different in Matthew and Luke) the servant who did not increase the investment of his master states that he knows the master (i.e., the aristocratic absentee landlord) is a severe person and demands a profit (Matt 25:24; Luke 10:21). The aristocrats were driven by the will to acquire. Second, was the desire for village peasants to provide subsistence for their families. The will to feed their families propelled them to the most intensive labor and thus to greater production of goods. Thus, the prayer "give us our bread" (Matt 6:11; Luke 11:3) represents a real anxiety. Their daily bread (or "bread of tomorrow") was often in jeopardy. Third, there was the wish for those at the market centers to trade goods of one kind either for goods of another kind or for money (coins). Finally, there was the value, on the part of the Jewish people for their sacred space, the Temple. This value kept goods flowing to Jerusalem.

The third item to be explained in the model is what Davies calls the "gates" (= G). Gates are "impediments to the rapid flow and exchange of resources, goods and services" (Davies 2005: 151). The gates in the economy of Lower Galilee in the early first century CE would be farming technology and methods. In other words, the primitive methods and technology would have limited the productivity of the land. The method is illustrated in the Parable of the Sower (Mark 4:1–9; Matt 13:1–9; Luke 8:4–8). The sower or planter simply cast the seeds on the ground in a rather careless fashion, some of which fell on unproductive soil. Many of the seeds were eaten by the birds and only a few of them germinated. Another gate to the ancient economy of Lower Galilee was the means of transport (by pack animal) of goods. The Good Samaritan was evidently a small merchant or trader carrying goods on his donkey (Luke 10:34) for trade in Jericho. But a donkey can carry only so much and the distance between markets made it impossible to trade every day. On the other hand, by this measure, taxes, such as taxes on transportation (see Levi in Mark 2:14) and taxes on land, are not gates in the economic sense since they force the flow of goods even though the peasants might have regretted and resented them. Sociologically speaking, taxes were a hardship and probably most of the time hated by the peasants. But economically speaking, they served a different function.

The reader will also note the reservoirs (= R). These are the places of resource accumulation and thesaurization (treasure building). Although Davies concedes that poor peasants can participate to a limited extent in reservoir building (by for example a small coin stash under the floor of their house), the significant reservoirs were with the temples and the governing elites. Thus, in the model the reservoirs are with Antipas and the aristocrats in Galilee and the Temple in Jerusalem. Jesus told a parable about an aristocrat who built up a sizeable reservoir (Luke 12:13–21). The story reminds one of the granary or barn that Queen Berenice owned in the village of Besara (= Beth Shearim), located in the northwest corner of the Great Plain (Josephus, *Vita* 119). Josephus indicates in his narrative that the queen owned (in 67 CE) several villages in the area (and the land adjacent to them) and had collected from them her hoard of grain for her barn(s) in Besara. Since Berenice was a descendant of Herod the Great, this granary and the large estate it served was probably inherited from him. Is it possible that Jesus even had King Herod in mind when he represented him as a greedy hoarder whose life was at last required of him by God? That Jesus did not approve of hoarding (= reservoirs) is also seen in his admonition to his disciples against thesaurization (Matt 6:19–21; Luke 12:33–34).

Finally, note that Davies gives great emphasis to the market exchanges. He stresses the villages' exchanges within themselves, the villages' exchanges with the major market centers (for us, Sepphoris and Tiberias), and the exchanges between the major market centers in the region with those out of the region. Although some historians hesitate to affirm a market economy in Lower Galilee (Oakman 1998: 84–97; Horsley 1996: 66–87), I accept this characteristic especially in light of recent archaeological discoveries. Archaeologists have revealed that at least four villages were producing and marketing their wares for the rest of Lower Galilee and even beyond: Kefar Hananya, Kefar Shikhin, Bethlehem of Galilee, and Kefar Reina.

The pottery of Kefar Hananya and Kefar Shikhin was already well known from the rabbinic sources (*m. Kelim* 2:2; *b. Bava Metzi'a* 74a; *b. Shabbat* 120b). Now, archaeologists have established that the tiny village of Kefar Hananya (located on the border between Lower Galilee and Upper Galilee) exported its common pottery up to 24 kilometers away into Galilee and the Golan. Further, they maintain that 75 percent of the first-century common table wares excavated at Sepphoris so far (cooking bowls) were made in Kefar Hananya. In addition, 15 percent of the storage jars or kraters discovered thus far in Sepphoris originated in the nearby village of Shikhin. The Shikhin storage jars account for the majority of pottery of that type in Galilee (Fiensy 2007: 51). The process by which these conclusions were made is called neutron activation analysis. The scientific test allows the excavators to determine the chemical content of the clay used in making the pottery. The clay content of many of the wares found in the villages and cities of Galilee indicates that much of the pottery came from the area of Kefar Hananya and that many of the large jars came from the tiny village of Shikhin (1.5 kilometers from Sepphoris).

Further, archaeological discovery has brought to light two quarry workshops in Lower Galilee—one in Bethlehem of Galilee (just southwest of Sepphoris) and the other in Kefar Reina (just east of Sepphoris). These villages were major producers of stone cups and other vessels. Stoneware has been discovered throughout Galilee in twelve villages and cities (Fiensy 2007: 51–2).

The conclusions usually drawn from these discoveries are: (1) the cities with their rich people must not have exploited the peasants who lived in the villages but rather must have given them opportunities for marketing their goods and thus increased their economic situation; (2) the villages not only engaged in farming but had industries as well. Thus, the socio-economic effects of the increase in marketization are often assumed to have been positive. Some archaeologists believe that increased marketization must have brought unprecedented prosperity to Lower Galilee.

But economists speak a word of caution. Karl Polanyi's analysis of the transformation from a subsistence economy to a market economy is a classic (Polanyi 1944). Much of what he wrote has to do with the "Great Transformation" that took place in Europe during the industrial revolution but his insights are also informative for our period.

Polanyi notes that when societies depart from a subsistence economy for a market economy, there are both economic and social consequences. Economically, subsistence is abandoned in favor of gain: "... for the motive of subsistence that of gain must be substituted" (1944: 41). At first this change might seem beneficial. But what if the market begins to pay less than one's goods had been worth when one traded in reciprocal exchanges? Now one is at the mercy of the going market price both for goods and for labor: "A market economy ... is an economy directed by market prices and nothing but market prices" (1944: 43).

The irony could become that subsistence is actually threatened. Polanyi stated that in traditional ("primitive") societies starvation was not a threat unless the whole community starved at the same time since one could always count on help from relatives and neighbors (which must be reciprocated later): "There is no starvation in societies living on the subsistence margin" (1944: 163). But a market economy pays individuals the going rate for both goods and labor and, therefore, in down-cycles human labor might be devalued if indeed one can even find a day's work (cf. Lenski 1966: 206).

This condition is reflected in one of Jesus's parables (Matt 20:3) in which day laborers must sell their labor in the market each day. But many of them find no takers for their labor.

Further, Polanyi noted the social effects of marketization. The increase in the value of markets tends to negate traditional institutions (such as family, neighborhoods, and religious convictions; 1944: 163). Everything now has a market price and these old associations are not valued very highly.

How advanced was the market economy in Lower Galilee in the time of Jesus and Antipas? I think it had started down the road described by Polanyi but had not advanced very far. The stresses were beginning in my judgment but were not yet causing a "Great Transformation"—to use Polanyi's expression—but only a small transformation (indeed, there was no great transformation anywhere in antiquity). There is no evidence for such a seismic socio-economic transformation in the first half of the century. It may be, however, that later the change did develop sufficiently that it helped aggravate the desire for war in 66 CE (Fiensy 2002). Although the ancient economy saw no transformation like the industrial revolution, it still witnessed from time to time economic stresses that were a milder form.

To Jesus are attributed words of rebuke aimed at religious leaders (sometimes they are scribes and other times Pharisees) for wanting a "greeting in the market place" (Matt 23:7; Mark 12:38; Luke 11:43, 20:46). Was at least part of Jesus's irritation that these religious leaders craved to be greeted in public the fact that it was in the markets of Sepphoris and Tiberias that the peasants were being taken advantage of? Instead of helping the plight of the peasants, perhaps the leaders basked in their social stature and overlooked injustice right under their noses.

Conclusions

Let us now return to our questions. Was the ancient economic system like that of modern, western, capitalist societies? No, the ancient system was agrarian and not industrial. It was based on the essential bifurcation of its society into aristocrats and peasants. It is, therefore, confusing to interpret economic references in the New Testament from a modern perspective (cf. Morris and Manning 2005: 21).

Were the economic conditions driving the peasants of Lower Galilee toward poverty, even starvation? No, there is no evidence that the economy in Lower Galilee was causing great social upheaval.[1] The system, however, was against the peasant agriculturalist. It was hard just to survive, let alone to thrive or get ahead in that kind of economic world. Yet, during the time of Jesus and Antipas, we see no great stress on the economic life of the average villager. That may have come later, just before the war of 66–73 CE.

Was Lower Galilee so prosperous that the economic boom "floated all boats" so to speak? That was not exactly so. There was a vital economy. The goods were flowing as the model shows. The agricultural society was also developing vibrant markets for locally handcrafted goods such as pottery and stoneware. Yet marketization, as it develops over time, can turn on the individual worker and place stress on both subsistence and traditional institutions. It may well have been better for the average farmer in Lower Galilee than in the rest of Palestine during the time of Jesus and Antipas. But Galilee's day was coming.

Did Jesus criticize the ancient economic system? He criticized not the system so much as the dominant partners of the system: the aristocrats. Consider the following:

How difficult it is for one who has wealth to enter the kingdom of God.
(Mark 10:23 and par.; *Gospel Nazarenes*;
Shepherd of Hermes, *Similitude* 9:20:1–4)

It is easier for a camel to go through the eye of the needle than for a rich person to enter the kingdom of God.
(Mark 10:25 and par.)

When Jesus talked about rich persons in such a critical way, he was referring to those 1,500 to 2,000 aristocrats living in Sepphoris and Tiberias. He said nothing that we know about the system as such. But he could be stingingly critical of the wealthy men and women who controlled it.

Further Reading

Davies, John K. (2005) "Linear and Nonlinear Flow Models for Ancient Economies" in J. G. Manning and I. Morris (eds) *The Ancient Economy: Evidence and Models*, Stanford: Stanford University Press.

Davies, John K. (2008) "Hellenistic Economies" in G. R. Bugh (ed.) *The Cambridge Companion to the Hellenistic World*, Cambridge: Cambridge University Press.

Fiensy, David A. (2007) *Jesus the Galilean: Soundings in a First Century Life*, Piscataway, NJ: Gorgias Press.

Groh, Dennis (1997) "The Clash Between Literary and Archaeological Models of Provincial Palestine" in D.R. Edwards and C.T. McCollough (eds) *Archaeology and the Galilee*, Atlanta: Scholars Press.

Jensen, Morten H. (2006) *Herod Antipas in Galilee*, Tübingen: Mohr Siebeck.

Oakman, E. Douglas (1994) "The Archaeology of First-Century Galilee and the Social Interpretation of the Historical Jesus" in *SBL Seminar Papers*, 33: 220–51, Atlanta, GA: Scholars Press.

Oakman, E. Douglas (1998) *Jesus and the Peasants,* Matrix. The Bible in Mediterranean Context, Eugene, OR: Wipf and Stock.

Overman, J.A. (1997) "Jesus of Galilee and the Historical Peasant" in D.R. Edwards and C.T. McCollough (eds) *Archaeology and the Galilee*, Atlanta: Scholars Press.

Note

1   This conclusion is mid-way between two other opposing views. Some argue that indebtedness was the norm for the poor, and in such a state of affairs, they were subjected to "brutal compulsion and oppression" (Hanson and Oakman 2008:13; Oakman 1994; 1996; 2008). Others maintain that Galilee was prospering economically and that it was an "egalitarian society" (Overman 1997: 67–73; Groh 1997: 29–37; Jensen 2006: 258).

14

Purity, Dirt, Anomalies, and Abominations

Ritva H. Williams

Purity and Impurity
Social and Physical Bodies
Israelite and Judean Purity Rules
Mark 7:1–22
Conclusion: Purity and Mark's Jesus Group
Further Reading
Notes

In the Gospels we encounter persons afflicted by unclean spirits (Mark 1:26–27; 5:1–20), lepers begging to be made clean (Mark 1:40; Matt 8:2; Luke 5:12), and controversies between Jesus and the Pharisees about eating with defiled hands (Mark 7:1–23; Matt 15:1–20). To get the point of these and many other New Testament narratives we need to understand the phenomenon of purity rules as systematic and symbolic expressions of a group's identity and core values. This chapter will present a model of purity and impurity drawn from cross-cultural anthropology as a framework for interpreting the debate about unwashed hands in Mark 7:1–23.

Purity and Impurity

Mary Douglas's groundbreaking book *Purity and Danger*[1] demonstrates that concerns about purity and impurity are not expressions of primitive human impulses or infantile psychological desires. She begins by defining "dirt" as "matter out of place." Douglas asserts that the idea of "dirt" is the consequence of

> … a set of ordered relations and a contravention of that order. Dirt, then, is never a unique isolated event. Where there is dirt there is a system. Dirt is the by-product of a systematic ordering and classification of matter, in so far as ordering involves rejecting inappropriate elements.
>
> (Douglas 2007 [1966]: 44)

Her point is that the human activity of ordering and classifying experience creates "dirt" understood as matter out of place. All social groups past and present engage in this activity; it is a cross-cultural human phenomenon that produces specific purity systems differing only in their details (2007 [1966]: 43).

Elaborating on Douglas's work, Neyrey describes purity as both a general human activity and the specific rules that it produces. At an abstract level, purity refers to the generic process of ordering, classifying, and evaluating persons, places, things, times, events, and experiences so that everyone and everything is in its proper place and time. What is in place is pure, what is not in place is impure or "dirt." This process results in specific purity systems and rules that provide members of social groups with a conceptual map of reality for discerning if, when and where something is acceptable or unacceptable, and how to deal with the latter (1986b: 91–2). Thus, Israelite, Judean, and early Christian purity rules are particular instances of the generic activity called purity.

To understand the concept of dirt as matter out of place, consider whether your bedroom is "clean" or "dirty." How do you know? In our house a clean bedroom is one in which the bed is made, freshly laundered clothing is folded neatly into drawers or hung on hangers in the closet, soiled clothes are stuffed in the hamper, books stand in rows on the shelf, toys live in the toy box, the carpet is vacuumed, and so forth. In a clean bedroom everything that belongs there has its designated place and is in that place. If and when these conditions do not apply (which was most of the time when our children were growing up) the room is dirty and targeted for cleaning. This involves returning everything to its proper place, and removing those things (like apple cores and candy wrappers) that do not belong there. Once that is accomplished the room is clean once again. Your definition of a clean bedroom might be somewhat different.

Another way to think about purity is to consider what is right, proper, or appropriate in a given situation, time or place. An object or person may be pure, clean, or appropriate in one situation but impure, unclean, or inappropriate in another. Soil in the flowerbed is not "dirt" because it is in its proper place providing nutrients to my petunias. When that same soil is tracked all over the living room carpet it is "dirt" and needs to be cleaned up. A hot sweaty man is not "dirty" as long as he is outside doing manual labor on a summer day, but he certainly would be if he showed up for a dinner party in that condition. When I was growing up it was not acceptable to wear pajamas to class; apparently now it is. The distinction between pure and impure, appropriate and inappropriate lies in the eye of the beholder that is always culturally conditioned, changing over time and may be contested.

Consider the following. What makes a dirty old man "dirty"? Is it his failure to bathe regularly or his inappropriate behavior? What makes a dirty joke "dirty"? Is it the content, or the audience, or the time and place in which it is shared? What is involved in "cleaning up" one's language? What makes certain words "dirty"? Is it the words themselves, or the contexts in which they are used, or perhaps who uses them? When, where and with whom might it be appropriate to use "dirty" words? Why are certain bodily functions regarded as "dirty" and even "gross" if performed in public even when they are perfectly normal, natural, and healthy? What is at stake in each of these instances is what is socially acceptable for particular persons in specific circumstances.

Many of the purity rules that unconsciously shape our everyday lives are relatively inconsequential; they do not produce much personal anxiety or public debate (e.g., Kleenex or back of the hand for wiping your nose). Other purity classifications raise soul-searching questions and generate moral, ethical, and theological controversy. "Is it a boy or girl?" is very often the first question asked as one enters the world. We expect to be able to tell the difference between the two sexes primarily on the basis of physical appearance. Yet, a person's sex involves more than outward appearance and emerges out of a complex process of chromosomal, genetic, and hormonal development. Occasionally a person is intersexed, having elements of both sexes. A person who is chromosomally male (XY) may be unable to process androgens (male hormones) and hence physically appears to be female, even having female external genitalia. Is this person a boy or a girl, a man or a woman? Should doctors intervene medically or surgically to help the person fit into one of those two categories? Should such intervention be based on chromosomal sex or apparent genital sex?

Situations such as this raise the issue of anomalies, that is, of experiences that blur and confuse the categories, lines, and boundaries social groups use to define where everyone and everything is supposed to fit. Anomalies may arouse a range of emotions from curiosity to discomfort to revulsion and even abhorrence. Anomalies that evoke strong feelings of disgust or hatred may be labeled abominations (Malina 2001: 166). Consider how you might respond when encountering a woman with a shaved head, a man wearing a dress, or a person whose sex you cannot determine by any of the normal visual or aural cues. How do you feel about persons who engage in violent acts on a hockey rink, at the shopping mall, in a combat zone, or a daycare center?

Bruce J. Malina (2001: 169–70) outlines five ways that social groups deal with anomalies. (1) Elites or opinion leaders can settle for one interpretation of reality, thus eliminating anomalies from public attention. The early church's adoption of the New Testament canon removed certain understandings of Jesus, such as found in Ebionism or Gnosticism, from its discourse by labeling them heretical. (2) Anomalies may be controlled physically by being removed from society permanently or temporarily as in the case of persons considered dangerous enough to warrant execution, exile, incarceration, or quarantine. (3) Groups underscore what is socially acceptable through clearly spelled out rules for avoiding anomalous persons, things, and behavior. Laws forbidding smoking in public places or same-sex marriage fall into this category. (4) Labeling what is anomalous as a public hazard furthers conformity by excluding it from serious discussion. Labeling an idea "humanistic" or "liberal" in certain circles has the effect of ensuring that it will be rejected out of hand. In other groups the use of terms such as "fundamentalist" or "evangelical" can have the same effect. (5) In ritual contexts anomalies can enrich meaning or call attention to other levels of existence. Computer role-playing games, for instance, provide ritual spaces in which persons can act out situations in ways that they could not or would not in the real world.

In summary, the point of purity as a generic human process is to generate specific systems of culturally defined purity rules that "have a place for everything and everyone, with everything and everyone in its place—and with anomalies properly excluded" (Malina 2001: 169).

Social and Physical Bodies

Returning to the work of Mary Douglas, we are reminded that purity systems are symbolic systems in which purity rules are replicated throughout the social order. She highlights the centrality of the human body as a symbol of society:

> The body is a model which can stand for any bounded system. Its boundaries can represent any boundaries which are threatened or precarious. The body is a complex structure. The functions of its different parts and their relation afford a source of symbols for other complex structures. We cannot possibly interpret rituals concerning excreta, breast milk, saliva and the rest unless we are prepared to see … the powers and dangers credited to social structure reproduced small on the human body.
>
> (Douglas 2007 [1966]: 142)

Douglas's point is that the individual human body functions symbolically as a microcosm of the social group. She finds that each culture draws on body symbolism selectively in response to its own special risks, problems, and context (2007 [1966]: 150).

Just as every social group has external boundaries, internal structures, and margins so does each physical body. The external boundary of the physical body is its skin. Purity rules that focus on bodily surfaces and orifices often replicate a group's anxiety about maintaining its political or cultural integrity (Douglas 2007 [1966]: 153; Neyrey 1988a: 73). Clothing, a kind of second skin, is often an indicator of social location (Neyrey 1988a: 72). What cultural values and anxieties are affirmed and reinforced by all those commercials promoting products that ensure that our breath, our armpits, and other bodily apertures always smell clean and fresh? Consider how hospital gowns that leave a good portion of a patient's backside exposed reveal what it means to be sick and in hospital.

Hierarchically organized internal social structures are replicated in the symbolic relationship of body parts (Douglas 2007 [1966]: 78; Neyrey 1988a: 73). Even a cursory investigation of how we use body parts in common speech reveals this symbolism. To be "high-minded" is to be noble, but to be ruled by one's belly or genitals is not. No one wants to receive a left-handed compliment or to be called any of the slang terms used for the sex organs or digestive orifices. The use of body metaphors to describe persons within groups and groups within society says something about their relative status and importance within the social system.

Just as everyone and everything should be clearly and precisely located in their properly delineated places within the social body, physical bodies ought to have clearly defined margins. "Too much" means that something spills over into areas where it does not belong, as in the case of the intersexed person. The same applies to persons who are too tall, too big, too loud, too emotional, and so forth. "Too little" of something—such as limited sight, hearing or mobility—is a sign of a body that is incomplete or defective (Neyrey 1988a: 73–4). How physical bodies that transgress their margins are treated reveals much about a culture's underlying values and anxieties.

In summary, purity rules construct culturally specific external boundaries, internal structures, and margins that enable members of a group to make sense of their experience. The purity rules that order the social body are replicated on the physical body so that each reinforces the group's core values.

Israelite and Judean Purity Rules

As Carol Meyer reminds us, "religious culture in ancient Israel was hardly unitary... for much if not all of the period of the Hebrew Bible there was no commonly accepted cultic norm and praxis" (2005: 13). From ancient Israel's plurality of religious voices emerged multiple conceptions of purity. The Torah recognizes different categories of impurity: (1) temporary contact contagion, (2) long-lasting/permanent internal pollution arising from (a) certain sins and (b) ingesting impurity.[2] Each of these purity systems has its own logic and symbolism.

Temporary contact contagion results from the loss of vital body fluids due to reproductive processes such as menstruation, ejaculation, and childbirth (Lev 12:1–8; 15:1–33), breakdown of the skin due to certain diseases (Lev 13:1–14:32), and death (Num 19:10–22). These situations are frequently unavoidable and often obligatory. All Israelites are commanded to reproduce (Gen 1:28; 9:7), and with the exception of the high priest to bury their deceased relatives (Lev 21:1–4, 10–15). Such activities, therefore, are not sins and do not make the persons involved sinners. Leaking, broken, or expired bodies are simply impure, defiling things and persons that come into physical contact with them. The resulting impurity is temporary and easily resolved by rituals of purification such as washing and waiting for a prescribed length of time. For the duration of the impurity, however, the person is ineligible to interact with God in Tabernacle or Temple. The logic is that of *imitatio dei*: in order to approach the single, eternal deity humans must separate themselves from what makes them least god-like: reproduction and death (Klawans, 2004: 2044). Outside of sacred space temporary contact contagion does not seriously impede social interaction, except in the case of quarantined lepers (Lev 11:45–46).

Long-lasting/permanent internal pollution arises from certain particularly heinous sexual sins (Lev 18:24–30), idolatry (Lev 19:31; 20:1–3), and murder (Num 35:33–34). This kind of impurity is not transmitted by physical contact, and cannot be resolved by rituals of washing or sacrifice. Sexual sin, idolatry and murder are "abominations" (*to'evah*) that result in a more or less permanent pollution. Such sinners will be put to death by the community (Lev 20:2, 10–15; Gen 9:6; Num 34:16–31) or cut off from the people by God (Lev 18:29; 20:3–6). The latter is traditionally understood to mean the divinely inflicted penalty of extirpation or extermination (Schwartz 2004: 221, n. 20–21). The performance of these abominations leaves behind a residue that pollutes the land which in turn will spew them out (Lev 18:24–25; 20:22; Num 35:33), and defiles the sanctuary so that ultimately even God abandons the people (Lev 20:3; Ezek 8–11). The logic here is that individual sins which rupture relationships within families, between neighbors, and with God can pollute and destroy entire communities.

Israelite rules for clean and unclean animals reveal concerns for both temporary contact contagion and long-lasting/permanent internal pollution. Physical contact with the carcasses of certain prohibited species such as quadrupeds and eight reptiles conveys a temporary defilement that is resolved by washing and waiting a prescribed amount of time (Lev 11:24–45). More significantly, eating so-called "unclean" animals is prohibited.

Moreover, birds and all creatures that swarm in the waters or on the land are labeled *sheketz*, i.e., detestable or abominable (Lev 11:10–20, 23, 41–45; but *to'evah* in Deut 14:3). No purification rituals are prescribed for resolving the pollution that results from ingesting these creatures. Instead the texts connect ingesting impurity with other behaviors that lead to being spewed out of the land (Lev 20:22–26; *sheketz* in Lev 11:10–12; *to'evah* in Deut 14:3). The logic here is that inappropriate or unacceptable foreign or alien elements entering the body (physical and social) from outside can also pollute or destroy its internal coherence and integrity.

Disputes over the nature of purity characterize the Second Temple Judaism (520 BCE–70 CE). In the Persian period, the language of purity was used to justify invalidating mixed marriages (Ezra 9:1–10:44; Neh 13:23–31). The sectarians at Qumran argued for stricter purity rules than those practiced in Jerusalem, expanded the list of sins that result in internal pollution, and connected sin more closely with contact contagion. Debates between Pharisees and Sadducees over purity are preserved in the *Mishnah* (ca. 200 CE), the compilation of oral law and commentary that provides the basis for rabbinic Judaism. It is from these texts that Malina and Neyrey have reproduced the various purity maps of early Judaism that appear in their publications (e.g., Neyrey 1986a: 67–69; 1988a: 67–9; Malina 2001: 170–80).

Judeans were not alone in the ancient Mediterranean to be concerned about purity and impurity. Throughout the Greco-Roman world the temporary contact contagion resulting from birth, death, disease, and sexual intercourse was deemed incompatible with the divine presence.

> Herodotus reports, "Birth, sexual intercourse, and death were not allowed in sanctuaries." Even certain clothes, foods, weapons or types of metal might restrict access to a sanctuary. In Rome, the celebrant had to purify at least his hands and feet and wear clean clothes ... People could not enter the *agora* at Athens unless they had been symbolically purified at the lustral basins at the entrances.
>
> (Harrington 2001: 55)

It is beyond the scope of this chapter to explore further the purity systems that were operative in the Mediterranean cultures of antiquity. This brief outline is intended to provide a context for the discussion of purity that we find in Mark 7.

Mark 7:1–22

The Gospel of Mark is an in-group document, written by and for third-generation Jesus group members to help them make sense of their experience. The Gospel tells the story of Jesus and his first followers in a way that is relevant to Mark's community (Malina and Rohrbaugh 2003: 15–17). The author's care in translating Aramaic terms and sentences for his audience's benefit (e.g., Mark 5:41; 7:34) suggests that they were predominantly Greek-speaking. Similarly, the gospel writer has to explain the details of "traditions of the elders" promoted by the Pharisees and scribes from Jerusalem (7:3–4) pointing to a Diaspora location for his community. The text presupposes knowledge of the Septuagint (a Greek translation of the Hebrew Scriptures), and promotes particular beliefs and values supported by those ancient texts. Jesus's responses to his adversaries provide a model for Mark's third-generation community to follow when confronted by similar questions, and assure them that their practices are firmly rooted in the traditions of Israel as taught by Jesus and his group.

Mark 7:1–2 introduces the controversy and the issue: some Pharisees and scribes from Jerusalem notice that Jesus's disciples eat with "unclean"—that is, unwashed—hands. The author inserts a digression in verses 3–4 explaining to his audience why this is an issue: "the Pharisees and all the Judeans" hold fast to the traditions of the elders that require hand washing before eating. These same traditions prescribe bathing when one comes back from the market, as well as washing cups, pots and kettles. Is Mark exaggerating when he says that "all the Judeans" observe these traditions? We really have no way of verifying such a statement, even though the *Mishnah* makes a similar claim: "Come and see how far purity has broken out in Israel that everyone eats ordinary foods in a state of purity" (*Shabbat* 13:1). Certainly the Pharisees and the Essenes in the first century observed such rituals. In Mark's time and locale hand washing must have been prevalent enough among Judeans that the followers of Jesus were conspicuous for not doing so (Harrington 2001: 173).

The Pharisaic purity system has sometimes been represented as expressing concern primarily for the purity of bodily surfaces (e.g., Neyrey 1988a: 77). Other studies suggest a more nuanced understanding. John Poirier's analysis of evidence drawn from the Synoptic Gospels, the Tosephta, and the Babylonian Talmud leads him to argue that

> … the Pharisees divided the body between an interior and exterior, and that the importance of hand washing was attached to the need to keep one's interior undefiled. A failure to do so would presumably disrupt one's personal religious practice.

(Poirier 1996: 233)

By religious practice, Poirier specifically means prayer and Torah-study. He contends that the Pharisaic commitment to eating ordinary food in a state of ritual purity arose from a desire to avoid *ingesting* pollution (1996: 226–7). Harrington's work on rabbinic holiness in the Greco-Roman world supports the conclusion that the Pharisees ritually purified themselves so as not to defile their food and so ingest impurity (2001: 172). She provides a cross-cultural parallel from India where those who chant the Veda establish a state of ritual purity prior to their recitation by bathing and not eating meat (Harrington 2001: 150). Hand washing before prayer and Scripture-study among Judeans is attested in the second-century BCE *Letter of Aristeas*. There it is understood as a token that the participants had done no evil (Salyer 1993: 147, n. 5); that is, their outwardly clean hands symbolized their internally pure hearts (cf. Ps 24:3–4). If Poirier and Harrington are correct, then the point of eating ordinary food in ritually purified vessels with ritually clean hands may have been to ensure internal purity. Perhaps they believed that this state of heightened holiness enabled them to interact with the divine word at a deeper or more intense level.

In Mark 7, hand washing is a synecdoche, a single hot button issue representing a larger problem (Neyrey1988a: 71; Salyer 1993: 147). This is made clear in the question put to Jesus: "Why do your disciples not walk according to the traditions of the elders, but eat with unclean hands?" (Mark 7:4). The Pharisees and scribes regard the disciples' impure hands as evidence that the Jesus people are outsiders to these Judean identity-defining traditions (Mark 7:3). The controversy is about the boundaries of God's people that determine "who is in and out, pure and impure, loyal and disloyal" (Neufeld 2000: 23). How can one tell?

Jesus responds aggressively to discredit the Pharisees and scribes as spokespersons for God's people. His recitation of Isaiah 29:13 is directed at his challengers, denouncing them as hypocrites who honor God with their lips, not their hearts, teaching human precepts as doctrine (Mark 7:6–7). Jesus's initial charge draws a contrast between lips and heart, between the gateway to the interior of the human person and the actual inner core. Since the Pharisees' piety arises not from their hearts but from their lips, they teach only human precepts in place of God's commandments. This is the point that Jesus makes in verse 8, "You abandon the commandment of God and hold to human tradition."

Jesus reiterates this charge in verse 9, and supports it in verses 10–13 with the example of *corban*. The tradition of *corban* allowed a person to designate property, money, and other goods as offerings to God. The object did not actually have to be offered, but could be simply set aside as if it were an offering with the effect of making it unavailable for normal usage. Jesus criticizes the manipulation of this practice to deny material assistance to parents either by declaring something *corban* only when one's parents attempted to make use of it and/or scribal refusal to permit the retraction of the vow in a time of financial need. Such scribal rulings meant that persons might simply not be permitted to do anything for their parents in contravention of the commandment to honor one's parents (Mark 7:12). In this way the traditions of the elders violate rather than uphold God's commandments.

Jesus then calls back the crowd and asserts, "there is nothing outside a person that by going in can defile, but the things that come out are what defile" (Mark 7:14–15). Jesus then leaves the public realm and enters the house where he is asked by his disciples to explain this parable (Mark 7:17). Jesus reiterates his position that whatever goes into a person from outside cannot defile because it enters not the heart but passes through the stomach and out into the latrine (Mark 7:18–19). Eating with unwashed hands does not defile the inner core of the person because what is ingested simply passes through the digestive tract and is excreted. Within Israel's purity system human feces are unseemly and must be buried outside the encampment, but they do not result in temporary contact contagion or impurity (Deut. 23:11–15). In Jesus's estimate the Pharisaic program of eating in a state of physical purity in order to avoid ingesting impurity is misguided; it has no effect on the heart or center of the person.

The gospel writer takes Jesus's argument a step further and infers that if impurity cannot be ingested, then all foods must be clean (Mark 7:19b). Here we see Mark addressing head-on the concerns of his third-generation Jesus group audience.[3] The principle asserted by Jesus in the context of the hand-washing debate is used to support the abandonment of Judean dietary practices. Mark may be drawing on a Hellenistic conception of food as being clean precisely because it passes through into excrement. If so, this may be another indicator of the geographic location and ethnic identity of Mark's audience (Salyer 1993: 153). The issue of what Jesus group members should ingest was controversial as we see in Paul's letters (1 Cor 7–10; Gal 2; Rom 14). Luke resolved the debate for his community through the revelation of Peter's vision in Acts 10. Mark does the same here for his community.

Jesus concludes his argument by insisting that what really defiles a person is what comes out of the human heart—evil intentions that manifest themselves in fornication, theft, murder, adultery, avarice, wickedness, deceit, licentiousness, envy (the evil eye), slander, pride, and folly (Mark 7:20–23). The impurity that really matters emerges from the inner core of the person and is manifested as sinful behavior, specifically in vices that roughly correspond to violations of the Ten Commandments. Table 14.1 is an adaptation of one proposed by Neyrey (1986b: 120).

Table 14.1 Adaption of the Ten Commandments by Neyrey

The Vice List in Mark 7:21-22	The Ten Commandments
Fornication, adultery, licentiousness	You shall not commit adultery
Theft	You shall not steal
Murder	You shall not murder
Avarice, envy (evil eye)	You shall not covet…
Deceit, slander	You shall not bear false witness
7:10-13 – Corban	Honor your father and your mother

Although wickedness, pride and folly do not fit the pattern, taken all together the vice list makes the point that purity as demonstrated in behavior that honors God's commandments is the hallmark of a godly people.

Conclusion: Purity and Mark's Jesus Group

Neyrey has correctly observed that "it would be erroneous to assert that Mark portrays Jesus as abrogating the general purity system or that Mark was himself unconcerned with purity issues" (1986b: 105). Rather Mark depicts Jesus putting in place an alternative purity system, one which has its roots in historical and Scriptural traditions shared with the Pharisees and scribes from Jerusalem. One might even contend that Mark's community regards Jesus as re-establishing God's originally intended purity system (Salyer 1993: 162, n.11).

My hypothesis is this. Both the Pharisees and Jesus were concerned about the long-lasting/permanent internal purity of physical and especially social bodies. They differed in their evaluation of what constituted the greatest danger to that purity. The Pharisees' project of eating in a state of physical cleanness so as to avoid ingesting impurity makes sense as a strategy to maintain the body's internal purity. They understood the social body, Israel, to be a holy people residing in a holy land, worshipping in holy space, hearing a holy word. Purity resides *within* this holy body which must be protected against pollution from outside. Their fear of ingesting impurity by eating with unwashed hands replicates anxieties about the social body assimilating and accommodating dominant Greco-Roman cultural values and practices. For the Pharisees, the written and oral Torah represent a double-walled fence protecting this body from alien and potentially defiling elements in the world around it.

The Markan Jesus is more concerned with the evil that emerges from the very core and center of the physical and social body. Impurity emerges from the human heart as sin, specifically violations of God's commandments. These defile the very core of the person and pose the greatest danger to the wholeness and integrity of the social body. In the context of first-century Galilee Jesus contended that the poor condition of the social body, e.g., an economics of exploitation evidence by failure to care for one's parents (Mark 7:9–13), was the consequence of internal corruption and pollution rather than the result of absorbing unclean foreign elements. For Mark's audience located outside of Judea, the point of Jesus's discourse is that immoral behavior by core members of the group is potentially more damaging to the reputation and survival of their particular Jesus group than assimilating aspects of the dominant culture or integrating non-Judeans into the social group. Thus we see that Jesus and Mark, like the Pharisees, are concerned about the purity of the body's interior, but differ in their assessment of what constitutes the greatest threat to that long-lasting internal purity. Since for Jesus (and Mark) the greater danger lies within the body itself, from their perspective attempts to construct a fence to protect it from external pollution are misguided.

Further Reading

Douglas, Mary (2007 [1966]) *Purity and Danger: An Analysis of Concepts of Pollution and Taboo*, Harmondsworth: Penguin.

Klawans, Jonathan (2004) "Concepts of Purity in the Bible," in Adele Berlin and Marc Zvi Brettler (eds) *The Jewish Study Bible*, Oxford: Jewish Publication Society, pp. 2041–47.

Levine, Amy-Jill (2006) *The Misunderstood Jew—The Church and the Scandal of the Jewish Jesus*, San Francisco: Harper SanFrancisco.

Neyrey, Jerome H. (1986) "The Idea of Purity in Mark's Gospel," *Semeia*, 35: 91–128.

Neyrey, Jerome H. (1988a) "A Symbolic Approach to Mark 7," *FF*, 4.3: 63–91.

Neyrey, Jerome H. (1988b) "Unclean, Common, Polluted and Taboo—A Short Reading Guide," *FF*, 4.4: 72–82.

Neyrey, Jerome H. (1996) "Readers Guides to Clean/Unclean, Pure/Polluted, and Holy/Profane: The Idea and System of Purity," in Richard L. Rohrbaugh (ed.) *The Social Sciences and New Testament Interpretation*, Peabody, MA: Hendrickson, pp. 159–82.

Sawyer, John F. A., and Mary Douglas (1996) *Reading Leviticus: A Conversation with Mary Douglas*, Sheffield: Sheffield Academic Press.

Salyer, Gregory (1993) "Rhetoric, Purity and Play: Aspects of Mark 7:1–23," *Semeia*, 64: 139–69.

Notes

1   First published in 1966 by Routledge & Kegan Paul; re-issued in the Routledge Classics series in 2002 and reprinted in 2004, 2006 (twice), and 2007. All quotations are taken from the 2007 reprint.

2   These categories derive from distinctions described by Jonathan Klawans (2000). Klawans distinguishes between "ritual" and "moral" impurity with ingested impurity as a category sharing some characteristics of the other two. Because "ritual" and "moral" are theologically loaded terms, I prefer to use other descriptors for these categories.

3   Amy-Jill Levine argues that had Jesus actually declared all foods clean then the account in Acts 10 and the controversy over table fellowship in Galatians 2 would make no sense at all (2006: 25–6).

15

Ritual and Christian Origins

Risto Uro

A Survey of Existing Studies
Recent Theories and Applications to Early Christianity
Conclusion
Further Reading
Notes

> Ritual is the hardest religious phenomenon to capture in texts or comprehend by thinking …
>
> Ronald L. Grimes (1995: 5)

Although countless in number and scope, studies and books on Christian origins seldom focus on rituals. Scholars of the New Testament and early Christianity have by and large been interested in other aspects of the emerging early Christian religion, such as the teachings of Jesus or Paul, the religious experiences of the first followers, and the development and variety of doctrinal ideas reflected in early Christian sources. Even social-scientific criticism of the New Testament and other early Christian texts has given surprisingly little consideration to the role of ritual in the formation of the early Christian movement and in the social life of early communities, although the study of ritual has a long history in anthropology and, during the past few decades, ritual studies has established itself as an independent field in religious and cultural studies (Grimes 1985; 1990; 1995; Bell 1992; 1997).

Most recent introductions to the social world of the New Testament and early Christianity pay little attention to the ritual behavior of early Christians and other contemporary groups (e.g., Rohrbaugh 1996; Esler 1995; 2000; Blasi, Duhaime, and Turcotte 2002; Neyrey and Stewart 2008). While some aspects related to ritual, such as purity, are discussed among the typical topics dealt with in these volumes (cultural values, social structures, kinship, economics, gender, etc.), ritual rarely receives independent treatment. There are, of course, important exceptions to this failure to focus on ritual in its own right and I will cite such studies later in this chapter. In general, however, one may conclude that New Testament scholars have been slow in accepting ritual as an analytical tool for and a key to the social world of the New Testament. Particularly little work has been done in utilizing theories about ritual and theoretical approaches advanced in various fields of ritual and religious studies for the analysis of the nascent Christian movements (see, however, DeMaris 2008 and other pioneering works listed below).

Even though ritual does not have as central a position in New Testament and early Christian studies as it has in religious studies and anthropology, it would be a mistake to state that scholars in these fields have completely ignored ritual practices in their historical work. The German history-of-religions school in the early twentieth century was deeply engaged in the analysis and comparison of the Hellenistic "background" of early Christian practices (e.g., Reitzenstein 1978) and, to some extent, a few New Testament scholars have continued this tradition in later periods (e.g., Wagner 1962; Klauck 1982; Wedderburn 1987). Several studies on theologies of baptism in the New Testament have been published (e.g., Beasley-Murray 1962; Frankemölle 1970; Hartman 1997). Liturgical scholars have been interested in the earliest developments of Christian worship, although most of their historical work has by necessity been concentrated on later centuries of the Christian church (e.g., Jones *et al.* 1992; Johnson 1999; Bradshaw 2002; 2004; Wainwright and Westerfield Tucker 2006). Historians of liturgy have not, until quite recently, turned to ritual theories to enrich their work. (For such cross-disciplinary work, however, see Stringer 2005; Bradshaw and Melloh 2007). Moreover, scholars using sociohistorical and social-scientific perspectives have touched upon ritual dimensions of early Christian community life in several ways, although, as noted above, ritual theories have not been at the center of their work.

In what follows, I will attempt to give a short summary of the earlier approaches to ritual in the study of the New Testament and early Christianity. I will also introduce some recent theories about ritual and consider their explanatory power and usefulness for the study of Christian origins.

A Survey of Existing Studies

During the last hundred years or so, scholars have applied a wide variety of perspectives and approaches in their analyses of early Christian rituals. For the purpose of this presentation (see also Uro 2009), I will divide such studies into three approaches: genealogical, functionalist, and symbolist. Note, however, that especially the last group of approaches is rather heterogeneous and comprises several different theoretical commitments and strategies.

Genealogical

A classic example of the genealogical approach is Hans Lietzmann's *Mass and Lord's Supper* (Lietzmann 1979), in which he traces the later eucharistic liturgies back to two basic archetypes, the agape meal, originating in the practice of the early community in Jerusalem, and the Eucharist, which had its origins in Pauline Christianity. Lietzmann's method is source critical, looking for seams, later additions, and alternative traditions in eucharistic texts.

The concerns for origin and dependence, which dominate Lietzmann's and many of his contemporaries' work, continue to be present in later studies on early Christian rituals, although the problems involved in this kind of approach are largely recognized in present-day scholarship. The underlying assumption, at least in many of the studies produced by the so-called history-of-religions school, is that by tracing a tradition back to its original source or earliest root (literary or oral), one has access to the authentic meaning of that tradition (see, e.g., King 2003). Since many representatives of the school were philologists, they relied heavily on linguistic details and treated religious traditions as if they were manuscripts deriving from a single autograph. This autograph could be seen as a kind of pure or uncontaminated beginning (or, vice versa, as a foreign or bad influence). Fueled by such interest, genealogical practices run counter to a realistic understanding of Christian beginnings. This is not to say that the quest for the origin and historical influences is antiquated, but scholars of religion increasingly realize that "all religions have composite origins and are continually reconstructed through ongoing processes of synthesis and erasure" (Stewart and Shaw 1994: 7, cited in Martin 2000: 281).

Functionalist

The explanatory power of the genealogical approach is weakened by still another problem. Even if one were able to determine the original source of a tradition or ritual, this source would not explain what prompted the tradition or ritual in the first place. Nor would it explain why it spread among people, why people keep on repeating it (see Sperber 1996, which offers an "epidemiology" of cultural representations). Functionalist explanations, which entered New Testament scholarship in the 1970s, intended to address these kinds of questions. In sociological and social-scientific studies, the emphasis of New Testament scholarship shifted from the search for the origin to the search for the social function of early Christian beliefs and practices, and from influence to social context. Many scholars were convinced that "the sort of questions to be asked about the early Christian movement are those about how it worked" (Meeks 1983: 7). Wayne Meeks's groundbreaking study, *The First Urban Christians*, includes a major chapter on ritual in Pauline churches, which discusses baptism and the Lord's Supper as well as what he calls minor rituals (prayer, hymns, reading of the Scriptures, etc.). Meeks is well informed about the various theoretical approaches to ritual in the anthropology of that time and uses insights from ritual studies in a creative way. The functionalistic reasoning is explicitly contrasted to the analysis of the origin or theological content in Meeks's treatment of Pauline rituals.

> These passages [allusions to baptisms in Paul] have often been analyzed for their ideational content and for their parallels, connections, and possible antecedents in the history of religions. Our purpose is different; we are trying to see what baptism did for ordinary Christians, disregarding the question of where its elements may have come from and even the profounder theological beliefs that Paul and the other early leaders associated with it ...
>
> (Meeks 1983: 154)

Meeks furthermore argues that Paul uses the symbolism of the supper "to enhance both internal coherence, unity, and equality of the Christian group" and "to protect its boundaries vis-à-vis other kinds of cultic association" (Meeks 1983: 160). In broad lines, this echoes the functionalist stance present already in Émile Durkheim's *Elementary Forms of Religious Life*: "rites are, above all, the means by which the social group periodically reaffirms itself" (Durkheim 2001: 287).

Functionalism (or structural functionalism) has been criticized in the social sciences since the latter half of the twentieth century (e.g., Penner 1971). It is generally recognized that, as a grand theory, functionalism creates a kind of feedback loop that leads to a circular argument: if every social phenomenon must serve some (positive) function to survive and nothing without such a function survives, how can we possibly argue against a functionalist explanation (Pyysiäinen 2001: 67)? On the other hand, understood as *one* explanation for ritual behavior, functionalist reasoning has hardly lost its relevance. It is very intuitive to think that collective rituals often provide a kind of glue that keeps social groups together (Boyer 2002: 30). Various recent neo-functionalist explanations, building on evolutionary perspectives, have in fact attempted to demonstrate how rituals can promote group cohesion, for example, by requiring members to engage in behavior that is too costly to fake (Irons 2001; Sosis and Ruffle 2003; Bulbulia 2007).

Symbolist

Discussion on ritual symbolism has been complex and multifaceted, and it would be impossible to capture the major debates and currents here. In New Testament scholarship, scholars have drawn basically on three different symbolist approaches (which are often mixed with structuralist arguments).

First, pollution and cleansing constitute a central theme in many rituals (Liénard and Boyer 2006). As noted at the beginning of this chapter, biblical scholars have often focused on this aspect of ritual behavior, not least because of the influential works by the British anthropologist Mary Douglas (2007 [1966]; 1970). The application of Douglas's insights to biblical material was facilitated by the fact that Douglas herself referred to Hebrew Bible purity rules in her *Purity and Danger* (especially to food laws in Lev 11). Douglas's idea about purity rules (and ritual in general) as symbols of the social structure was further developed in her grid/group model, which sets out four ideal types of societies with corresponding cosmologies and emphases on ritual and social order (Douglas 1970). This model has been used by some New Testament scholars in their analyses of early Christian communities (Malina 1986; Neyrey 1986a; 1986b).

Second, Victor Turner's famous tripartite processual scheme (separation, liminality, reintegration; see Turner 1967; 1969; 1974), adapted from Arnold van Gennep's analysis of rites of passage (see van Gennep 1960), is also often classified to the symbolist tradition, although it owes a great deal to structuralism as well. Turner's idea about the dialectic between the social order and a period of social disorder and liminality (antistructure), which he termed *communitas*, has important affinities with Douglas's analysis of different degrees of group (experience of a bounded unit) and grid (rules that bind a person to others) in society (Bell 1997: 43), but New Testament scholars have not explored these affinities in any depth. Several scholars have, however, sought to apply Turner's processual model to early Christian sources. This has been done basically in two ways. Some scholars have attempted to recognize Turner's tripartite scheme in the structure of some early Christian texts (McVann 1994; see also Draper 2000), while others have analyzed early Christian religious life and theologies, especially as reflected in Pauline letters, in light of Turner's insights (Meeks 1983; for a comprehensive analysis of the "liminal" theology of Paul, see Strecker 1999).

Third, both Turner's and Douglas's approach assumes that ritual symbols play an important role in mirroring and maintaining (as well as resisting) social equilibrium. Some theorists, however, have moved beyond such a structural-functionalist framework toward a more semiotic (or symbolic-cultural) understanding of ritual symbolism. Catherine Bell calls such theorists (loosely) culturalists (or symbolic-culturalists) and her description of the shift in the interpretation of symbols is worth quoting in full:

> In contrast to how functionalism closely links symbols to social organization, culturalists tend to see these links as weak and indirect and emphasize instead the autonomy and languagelike nature of a cultural system of symbols. In other words, culturalists interpret the symbols and symbolic action so important to ritual less in terms of their connection to social organization and more in terms of an independent system organized like a language for the primary purpose of communication. This has shifted interpretation from a focus on what social reality may be represented (or maintained) by a symbol to a focus on what the symbol means (communicates) within the context of the whole system of symbols in which it is embedded.
>
> (Bell 1997: 61)[1]

Ritual has often been understood as a form of communication, though this can be done in a number of different ways (Laidlaw and Humphrey 2006; Thomas 2006). According to Bell's analysis, ritual theorists have followed up two different paths in their use of the language analogy. While some have emphasized the semiotic (or hermeneutic) side of ritual sign language and been mainly concerned with the *interpretation* of ritual symbols (Turner 1969; Geertz 1973), other theorists, taking a cue from Edmund Leach's direct appeal to the field of linguistics (Leach 1976), have made an attempt to seek the (universal) "grammar" of ritual actions (Staal 1989; Lawson and McCauley 1990; McCauley and Lawson 2002). The representatives of the latter approach aim at a more explanatory and less interpretative methodology and separate themselves clearly from the symbolist tradition. I will discuss Lawson and McCauley's theory in more detail below.

A good example of the first (semiotic or hermeneutic) approach in New Testament scholarship is Gerd Theissen's book *A Theory of Primitive Christian Religion*, which includes a lengthy chapter on early Christian rituals (Theissen 1999). Theissen's analysis of ritual combines both functionalist and semiotic perspectives. Like Meeks, Theissen sees the Eucharist as a rite of integration renewing the cohesion of the group. At the same time, in Theissen's semiotic interpretation, both baptism and the Eucharist form a "ritual sign language" loaded heavily with symbolic meanings. In contrast to the ritual sacrifices of antiquity, Christian rituals contain "a consistent reduction of violence." Drawing on psychoanalytic concepts, Theissen argues that this reduction happens through a kind of sublimation. "The rites express in an unacknowledged way the hidden anti-social nature of human beings" (Theissen 1999: 135). To put it in symbolic terms, for Theissen, baptism is "a symbolic suicide" and the Eucharist "symbolic cannibalism."

It goes without saying that many rituals include signs, sounds, words, gestures, smells, or physical elements that can be interpreted symbolically. What is more problematical is the assumption that ritual symbolism has a language-like nature which would make it possible to translate or decode a symbol or set of symbols into some other language. Dan Sperber criticized this "cryptological" view of symbolism more than thirty years ago in an important book (Sperber 1974). Ritual activities often trigger symbolic mechanisms in people's minds and this property of ritual can be used as a tool for consolidating religious traditions and dogmatic systems (Sørensen 2005; Ketola 2008: 41). But it is important to notice that not all ritual activities evoke symbolic interpretations with a similar force. The main focus of the healing rituals, for example, is not in the symbolic meanings of various components of the ritual action but in the efficacy of the ritual. Symbolism is, therefore, a response or approach to ritual behavior (albeit widely taken) rather than an integral part of ritual itself.

Recent Theories and Applications to Early Christianity

The general approaches described in the previous section (genealogical, functionalist, and symbolist) can be understood as belonging to a phase of scholarship which is called by the editors of *Theorizing Rituals* "the age of grand theories" (Kreinath, Snoek, and Stausberg 2006). Instead of presenting just another theory of ritual(s), the editors of this massive two-volume work (consisting of an annotated bibliography and a collection of essays on basic themes) call for "theorizing rituals," by which they mean a move from "theories that seek to explain everything" to a view that no single theory suffices to account for the complexity of the phenomena. Two recent books written by biblical scholars clearly represent this type of pluralistic approach in their attempts to understand and explain ritual behavior in the biblical world (Klingbeil 2007; DeMaris 2008).

Ritual as Embodied Power Negation

It would be impossible to make, within the limits of the present chapter, a comprehensive survey of the recent trends and developments within the field of ritual studies. The above-mentioned volumes on *Theorizing Rituals* and Bell's supplementary considerations to the entry on "Ritual" in the second edition of *Encyclopedia of Religion* (Bell 2005) provide the best guides for those who want to familiarize themselves with the major currents and developments. One important dividing line in the recent discussion is the one between theories that "remain heavily rooted in cultural explanation" (Bell 2005) and those seeking to advance empirically testable theories and models with clearly defined predictions. Bell is herself perhaps the most profiled representative of the first camp. Bell's approach to rituals draws on, among other things, various sociocultural theories of practice (e.g., Bourdieu 1977) and takes the body as the central category of analysis (see also Vial 1999). Since the body is seen by Bell (and by so many other culturalists following Foucault) as the socialized body or "political body," her analysis of ritual focuses on the way in which "power is negotiated in ritual and how ritual strategies construct distinct forms of domination and resistance" (Bell 1992: 211). An excellent example of an analysis along these lines is Stanley Stowers's study on the sacrificers and non-sacrificers in the social world of early Christians (Stowers 1995). Stowers demonstrates how the sacrificial system of Greek religion was involved in the construction of gender and kinship and how ritual practices created a particular environment within which the participants came to embody and negotiate power relations.

Cognitive Approaches to Ritual

The latter type of theorizing about rituals, that is, relying on empirically testable models and theories, has been conducted mainly by cognitive theorists or scholars working in the field of the cognitive science of religion. While members of the "cultural camp" tend to reject any suggestion that ritual is universal, cognitive scholars are interested in cross-culturally recurrent patterns in religious thought and practice seeking to explain these regularities in terms of the architecture of the human mind (Pyysiäinen 2001; Tremlin 2006; Barrett 2007; Luomanen, Pyysiäinen, and Uro 2007).

Scholars using cognitive perspectives have focused on several aspects of ritual behavior. One is the compulsiveness of ritual behavior, which has made some researchers ask whether there is a common cognitive mechanism behind obsessive neuroses and collective ritualized behavior, a claim that was made by Freud (e.g., Freud 1963; see also Dulaney and Fiske 1994; Fiske and Haslam 1997). Pascal Boyer has argued that rituals are compulsive for humans because they are "snares for thought" that produce highly salient effects by activating special mechanisms in the mental "basement" (Boyer 2002). In collaboration with Pierre Liénard, Boyer has further argued that ritualization is best explained as an occasional by-product of specific human precaution systems including the detection of and reaction to inferred threats to fitness (distinct from systems responding to manifest danger) (Boyer and Liénard 2006; Liénard and Boyer 2006). Uro has applied Boyer's and others' theories to early Jewish and Christian beliefs about corpse impurity and relic veneration (Uro 2007b), and similar cognitive and psychological research is currently inspiring fresh insights on early Jewish and early Christian morality and magic (Czachesz 2008; 2009; Kazen 2007).

Another central theme in cognitive approaches to ritual is memory. Anthropologist Harvey Whitehouse has advanced a theory of two modes of religiosity, doctrinal and imagistic (Whitehouse 1995; 2000; 2004). Whitehouse argues that all religious traditions tend to gravitate around two modes: the doctrinal mode, characterized by large-scale organizations, orthodoxy, and routinized rituals; and the imagistic mode, distinguished by small-scale communities with an emphasis on emotionally-arousing rituals (see Table 15.1). What makes Whitehouse's theory cognitive is that these modes of the world's religious traditions is explained by two different memory systems: semantic memory (storing concept-based knowledge) and episodic memory (storing autobiographical knowledge), the former dominating the codification and the transmission of religious knowledge in the doctrinal mode, the latter dominating the imagistic mode. The modes of religiosity theory has attracted considerable attention and has been tested and criticized by a large number of ethnographers, anthropologists, psychologists, and historians of religion (Whitehouse and Laidlaw 2004; Whitehouse and McCauley 2005; Whitehouse and Martin 2004). It seems that in Whitehouse's theory the causal link between the cognitive mechanisms and the modes of religiosity is rather vague (see Wiebe 2004), but the theory has in any case opened up a new avenue in combining both cultural and cognitive factors in a single theory (for an application to the Valentinian movement in early Christianity, see Uro 2007a).[2]

An alternative cognitive theory focusing on the role of ritual in the social dynamics of religious movements is the ritual competence or ritual form theory developed by McCauley and Lawson (see Lawson and McCauley 1990; for social dynamics, see especially McCauley and Lawson 2002). Drawing on generative linguistics, Lawson and McCauley argue that people all over the world, irrespective of their culture, have intuitive competence to

Table 15.1 The two modes of religiosity according to Whitehouse (modified from Whitehouse 2004)

Imagistic	Doctrinal
Low frequency rituals	High frequency rituals
High emotion	Low emotion
Episodic memory	Semantic memory
Spontaneous exegesis	learned exegesis
Dynamic leadership	Passive or absent leadership
Noncentralized	Centralized

judge whether the "grammar" of a ritual is correct or incorrect. McCauley and Lawson's theory is based on the observation that the action representation system of ritual follows the general pattern of *any* action (versus something just happening). The basic components of action are agent, action/ instrument, and patient (see the action representation system illustrated in Figure 15.2). Religious rituals are distinguished from other (ritual) actions by the presence of "culturally postulated superhuman agents" (CPS agents), associated with one of these components. Using these constituent parts, McCauley and Lawson divide religious rituals into two ritual profiles: (1) special agent rituals, and (2) special patient/instrument rituals, depending on which component a CPS agent is associated with.

With their model, McCauley and Lawson believe that they can provide fairly accurate predictions about the properties of a ritual in any religious tradition. They claim that they can predict whether a ritual is reversible, whether it is repeatable, and how much sensory pageantry or sensory stimulation is associated with any given ritual. The model, for example, predicts that special agent rituals are often central in religious systems and cannot be repeated, that elevated levels of sensory arousal become associated with special agent rituals, and that a balanced ritual system includes rituals from both profiles (special agent rituals and special patient/instrument rituals).

As in the case of Whitehouse, the theory advanced by Lawson and McCauley is open to criticism (for a critical discussion and application to first-century Judaism, see Ketola 2007). Yet if it is not understood as a grand theory—a theory that seeks to explain everything—it can be used as a helpful tool, for example, for an analysis of the ritual structure of the baptisms practiced by John and early Christians. Although we have plenty of information about ritual bathing in second temple Judaism (Lawrence 2006), it is generally acknowledged that the baptism of John was a ritual innovation in the sense that it was not a self-baptism but an act in which someone (agent) was baptizing someone else (patient) (see, e.g., Taylor 1997: 50). Thus, in terms of Lawson and McCauley's theory the baptism of John could be understood as a special agent ritual, in which a superhuman agent is associated with the agent of the ritual action (that is, with a charismatic person acting in God's name; for a more detailed discussion, see Uro 2009). According to Lawson and McCauley's prediction, special agent rituals are unrepeatable, since "when the gods act … the effects are superpermanent" (McCauley and Lawson 2002: 122). Scholars debate over whether the baptism of John should be interpreted as a rite that was performed only once per person (e.g., Scobie 1964: 91–2; Webb 1991: 183, 216; Taylor 1997: 69–72), and there is a real danger that we anachronistically read too much later Christian theology into the ritual activity of the historical John.

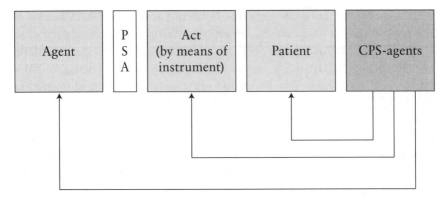

CPS-agent = culturally postulated superhuman agent
PSA = Principle of Superhuman Agency

Figure 15.2 Action representation system (McCauley and Lawson 2002)

However, the ritual competence theory may be helpful in explaining the evolution of early Christian baptism from purification rites to a rite that was normally performed only once for each individual. It may, for example, shed some light on the theological problems that arose when the "superpermanent change" brought about in baptism seemed to disappear in people's life, as happened in the case of lapsing (Heb 6:4, 6; Herm. *Vis.* 2.2.4; 3.5.5; *Mand.* 4.3.3–5; see DeMaris 2008: 28–9). Lawson and McCauley's strict definition of religious ritual as actions in which CPS agents play a role and which bring about some change in the religious world clearly leaves out many important aspects (McCauley and Lawson 2002: 13), but combined with other approaches their theory may prove to be fruitful in the analysis of early Christian rituals. One may, for example, ask how ritual actions may be interpreted from the point of view of "magical agency" (corresponding to Lawson and McCauley's analysis of ritual as actions) or from the point of view of symbolic meanings, that is, from their ability to express the content of doctrinal systems and beliefs (corresponding to a view of ritual as communication) (Sørensen 2005). Or one may ask how the "grammar" of ritual actions is related to the use of political power (see Bell 1997; Vial 1999).

Conclusion

The analysis of early Christian rituals involves a complexity of issues and problems which cannot be solved by any magic bullet theory. This is so because ritual scholars themselves are becoming increasingly aware that the age of grand theories is over.[3] Moreover, it is improbable that all different types of social or individual behavior traditionally categorized under the concept "ritual" (such as rites of passage, calendrical rites, rites of exchange, etc.) form an analytically coherent set of phenomena which could be captured in one single definition or theoretical framework. Ritual, like marriage or religion, is not an analytical category but rather a family-resemblance category (Liénard and Boyer 2006). Theoretical and methodological problems in the study of early Christian ritual can be best addressed by a piecemeal approach in which different aspects of early Christian behavior, as reflected in our sources, are examined in view of the insights and knowledge gained from ritual and cognate studies. This entails a pluralistic approach which combines historical, archaeological, and cultural analyses informed by theoretical approaches developed in a host of different fields, such as the social sciences, psychology, the cognitive science of religion, and evolutionary and ecological sciences. Instead of entrenching in different camps (for example, cultural versus cognitive studies), scholars should strive for cooperation.[4]

Further Reading

Boyer, P. (2002) *Religion Explained: The Human Instincts that Fashion Gods, Spirits and Ancestors*, London: Vintage.

DeMaris, R. E. (2008) *The New Testament in Its Ritual World*, London: Routledge.

Grimes, R. L. (1985) *Research in Ritual Studies: A Programmatic Essay and Bibliography*, ATLA Bibliography Series 14, Metuchen, NJ: ATLA and Scarecrow Press.

Grimes, R. L. (1990) *Ritual Criticism: Case Studies in Its Practice, Essays on Its Theory*, Columbia, SC: University of South Carolina Press.

Grimes, R. L. (1995) *Beginnings in Ritual Studies*, rev. edn, Columbia, SC: University of South Carolina Press.

Kreinath, J., J. Snoek, and M. Stausberg (eds) (2006) *Theorizing Rituals: Issues, Topics, Approaches, Concepts*, Numen Book Series, Studies in the History of Religions 114–1, Leiden: Brill.

Kreinath, J., J. Snoek, and M. Stausberg (2007) *Theorizing Rituals: Annotated Bibliography of Ritual Theory, 1966–2005,* Numen Book Series, Studies in the History of Religions 114–2, Leiden: Brill.

McCauley, R. N., and T. E. Lawson, (2002) *Bringing Ritual to Mind: Psychological Foundations of Cultural Forms*, Cambridge: Cambridge University Press.

Meeks, W. A. (1983) *The First Urban Christians: The Social World of the Apostle Paul*, New Haven, CT: Yale University Press.

Theissen, G. (1999) *A Theory of Primitive Christian Religion*, trans. J. Bowden, London: SCM.

Whitehouse, H. (2004) *Modes of Religiosity: A Cognitive Theory of Religious Transmission*, Walnut Creek, CA: AltaMira.

Notes

1   It should be noted that according to Bell no clear line can be drawn between functional-structuralists and symbolic-culturalists. Victor Turner, Mary Douglas, and Edmund Leach, for example, can be fitted into both groups (Bell 1997: 62). The distinction is, however, helpful in delineating some important changes in ritual theorizing during the last decades reflected also in New Testament scholarship.

2   For a different cognitive approach on ritual and memory moving beyond the "two modes" dichotomy, see Czachesz (forthcoming).

3   In a way, Rappaport's ambitious and massive synthesis of ritual is a culmination of this age, while it, at the same time, builds a bridge between evolutionary biology and the social sciences (Rappaport 1999).

4   I am grateful to István Czachesz, Jutta Jokiranta, Petri Luomanen, and Timo Vanhoja for helpful comments on an earlier version of this chapter.

Glossary

Agrarian economy refers to an economy that is based on land ownership and farm production. Land and production are controlled by a small elite for personal use and distribution at the expense of peasant farmers who work the land.

Altered states of consciousness (ASC) refer to those experiences in humankind in which varied phases of waking and sleeping states are encountered and in which sensations, perceptions, and emotions are altered—they may be altered/induced by various physiological, psychological, and pharmacological agents. Thus, dreaming, sleeping, hypnagogic (drowsiness before sleep), hypnopompic (semi-consciousness preceding waking), hyperalert, lethargic, rapture, hysteria, fragmentation, regressive, meditative, trance, reverie, daydreaming, internal scanning, stupor, coma, expanded consciousness, and normal consciousness are all considered manifestations of consciousness. Some cultures celebrate these states and employ them regularly, either professionally or privately, to gain understanding of the world, cosmos, and mind that would not be accessible during alert waking consciousness. *See polyphasic cultures.*

Apostle comes from the Greek word *apostolos*, meaning one sent out to proclaim a message or one sent as an official representative of a person, movement, or organization. It comes to be applied to those who have some intimate knowledge of Jesus and are his followers—the twelve apostles of Jesus are chosen to disseminate the good news of Jesus. In the initial stages of the Jesus movement and later in Paul no distinction seems to have been made on the basis of gender; both men and women exercised the role of an apostle. Paul, in Romans 16, refers to Junia (a female) as an apostle entrusted with teaching, a possibility that disappears later. For the writer of 1 Timothy women must be submissive and not exercise the role of teacher in the church.

Balanced reciprocity is a type of exchange of goods and services in which both parties receive equal amounts. It is a fair exchange in which what one puts in is also what one receives. *See negative reciprocity, generalized reciprocity.*

Brokers are social entrepreneurs whose task it is to bring people together for the purpose of the exchange of goods and services between patrons and clients. They must be proficient at networking, experts at bringing people together, and willing to manipulate social relations for a profit. They must also have sufficient power and influence to effect exchanges between patrons and clients. A stockbroker, for example, stands between the financial world and the clients, providing expert advice, buying and selling, and negotiating contracts that stand to benefit the clients. *See patronage.*

Constructionism is a term used by sociologists to describe how ethnic groups construct their identity in relation to others. Observable cultural features such as language, dress, and food—"cultural stuff"—do not produce ethnic identity but rather are used by groups to describe themselves and thereby to differentiate and separate themselves from other groups in their immediate social environment. An ethnic identity is not natural, inherent, fixed, and unchangeable, but freely chosen, fluid, and changeable—continually constructed—in new contexts in relation to outsiders' views. It is self-imposed, and dramatic events such as migration, oppression, or persecution intensify such social boundary marking.

Emic is a term used by cultural anthropologists to refer to insiders' perspective and analysis of the behaviors, attitudes, values, and customs of the culture in which they participate. *See etic.*

Eschatology is a Greek term that means literally the study of "last things" or the study of the processes by which the end of current human existence will unfold itself. Eschatological is the adjective and is used to describe attitudes, beliefs, and patterns of behaving in the time before the end.

Ethno-symbolism refers to an ethnic group's longing for its past "golden age" that it captures through its myths of origins and election along with its capacity to endure and adapt to new exigencies.

Etic is a term used by cultural anthropologists to refer to the outsiders' perspective and analysis of the behaviors, attitudes, values, and customs of cultures in which they do not participate. *See emic.*

Exteroception relates to studies in altered states of consciousness and refers to the senses of touch, vision, hearing, taste, and smell that humans use to navigate their physical environments/worlds. *See interoception.*

First-order resources are such things as land, money, food, and protection, and are distributed by patrons in exchange for labor and honor.

First space is a term developed by Lefebvre; it refers to "perceived space" and includes material spatial practices such as agricultural production of peasants, taxation, and tithing to the elite who controlled production. A contrast is made between the material practices required for use in the household and the local community. Second space refers to conceived space or how space is represented through images and representations of spatiality. These include the thought processes and ideology that govern the material practices of First space. In Judean society this ideology finds its expression in Torah regulations and oral traditions that legitimize these material practices making them appear as if they are natural— again determined by the elite to keep people in their place according to class, race, and gender. Third space refers to the non-elites and how they conceived of lived space—it represents a critical perspective from the underground or the margins in protest against oppressive systems.

Gendered space refers to physical spaces, practices, texts, and conduct conceived of in different ways for men and women. They have been labeled as belonging to either the domain of the male or of the female: home versus work place; private versus public; etc. These categories always express power relationships between males and females, and in a patriarchal society are oppressive to women.

Generalized reciprocity is characterized by exchanges that are based on altruism—there is no desire to gain anything in return. It is sharing what one has with one's family and kinship group without thought of keeping an account of what one has given or received. There is no expectation of immediate repayment. *See balanced reciprocity; negative reciprocity.*

Gentile is a term of Latin origins (*gentilis*, of or belonging to a tribe) that comes to translate the New Testament Greek word *ethnē*—a word for "group." It could refer to almost any kind or size of collectivity, from swarms of bees and flocks of birds to bands of bandits, collections of males and females, trade associations, the inhabitants of a village, citizens of cities or regions, and migrants from a particular place. In Jewish literature it is used to refer to outsiders, that is, peoples with a non-Israelite heritage.

High context refers to societies that communicate in conversation and writing with the presumption that they share a well-defined and explicit set of truths, values, customs, practices, and attitudes. So, for example in the Gospels, long explanations detailing sowing seed into the ground would not be required. In North American society no explanation is needed when "Katrina" is mentioned in conversation or writing—it constitutes a common body of knowledge.

Honor is a social value that determines how people relate to each other in the areas of power, gender, status, and religion. It determines relationships between peasants and the elite, men and women, parents and children based on observing the other critically in the public sphere. Honor is the value that persons have in their own eyes confirmed by public evaluation. It is a claim of worth along with the social acknowledgement of that worth.

Instrumentalism refers to the process by which an ethnic group advances its socio-political interests through strategic and deliberate constructions of its identity that help to realize those interests. An example would be to stress one's minority status in order to gain benefits politically and economically from such status.

Interoception relates to discussions of altered states of consciousness and refers to the sensory receptors inside the body that monitor what is happening internally, such as pain, memory, identity, emotions, the unconscious sense of time and space. *See exteroception.*

Johannine is an adjective that refers specifically to the Gospel of John and its characteristic features and generally the other writings thought to be in its orbit, 1 John, 2 John, 3 John, and Revelation. These writings are seen by some to be the product of a Johannine school.

Josephus, Flavius Josephus (37–100 CE) is an important Jewish historian and apologist. Two of his most important works are the *Jewish War* (circa 75 CE), which recounts the Jewish revolt against Rome (66–70 CE), and *Antiquities of the Jews* (circa 94 CE), which recounts a history of the Jewish people and the world from their inception. The works are valuable in the information that they provide about the vicissitudes of first-century CE Judaism.

Landscape is an encompassing term that includes such things as perceptions that people have of time and place; time is understood in terms of the memories of a community that are attached to the place where the community or individuals within the community live. An example is "home." Home fits in a landscape as a meaningful space within which people reside. Landscape is not a neutral term devoid of disposition but incorporates expressions of a complex interaction among human ideas, social structures, and the physical features of the environment.

Law, the Law refers to the Deuteronomic code (Deuteronomy 12–26) and Pentateuch of the ancient Israelites in which were laid out the rules of conduct recognized by the Israelite community as binding and enforceable by authority. It addressed such matters as marriage, divorce, sexuality, matters of purity and impurity, feasts, festivals, holy days, worship, idolatry, loyalty to God, and many other matters of community decorum. *See Torah.*

Limited good is the view that all goods whether they be land, money, honor, protection, food, political influence, or economic clout were in short supply and in fixed quantities. In other words, if someone held an overabundance of food, someone else would be without it. A person's or family's gain came at the expense of others.

Lukan or Lucan is an adjective that refers specifically to the Gospel of Luke and its characteristic features and generally to the writings in the orbit of the author of Luke, and the Acts of the Apostles.

Markan or Marcan is an adjective that refers specifically to the Gospel of Mark and its characteristic features.

Material monism relates to the issue of defining exactly what an altered state of consciousness is and how it is produced. States of consciousness are produced by processes that are governed by bodies and nervous systems that are unique and which operate in accordance with certain physical laws and environments. Immense variation of experience is possible that is neither exclusively brain focused nor socially focused but part of the biopsychosocial existence of humans interacting with their world.

Matthean is an adjective that refers specifically to the Gospel of Matthew and its characteristic features.

Monophasic cultures are those that do not give credence to altered states of consciousness and as a result have few healthy altered states of consciousness as part of their repertoire. They derive their view of reality exclusively from the usual waking condition. Those who tend to have them are usually denigrated, especially if drugs are used to achieve an altered state of consciousness. *See polyphasic cultures.*

Negative reciprocity is characterized by a high amount of self-interest and the desire to obtain something for nothing from the other party in the give and take of acquiring goods and services. It is to take advantage of another through manipulation, coercion, or trickery. *See generalized reciprocity; balanced reciprocity.*

Neutron activation analysis refers to the process of determining, on the basis of the chemical content of clay, where pottery originated.

Paraclete is one of the functional names given to the Holy Spirit in the Gospel of John and means "one called alongside to help." As such it reminds the disciples of what Jesus has taught them, it testifies in behalf of Jesus, it furthers Jesus's work in the world concerning sin, righteousness, and judgment, and it guides the disciples in truth.

Pastoral Epistles are letters purportedly written by Paul of Tarsus to Timothy and Titus, two congregational leaders or pastors (Timothy and Titus). Authorship of these letters is contested: some argue for Pauline authorship but most find the letters coming from a later hand, as late as the early second century CE.

Patronage is a system of exchange for goods and services between people who are not social equals. It involves material support but also power, protection, and influence. Patrons promote their clients' interests and in turn clients offer praise for their patrons. Clients may also provide military service for their patrons. *See brokers.*

Patron–client interaction provides a structure in which various kinds of resources such as economic, political, and legal are provided in exchange for praise, loyalty, and other forms of honor-enhancing support.

Peasant refers to persons who work the land and whose surpluses are transferred to a group of elite who use the surpluses to support their own lifestyles and to distribute as they please. Peasants do not work the land to become wealthy but to feed themselves.

Philo, Philo of Alexandria (20–50 CE) was an Israelite philosopher who used the interpretive methods from Stoicism along with allegory (an emblematic way of illustrating meaning other than the literal) to synthesize Jewish history, belief, practice, and thought with Greek philosophy. In short, he wrote to make the Judaism of his day palatable to cultural detractors curious about its origins, ancestors, practices, and rituals. He wrote approximately forty short books—*On Sobriety, On Dreams, The Life of Moses, Questions and Answers On Genesis*—to name just a few.

Political economy refers to political leaders holding dominance over the economic activity of their subjects and personally benefitting from the control of economic activity often exerted through controlling land and production.

Polyphasic cultures are those that regularly activate and employ altered states of consciousness to interact with the world and the cosmos. They value and cultivate these states, honor those who master them, and derive much understanding from them about the mind, world, and cosmos. Altered states of consciousness are clearly defined, ritualized, and regulated—not everyone may legitimately use them. *See monophasic cultures.*

Primordialism is a theory that refines the notion of ethnicity and refers to members of ethnic groups having powerful, deep-seated feelings for each other, feelings that they believe are natural, sacred, and that have existed from the beginning. Language, land, family, custom, and religion serve to intensify these feelings and are culturally generated. Hence primordialism is also known as cultural primordialism. *See sociobiological primordialism.*

Pseudonymity, pseudonymous means literally "false name" but refers to the literary practice of attaching the name of a venerated person from the past to letters (or any other style of writing), a common practice in the ancient world. *See Pastoral Epistles.*

Q (from the German *Quelle* meaning source) is the designation for an early source thought to have been used by Matthew and Luke in the writing of their gospels.

Septuagint (LXX) refers to the translation of the Hebrew Scriptures into Greek around 285 BCE. Septuagint comes from a tradition recounted in the *Letter of Aristeas* that seventy-two Jewish scholars had produced it.

Sociobiological primordialism is an alternative to cultural primordialism and notes that humans tend to exhibit certain kinds of behavior—altruism, aggression, war, and criminality—and that these tend to run in families. Such traits are seen as biologically inherited because they contribute to humans adapting to the environment for their benefit. *See primordialism.*

Synoptic Gospels means literally to be "seen together with one eye" and refers to the Gospels of Matthew, Mark, and Luke. Because they relate so many of the same stories and sayings, they are placed side by side in parallel columns and viewed together as one.

Temple, the Temple refers to the large, ornate structure in Jerusalem in which worship, prayer, study of the Torah, and sacrifice took place. It served as the focal point of Jewish religious life until its destruction in 70 CE by the Romans.

Thesaurization is the process by which land owners and the aristocrats built treasure houses for accumulating goods such as grain, wine, or oil.

Torah is a term in Hebrew that means "learning" and "instruction" and is often translated as "law." It used to designate either the laws given to Moses on Mount Sinai or the Pentateuch, the five books of Moses thought to have been written by Moses. The Pentateuch includes Genesis, Exodus, Leviticus, Numbers, and Deuteronomy.

Bibliography

Aasgaard, R. (2004) *"My Beloved Brothers and Sisters!" Christian Siblingship in Paul*, London: T & T Clark International.

—— (2008) "Like a Child: Paul's Rhetorical Uses of Childhood," in M. J. Bunge (ed.) *The Child in the Bible*, Grand Rapids, MI: Eerdmans, pp. 249–77.

Alvarado, C. S. (2000) "Out-of-Body Experiences," in E. Cardeña, S. J. Lynn, and S. Krippner (eds) *Varieties of Anomalous Experience: Examining the Scientific Evidence*, Washington, DC: American Psychological Association.

American Anthropological Association Statement on Race (1998) May 17, http://www.aaanet.org/stmts/racepp.htm (accessed December 11, 2008).

Angier, N. (2000) "Do races differ? Not really, DNA shows," *New York Times* (August 22).

Armstrong, J. (1982) *Nations before Nationalism,* Chapel Hill, NC: University of North Carolina Press.

Ashton, J. (2000) *The Religion of Paul the Apostle*, New Haven, CT: Yale University Press.

Assmann, Jan (1992) *Das kulturelle Gedächtnis: Schrift, Erinnerung und politische Identität in frühen Hochkulturen*, Munich: Beck.

—— (2006) *Religion and Cultural Memory: Ten Studies,* trans. Rodney Livingstone, Stanford, CA: Stanford University Press.

Augsburger, David W. (1986) *Pastoral Counseling Across Cultures*, Philadelphia: Westminster Press.

Aune, David E. (1987) *The New Testament in its Literary Environment*, Philadelphia: Westminster Press.

Austin, J. H. (1998) *Zen and the Brain: Towards an Understanding of Meditation and Consciousness*, Cambridge, MA: MIT Press.

Balch D. L. (1981) *Let Wives be Submissive: The Domestic Code in 1 Peter*, SBLMS 26, Chico, CA: Scholars.

—— (1992) "Neopythagorean Moralists and the New Testament Household Codes," in *ANRW*, II 26.1, pp. 389–404.

Barrett, J. L. (2007) "Cognitive Science of Religion," *Religion Compass*, 1: 1–19.

Bartchy, Scott. S. (1999) "Undermining Ancient Patriarchy: Paul's Vision of a Society of Siblings," *BTB*, 29: 68–78.

—— (2008) "Who should be Called 'Father'? Paul of Tarsus between the Jesus Tradition and *Patriae Potestas*," in J. H. Neyrey and E. C. Stewart (eds) *The Social World of the New Testament: Insights and Models*, Peabody, MA: Hendrickson, pp. 165–80.

Barth, F. (1969) *Ethnic Groups and Boundaries: The Social Organization of Cultural Difference*, Boston: Little, Brown. Reprinted 1998.

—— (1994) "Enduring and Emerging Issues in the Analysis of Ethnicity," in H. Vermeulen and C. Govers (eds) *The Anthropology of Ethnicity: Beyond "Ethnic Groups and Boundaries,"* Amsterdam: Het Spinhuis, pp. 11–32.

Bartlett, F. C. (1932) *Remembering: A Study in Experimental and Social Psychology*, London: Cambridge University Press. Reprinted 1995, Cambridge: Cambridge University Press.

Barton, Carlin A. (2001) *Roman Honor: The Fire in the Bones*, Berkeley, CA: University of California Press.

—— (2002) "Being in the Eyes: Shame and Sight in Ancient Rome," in David Frederick (ed.) *The Roman Gaze: Vision, Power, and the Body*, Baltimore: Johns Hopkins University Press.

Bassler, Jouette M. (1982) *Divine Impartiality: Paul and a Theological Axiom*, SBLDS 59, Chico, CA: Scholars Press.

—— (1996) *1 Timothy, 2 Timothy, Titus*, Nashville: Abingdon Press.

Batten, Alicia (2004) "God in the Letter of James: Patron or Benefactor?" *NTS*, 50: 257–72.

Baxter, A. G., and J. A. Ziesler (1985) "Paul and Arboriculture: Romans 11.17–24," *JSNT*, 24: 25–32.

Beals, R. L., and H. Hoijer (1965) *An Introduction to Anthropology*, New York: Macmillan.

Beasley-Murray, G. R. (1962) *Baptism in the New Testament*, London: Macmillan.

Bedford, P. R. (2005) "The Economy of the Near East in the First Millennium BC," in J. G. Manning and I. Morris (eds) *The Ancient Economy: Evidence and Models*, Stanford: Stanford University Press.

Beg, Muhammad Abdul Jabbār (1977) "The Status of Brokers in Middle Eastern Society in the Pre-Modern Period," *The Muslim World*, 67: 87–90.

Bell, C. (1992) *Ritual Theory, Ritual Practice*, Oxford: Oxford University Press.

—— (1997) *Ritual: Perspectives and Dimensions*, Oxford: Oxford University Press.

—— (2005) "Ritual (Further Considerations)," in L. Jones (ed.) *Encyclopedia of Religion*, 2nd edn, Detroit: Macmillan.

Bentall, R. P. (2000) "Hallucinatory Experiences," in E. Cardeña, S. J. Lynn, and S. Krippner (eds) *Varieties of Anomalous Experience: Examining the Scientific Evidence*, Washington, DC: American Psychological Association.

Blackmore, S. (2005a) *Consciousness: A Very Short Introduction*, Oxford: Oxford University Press.

—— (2005b) "Out-of-Body Experiences," in J. Henry (ed.) *Parapsychology: Research on Exceptional Experiences*, London: Routledge.

Blasi, A., J. Duhaime, and P. A. Turcotte (eds) (2002) *Handbook of Early Christianity: Social Science Approaches*, Walnut Creek, CA: AltaMira.

Boissevain, Jeremy (1974) *Friends of Friends: Networks, Manipulators and Coalitions,* Oxford: Basil Blackwell.

Bonanno, George (1990) "Remembering and Psychotherapy," *Psychotherapy,* 27: 175–86.

Bookidis, Nancy (2005) "Religion in Corinth: 146 B.C.E. – 100 C.E.," in D. Schowalter and S. J. Friesen (eds) *Urban Religion in Roman Corinth: Interdisciplinary Approaches,* Cambridge, MA: Harvard University Press, pp. 141–64.

Bornkamm, G. (1991) "The Letter to the Romans as Paul's Last Will and Testament," in K. P. Donfried (ed.) *The Romans Debate,* Peabody, MA: Hendrickson, pp. 16–28. Reprinted in *ABR,* (1963) 11: 2–14.

Bourdieu, P. (1977) *Outline of a Theory of Practice,* trans. R. Nice, Cambridge: Cambridge University Press.

Bourguignon, E. (1979) *Psychological Anthropology: An Introduction to Human Nature and Cultural Differences,* New York: Holt, Rinehart and Winston.

Bowditch, P. L. (2001) *Horace and the Gift Economy of Patronage,* Berkeley, CA: University of California Press.

Boyer, P. (2002) *Religion Explained: The Human Instincts that Fashion Gods, Spirits and Ancestors,* London: Vintage.

—— and P. Liénard (2006) "Why Ritualized Behavior? Precaution Systems and Action Parsing in Developmental, Pathological and Cultural Rituals," *Behavioral and Brain Sciences,* 29, no. 6: 595–650.

Bradshaw, P. F. (2002) *The Search for the Origins of Christian Worship: Sources and Methods for the Study of Early Liturgy,* 2nd edn, London: SPCK.

—— (2004) *Eucharistic Origins,* Oxford: Oxford University Press.

—— and J. Melloch (eds) (2007) *Foundations in Ritual Studies: A Reader for Students of Christian Worship,* Grand Rapids, MI: Baker.

Braund, D. (1989) "Function and Dysfunction: Personal Patronage in Roman Imperialism," in A. Wallace-Hadrill (ed.) *Patronage in Ancient Society,* London: Routledge, pp. 37–52.

Brenenbaum, H., J. Kerns, and C. Raghaven (2000) "Anomalous Experiences, Peculiarity, and Psychopathology," in E. Cardeña, S. J. Lynn, and S. Krippner (eds) *Varieties of Anomalous Experience: Examining the Scientific Evidence,* Washington, DC: American Psychological Association.

Brett, M. G. (ed.) (1998) *Ethnicity and the Bible,* Biblical Interpretation Series 19, Leiden: Brill.

Brown, Peter (1982) *Society and the Holy in Late Antiquity,* Berkeley, CA: University of California Press.

Brown, R. E. (1982) "The Roman Church Near the End of the First Christian Generation (A.D. 58 – Paul to the Romans)," in R. E. Brown and J. P. Meier, *Antioch and Rome: New Testament Cradles of Catholic Christianity,* New York: Paulist Press, pp. 105–27.

Brown, Tricia Gates (2003) *Spirit in the Writings of John: Johannine Pneumatology in Social-Scientific Perspective,* JSNTSup 253, London, New York: T & T Clark.

Bruce, F. F. (1976) *Commentary on the Book of Acts,* Grand Rapids, MI: Eerdmans.

—— (1991) "The Romans Debate—Continued," in K. P. Donfried (ed.) *The Romans Debate,* Peabody, MA: Hendrickson, pp. 175–94; reprinted in *BJRL* (1981–1982) 64: 334–59.

Bruner, Frederick Dale (2004) *Matthew: A Commentary*, Volume 1, *The Christbook: Matthew 1–12*, rev. edn, Grand Rapids, MI: Eerdmans.

Bruner, Jerome, and Carol Fleisher Feldman (1996) "Group Narrative as a Cultural Context of Autobiography," in David C. Rubin (ed.) *Remembering Our Past: Studies in Autobiographical Memory*, Cambridge: Cambridge University Press, pp. 291–317.

Buell, D. K., (2000) "Ethnicity and Religion in Mediterranean Antiquity and Beyond," *RelSRev,* 26: 243–9.

—— (2005) *Why This New Race? Ethnic Reasoning in Early Christianity,* New York: Columbia University Press.

—— and C. Johnson Hodge (2004) "The Politics of Interpretation: The Rhetoric of Race and Ethnicity in Paul," *JBL*, 123: 235–51.

Bulbulia, J. (2007) "Evolution of Religion" in L. Barrett and R. Dunbar (eds) *Oxford Handbook of Evolutionary Psychology*, Oxford: Oxford University Press.

Butlin, R. A. (1993) *Historical Geography Through the Gates of Space and Time*, London: Arnold.

Campbell, John K. (1964) *Honour, Family and Patronage*, Oxford: Oxford University Press.

Cardeña, E., S. J. Lynn, and S. Krippner (2000) "Introduction: Anomalous Experiences in Perspective," in E. Cardeña, S. J. Lynn, and S. Krippner (eds) *Varieties of Anomalous Experience: Examining the Scientific Evidence*, Washington, DC: American Psychological Association.

Carney, Thomas F. (1975) *The Shape of the Past: Models and Antiquity*, Lawrence, KS: Coronado.

Carruthers, Mary (1990) *The Book of Memory: A Study of Memory in Medieval Culture*, Cambridge: Cambridge University Press.

Carter, R. (2002) *Exploring Consciousness*, Berkeley, CA: University of California Press.

Carter, W. (2001) *Matthew and Empire: Initial Explorations,* Harrisburg, PA: Trinity Press International.

Casey, Edward S. (1987) *Remembering: A Phenomenological Study*, Bloomington, IN: Indiana University Press.

—— (1993) *Getting Back into Place: Toward a Renewed Understanding of the Placeworld*, Bloomington, IN: Indiana University Press.

Chance, J. Bradley (2007) *The Acts of the Apostles*, Smyth & Helwys Bible Commentary 23, Macon, GA: Smyth & Helwys.

Chandra Shekar, C. R. (1989) "Possession Syndrome in India," in C. A. Ward (ed.) *Altered States of Consciousness and Mental Health: A Cross-Cultural Perspective*, London: Sage.

Chow, J. K. (1992) *Patronage in Corinth: A Study of Social Networks in Corinth*, JSNTSup 75, Sheffield: JSOT Press.

Clarke, Andrew D. (1993) *Secular and Christian Leadership in Corinth: A Sociohistorical and Exegetical Study of 1 Corinthians 1–6*, Leiden: Brill.

Cohen, S. J. D. (1999) *The Beginnings of Jewishness: Boundaries, Varieties, Uncertainties,* Berkeley, CA: University of California Press.

Collins, J. J. (1986) *Between Athens and Jerusalem: Jewish Identity in the Hellenistic Diaspora*, New York: Crossroad.

Collins, Raymond F. (1999) *First Corinthians*, Collegeville, MN: Liturgical Press.

Connerton, Paul (1989) *How Societies Remember*, Cambridge: Cambridge University Press.

Conzelmann, Hans (1987) *Acts of the Apostles*, Philadelphia: Fortress.

Craffert, P. F. (2008) *The Life of a Galilean Shaman: Jesus of Nazareth in Anthropological-Historical Perspective*, Eugene, OR: Cascade.

Cranford, M. (1993) "Election and Ethnicity: Paul's View of Israel in Romans 9.1–13," *JSNT*, 50: 27–41.

—— (1995) "Abraham in Romans 4: The Father of All Who Believe," *NTS*, 41: 71–88.

Crapanzano, V. (2001) "The Etiquette of Consciousness," *Social Research*, 68, no. 3: 627–49.

Crook, Zeba A. (2004a) *Reconceptualising Patronage: Patronage, Loyalty, and Conversion in the Religions of the Ancient Mediterranean*, BZNW 130, Berlin: De Gruyter.

—— (2004b) "BTB Readers Guide: Loyalty," in *BTB*, 34: 167–77.

—— (2007) "Constructing a Model of Ancient Prayer," in A. C. Hagedorn, Zeba A. Crook, and E. Stewart (eds) *In Other Words: Essays on Social Science Methods and New Testament in Honor of Jerome H. Neyrey, S. J.*, Sheffield: Sheffield Phoenix, pp. 48–66.

—— (2008) "Grace as Benefaction in Galatians 2:9, 1 Corinthians 3:10, and Romans 12:3; 15:15," in D. Neufeld (ed.) *The Social Sciences and Biblical Translation*, SBLSymS 41, Atlanta: Scholars Press, pp. 25–38.

Crossan, John Dominic (1991) *The Historical Jesus: The Life of a Mediterranean Jewish Peasant*, San Francisco: Harper.

—— (1994) *Jesus: A Revolutionary Biography*, San Francisco: Harper.

Czachesz, I. (2008) "Magic and Mind: Toward a Cognitive Theory of Magic, with Special Attention to the Canonical and Apocryphal Acts of the Apostles," *Annali di storia dell' esegesi*, 24, no. 1: 295–321.

—— (2009) "Explaining Magic: Earliest Christianity as a Test Case," in L. H. Martin and J. Sørensen (eds) *Past Minds: Studies in Cognitive Historiography*, London: Equinox.

—— (forthcoming) "Rituals and Memory in Early Christianity," in A. W. Geertz and J. Sørensen (eds) *Religious Ritual, Cognition and Culture*, London: Equinox.

Damon, C. (1997) *The Mask of the Parasite: A Pathology of Roman Patronage*, Ann Arbor, MI: University of Michigan Press.

D'Angelo, Mary Rose (2003) "'Knowing How to Preside over His Own Household': Imperial Masculinity and Christian Asceticism in the Pastorals, *Hermas*, and Luke-Acts," in Stephen D. Moore and Janice Capel Anderson (eds) *New Testament Masculinities*, Atlanta: Society of Biblical Literature, pp. 265–96.

Danker, Frederick W. (1982) *Benefaction: Epigraphic Study of a Graeco-Roman and New Testament Semantic Field*, St Louis: Clayton.

Davies, John K. (1987) "Family and State in the Mediterranean," in D. Gilmore (ed.) *Honor and Shame and the Unity of the Mediterranean*, Special Publication of the American Anthropological Association 22, Washington, DC: American Anthropological Association.

—— (2005) "Linear and Nonlinear Flow Models for Ancient Economies" in J. G. Manning and I. Morris (eds) *The Ancient Economy: Evidence and Models*, Stanford, CA: Stanford University Press.

—— (2008) "Hellenistic Economies," in G. R. Bugh (ed.) *The Cambridge Companion to the Hellenistic World*, Cambridge: Cambridge University Press.

Davies, S. L. (1995) *Jesus the Healer: Possession, Trance, and the Origins of Christianity*, London: SCM.

Davies, W. D. (1974) *The Gospel and the Land*, Berkeley, CA: California University Press.

—— (1984) "Paul and the Gentiles: A Suggestion Concerning Romans 11:13–24," in W. D. Davies (ed.) *Jewish and Pauline Studies*, Philadelphia: Fortress Press.

De Ste Croix, G. E. M. (1981) *The Class Struggle in the Ancient Greek World*, Ithaca, NY: Cornell University.

Deacon, Terrence W. (1997) *The Symbolic Species: The Co-Evolution of Language and the Brain*, New York: Norton.

Delany, Carol (1987) "Seeds of Honor, Fields of Shame," in D. Gilmore (ed.) *Honor and Shame and the Unity of the Mediterranean*, Special Publication of the American Anthropological Association 22, Washington, DC: American Anthropological Association.

DeLoache, Judy S. (2004) "Becoming Symbol-Minded," *Trends in Cognitive Sciences*, 8: 66–70.

DeMaris, R. E. (2002) "The Baptism of Jesus: A Ritual-Critical Approach," in Wolfgang Stegemann, Bruce J. Malina, and Gerd Theissen (eds) *The Social Setting of Jesus and the Gospels*, Minneapolis: Fortress, pp. 137–57.

—— (2008) *The New Testament in Its Ritual World*, London: Routledge.

Denzey, N. (2002) "The Limits of Ethnic Categories," in A. J. Blasi, J. Duhaime, and P. A. Turcotte (eds) *Handbook of Early Christianity*, Walnut Creek, CA: Altamira Press, pp. 489–507.

Dibelius, M. (1956) *Studies in the Acts of the Apostles*, London: SCM.

Dixon, Suzanne (1988) *The Roman Mother*, Norman, OK: University of Oklahoma Press.

Donald, Merlin (2001) *A Mind So Rare: The Evolution of Human Consciousness*, New York: Norton.

Donfried, K. P. (1991a) "A Short Note on Romans 16," in K. P. Donfried (ed.) *The Romans Debate*, Peabody, MA: Hendrickson, pp. 44–52. Reprint of *JBL*, (1970) 89: 441–9.

—— (1991b) "False Presuppositions in the Study of Romans," in K. P. Donfried (ed.) *The Romans Debate*, Peabody, MA: Hendrickson, pp. 102–25. Reprint of *CBQ*, (1974) 36: 332–58.

Douglas, M. (1970) *Natural Symbols: Explorations in Cosmology*, London: Barrie & Jenkins.

—— (2007 [1966]) *Purity and Danger: An Analysis of the Concepts of Pollution and Taboo*, London: Ark.

Draper, J. A. (2000) "Ritual Process and Ritual Symbol in Didache 7–10," *VC*, 54: 121–58.

Drummond, A. (1989) "Early Roman Clientes," in A. Wallace-Hadrill (ed.) *Patronage in Ancient Society*, London: Routledge, pp. 89–115.

Duby, Georges (1988) "The Emergence of the Individual," in Georges Duby (ed.) *A History of Private Life: II. Revelations of the Medieval World*, trans. Arthur Goldhammer, Cambridge, MA: Belknap Press, pp. 507–630.

Dulaney, S., and A. P. Fiske (1994) "Cultural Rituals and Obsessive-Compulsive Disorder: Is There a Common Psychological Mechanism?" *Ethos*, 22, no. 3: 243–83.

Duling, D. C. (1992) "Matthew's Son of David in Social-Scientific Perspective: Kinship, Kingship, Magic, and Miracle," *BTB*, 22: 99–116.

—— (1995) "The Matthean Brotherhood and Marginal Scribal Leadership," in Philip Esler (ed.) *Modelling Early Christianity: Social-Scientific Studies of the New Testament in its Context*, London: Routledge, pp. 159–82.

—— (2003a) *The New Testament: History, Literature, and Social Context*, 4th edn, Belmont, CA: Thomson/Wadsworth.

—— (2003b=2008a) "'Whatever Gain I Had …': Ethnicity and Paul's Self-Identification in Phil. 3:5–6, " in D. B. Gowler, G. Bloomquist, and D. F. Watson (eds) *Fabrics of Discourse: Essays in Honor of Vernon K. Robbins,* Harrisburg, PA: Trinity Press International, pp. 222–41. Reprinted in *HvTSt*, (2008) 64, no. 2: 799–818.

—— (2005a) "Empire: Theories, Methods, Models," in John Riches and David C. Sim (eds) *The Gospel of Matthew in its Roman Imperial Context*, London: T & T Clark International, pp. 49–74.

—— (2005b) "Ethnicity, Ethnocentrism, and the Matthean *Ethnos*," *BTB*, 35: 125–43. Also online: http://academic.shu.edu/btb/vol35/4/04%20Duling.pdf.

—— (2006=2008b) "2 *Corinthians 11:22: Historical Context, Rhetoric, and Ethnic Identity,*" in John Fotopoulos (ed.) *The New Testament and Early Christian Literature in Greco-Roman Context: Studies in Honor of David E. Aune,* Supplements to *Novum Testamentum*, Leiden: Brill. Reprinted (2008) *HTS*, 64, no. 2: 819–43.

Dunn, J. D. G. (1996) *The Epistles to the Colossians and to Philemon: A Commentary on the Greek Text*, NIGTC, Grand Rapids, MI: Eerdmans.

Durkheim, É. (2001) *The Elementary Forms of Religious Life*, trans. C. Cosman, Oxford World's Classics, Oxford: Oxford University Press. French original 1912.

Edwards, D. R. (1992) "The Socio-Economic and Cultural Ethos of the Lower Galilee in the First Century: Implications for the Nascent Jesus Movement," in L. I. Levine (ed.) *The Galilee in Late Antiquity*, New York: Jewish Theological Seminary of America.

Ehrsson, H. H. (2007) "The Experimental Induction of Out-of-Body Experiences," *Science*, 317 (24 August): 1048.

Eilers, C. (2002) *Roman Patrons of Greek Cities*, Oxford: Oxford University Press.

Eisenbaum, P. (2000) "Paul as the New Abraham," in R. A. Horsley (ed.) *Paul and Politics: Essays in Honor of Krister Stendahl*, Harrisburg, PA: Trinity International Press, pp. 130–45.

Eisenstadt, S. N., and Louis Roniger (1980) "Patron–Client Relations as a Model of Structuring Social Exchange," *Comparative Studies in Society and History*, 22: 42–77.

—— (1984) *Patrons, Clients, and Friends: Interpersonal Relations and the Structure of Trust in Society*, Cambridge: Cambridge University Press.

Eliade, Mircea (1959) *The Sacred and the Profane*, New York: Harper and Row.

Elliott, John H. (2004) "No Kingdom of God for Softies? or, What Was Paul Really Saying? 1 Corinthians 6:9–10 in Context," *BTB*, 34: 17–40.

—— (2007) "Jesus the Israelite was neither a 'Jew' nor a 'Christian': On Correcting Misleading Nomenclature," *Journal for the Study of the Historical Jesus*, 5, no. 2: 119–55.

Esler, P. F. (ed.) (1995) *Modelling Early Christianity: Social Scientific Studies of the New Testament in Its Context*, London: Routledge.

—— (1998) *Galatians*, New Testament Readings, London: Routledge.

—— (ed.) (2000) *The Early Christian World*, London: Routledge.

—— (2003a) *Conflict and Identity in Romans: The Social Setting of Paul's Letter,* Minneapolis, MN: Fortress Press.

—— (2003b) "Ancient Oleiculture and Ethnic Differentiation: The Meaning of the Olive-Tree Image in Romans 11," *JSNT*, 26, no. 1: 103–24.

—— (2006) "Paul's Contestation of Israel's (Ethnic) Memory of Abraham in Galatians 3," *BTB*, 36: 23–34.

Fabrega, Horacio (1974) *Disease and Social Behavior: An Interdisciplinary Perspective*, Cambridge, MA: MIT Press.

Farmer, Sarah Bennett (1999) *Martyred Village: Commemorating the 1944 Massacre at Oradour sur Glane*, Berkeley, CA: University of California Press.

Fentress, James, and Chris Wickham (1992) *Social Memory*, Oxford: Blackwell.

Fiensy, David A. (1991) *The Social History of Palestine in the Herodian Period: The Land Is Mine,* Lewiston, NY: Edwin Mellen Press.

—— (1997) "Jesus' Socioeconomic Background," in J. H. Charlesworth and L. Johns (eds) *Hillel and Jesus*, Minneapolis: Fortress.

—— (2002) "Jesus and Debts: Did He Pray About Them?" *ResQ*, 44: 233–9.

—— (2007) *Jesus the Galilean: Soundings in a First Century Life,* Piscataway, NJ: Gorgias Press.

Finley, M. I. (1973) *The Ancient Economy*, Berkeley, CA: University of California Press.

Fischer, R. (1971) "A Cartography of the Ecstatic and Meditative States," *Science*, 174 (4012) 26 November: 52–60.

Fisher, N. R. E. (1992) *Hybris: A Study in the Values of Honor and Shame in Ancient Greece*, Warminster: Aris and Phillips.

Fiske, A. P., and N. Haslam (1997) "Is Obsessive Compulsive Disorder a Pathology of the Human Disposition to Perform Socially Meaningful Rituals? Evidence of Similar Content," *Journal of Mental Disease*, 185, no. 4: 211–22.

Foerster, W. (1964) "*Exousia*," *TDNT* 2: 562–75.

Forbes, C. (1986) "Comparison, Self-Praise, and Irony: Paul's Boasting and the Conventions of Hellenistic Rhetoric," *NTS*, 32: 1–30.

Foster, George M. (1965) "Peasant Society and the Image of Limited Good," *AQ*, 67: 293–315.

—— (1972) "A Second Look at Limited Good," *AQ* 45: 57–64.

Foucault, M. (1980) *Power/Knowledge: Selected Interviews and other Writings 1972–1977*, ed. Colin Gordon, Brighton: Harvester.

Frankemölle, H. (1970) *Das Taufverständnis des Paulus: Taufe, Tod und Auferstehung nach Röm 6*, SBS 47, Stuttgart: Verlag Katholisches Bibelwerk.

Freidson, Eliot (1970) *The Profession of Medicine: A Study of the Sociology of Applied Knowledge*, New York: Harper & Row.

Freud, S. (1963) "Obsessive Acts and Religious Practices," in P. Rieff (ed.) *Character and Culture*, New York: Collier.

Freyne, S. (1980) *Galilee from Alexander the Great to Hadrian, 323 B.C.E. to 135 C.E.*, Wilmington, DE: Glazier.

—— (1995) "Jesus and the Urban Culture of Galilee," in T. Fornberg and D. Hellholm (eds) *Texts and Contexts: Biblical Texts and their Textual and Situational Contexts*, Oslo: Scandinavian University Press, pp. 596–622.

—— (2004) *Jesus a Jewish Galilean*, New York: Continuum.

Gamble, H., Jr. (1977) *The Textual History of the Letter to the Romans*, Studies and Documents 42, Grand Rapids, MI: Eerdmans.

Garnsey, Peter, and G. Woolf (1989) "Patronage of the Rural Poor in the Roman World," in A. Wallace-Hadrill (ed.) *Patronage in Ancient Society*, London: Routledge, pp. 153–70.

Geary, P. J. (1999) "Barbarians and Ethnicity," in G. W. Bowersock, P. Brown, and O. Grabar (eds) *Late Antiquity: A Guide to the Postclassical World*, Cambridge, MA: Harvard University Press, pp. 107–29.

Geertz, C. (1963) "The Integrative Revolution," in C. Geertz (ed.) *Old Societies and New States*, New York: Free Press, pp. 108–13.

—— (1973) *Interpretation of Cultures: Selected Essays by C. Geertz*, London: Hutchinson.

—— (1976) "'From the Native's Point of View': On the Nature of Anthropological Understanding," in Keith H. Basso and Henry A. Selby (eds) *Meaning and Anthropology*, Albuquerque, NM: University of New Mexico Press, pp. 221–37.

Gellner, E. (2006) *Nations and Nationalism*, 2nd edn, Oxford: Blackwell.

Gilmore, David D. (ed.) (1987) *Honor and Shame and the Unity of the Mediterranean*, Special Publication of the American Anthropological Association 22, Washington, DC: American Anthropological Association.

Glancy, Jennifer A. (2002) *Slavery in Early Christianity*, Oxford: Oxford University Press.

—— (2003) "Protocols of Masculinity in the Pastoral Epistles," in Stephen D. Moore and Janice Capel Anderson (eds) *New Testament Masculinities*, Atlanta: Society of Biblical Literature, pp. 235–64.

Gray, J. (2003) "Iconic Images: Landscape and History in the Local Poetry of the Scottish Borders," in J. P. Stewart and A. Strathern (eds) *Landscape, Memory and History: Anthropological Perspectives*, London: Pluto Press, pp. 16–46.

Gray, M. (2001) "The Pilgrimage as Ritual Space," in A. T. Smith and A. Brookes (eds) *Holy Ground: Theoretical Issues Relating to the Landscape and Material*

Culture of Ritual Space, British Archaeological Reports International Series 956, Oxford: Archeopress, pp. 91–7.

Green, J. B. (1995) *The Theology of the Gospel of Luke*, Cambridge, Cambridge University Press.

Green, John T. (1989) *The Role of the Messenger and Message in the Ancient Near East*, BJS 169, Atlanta: Scholars.

Greyson, B. (2000) "Near-Death Experiences," in E. Cardeña, S. J. Lynn, and S. Krippner (eds) *Varieties of Anomalous Experience: Examining the Scientific Evidence*, Washington, DC: American Psychological Association.

Grimes, R. L. (1985) *Research in Ritual Studies: A Programmatic Essay and Bibliography*, ATLA Bibliography Series 14, Metuchen, NJ: ATLA and Scarecrow Press.

—— (1990) *Ritual Criticism: Case Studies in Its Practice, Essays on Its Theory*, Columbia, SC: University of South Carolina Press.

—— (1995) *Beginnings in Ritual Studies*, rev. edn, Columbia, SC: University of South Carolina Press.

Guijarro, S. (1997) "The Family in First-Century Galilee," in H. Moxnes (ed.) *Constructing Early Christian Families: Family as Social Reality and Metaphor*, London: Routledge, pp. 42–64.

Gundry-Volf, J. M. (2001) "The Least and the Greatest: Children in the New Testament," in M. J. Bunge (ed.) *The Child in Christian Thought*, Grand Rapids, MI: Eerdmans, pp. 29–60.

Haenchen, Ernst (1971) *The Acts of the Apostles: A Commentary*, trans. B. Noble and G. Shinn, Oxford: Basil Blackwell.

Halbwachs, Maurice (1980) *The Collective Memory*, trans. Francis J. Ditter and Vida Yazdi Ditter, New York: Harper & Row.

—— (1992) *On Collective Memory*, ed. and trans. Lewis A. Coser, Chicago: University of Chicago Press.

Hall, J. M. (1997) *Ethnic Identity in Greek Antiquity*, Cambridge: Cambridge University Press.

Hall, R. G. (1988) "Epispasm and the Dating of Ancient Jewish Writings," *JSP*, 2: 1–86.

Halperin, David M. (2002) "The First Homosexuality?" in Martha C. Nussbaum and Juha Sihvola (eds) *The Sleep of Reason: Erotic Experience and Sexual Ethics in Ancient Greece and Rome*, Chicago: University of Chicago Press, pp. 226–68.

Hamilton, M. (1995) "Who Was a Jew? Jewish Ethnicity During the Achaemenid Period," *ResQ*, 37/2. http://www.acu.edu/sponsored/restoration_quarterly/archives/1990s/vol_37_no_2_contents/hamilton.html (accessed 12/11/08).

Hanson, K. C., (1996) "'How Honorable! How Shameful!' A Cultural Analysis of Matthew's Makarisms and Reproaches," *Semeia*, 68: 81–111.

—— and Douglas E. Oakman (1998) *Palestine in the Time of Jesus: Social Structures and Social Conflicts*, 1st edn, Minneapolis: Fortress.

—— and Douglas E. Oakman (2008) *Palestine in the Time of Jesus: Social Structures and Social Conflicts*, 2nd edn, Minneapolis: Fortress.

Harmon, A. (2007) "In DNA Era, New Worries About Prejudice," *New York Times* (Nov. 11).

Harrill, J. A. (2006) *Slaves in the New Testament: Literary, Social, and Moral Dimensions*, Minneapolis: Fortress.

Harrington, Hannah K. (2001) *Holiness—Rabbinic Judaism and the Graeco-Roman World*, London: Routledge.

Hartman, L. (1997) '*Into the Name of the Lord': Baptism in the Early Church*, Studies of the New Testament and Its World, Edinburgh: T & T Clark.

Harvey, D. (1989) *The Condition of Postmodernity*, Oxford: Blackwell.

Hays, Richard (2004) "Paul on the Relations Between Men and Women," in Amy-Jill Levine and Marianne Blickenstaff (eds) *A Feminist Companion to Paul*, Cleveland, OH: Pilgrim Press, pp. 137–47.

Heers, Jacques (1977) *Family Clans in the Middle Ages: A Study of Political and Social Structure in Urban Areas*, trans. B. Herbert, Amsterdam: North-Holland.

Heidebrecht, Doug (2004) "Reading 1 Timothy 2:9–15 in its Literary Context," *Direction*, 33, no. 2: 171–84.

Hemelrijk, Emily A. (1999) *Matrona Docta: Educated Women in the Roman Elite from Cornelia to Julia Domna*, New York: Routledge.

Hengel, M. (1968) "Das Gleichnis von den Weingärtnern Mc 12:1–12 im Licht der Zenonpapyri und der rabbinischen Gleichnisse," *ZNW*, 59: 1–39.

Herz, J. (1928) "Grossgrundbesitz in Palästina im Zeitalter Jesu," *PJ*, 24: 98–113.

Hitchner, R. B. (2005) "The Advantages of Wealth and Luxury: The Case for Economic Growth in the Roman Empire," in J. G. Manning and I. Morris (eds) *The Ancient Economy: Evidence and Models*, Stanford, CA: Stanford University Press.

Hobson, J. A. (2007) "States of Consciousness: Normal and Abnormal Variation," in P. D. Zelazo, M. Moscovitch, and E. Thompson (eds), *The Cambridge Handbook of Consciousness*, Cambridge: Cambridge University Press.

Holland, G. S. (1993) "Speaking Like a Fool: Irony in 2 Corinthians 10–13," in *Rhetoric and the New Testament: Essays from the 1992 Heidelberg Conference*, JSNTSup 90: Sheffield: JSOT Press, pp. 250–64.

Hollenbach, Paul W. (1982) "Jesus, Demoniacs, and Public Authorities: A Socio-Historical Study," *JAAR*, 49: 567–88.

Hollinger, D. A. (2003) "Amalgamation and Hypodescent: The Question of Ethnoracial Mixture in the History of the United States," *AHR*, 108, no. 5: 1363–90.

"Honor" (1968–79) in D. Sills (ed.) *International Encyclopedia of the Social Sciences*, 18 vols, New York: Free Press, vol. 6, pp. 503–11.

Hood, R. T. (1961), "The Genealogies of Jesus," in A. Wikgren (ed.) *Early Christian Origins: Studies in Honor of H. R. Willoughby*, Chicago: Quadrangle Books, pp. 1–15.

Horowitz, D. (1985) *Ethnic Groups in Conflict*, Berkeley, CA: University of California Press.

Horrell, David G. (2004) "Domestic Space and Christian Meetings at Corinth: Imagining New Contexts and the Buildings East of the Theatre," *NTS*, 50: 349–69.

Horsley, Richard A. (1996) *Archaeology, History, and Society in Galilee: The Social Context of Jesus and the Rabbis*, Valley Forge, PA: Trinity Press.

Hurford, James R. (1998) Review of Terrence Deacon, "The Symbolic Species: The Co-Evolution of Language and the Brain," *Times Literary Supplement*, October 23: 34.

Hutchinson, J., and A. D. Smith (1996) *Ethnicity*, Oxford Reader, Oxford: Oxford University Press.

Huxley, A. (1972) "Visionary Experiences," in J. White (ed.) *The Highest State of Consciousness*, New York: Anchor Books.

Huxley, J., and A. C. Haddon (1935) *We Europeans: A Survey of "Racial" Problems, With a Chapter on Europe Overseas*, London: Jonathan Cape.

Irons, W. (2001) "Religion as Hard-To-Fake Sign of Commitment," in R. Nesse (ed.) *Evolution and the Capacity for Commitment*, New York: Russell Sage Foundation.

Isaac, B. (2004) *The Invention of Racism in Classical Antiquity*, Princeton, NJ: Princeton University Press.

Ivarsson, Fredrik (2007) "Vice Lists and Deviant Masculinity: The Rhetorical Function of 1 Corinthians 5:10–11 and 6:9–10" in Todd Penner and Caroline Vander Stichele (eds) *Mapping Gender in Ancient Religious Discourses*, Leiden: Brill.

James, W. ([1902] 1994) *The Varieties of Religious Experience*, New York: Modern Library.

Jenkins, R. (1994) "Rethinking Ethnicity: Identity, Categorization and Power," *Ethnic and Racial Studies*, 17: 197–223.

—— (1996) "Ethnicity Etcetera: Social Anthropological Points of View," *Ethnic and Racial Studies*, 19: 807–22.

—— (1997) *Rethinking Ethnicity: Arguments and Explorations*, London: Sage.

—— (2001) "Ethnicity, Anthropological Aspects," in N. J. Smelser and P. B. Baltes (eds) *International Encyclopedia of the Social and Behavioural Sciences*, Oxford: Pergamon, pp. 4824–8.

Jewett, R. (1988) "Paul, Phoebe, and the Spanish Mission," in J. Neusner *et al.* (eds) *The Social World of Formative Judaism and Christianity: Essays in Tribute to Howard Clark Kee*, Philadelphia: Fortress, pp. 142–61.

—— (2007) *Romans: A Commentary*, Hermeneia, Minneapolis, MN: Fortress.

Johnson, M. E. (1999) *The Rites of Christian Initiation: Their Evolution and Interpretation*, Collegeville, MN: Liturgical Press.

Johnson, S. E. (1987) *Paul the Apostle and His Cities*, Wilmington, DE: Glazier.

Johnson, T., and C. Dandeker (1989) "Patronage: Relation and System," in A. Wallace-Hadrill (ed.) *Patronage in Ancient Society*, London: Routledge, pp. 219–41.

Johnson Hodge, C. (2007)*"If Sons, Then Heirs": A Study of Kinship and Ethnicity in Paul's Letter to the Romans*, Oxford: Oxford University Press.

—— (2008) "Olive Trees and Ethnicities: Judeans and Gentiles in Romans 11:17–24," in J. Zangenburg and M. Labahn (eds) *Christians as a Religious Minority in a Multicultural City: Modes of Interaction and Identity Formation in Early Imperial Rome*, Leiden: Brill, pp. 77–89.

Jones, C., G. Wainwright, E. J. Yarnold, and P. F. Bradshaw (eds) (1992) *The Study of Liturgy*, London: SPCK.

Jones, C. P. (1996) "Ethnoi and genoi in Herodotus," *CQ*, 46: 315–20.

Jones, M. (2003) "The Concept of 'cultural landscape'—Discourse and Narratives," in H. Palang and G. Fry (eds) *Landscape Interfaces: Cultural Heritage in Changing Landscapes,* Dordrecht: Kluwer, pp. 21–52.

Joshel, Sandra R., and Sheila Murnaghan (1998) *Women and Slaves in Greco-Roman Culture: Differential Equations*, New York: Routledge.

Kallio, S., and A. Revonsuo (2003) "Hypnotic Phenomena and Altered States of Consciousness: A Multilevel Framework of Description and Explanation," *Contemporary Hypnosis*, 20, no. 3: 111–64.

Karris, R. J. (1991) "Romans 14:1–15:13 and the Occasion of Romans," in K. P. Donfried (ed.) *The Romans Debate,* Peabody, MA: Hendrickson, pp. 65–84. Reprinted from *CBQ*, (1973) 25: 155–78.

Kautsky, J. H. (1982) *The Politics of Aristocratic Empires*, Chapel Hill, NC: University of North Carolina Press.

Kazen, T. (2007) "Empathy and Ethics: Bodily Emotion as Basis for Moral Admonition," paper presented at the SBL International Meeting, Vienna, Austria, July 22–26.

Kennedy, George A. (1984) *New Testament Interpretation through Rhetorical Criticism*, Chapel Hill, NC: University of North Carolina Press.

—— (1994) *A New History of Classical Rhetoric,* Princeton, NJ: Princeton University Press.

Ketola, K. (2007) "A Cognitive Approach to Ritual Systems in First-Century Judaism," in P. Luomanen, I. Pyysiäinen, and R. Uro (eds) *Explaining Early Judaism and Christianity: Contributions from Cognitive and Social Science*, Leiden: Brill.

—— (2008) *The Founder of the Hare Krishnas as Seen by Devotees: A Cognitive Study of Religious Charisma*, Numen Book Series, Studies in the History of Religions 120, Leiden: Brill.

Kihlstrom, J. F. (1984) "Conscious, Subconscious, Unconscious: A Cognitive Perspective," in K. S. Bowers and D. Meichenbaum (eds) *The Unconscious Reconsidered*, New York: John Wiley & Sons.

King, K. L. (2003) *What Is Gnosticism?* Cambridge, MA: Harvard University Press.

Kirk, Alan, and Tom Thatcher (eds) (2005) *Memory, Tradition, and Text: Uses of the Past in Early Christianity*, Semeia Studies 52, Leiden: Brill.

Klauck, H. J. (1982) *Herrenmahl und hellenistischer Kult: Eine religionsgeschichtliche Untersuchung zum ersten Korintherbrief*, NTAbh, n.s., 15, Münster: Aschendorff.

Klawans, Jonathan (2000) *Impurity and Sin in Ancient Judaism*, Oxford: Oxford University Press.

—— (2004) "Concepts of Purity in the Bible," in Adele Berlin and Marc Zvi Brettler (eds) *The Jewish Study Bible*, Oxford: Jewish Publication Society/Oxford University Press, pp. 2041–47.

Klingbeil, G. A. (2007) *Bridging the Gap: Ritual and Ritual Texts in the Bible*, BBR Supplements 1, Winona Lake, IN: Eisenbrauns.

Kloppenborg, J. (2003) Personal Communication. Evidence for Voluntary Associations Called *Ethnē*.

Koester, H. (2000) *History and Literature of Early Christianity*, 2nd edn, *Introduction to the New Testament*, Berlin: Walter De Gruyter.

Kowalski, Seweryn (1957) (trans.) *Pismo Święte Nowego Testamentu*, Warsaw: Pax.

Kraemer, R. S. (1989) "On the Meaning of the Term 'Jew' in Graeco-Roman Inscriptions," *HTR*, 82: 35–43.

Kreinath, J., J. Snoek, and M. Stausberg (eds) (2006) *Theorizing Rituals: Issues, Topics, Approaches, Concepts,* Numen Book Series, Studies in the History of Religions 114-1, Leiden: Brill.

—— (2007) *Theorizing Rituals: Annotated Bibliography of Ritual Theory, 1966–2005,* Numen Book Series, Studies in the History of Religions 114-2, Leiden: Brill.

Kriel, J. R. (2000) *Matter, Mind, and Medicine: Transforming the Clinical Method,* Amsterdam: Ropodi.

—— (2002) "And the Flesh Became Mind: Evolution, Complexity and the Unification of Animal Consciousness," in C. W. Du Toit (ed.) *Brain, Mind and Soul: Unifying the Human Self,* Pretoria: UNISA.

Krippner, S. (1972) "Altered States of Consciousness," in J. White (ed.) *The Highest State of Consciousness,* New York: Anchor Books.

—— (1997a) "Dissociation in Many Times and Places," in S. Krippner and S. M. Powers (eds) *Broken Images, Broken Selves: Dissociative Narratives in Clinical Practice,* Washington, DC: Brunner/Mazel.

—— (1997b) "The Varieties of Dissociative Experiences," in S. Krippner and S. M. Powers (eds) *Broken Images, Broken Selves: Dissociative Narratives in Clinical Practice,* Washington, DC: Brunner/Mazel.

Laidlaw, J., and C. Humphrey (2006) "Action" in J. Kreinath, J. Snoek, and M. Stausberg (eds) *Theorizing Rituals: Issues, Topics, Approaches, Concepts,* Numen Book Series, Studies in the History of Religions 114-1, Leiden: Brill.

Lambek, M. (1989) "From Disease to Discourse: Remarks on the Conceptualization of Trance and Spirit Possession," in C. A. Ward (ed.) *Altered States of Consciousness and Mental Health: A Cross-Cultural Perspective,* London: Sage.

Lambrecht, J. (2001) "The Fool's Speech and its Context: Paul's Particular Way of Arguing in 2 Cor 10–13," *Bib,* 82: 305–24.

Lampe, P. (1991) "The Roman Christians of Romans 16," in K. P. Donfried (ed.) *The Romans Debate,* Peabody, MA: Hendrickson, pp. 216–30.

Landé, C. H. (1977) "Introduction: The Dyadic Basis of Clientalism," in S. W. Schmidt *et al.* (eds) *Friends, Followers, and Factions: A Reader in Political Clientalism,* Berkley, CA: University of California Press, pp. xiii–xxxvii.

Langlands, Rebecca (2006) *Sexual Morality in Ancient Rome,* New York: Cambridge University Press.

Laughlin, C. D. (1990) *Brain, Symbol & Experience: Towards a Neurophenomenology of Human Consciousness,* Boston: Shambhala.

—— (1997) "The Cycle of Meaning: Some Methodological Implications of Biogenetic Structural Theory," in S. D. Glazier (ed.) *Anthropology of Religion: A Handbook,* Westport, CT: Greenwood.

Laughlin, C. D., J. McManus, and E. G. d'Aquili (1990) *Brain, Symbol & Experience: Towards a Neurophenomenology of Human Consciousness,* Boston: Shambhala.

Lawrence, J. D. (2006) *Washing in Water: Trajectories of Ritual Bathing in the Hebrew Bible and Second Temple Literature*, SBL Academia Biblica 23, Atlanta: Society of Biblical Literature.

Lawson, T. E., and R. N. McCauley (1990) *Rethinking Religion: Connecting Cognition and Culture*, Cambridge: Cambridge University Press.

Leach, E. (1976) *Culture and Communication*, Cambridge: Cambridge University Press.

Lefebvre, H. (1991) *The Production of Space*, Oxford: Blackwell.

Lenggenhager, B., T. Tadi, T. Metzinger, and O. Blanke (2007) "Video Ergo Sum: Manipulating Bodily Self-Consciousness," *Science*, 317 (24 August): 1096–9.

Lenski, G. E. (1966) *Power and Privilege: A Theory of Social Stratification*, 1st edn, New York: McGraw-Hill.

—— (1984) *Power and Privilege: A Theory of Social Stratification*, 2nd edn, Chapel Hill, NC: University of North Carolina Press.

Leon, H. J. (1995=1960) *The Jews of Ancient Rome,* with a new introduction by Carolyn A. Osiek (1995), Peabody, MA: Hendrickson.

Levine, Amy-Jill (2006) *The Misunderstood Jew—The Church and the Scandal of the Jewish Jesus*, San Francisco: Harper SanFrancisco.

Lewellen, Ted C. (1983) *Political Anthropology: An Introduction*, South Hadley, MA: Bergin and Harvey.

Liénard, P., and P. Boyer (2006) "Whence Collective Rituals? A Cultural Selection Model of Ritualized Behavior," *American Anthropologist*, 108, no. 4: 814–27.

Lietzmann, H. (1979) *Mass and Lord's Supper: A Study in the History of the Liturgy*, trans. D. H. G. Reeve, with introduction and further inquiry by R. D. Richardson, Leiden: Brill.

Lightfoot, R. H. (1938) *Locality and Doctrine in the Gospels*, London: Hodder and Stoughton.

Llewelyn, S. R. (ed.) (2002) *New Documents Illustrating Early Christianity 9*, Grand Rapids, MI: Eerdmans.

Locke, R. G., and E. F. Kelly (1985) "A Preliminary Model for Cross-Cultural Analysis of Altered States of Consciousness," *Ethos*, 13, no. 1: 3–55.

Lohmeyer, E. (1936) *Galiläa und Jerusalem*, Göttingen : Vandenhoeck & Ruprecht.

Lomas, K., and T. Cornell (2003) *'Bread and Circuses': Euergetism and Municipal Patronage in Roman Italy*, London: Routledge.

Louw, Johannes P., and Eugene A. Nida (eds) (1988) *Greek–English Lexicon of the New Testament based on Semantic Domains*, 2 vols, New York: United Bible Societies.

Lowenthal, David (1985) *The Past is a Foreign Country*, New York: Cambridge University Press.

Ludwig, Arnold M. (1968) "Altered States of Consciousness," in R. Prince (ed.) *Trance and Possession States*, Montreal: Burke Memorial Society.

Luomanen, P., I. Pyysiäinen, and R. Uro (2007) "Introduction: Social and Cognitive Perspectives in the Study of Christian Origins and Early Judaism," in P. Luomanen, I. Pyysiäinen, and R. Uro (eds) *Explaining Early Judaism and Christianity: Contributions from Cognitive and Social Science*, Leiden: Brill.

Luz, Ulrich (2007) *Matthew 1–7: A Commentary,* trans. James E. Crouch, Minneapolis: Fortress.

MacDonald, M. Y. (1990) "Early Christian Women Married to Unbelievers," *SR,* 19: 221–34.

—— (2007) "Slavery, Sexuality and House Churches: A Reassessment of Colossians 3:18–4:1 in Light of New Research on the Roman Family," *NTS,* 53: 94–113.

—— (2008) "A Place of Belonging: Perspectives on Children from Colossians and Ephesians," in M. J. Bunge (ed.) *The Child in the Bible,* Grand Rapids, MI: Eerdmans, pp. 278–304.

MacMullen, Ramsay (1974) *Roman Social Relations,* New Haven, CT: Yale University Press.

Malbon, E. S. (1986) *Narrative Space and Mythic Meaning in Mark,* San Francisco: Harper & Row.

Malina, Bruce J. (1986) *Christian Origins and Cultural Anthropology: Practical Models for Biblical Interpretation,* Atlanta, GA: John Knox Press.

—— (1988) "Patron and Client: The Analogy Behind Synoptic Theology," in *Forum,* 4.1: 2–32.

—— (1995) *On the Genre and Message of Revelation: Star Visions and Sky Journeys,* Peabody, MA: Hendrickson.

—— (1996) *The Social World of Jesus and the Gospels,* London: Routledge.

—— (2001) *The New Testament World: Insights from Cultural Anthropology,* 3rd edn, Louisville, KY: Westminster John Knox Press.

—— (2007) "Who Are We? Who Are They? Who Am I? Who are You (Sing.)?: Explaining Identity, Social and Individual," *Annali di storia dell'esegesi,* 24, no. 1: 103–9.

—— and Jerome H. Neyrey (1991) "Honor and Shame in Luke-Acts: Pivotal Values of the Mediterranean World," in J. Neyrey (ed.) *The Social World of Luke-Acts: Models for Interpretation,* Peabody, MA: Hendrickson.

—— and Jerome H. Neyrey (1996) *Portraits of Paul: An Archeology of Ancient Personality,* Peabody, MA: Hendrickson.

—— and Richard L. Rohrbaugh (1992) *Social-Science Commentary on the Synoptic Gospels,* 1st edn, Minneapolis: Fortress.

—— and Richard L. Rohrbaugh (2003) *Social-Science Commentary on the Synoptic Gospels,* 2nd edn, Minneapolis: Fortress.

Malkin, I. (ed.) (2001) *Ancient Perceptions of Greek Ethnicity,* Washington, DC: Center for Hellenic Studies/Cambridge, MA: Harvard University Press.

Malkki, Liisa H. (1995) *Purity and Exile: Violence, Memory, and National Cosmology among Hutu Refugees in Tanzania,* Chicago: University of Chicago Press.

Mann, M. (1986) *The Sources of Social Power,* Cambridge: Cambridge University Press.

Manson, T. W. (1991 [1962]) "St. Paul's Letter to the Romans," in K. P. Donfried (ed.) *The Romans Debate,* Peabody, MA: Hendrickson, pp. 1–15. Reprinted from *Studies in the Gospels and Epistle,* ed. M. Black, Manchester: Manchester University Press, 1962, pp. 225–41.

Marks, L. E. (2000) "Synesthesia," in E. Cardeña, S. J. Lynn, and S. Krippner (eds) *Varieties of Anomalous Experience: Examining the Scientific Evidence*, Washington, DC: American Psychological Association.

Marshall, Howard I. (1978) *The Gospel of Luke: A Commentary on the Greek Text*, Grand Rapids, MI: Eerdmans.

Marshall, P. (1983) "A Metaphor of Social Shame: *Thriambevein*," *NovT*, 25: 302–17.

Martin, Dale B. (2003) "Slave Families and Slaves in Families," in D. L. Balch and C. Osiek (eds) *Early Christian Families in Context: An Interdisciplinary Dialogue*, Religion, Marriage, and Family [Series], Grand Rapids, MI: Eerdmans, pp. 207–30.

—— (2006) "Heterosexism and the Interpretation of Romans 1:18–32," in Mathew Kuefler (ed.) *The Boswell Thesis: Essays on Christianity, Social Tolerance, and Homosexuality*, Chicago: University of Chicago Press.

Martin, L. H. (2000) "Of Religious Syncretism, Comparative Religion and Spiritual Quests," *Method & Theory in the Study of Religion*, 12: 277–86.

Marxsen, W. (1964) *Introduction to the New Testament*, trans. G. Buswell, Philadelphia: Fortress Press.

Matlock, B. (2007) "'Jews by Nature': Paul, Ethnicity, and Galatians," in D. Burns and J. W. Rogerson (eds) *In Search of Philip R. Davies: Whose Festschrift Is It Anyway?* London: T & T Clark. http://tandtclark.typepad.com/Davies_FS_Files/Davies_FS_Matlock.pdf (accessed 12/11/08).

McCauley, R. N., and T. E. Lawson (2002) *Bringing Ritual to Mind: Psychological Foundations of Cultural Forms*, Cambridge: Cambridge University Press.

McDowell, L. (1999) *Gender, Identity and Place: Understanding Feminist Geographies*, Cambridge: Polity.

McVann, M. (1994) "Reading Mark Ritually: Honor-Shame and the Ritual of Baptism," *Semeia*, 67: 179–98.

Meeks, W. A. (1983) *The First Urban Christians: The Social World of the Apostle Paul*, New Haven, CT: Yale University Press.

—— (1986) *The Moral World of the First Christians*, Philadelphia, PA: Westminster.

—— (1987) "Judgment and the Brother: Romans 14:1–15:13," in G. F. Hawthorne and O. Betz (eds) *Tradition and Interpretation in the New Testament: Essays in Honor of E. Earle Ellis*, Grand Rapids, MI: Eerdmans, pp. 290–300.

Meggitt, Justin J. (1998) *Paul, Poverty and Survival*, Edinburgh: T & T Clark.

Meyer, Ben F. (1979) *The Aims of Jesus*, London: SCM.

Meyer, Carol (2005) *Households and Holiness: The Religious Culture of Israelite Women*, Minneapolis: Fortress Press.

Millett, Paul (1989) "Patronage and its Avoidance in Classical Athens," in A. Wallace-Hadrill (ed.) *Patronage in Ancient Society*, London: Routledge, pp. 5–47.

Milnor, Kristina (2005) *Gender, Domesticity, and the Age of Augustus: Inventing Private Life*, New York: Oxford University Press.

Minear, P. (1971) *The Obedience of Faith. The Purposes of Paul in the Epistle to the Romans*, Studies in Biblical Theology 2/19, London: SCM Press.

Moerman, Daniel E. (1979) "Anthropology of Symbolic Healing," *Current Anthropology*, 20: 59–80.

—— (2002) *Meaning, Medicine and the "Placebo Effect,"* Cambridge: Cambridge University Press.

Montague, A. (1942) *Man's Most Dangerous Myth: The Fallacy of Race*, New York: Columbia University Press.

Morris, Ian (1991) "The Early Polis as City and State," in John Rich and A. Wallace-Hadrill (eds) *City and Country in the Ancient World*, London: Routledge, pp. 24–57.

—— and J. G. Manning (2005) "Introduction," in J. G. Manning and I. Morris (eds) *The Ancient Economy: Evidence and Models*, Stanford, CA: Stanford University Press.

Mouritsen, H. (1988) *Elections, Magistrates and Municipal Élite: Studies in Pompeian Epigraphy*, Analecta Romana Instituti Danici, Supp. XV, Rome: 'L'Erma' di Bretschneider.

Moxnes, Halvor (1988) *The Economy of the Kingdom: Social Conflicts and Economic Relations in Luke's Gospel*, Philadelphia: Fortress.

—— (1997) (ed) *Constructing Early Christian Families: Family as Social Reality and Metaphor*, London: Routledge.

—— (2001) "Kingdom Takes Place," in John J. Pilch (ed.) *Social Scientific Models for Interpreting the Bible*, Biblical Interpretation Series 53, Leiden: Brill, pp. 176–209.

—— (2003) *Putting Jesus in His Place: A Radical Vision of Household and Kingdom*, Louisville, KY: Westminster John Knox.

—— (2007) "Where is 'Following Jesus'? Masculinity and Place in Luke's Gospel," in Anselm Hagedorn, Z. A. Crook, and E. C. Stewart (eds) *In Other Words: Essays on Social Science Methods and the New Testament in Honor of Jerome H. Neyrey*, Sheffield: Phoenix Press, pp. 155–70.

Murphy-O'Connor, Jerome (2002) *St. Paul's Corinth: Texts and Archaeology*, 3rd edn, Collegeville: Liturgical Press.

Muthuraj, J. G. (1997) "The Meaning of *ethnos* and *ethnē* and its Significance to the Study of the New Testament," *Bangalore Theological Forum*, 29, no. 10: 3–36.

Namer, Gérard (1987) *Mémoire et société*, Paris: Méridiens Lincksieck.

Nanos, Mark D. (1996) *The Mystery of Romans: The Jewish Context of Paul's Letter*, Minneapolis, MN: Fortress.

Neils, J. (1992) *Goddess and Polis: The Panathenaic Festival in Ancient Athens*, Hanover, NH: Hood Museum of Art, Dartmouth College; Princeton, NJ: Princeton University Press.

Netting, Robert McC., R. R. Wilk, and E. J. Arnould (1984) *Households: Comparative and Historical Studies of the Domestic Group*, Berkeley, CA: University of California Press.

Neufeld, Dietmar (2000) "Jesus's Eating Transgressions and Social Impropriety in the Gospel of Mark: A Social-Scientific Approach," *BTB*, 30: 15–26.

—— (2008a) "Sins and Forgiveness: Release and Status Reinstatement of the Paralytic in Mark 2:1–12," in Dietmar Neufeld (ed.) *The Social Sciences and Biblical Translation*, SBLSymS 41, Atlanta: Society of Biblical Literature.

—— (2008b) (ed.) *The Social Sciences and Biblical Translation*, SBLSymS 41, Atlanta: Society of Biblical Literature.

Newberg, A., E. d'Aquili, and V. Rause (2001) *Why God Won't Go Away: Brain Science and the Biology of Belief*, New York: Ballantine.

Neyrey, Jerome H., (1986a) "Body Language in 1 Corinthians: The Use of Anthropological Models for Understanding Paul and His Opponents," *Semeia*, 35: 129–70.

—— (1986b) "The Idea of Purity in Mark's Gospel," *Semeia*, 35: 91–128.

—— (1988a) "A Symbolic Approach to Mark 7," *FF*, 4, no. 3: 63–91.

—— (1988b) "Unclean, Common, Polluted and Taboo—A Short Reading Guide," *FF*, 4, no. 4: 72–82.

—— (1991) (ed.) *The Social World of Luke-Acts*, Peabody, MA: Hendrickson.

—— (1996) "Readers Guides to Clean/Unclean, Pure/Polluted, and Holy/Profane: The Idea and System of Purity," in Richard L. Rohrbaugh (ed.) *The Social Sciences and New Testament Interpretation*, Peabody, MA: Hendrickson, pp. 159–82.

—— (1998) *Honor and Shame in the Gospel of Matthew*, Louisville, KY: Westminster John Knox.

—— (2001) "Prayer, in Other Words: New Testament Prayers in Social Scientific Perspective," in John J. Pilch (ed.) *Social Scientific Models for Interpreting the Bible: Essays by the Context Group in Honor of Bruce J. Malina*, Leiden: Brill, pp. 349–80.

—— (2004) *Render to God: New Testament Understandings of the Divine*, Minneapolis: Fortress.

—— (2007) "'I am the Door' (John 10:7, 9): Jesus the Broker in the Fourth Gospel," *CBQ*, 69: 271–91.

—— and E. C. Stewart (eds) (2008) *The Social World of the New Testament: Insights and Models*, Peabody, MA: Hendrickson.

Oakes, Peter (2009) *Reading Romans in Pompeii: Paul's Letter at Ground Level*, London: SPCK/Minneapolis: Fortress.

Oakman, Douglas E. (1986) *Jesus and the Economic Questions of His Day*, Lewiston, NY: Mellon.

—— (1994) "The Archaeology of First-Century Galilee and the Social Interpretation of the Historical Jesus," in *SBL Seminar Papers*, Atlanta: Scholars Press, vol. 33, pp. 220–51.

—— (1996) "The Ancient Economy," in Richard L. Rohrbaugh (ed.) *The Social Sciences and New Testament Interpretation*, Peabody, MA: Hendrickson.

—— (2008) *Jesus and the Peasants,* Matrix: The Bible in Mediterranean Context, Eugene, OR: Wipf and Stock.

Økland, J. (2004) *Women in their Place: Paul and the Corinthian Discourse of Gender and Sanctuary Space,* JSNTSup 269, London: T & T Clark.

Olick, Jeffrey K. (1999) "Collective Memory: The Two Cultures," *ST* 17: 333–48.

—— and Joyce Robbins (1998) "Social Memory Studies: From 'Collective Memory' to the Historical Sociology of Mnemonic Practices," *Annual Review of Sociology*, 24: 105–40.

Olwig, K. R. (1996) "Recovering the Substantive Nature of Landscape," *Annals of the Association of American Geographers*, 84: 630–53.

Osiek, C., (1995) "Introduction," in H. J. Leon, *The Jews of Ancient Rome,* updated edn, Peabody, MA: Hendrickson.

—— (2002) "The Bride of Christ (Eph 5:22–33): A Problematic Wedding," *BTB*, 32: 29–39.

—— (2005) "Family Matters," in Richard A. Horsley (ed.) *Christian Origins, A People's History of Christianity*, vol. 1, Minneapolis: Fortress Press, pp. 201–20.

—— and D. L. Balch (1997) *Families in the New Testament World: Households and House Churches*, The Family, Religion, and Culture, Louisville, KY: Westminster John Knox.

—— and M. Y. MacDonald, with J. H. Tulloch (2006) *A Woman's Place: House Churches in Earliest Christianity*, Minneapolis: Fortress Press.

Parkin, R. (1997) *Kinship: An Introduction to the Basic Concept*, Oxford: Blackwell Publishers.

Parkin, T. G. (2003) *Old Age in the Roman World: A Cultural and Social History*, Baltimore: Johns Hopkins University Press.

Parks, Ward (1991) "The Textualization of Orality in Literary Criticism," in A. N. Doane and Carol Braun Pasternack (eds) *Vox intexta: Orality and Textuality in the Middle Ages*, Madison, WI: University of Wisconsin Press, pp. 46–61.

Penner, H. H. (1971) "The Poverty of Functionalism," *HR*, 11: 91–7.

Penner, Todd, and Caroline Vander Stichele (2005) "Unveiling Paul: Gendering Ethos in 1 Corinthians 11:2–16," in Thomas H. Olbricht and Anders Eriksson (eds) *Rhetoric, Ethic, and Moral Persuasion in Biblical Discourse*, New York: T & T Clark International, pp. 214–37.

Peristiany, J. G. (1966) *Honour and Shame: The Values of Mediterranean Society*, Chicago: Chicago University Press.

—— and J. Pitt-Rivers (1992) *Honor and Grace in Anthropology*, Cambridge: Cambridge University Press.

Perring, Dominic (1991) "Spatial Organisation and Social Change in Roman Towns," in John Rich and A. Wallace-Hadrill (eds) *City and Country in the Ancient World*, London: Routledge, pp. 273–93.

Pilch, John J., (1981) "Biblical Leprosy and Body Symbolism," *BTB*, 11: 119–33.

—— (1989) "Reading Matthew Anthropologically: Healing in Cultural Perspective," *List*, 24: 278–89.

—— (1993) "Visions in Revelation and Alternate Consciousness: A Perspective from Cultural Anthropology," *List*, 28 no. 3: 231–44.

—— (1995) "The Transfiguration of Jesus: An Experience of Alternate Reality," in P. F. Esler (ed.) *Modelling Early Christianity: Social-Scientific Studies of the New Testament in Its Context*, London: Routledge.

—— (1998) "Appearances of the Risen Jesus in Cultural Context: Experiences of Alternate Reality," *BTB*, 28: 52–60.

—— (2000) *Healing in the New Testament: Insights from Medical and Mediterranean Anthropology*, Minneapolis: Fortress Press.

—— (2002a) "Alternate State of Consciousness in the Synoptics," in Wolfgang Stegemann, Bruce J. Malina, and G. Theissen (eds) *The Social Setting of Jesus and the Gospels*, Minneapolis: Fortress.

—— (2002b) "Paul's Ecstatic Trance Experience Near Damascus in Acts of the Apostles," *HvTSt*, 58, no. 2: 690–707.

—— (2004) *Visions and Healings in the Acts of the Apostles: How the Early Believers Experienced God*, Collegeville, MN: Liturgical Press.

—— (2005) "Holy Men and Their Sky Journeys: A Cross-Cultural Model," *BTB*, 35: 106–11.

—— (2007a) "Disease," *NIDB*, 2: 135–40.

—— (2007b) "Flute Players, Death, and Music in the Afterlife (Matthew 9:18–19, 23–26)," *BTB*, 37: 12–19.

—— (2008a) "Leprosy," *NIDB* 3: 635–7.

—— (2008b) "The Usefulness of the 'Meaning Response' Concept For Interpreting Translations of Matthew's Gospel," in Dietmar Neufeld (ed.) *The Social Sciences and Biblical Interpretation*, Atlanta: Society of Biblical Literature, pp. 97–108.

—— and Bruce J. Malina (eds) (1993) *Biblical Social Values and Their Meaning: A Handbook*, Peabody, MA: Hendrickson.

Pitt-Rivers, Julian (1966) "Honour and Social Status," in J. G. Peristiany (ed.) *Honour and Shame: The Values of Mediterranean Society,* Chicago: Chicago University Press.

Plevnik, J. (1993) "Honor/Shame," in J. J. Pilch and B. J. Malina (eds) *Biblical Social Values and Their Meaning: A Handbook*, Peabody, MA: Hendrickson, pp. 95–104.

Poirier, John C. (1996) "Why Did the Pharisees Wash Their Hands?" *JJS,* 47, no. 2: 217–33.

Polanyi, K. (1944) *The Great Transformation,* Boston, MA: Beacon Press.

Pomeroy, S. B. (ed.) (1999) *Plutarch's Advice to the Bride and Groom and A Consolation to His Wife*, Oxford: Oxford University Press.

Prager, Jeffrey (1998) *Presenting the Past: Psychoanalysis and the Sociology of Misremembering*, Cambridge, MA: Harvard University Press.

Pyysiäinen, I. (2001) *How Religion Works: Towards a New Cognitive Science of Religion*, Cognition and Culture 1, Leiden: Brill.

Ramachandran, V. S. (2004) *A Brief Tour of Human Consciousness: From Imposter Poodles to Purple Numbers*, New York: Pi Press.

Rappaport, R. A. (1999) *Ritual and Religion in the Making of Humanity*, Cambridge: Cambridge University Press.

Rawson, B. (2003) *Children and Childhood in Roman Italy*, Oxford: Oxford University Press.

Redfield, R. (1956) *Peasant Society and Culture*, Chicago: University of Chicago.

Reitzenstein, R. (1978) *Hellenistic Mystery Religions: Their Basic Ideas and Significance*, trans. J. E. Steely, Pittsburgh, PA: Pickwick.

Rich, John, and Andrew Wallace-Hadrill (eds) (1991) *City and Country in the Ancient World*, London: Routledge.

Richardson, P. (1998) "Augustan-Era Synagogues in Rome," in K. P. Donfried and P. Richardson (eds) *Judaism and Christianity in First-Century Rome,* Grand Rapids, MI: Eerdmans, pp. 17–29.

Rohrbaugh, Richard L. (1991) "The Pre-Industrial City in Luke-Acts: Urban Social Relations," in Jerome H. Neyrey (ed.) *The Social World of Luke-Acts*, Peabody, MA: Hendrickson, pp. 125–49.

—— (1995) "Legitimating Sonship—A Test of Honour: A Social-Scientific Study of Luke 4:1–30," in P. Esler (ed.) *Modelling Early Christianity: Social-Scientific Studies of the New Testament in its Context*, London: Routledge.

—— (ed.) (1996) *The Social Sciences and New Testament Interpretation*, Peabody, MA: Hendrickson.

—— (2000) "Gossip in the New Testament," in John J. Pilch (ed.) *Social Scientific Models for Interpreting the Bible: Essays by The Context Group in Honor of Bruce J. Malina*, Leiden: Brill.

—— (2007) *The New Testament in Cross-Cultural Perspective*, Matrix. The Bible in Mediterranean Context, Eugene, OR: Wipf and Stock.

Romano, D. G. (2005) "Urban and Rural Planning in Roman Corinth," in D. Schowalter and S. J. Friesen (eds), *The Social World of Luke-Acts*, Peabody, MA: Hendrickson, pp. 25–59.

Rosen, R. M., and I. Sluiter (eds) (2006) *City, Countryside and the Spatial Organization of Value in Classical Antiquity,* Mnemosyne 279, Leiden: Brill.

Rosenzweig, Roy, and David Thelen (1998) *The Presence of the Past: Popular Uses of History in American Life*, New York: Columbia University Press.

Rostovtzeff, M. (1922) *A Large Estate in Egypt in the Third Century B.C*, Madison, WI: University of Wisconsin Press.

—— (1957) *Social and Economic History of the Roman Empire*, Oxford: Clarendon.

Rubin, David C. (1995) *Memory in Oral Traditions: The Cognitive Psychology of Epic, Ballads, and Counting-out Rhymes*, Oxford: Oxford University Press.

Rutgers, L. V. (1995) *The Jews in Late Ancient Rome: Evidence of Cultural Interactions in the Roman Diaspora,* Leiden: Brill.

—— (1998) "Roman Policy toward the Jews: Expulsions from the City of Rome during the First Century C.E.," in K. P. Donfried and P. Richardson (eds) *Judaism and Christianity in First-Century Rome,* Grand Rapids, MI: Eerdmans, pp. 93–116.

Sahlins, M. (1972) *Stone Age Economics*, Chicago: Aldine Atherton.

Saldarini, A. (1994*) Matthew's Christian–Jewish Community,* Chicago: University of Chicago Press.

Saller, Richard P. (1982) *Personal Patronage Under the Early Empire*, Cambridge: Cambridge University Press.

—— (1989) "Patronage and Friendship in Early Imperial Rome: Drawing the Distinction," in A. Wallace-Hadrill (ed.) *Patronage in Ancient Society*, London: Routledge, pp. 49–62.

—— (1998) "Symbols of Gender and Status Hierarchies in the Roman Household," in Sandra R. Joshel and Sheila Murnaghan (eds) *Women and Slaves in Greco-Roman Culture: Differential Equations*, New York: Routledge, pp. 85–91.

—— (1999) *"Pater Familias, Mater Familias*, and the Gendered Semantics of the Roman Household," *CP*, 94: 182–97.

—— (2005) "Framing the Debate Over Growth in the Ancient Economy," in J. G. Manning and I. Morris (eds) *The Ancient Economy: Evidence and Models*, Stanford, CA: Stanford University Press.

—— (2007) "Household and Gender," in W. Sheidel, I. Morris, and R. Saller (eds) *The Cambridge Economic History of the Greco-Roman World*, Cambridge: Cambridge University, pp. 87–112.

Salyer, Gregory (1993) "Rhetoric, Purity, and Play—Aspects of Mark 7:1–23," *Semeia*, 64: 139–69.

Sampley, J. P. (1995) "The Weak and the Strong: Paul's Careful and Crafty Rhetorical Strategy in Romans 14:1–15:13," in L. M. White and O. L. Yarbrough (eds), *The Social World of the First Christians: Essays in Honor of Wayne A. Meeks*, Minneapolis, MN: Augsburg Fortress, pp. 40–52.

Sapir, Edward (1949) *Selected Writings of Edward Sapir*, ed. David G. Mandelbaum, Berkeley, CA: University of California Press.

Satlow, M. (2001) *Jewish Marriage in Antiquity*, Princeton, NJ: Princeton University Press.

Sawyer, Deborah F. (2002) *God, Gender and the Bible*, London: Routledge.

Sawyer, John F. A., and Mary Douglas (1996) *Reading Leviticus: A Conversation with Mary Douglas*, Sheffield: Sheffield Academic Press.

Schama, S. (1995) *Landscape and Memory*, London: HarperCollins.

Schermerhorn, R. A. (1978) *Comparative Ethnic Relations*, New York: Random House.

Schmidt, Steffen W., Laurs Guasti, Carl H. Landé, and James C. Scott (eds) (1977) *Friends, Followers, and Factions: A Reader in Political Clientelism*, Berkeley, CA: University of California Press.

Schneider, J. (1971) "Of Vigilance and Virgins: Honor, Shame and Access to Resources in Mediterranean Societies," *Ethnology*, 10: 1–24.

Schüssler Fiorenza, E. (1999) *Rhetoric and Ethic: The Politics of Biblical Studies*, Minneapolis: Fortress.

Schwartz, Barry (1982) "The Social Context of Commemoration: A Study in Collective Memory," *Social Forces*, 61: 374–402.

—— (1996) "Memory as a Cultural System: Abraham Lincoln in World War II," *ASR*, 61: 908–27.

—— (1998) "Frame Image: Towards a Semiotics of Collective Memory," *Semiotica*, 121: 1–38.

—— Barry (2000) *Abraham Lincoln and the Forge of National Memory*, Chicago: University of Chicago Press.

—— (2005) "Jesus in First-century Memory—A Response," in Alan Kirk and Tom Thatcher (eds) *Memory, Tradition, and Text: Uses of the Past in Early Christianity*, Semeia Studies 52, Leiden: Brill, pp. 249–61.

Schwartz, Baruch H. (2004) "Introduction and Notes to Leviticus," in Adele Berlin and Marc Zvi Brettler (eds) *The Jewish Study Bible*, Oxford: Jewish Publication Society, pp. 221–40.

Scobie, C. H. H. (1964) *John the Baptist*, London: SCM Press.

Scott, Bernard Brandon (1989) *Hear Then the Parable: A Commentary on the Parables of Jesus*, Minneapolis: Fortress.

Scott, G. M., Jr. (1990) "A Resynthesis of the Primordial and Circumstantial Approaches to Ethnic Group Solidarity: Towards an Explanatory Model," *Ethnic and Racial Studies*, 13: 147–71.

Shils, E. (1957) "Primordial, Personal, Sacred and Civil Ties," *British Journal of Sociology*, 8: 130–45.

Sjoberg, Gideon (1960) *The Preindustrial City: Past and Present*, New York: Free Press.

Skinner, Marilyn (2005) *Sexuality in Greek and Roman Culture*, Malden, MA: Blackwell.

Smith, J. Z. (1987) *To Take Place: Toward Theory in Ritual*, Chicago: Chicago University Press.

Soja, E. W. (1996) *Thirdspace: Journeys to Los Angeles and other Real-and-Imagined Places*, Oxford: Blackwell.

—— (1999) "Thirdspace: Expanding the Scope of the Geographical Imagination," in D. Massey *et al.* (eds) *Human Geography Today*, Cambridge: Polity, pp. 260–78.

Sollors, W. (1996) *Theories of Ethnicity: A Classical Reader*, Basingstoke: Macmillan.

Sørensen, J. (2005) "Charisma, Tradition, and Ritual: A Cognitive Approach to Magical Agency," in H. Whitehouse and R. N. McCauley (eds) *Mind and Religion: Psychological and Cognitive Foundations of Religiosity*, Walnut Creek, CA: AltaMira.

Sosis, R., and B. J. Ruffle (2003) "Religious Ritual and Cooperation: Testing for a Relationship on Israeli Religious and Secular Kibbutzim," *Current Anthropology*, 44, no. 5: 713–22.

Spanos, N. P. (1989) "Hypnosis, Demonic Possession, and Multiple Personality: Strategic Enactments and Disavowals of Responsibility for Actions," in C. A. Ward (ed.) *Altered States of Consciousness and Mental Health: A Cross-Cultural Perspective*, London: Sage.

Sperber, D. (1974) *Rethinking Symbolism*, Cambridge: Cambridge University Press.

—— (1996) *Explaining Culture: A Naturalistic Approach*, Oxford: Blackwell.

Squire, Larry R., and Eric R. Kandel (1999) *Memory: From Mind to Molecules*, New York: Scientific American Library.

Staal, F. (1989) *Rules without Meaning: Ritual, Mantras and the Human Sciences*, Bern: Peter Lang.

Standhartinger, A. (2000) "The Origin and Intention of the Household Code in the Letter to the Colossians," *JSNT*, 79: 117–30.

Stanley, C. D. (1998) "'Neither Israelite nor Greek': Ethnic Conflict in Graeco-Roman Society [Gal 3:28]," *JSNT*, 64: 101–24.

Stegemann, Ekkehard W., and Wolfgang Stegemann (1999) *The Jesus Movement: A Social History of Its First Century*, trans. O. C. Dean, Jr., Minneapolis: Fortress.

Stewart, C., and R. Shaw (1994) "Introduction: Problematizing Syncretism" in C. Stewart and R. Shaw (eds) *Syncretism/Anti-syncretism: The Politics of Religious Synthesis*, London: Routledge.

Stewart, Eric C. (2007) "The City in Mark," in A. Hagedorn, Z. A. Crook, and E. C. Stewart (eds) *In Other Words: Essays on Social Science Methods and the New*

Testament in Honor of Jerome H. Neyrey, The Social World of Biblical Antiquity, Second Series 1. Sheffield: Sheffield Phoenix, pp. 202–20.

—— (2009) *Gathered Around Jesus: An Alternative Spatial Practice in the Gospel of Mark*, Eugene, OR: Cascade.

Stewart, P. J., and A. Strathern (2003) "Introduction," in P. J. Stewart and A. Strathern (eds) *Landscape, Memory and History: Anthropological Perspectives*, London: Pluto Press.

Stirewalt, M. L., Jr. (1991) "The Form and Function of the Greek Letter-Essay," in K. P. Donfried (ed.) *The Romans Debate,* Peabody, MA: Hendrickson, pp. 147–71.

Stowers, S. (1995) "Greeks Who Sacrifice and Those Who Do Not: Toward an Anthropology of Greek Religion," in L. M. White and L. O. Yarbrough (eds) *The Social World of the First Christians: Essays in Honor of Wayne Meeks*, Minneapolis, MN: Fortress.

Strecker, Christian (1999) *Die liminale Theologie des Paulus: Zugänge zur paulinishcen Theologie aus kulturanthropologischer Perspektive*, FRLANT 185, Göttingen: Vandenhoeck & Ruprecht.

Stringer, M. D. (2005) *A Sociological History of Christian Worship*, Cambridge: Cambridge University Press.

Swancutt, Diana (2004) "Sexy Stoics and the Rereading of Romans 1:18–2:16," in Amy-Jill Levine and Marianne Blickenstaff (eds) *A Feminist Companion to Paul*, Cleveland, OH: Pilgrim Press, pp. 42–73.

Talbert, C. H. (2007) *Ephesians and Colossians*, Paideia Commentaries on the New Testament, Grand Rapids, MI: Baker Academic.

Tart, C. T. (1969) "Introduction to Section 1: Some General Views on Altered States of Consciousness," in C. T. Tart (ed.) *Altered States of Consciousness: A Book of Readings*, New York: John Wiley & Sons.

—— (1980) "A Systems Approach to Altered States of Consciousness," in J. M. Davidson and R. J. Davidson (eds) *The Psychobiology of Consciousness*, New York: Plenum.

Tattersall, Ian (2002) *The Monkey in the Mirror: Essays on the Science of What Makes Us Human*, New York: Harcourt.

Taylor, Charles (1989) *Sources of the Self: The Making of the Modern Identity*, Cambridge, MA: Harvard University Press.

Taylor, J. E. (1997) *The Immerser: John the Baptist within Second Temple Judaism*, Grand Rapids, MI: Eerdmans.

Thatcher, Tom (2008) "Beyond Texts and Traditions: Werner Kelber's Media History of Christian Origins," in Tom Thatcher (ed.) *Jesus: the Voice and the Text: Beyond the Oral and the Written Gospel*, Waco, TX: Baylor University Press, pp. 1–28.

Theissen, G. (1999) *A Theory of Primitive Christian Religion*, trans. J. Bowden, London: SCM.

Thiselton, Anthony C. (2000) *The First Epistle to the Corinthians: A Commentary on the Greek Text*, Grand Rapids, MI: Eerdmans.

Thomas, G. (2006) "Communication," in J. Kreinath, J. Snoek, and M. Stausberg (eds) *Theorizing Rituals: Issues, Topics, Approaches, Concepts*, Numen Book Series, Studies in the History of Religions, Leiden: Brill, pp. 114–19.

Thompson, John B. (1996) "Tradition and Self in a Mediated World," in Paul Heelas, Scott Lash, and Paul Morris (eds) *De-traditionalization: Critical Reflections on Authority and Identity in a Time of Uncertainty*, Oxford: Blackwell, pp. 89–108.

Throop, C., and C. D. Laughlin (2007) "Anthropology of Consciousness," in P. D. Zelazo, M. Moscovitch, and E. Thompson (eds) *The Cambridge Handbook of Consciousness*, Cambridge: Cambridge University Press.

Tobin, T. (1995) "What Shall We Say That Abraham Found? The Controversy behind Romans 4," *HTR*, 88: 437–52.

Tremlin, T. (2006) *Minds and Gods: The Cognitive Foundations of Religion*, Oxford: Oxford University Press.

Triandis, Harry C. (1990) "Cross-Cultural Studies in Individualism and Collectivism," in R. A. Diensbier and J. J. Berman (eds) *Nebraska Symposium on Motivation 1989*, Lincoln, NE: University of Nebraska Press, pp. 41–133.

Turner, V. (1967) *The Forest of Symbols: Aspects of Ndembu Ritual*, Ithaca, NY: Cornell University Press.

—— (1969) *The Ritual Process: Structure and Anti-Structure*, Chicago: Aldine.

—— (1974) *Dramas, Fields, and Metaphors: Symbolic Action in Human Society*, Ithaca, NY: Cornell University Press.

Turner, V. W., and E. Turner (1978) *Image and Pilgrimage in Christian Culture: Anthropological Perspectives*, Oxford: Blackwell.

UNESCO (1950) "The Race Question," July 18. http://unesdoc.unesco.org/images/0012/001229/122962eo.pdf (accessed 12/11/08).

Uro, R. (2007a) "A Cognitive Approach to Gnostic Rituals," in P. Luomanen, I. Pyysiäinen, and R. Uro (eds) *Explaining Christianity Origins and Early Judaism: Contributions from Cognitive and Social Science*, Leiden: Brill.

—— (2007b) "Pure Mind: Ritual, Purity, and Early Christian Taboos," paper presented at the SBL International Meeting, Vienna, Austria, July 22–26.

—— (2009) "Towards a Cognitive History of Early Christian Rituals," in I. Czachesz and T. Bíró (eds) *Changing Minds: Religion and Cognition through Ages,* Groningen Studies in Cultural Changes. Leiden: Peeters.

US Census Bureau Race Data: Racial and Ethnic Classifications Used in Census 2000 and Beyond 2008. http://www.census.gov/population/www/socdemo/race/racefactcb.html (accessed 12/11/08).

Vaitl, D., *et al.* (2005) "Psychobiology of Altered States of Consciousness," *Psychological Bulletin*, 131, no. 1: 98–127.

Valantasis, R. (1995) "Constructions of Power in Asceticism," *JAAR*, 63: 775–821.

Van den Berghe, P. L. (1987) *The Ethnic Phenomenon*, Westport, CT: Praeger.

Van Gennep, A. (1960) *The Rites of Passage*, trans. M. B. Vizedom and G. L. Caffee, Chicago: University of Chicago Press.

Varshney, A. (1995) *Ethnic Conflict and Rational Choice: A Theoretical Engagement*, Cambridge, MA: Center for International Affairs, Harvard University Press.

Verboven, Koenraad (2002) *The Economy of Friends: Economic Aspects of Amicitia and Patronage in the Late Republic*, Collection Latomus 269, Brussels: Éditions Latomus.

Verner, D. (1983) *The Household of God: The Social World of the Pastoral Epistles*, SBLDS 71, Chico, CA: Scholars.

Veyne, Paul (1989) "'Humanitas': Romani e no[i]," in Andrea Giardina (ed.) *L'uomo Romano*, Bari: Laterza, pp. 385–415. English translation: "'Humanitas': Romans and Non-Romans," in Andrea Giardina (ed.) *The Romans*, trans. Lydia G. Cochrane, Chicago: University of Chicago Press, 1993, pp. 342–69.

Vial, T. M. (1999) "Opposites Attract: The Body and Cognition in a Debate over Baptism," *Numen*, 46: 121–45.

Von Rad, G., K. G. Kuhn, and W. Gutbrod (1965) "*Ioudaios*," *TDNT*, 3: 356–91.

Wagner, G. (1962) *Das religionsgeschichtliche Problem von Römer 6,1–11*, ATANT 39, Zürich: Zwingli.

Wagner-Pacifici, Robin (1996) "Memories in the Making: The Shape of Things That Went," *QS*, 19: 301–21.

Wainwright, G., and K. B. Westerfield Tucker (eds) (2006) *The Oxford History of Christian Worship*, Oxford: Oxford University Press.

Wallace-Hadrill, A. (1989a) *Patronage in Ancient Society*, London: Routledge.

—— (1989b) "Patronage in Roman Society; From Republic to Empire," in A. Wallace-Hadrill (ed.) *Patronage in Ancient Society*, London: Routledge, pp. 63–87.

Walsh, B. J., and S. C. Keesmaat (2004) *Colossians Remixed: Subverting the Empire*, Downers Grove, IL: InterVarsity Press.

Walsh, R. (2007) *The World of Shamanism: New Views of an Ancient Tradition*, Woodbury: Llewellyn.

Walters, J. C. (1993) *Ethnic Issues in Paul's Letter to the Romans*, Valley Forge, PA: Trinity Press International.

—— (1998) "Romans, Jews, and Christians: The Impact of the Romans on Jewish/Christian Religions in First-Century Rome," in K. P. Donfried and P. Richardson (eds) *Judaism and Christianity in First-Century Rome*, Grand Rapids, MI: Eerdmans, pp. 175–95.

Ward, C. A. (1989a) "Altered States of Consciousness and Mental Health: Theoretical and Methodological Issues," in C. A. Ward (ed.) *Altered States of Consciousness and Mental Health: A Cross-Cultural Perspective*, London: Sage.

—— (1989b) "Altered States of Consciousness and Psychopathology," in C. A. Ward (ed.) *Altered States of Consciousness and Mental Health: A Cross-Cultural Perspective*, London: Sage.

—— (1989c) "The Cross-Cultural Study of Altered States of Consciousness and Mental Health," in C. A. Ward (ed.) *Altered States of Consciousness and Mental Health: A Cross-Cultural Perspective*, London: Sage.

Warner, W. L., and P. S. Lunt (1942) "Ethnicity (1942)," an excerpt from *The Status* (1942) in W. Sollors (ed.) (1996) *Theories of Ethnicity: A Classical Reader*, Basingstoke: Macmillan, pp. 13–14.

Watkins, J. G., and H. H. Watkins (1986) "Hypnosis, Multiple Personality, and Ego States as Altered States of Consciousness," in B. B. Wolman and M. Ullman (eds) *Handbook of States of Consciousness*, New York: Van Nostrand Reinhold.

Watson, F. (1991) "The Two Roman Congregations: Romans 14:1–15:13," in K. P. Donfried (ed.) *The Romans Debate*, Peabody, MA: Hendrickson, pp. 203–15.

Webb, R. L. (1991) *John the Baptizer and Prophet: A Socio-Historical Study*, JSNTSup 62, Sheffield: Sheffield Academy Press.

Wedderburn, A. J. M. (1987) *Baptism and Resurrection: Studies in Pauline Theology against Its Graeco-Roman Background*, WUNT 44, Tübingen: Mohr (Siebeck).

Welborn, L. L. (1999) "The Runaway Paul," *HTR*, 92: 115–63.

Weldon, Mary Susan, and Krystal D. Bellinger (1997) "Collective Memory: Collaborative and Individual Processes in Remembering," *Journal of Experimental Psychology: Learning, Memory, and Cognition*, 23: 1160–75.

White, L. (1994) "One Drop of Blood," *The New Yorker* (July 24) http://www.afn.org/~dks/race/wright.html (accessed 5/5/08).

White, R. A. (1997) "Dissociation, Narrative, and Exceptional Human Experiences," in S. Krippner and S. M. Powers (eds) *Broken Images, Broken Selves: Dissociative Narratives in Clinical Practice*, Washington DC: Brunner/Mazel.

Whitehouse, H. (1995) *Inside the Cult: Religious Innovation and Transmission in Papua New Guinea*, Oxford: Clarendon.

—— (2000) *Arguments and Icons*, Oxford: Oxford University Press.

—— (2004) *Modes of Religiosity: A Cognitive Theory of Religious Transmission*, Walnut Creek, CA: AltaMira.

—— and J. Laidlaw (eds) (2004) *Ritual and Memory: Toward a Comparative Anthropology of Religion*, Walnut Creek, CA: AltaMira.

—— and L. H. Martin (eds) (2004) *Theorizing Religions Past: Archaeology, History, and Cognition*, Walnut Creek, CA: AltaMira.

—— and R. N. McCauley (eds) (2005) *Mind and Religion: Psychological and Cognitive Foundations of Religiosity*, Walnut Creek, CA: AltaMira.

Whitelam, K. W. (1996) *The Invention of Ancient Israel: The Silencing of Palestinian History*, London: Routledge.

Wiebe, D. (2004) "Critical Reflections on the Mode of Religiosity Argument," in H. Whitehouse and L. H. Martin (eds) *Theorizing Religions Past: Archaeology, History, and Cognition*, Walnut Creek, CA: AltaMira.

Wiefel, W. (1991) "The Jewish Community in Ancient Rome and the Origins of Roman Christianity," in K. P. Donfried (ed.) *The Romans Debate*, Peabody, MA: Hendrickson, pp. 85–101.

Wikan, U. (1990) "Shame and Honour: A Contestable Pair," *Man* 19: 635–52.

Williams, Craig (1999) *Roman Sexualities: Ideologies of Masculinity in Classical Antiquity*, New York: Oxford University Press.

Williams, R. H. (1999) "Bishops as Brokers of Heavenly Goods: Ignatius to the Ephesians," *Proceedings EGL & MWBS* 19: 119–28.

—— (2006) *Stewards, Prophets, Keepers of the Word: Leadership in the Early Church*, Peabody, MA: Hendrickson.

Wilson, E. O. (1978) *On Human Nature*, Cambridge, MA: Harvard University Press.

Windisch, H. (1924) *Der zweite Korintherbrief*, KEK 6; Göttingen: Vandenhoeck & Ruprecht.

Wink, Walter (1992) *Engaging the Powers: Discernment and Resistance in a World of Domination*, Minneapolis: Fortress.

Winkelman, M. (2000) *Shamanism: The Neural Ecology of Consciousness and Healing*, Westport, CT: Bergin & Garvey.

—— (2004) "Shamanism," in C. R. Ember and M. Ember (eds) *Encyclopedia of Medical Anthropology: Health and Illness in the World's Cultures,* Vol. 1: *Topics,* New York: Springer Science.

Winter, B. W. (2003) *Roman Wives, Roman Widows: The Appearance of New Women and the Pauline Communities,* Grand Rapids, MI: Eerdmans.

Witherington, Ben (1998) *The Acts of the Apostles. A Socio-Rhetorical Commentary,* Grand Rapids: MI: Eerdmans.

Wolf, E. (1966) *Peasants,* Englewood Cliffs, NJ: Prentice Hall.

Wujek, J. (1963) (trans.) *Pismo Święte,* corrected and edited with introduction and commentary by S. Styś and W. Lohn, Pulaski, WI: Franciscan Publishers.

Wulff, D. M. (1997) *Psychology of Religion: Classic and Contemporary,* New York: John Wiley & Sons.

Yang, P. Q. (2000) *Ethnic Studies: Issues and Approaches,* Albany, NY: State University of New York Press.

Young, Allan (1982) "The Anthropology of Illness and Sickness," *Annual Review of Anthropology,* 11: 257–85.

Zangwill, O. L. (1987) "Isolation Experiments," in R. L. Gregory (ed.) *The Oxford Companion to the Mind,* Oxford: Oxford University Press.

Zenner, Walter P. (1990) "Jewish Retainers as Power Brokers," *JQR,* 81: 127–49.

Zerubavel, Yael (1997) *Recovered Roots: Collective Memory and the Making of Israeli National Tradition,* Chicago: University of Chicago Press.

Zinberg, N. E. (1977) "The Study of Consciousness States: Problems and Progress," in N. E. Zinberg (ed.) *Alternate States of Consciousness,* New York: Free Press.

Zmijewski, J. (1978) *Der Stil der paulinischen "Narrenrede": Analyse der Sprachgestaltung in 2 Kor 11,1–12,10 als Beitrag zur Methodik von Stiluntersuchungen neutestamentlicher Texte,* BBB 52, Cologne/Bonn, Germany: Peter Hanstein.

Index of Ancient Sources

Index of Modern Authors

Index of Subjects

Related titles from Routledge

The Bible: The Basics

John Barton

'This book introduces some of the enduring and endlessly interesting questions about the Bible and its cultural influence. The writing is clear and fluid, but never overly simplifying ... highly recommended.'

Tod Linafelt, Georgetown University, USA

'With characteristic lucidity and freshness, John Barton offers firm foundations for the modern student. He addresses key questions that remain relevant for the twenty-first century in a balanced and thoroughly accessible way.'

George Brooke, University of Manchester, UK

The Bible: The Basics is a compelling introduction to the Bible as both a sacred text, central to the faith of millions, and a classic work of Western literature, containing a tapestry of genres, voices, perspectives and images. This masterly guide skilfully addresses both aspects of the Bible's character by exploring:

- the rich variety of literary forms, from poetry to prophecy
- and epistles to apocalypses
- the historical, geographic and social context of the Bible
- contemporary attitudes to the Bible held by believers and
- non-believers
- the status of biblical interpretation today

Including maps, a chronology and detailed suggestions for further reading, this is an ideal starting point for people of any faith or none who are studying the Bible in any setting or simply want to know more about the best-selling book of all time.

ISBN13: 978–0–415–41135–6 (hbk)
ISBN13: 978–0–415–41136–3 (pbk)
ISBN13: 978–0–203–85998–8 (ebk)

Available at all good bookshops
For ordering and further information please visit:
www.routledge.com

Christian Ethics: The End of the Law

David S. Cunningham

'David Cunningham's enjoyable and highly readable textbook is an excellent introduction to contemporary Christian ethics and is ideally suited for those who have little prior knowledge of Christian belief. His use of literature, film, and music is notably refreshing, as is the imaginative way he draws on the virtues to illuminate practical judgements in different parts of everyday life. This book will deservedly find its way onto the reading lists of many introductory courses on Christian ethics.'

Robert Song, University of Durham, UK

Christian Ethics provides a biblical, historical, philosophical and theological guide to the field of Christian ethics. Prominent theologian David S. Cunningham explores the tradition of 'virtue ethics' in this creative and lively text, which includes literary and musical references as well as key contemporary theological texts and figures.

Three parts examine:

- the nature of human action and the people of God as the 'interpretative community' within which ethical discourse arises
- the development of a 'virtue ethics' approach, and places this in its Christian context
- significant issues in contemporary Christian ethics, including the ethics of business and economics, politics, the environment, medicine and sex.

This is the essential text for students of all ethics courses in theology, religious studies and philosophy.

ISBN13: 978–0–415–37599–3 (hbk)
ISBN13: 978–0–415–37600–6 (pbk)
ISBN13: 978–0–203–92975–9 (ebk)

Related titles from Routledge

The New Testament in its Ritual World

Richard E. DeMaris

'...this valuable work forces New Testament scholars to give more attention to the neglected ritual world of the New Testament.'

V. Henry T. Nguyen, Loyola Marymount University

What was life like among the first Christians? For the last thirty years, scholars have explored the historical and social contexts of the New Testament in order to sharpen their understanding of the text itself. This interest has led scholars to focus more and more on the social features of early Christian communities and less on their theologies or doctrines.

Scholars are keen to understand what these communities were like, but the ritual life of early Christians remains largely unexplored. Studies of baptism and eucharist do exist, but they are very traditional, showing little awareness of the ritual world, let alone the broader social environment, in which Christians found themselves. Such studies make little or no use of the social sciences, Roman social history, or the archaeological record.

This book argues that ritual was central to, and definitive for, early Christian life (as it is for all social orders), and explores the New Testament through a ritual lens. By grounding the exploration in ritual theory, Greco-Roman ritual life, and the material record of the ancient Mediterranean, it offers new and insightful perspectives on early Christian communities and their cultural environment. In doing justice to a central but slighted aspect of community life, it outlines an alternative approach to the New Testament, one that reveals what the lives of the first Christians were actually like.

ISBN13: 978–0–415–43825–4 (hbk)
ISBN13: 978–0–415–43826–1 (pbk)
ISBN13: 978–0–203–93079–3 (ebk)